100 GREAT BUSINESSES

and the Minds Behind Them

100 GREAT BUSINESSES

BUSINESSES

and the Minds Behind Them

EMILY ROSS & ANGUS HOLLAND

SOURCEBOOKS, INC.®
NAPERVILLE, ILLINOIS

Published by Sourcebooks, Inc.
P.O. Box 4410, Naperville, Illinois   60567-4410
(630) 961-3900
FAX: (630) 961-2168
www.sourcebooks.com

Originally published in 2004

Library of Congress Cataloging-in-Publication Data
Ross, Emily.
  100 great businesses and the minds behind them / Emily Ross and Angus
Holland.
     p. cm.
  ISBN-13: 978-1-4022-0631-3
  ISBN-10: 1-4022-0631-3
 1. Success in business—Case studies. 2. Business enterprises—Case studies.
3. Entrepreneurship—Case studies. I. Title: One hundred great businesses
and the minds behind them. II. Holland, Angus. III. Title.

HF5386.R665 2005
650.1—dc22

                                                        2005024998

Printed and bound in the United States of America.
  VP   20 19 18 17 16 15 14 13 12 11 10

CONTENTS

ACKNOWLEDGMENTS

Thank you to the many inspiring companies and individuals who cooperated with us and to the authors and experts around the world who verified our information. Thank you particularly to Josh Abramson, Julie Aigner-Clark, Garry Barker, Gert Boyle, Alison Brennan, Nathan Cochrane, Meredith Curnow, John Demsey, Jessica Dettmann, Diana Duran, Andrew Dyson, Bill Echols, Kristi Ernsting, Tony Featherstone, Dana Fries, John Fread, Amanda Gome, Allen Goldberg, Liz Hulls, David James, Laurie Kahn-Leavitt, Neville Kenyon, Jenny Shorland, Sharon Krum, Liz Lange, Dave Liniger, Karyn Lovegrove, Peter Lynch, Amanda Mackevicius, Nathalie Moar, Gela Nash-Taylor, Neighborhood House, Mark Pendergrast, Yvonne Pendleton, Richard Rogers, Sally Ross, the entire Holland and Ross clans, Lucinda Schmidt, Jenny Shorland, Isadore Sharp, Nury Echeverria-Silva, Amita Tandukar, Andrew Tobias, Bill Tikos, Doug Tompkins, Toby Hagon, Tony Atherton, Megan Ryan, Les Winograd, and Lindy Woodhead.

A NOTE ON THE TEXT

We have deliberately not jammed the text with numbered endnotes, which, due to the research needed to write the entries, would have rendered the book unreadable. Instead, quotations are referenced at the end of each entry. Any quotations and key sources of research material not referenced at the end of an entry come from interviews conducted by the authors. We thank all the companies that participated in this book, with particular thanks to the founders who gave up their time. In the handful of cases where companies were unable to participate, we made every effort to verify the information presented was correct at the time of going to press.

All financial figures are in U.S. dollars unless otherwise specified.

INTRODUCTION

The typical business success story starts like this: Mr X has a brilliant idea in the bath one morning. He calls a friend, and together they build the invention in the garage. Then they go out and sell it from the back of Mr X's car, and before they know it, they are both millionaires.

We like these stories because they make us think we could easily do the same thing. All we need is that great idea, right?

Miracles do happen. Nike's Phil Knight did start out selling running shoes from the back of his car. Pierre Omidyar did just happen to have an idea for an Internet site—eBay—that made him a billionaire several times over. James Dyson became one of Britain's richest men after inventing a new kind of vacuum cleaner in his shed.

But these fairy tales tend to skip over the details, the parts of the story where, for example, Dyson had to build 5,127 vacuum cleaner prototypes before he actually got the thing to work properly, where FedEx founder Fred Smith nearly went broke several times over in the early years, and why Debbi Fields of Mrs. Fields Cookies fame now has little to do with the company that bears her name.

Having a great idea is the easy part. As the one hundred businesses in this book all demonstrate, the real talent lies in knowing what to do next: how to finance and build the product, when and how to market it, and—most importantly—how to persist with it and continue to believe in it through the inevitable difficult times. Like Lonnie Johnson, the rocket scientist who had to spend eight years knocking on doors before somebody agreed to build his invention, the Super Soaker water gun.

Our case studies cover a range of companies, from recent start-ups to firms over one hundred years old, from the origins of Corn Flakes to the birth of satellite radio; the genius of MTV to the Red

Bull energy drink phenomenon; from the Walkman to the Nike sneaker. What they all have in common is a talent for innovation, which can take many forms: inventing a whole new product, taking somebody else's idea and making it work better, or simply taking over the market by selling products cheaper than anybody else— take a bow, Samuel Walton.

There's the story of the home recipe for Liquid Paper that turned into a global company, why one of the world's richest men (with a $40 billion fortune) still drives a non-descript Volvo, and how the fortuitous purchase of a nude picture of Marilyn Monroe kick-started the biggest-selling men's magazine in the world. This book is about the brains behind the Barbie doll, about the woman who started Weight Watchers because, she recalled, "even her poodle was fat," those clever girls that created the Juicy Couture tracksuit, and the man that reinvented the circus and became a billionaire in the process.

Some of the businesses and personalities in this book, such as Microsoft and Revlon, Oprah Winfrey and Amazon.com's Jeff Bezos, are well-known. Then there are the businesses you might have seen down at the mall, such as Build-A-Bear Workshop and Dippin' Dots ice cream, and wondered, where did they get the idea for *that*? And there will probably be a few companies here that you've never heard of in a million years—such as Research in Motion and id Software—though chances are you own one of their products. As object lessons, all are inspiring in their own way.

We sought out people who do something better than everyone else, who work out how to create and market products that consumers really want, who appear at just the right time to ride (or create) a wave of popularity, or who manage to turn disaster into victory with an extreme makeover, as demonstrated by the ailing Finnish rubber boot manufacturer now better known as the world leader in mobile phones—Nokia. We looked for companies that created something we didn't even know we needed, such as

Rollerblade, TiVo and *American Idol*. We came across companies that created their own communities, such as Pierre Omidyar's eBay, which now has a population larger than Britain's, and Craigslist, which grew from an email bulletin to a few friends into the world's biggest free listing service. We have also examined companies such as Esprit and Levi's, which are no longer the ultra fashionable brands they once were, yet have managed to endure nevertheless.

Few of the people behind these companies have much in common—which is one of the main themes of this book. If nothing else, reading through the one hundred profiles here demonstrates that there is no single path to becoming an entrepreneur and no single type of successful business. Nor is there a "correct" way to make a business work. Each entrepreneur has their own set of circumstances, their own personality, quirks, and survival skills. They develop their own leadership style to suit their circumstances.

The cult of personality can come into play—think of Virgin founder Richard Branson (the man described as a "suit dressed up as a sweater") or the oracle of Omaha and second-richest man in the world, Warren Buffett, whom millions treat as a guru. Other business leaders cultivate reputations as bosses from hell, such as Revlon founder Charles Revson, who once exclaimed: "I built this business being a bastard, I run it by being a bastard, and I'll always be a bastard."

Bottom line: Is it really possible to learn from the experiences of entrepreneurs and replicate their success?

Probably not in the case of Apple's Steve Jobs, who was blessed with charisma famously described as a "reality distortion field." Or Michael Dell, who even in high school was earning more than his teacher thanks to his business sidelines. If you were going to be another Dell or Jobs, you'd probably know it already.

But there are plenty of late starters, too. Craig Newmark was in his early forties when he started Craigslist almost by accident. Maxine Clark had already been in retailing for more than twenty years when she had the idea for Build-A-Bear Workshop. Not to mention Ray Kroc, for whom McDonald's was the last roll of the dice, after many dismal years on the road as a salesman.

Many of today's billionaires are not born leaders, or even particularly good salespeople. Instead, their talents lie in taking risks, hiring the right people to help them, and in recognizing the skills they need to learn to succeed. When opportunity knocks, they listen.

The simple truth is that there are as many ways to succeed in business as there are great businesses.

Section 1

THE CROWD-PLEASERS

Pixar

Move over, Disney

A<small>SK A TYPICAL</small> P<small>IXAR</small> <small>EMPLOYEE WHAT THEIR COMPANY'S</small> greatest achievement has been over the past decade and the answer could well be "realistic fur"—more specifically, the luxuriant blue pelt that covered Sullivan, the hulking lead character in Pixar's 2001 hit feature, *Monsters Inc.* Getting the computer animation programs to make each hair wave about in a lifelike manner was apparently quite an achievement. But so too was giving each ant a different set of facial features in 1998's *A Bug's Life*. And another employee could well argue that the most difficult task of all was creating the underwater scenes in Pixar's 2003 hit, *Finding Nemo*: water is notoriously difficult to animate, particularly when it sloshes in and out of the mouth of a whale.

Pixar is the world leader in computer animation, a position it has held since its debut feature film, *Toy Story*, in 1995. But ask Ed Catmull, president of Pixar Animation Studios, the same question and he is likely to give you a completely different answer. Yes, Pixar is in many ways a technology company, forever seeking out more sophisticated effects. But technology alone does not make great movies. The studio's greatest achievement, according to Catmull, is telling great stories. The technology makes it happen, but it is the narrative and the characters that engage an audience. "Everything that we do on a film is driven by that story," he has said.

Pixar's ability to combine the traditional elements of good film-making (character and plot) with technology that gives audiences a new view of the world (from a toy's or a bug's perspective) has proved a winning formula with audiences of every one of its releases to date.

The company came to world attention in 1995, but its story goes back to 1974 when Catmull, studying at a vocational school called the New York Institute of Technology, first loosely pulled together the team that would later become Pixar. Catmull, who grew up in Salt Lake City, had, as a child, dreamed of working for Disney, but wasn't artistically gifted and ended up in computers. In 1979 Catmull took a job as vice president of the computer division at George Lucas's Lucasfilm, where he hired former top Disney animator John Lasseter in 1984. In 1986, George Lucas decided to sell off that side of his business, so Apple's Steve Jobs stepped in to buy it for $10 million and called the new company Pixar. (Today Jobs owns 51 percent of the company and is chairman and CEO, Catmull is president, and Lasseter is executive vice president, creative.)

In 1991, Jobs cut a deal with Disney to finance, market, and distribute Pixar's products, with Disney fronting most of the money in return for most of the profits. *Toy Story* opened in November 1995 and became the highest-grossing film of the year. On November 28, 1995, Jobs took Pixar public, raising $140 million.

Then in February 1997 Pixar cut a new distribution deal with Disney that tied the two together for five more movies but with expenses and profits roughly split 50/50. Pixar then continued on its winning streak, releasing a string of hits including *Toy Story 2* and *Monsters Inc.*; 2003's *Finding Nemo* was the highest-grossing animated feature of the year. In early 2004, Pixar suggested that it would look around for a new partner when the Disney deal expired, much to Disney's dismay (by then Pixar's movies had earned some $2.5 billion and seventeen Oscars; in late 2004 Pixar then released another hit, *The Incredibles*). Pixar's product has also proved incredibly profitable, in 2004 returning $141 million income on a revenue of $273 million.

So what is the secret formula that has taken an upstart to the top of its field? Just follow these simple rules:

First, nurture talent. Ed Catmull was once asked what he would prefer—a great idea, or great people? The answer, he said, was obvious: great people, because if you gave a good idea to the wrong people, they would screw it up, but if you gave the wrong idea to the right people, they would fix it. His other mottos: Don't get complacent because your competitors copy you; they might do a better job of it. Hire based on potential rather than position. Hire people on an upward trajectory in their careers. Hire people who are better than you are.

Experiment (in moderation). Pixar still makes short films that will not make any money, but allow artists to try out new techniques that can then be used on commercial features.

Focus on the detail. Behind the engaging storylines and clever effects, much of Pixar's work is painstaking slog. One four-minute scene in *A Bug's Life* took fifteen staffers four months to produce.

Focus on the main goal, which, in Pixar's case, is producing entertaining movies—not just cutting-edge computer-generated images. "If you don't have a clear vision you can get lost in the technology," says John Lasseter. "You can end up spending a lot of time and money and not achieve what you want."

Encourage creativity and productivity. Physically, Pixar is like one of those companies you thought only existed in Silicon Valley at the peak of the dot-com bubble, only better. The 775 employees at Emeryville, California, don't just get foosball tables and Coca-Cola in the fridge: there is a swimming pool, a soccer field, a 250-seat cinema, a gym, and a proper sit-down restaurant. It is so big some employees get about on scooters and skateboards. More importantly, though, the building's designers (who included CEO Steve Jobs) placed kitchenettes, mail stations, and meeting rooms in spots that encouraged employees to bump into each other and exchange ideas—something impossible in less lavish workplaces.

Steve Jobs has said he can see Pixar becoming the next Disney. An audacious vision, but not completely unrealistic, with Pixar producing a string of hits while Disney's efforts have been less reliable of late. But could Pixar grow into a major corporation and still have employees who ride around on skateboards? Can they maintain the culture that has incubated such creativity? There's a first time for everything.

NOTES

"Everything that we do..." Interview by Dan Rather, *60 Minutes II*, CBS, 10.15.03.
"If you don't have..." Ross, Jonathan. "John Lasseter on John Lasseter." *The Guardian*, 11.19.01.

REFERENCES

ABC News, *Boston Globe*, *BusinessWeek*, CBS, *Charlotte Observer*, *Financial Times*, *Fortune*, *The Guardian*, *Herald Sun*, *New York Times*, *Sunday Tribune*, *Time*, *Variety*

Julie Aigner-Clark and Bill Clark, Baby Einstein

Start 'em young

JULIE AIGNER-CLARK, THE MULTIMILLIONAIRE CREATOR OF THE Baby Einstein brand of videos, books, and other baby products, did not realize she was creating an international brand, a whole new product category, and a parenting phenomenon when she began making a homemade video for her baby daughter Aspen. She couldn't find anything in the stores suitable for her baby, so the former school teacher decided to produce one herself, turning her basement into a makeshift studio.

Aigner-Clark wanted to make a video that would introduce her daughter Aspen to music, art, literature, and poetry in a gentle, baby-friendly way. She created the Baby Einstein Language Nursery, a video that starred Aspen's favorite toys, nursery rhymes, multilingual counting, Aigner-Clark's soft, slow, gentle voiceover, and a simplified classical soundtrack. "I guess I just hit on an idea that nobody had come up with, or they didn't know how to do it," she says. "It was literally me pushing 'play' on the Betacam and dragging a cat across a table with a fishing line."

With $10,000 of her and husband Bill Clark's savings, they created a product that some have described as very much on the amateur side, others as "crack cocaine for children." The Baby Einstein video immediately found a following in Aigner-Clark's circle of friends. She had found a guilt-free way to entertain, and some would argue, educate the youngest demographic there is, while Mommy took a shower, made a phone call, or grabbed a few extra minutes' sleep.

In the space of five years, the Baby Einstein brand evolved from a video distributed among friends to a developmental media company sold to the Walt Disney Company in late 2001 for an estimated $25 million. The company had only just moved out of the family home into office space when the Disney deal was struck.

Despite being told by her family she was mad to invest her savings in a baby video, Aigner-Clark, a self-confessed very persistent woman, had an instinct about the video. "I am a full-time mom. I know what they like looking at and I know what they like listening to. I think it was instinctive as a mom." She also says her secret weapon was a "fabulous, optimistic husband who was a true entrepreneur." He persuaded Julie to invest the $10,000 in the venture.

The Baby Einstein idea and actually making the video was the easy part. Then things got tougher. Aigner-Clark was enjoying being home with her baby and was happy being a full-time mom. The next phase, finding distributors and reaching her target market, was much harder, and where Aigner-Clark's persistence came in handy. "I knew nothing about marketing," she says.

Aigner-Clark researched potential retailers and decided that The Right Start was the ideal retailer for the product. It would be able to sell at a higher price, and avoid the Baby Einstein brand being lost on the shelves of bigger retailers, surrounded by products with multimillion-dollar marketing budgets. She posted off copies of her tape to The Right Start and heard nothing. In desperation, she flew to New York City to the annual Toy Fair in 1997 and literally walked the floor searching amongst the 15,000 delegates for staff from The Right Start. On the second day she found them thanks to their nametags. "I charged up to these women and probably scared the hell out of them," says Aigner-Clark. "I just said 'Oh, my God, you have to watch this video. It's so perfect for the store.'" Unfortunately, her main contact at the fair left the company soon after, and Aigner-Clark had to pester the new buyer for several weeks until she finally watched the Baby Einstein tape. It was tested in ten stores, sold brilliantly, and was quickly distributed all over the country. Four months after launching the first video, The Right Start called Aigner-Clark and asked her to make more. "That was exciting. People really wanted what I was making," she says.

In the early years, Aigner-Clark would be sorting videos for shipping while her daughter took her daily naps. The company operated entirely on cash flow and never took on any debt. This all-cash way was essential, especially for Bill, who had started up a software company in the 1980s and had had negative experiences with venture capitalists. Neither Bill nor Julie wanted the "having-to-answer-to-them sessions" that outside stakeholders would want to have. By owning the whole business, "we would manage our time as we saw fit, sleep easier at night, and be independent," says Bill.

Bill Clark believes that the "all-cash way" gave Baby Einstein a competitive advantage. He emphasizes the importance of keeping overheads as low as possible to the success of Baby Einstein. He figures it is harder to predict revenue in those early years, so sticking to budgets is essential for survival. For Baby Einstein, that has meant reviewing forecast expenses if sales are looking tight, such as canceling a trade show, or cutting back on advertising or direct mail to ensure that costs do not blow out. Another trick that Bill recommends as part of the all-cash way is to negotiate discounts with suppliers for paying bills within twenty days.

The company had respectable sales of $100,000 in the first year—enough to cover costs and produce more videos including *Baby Bach, Baby Mozart, Baby Van Gogh,* and *Baby Shakespeare.* Aigner-Clark was now making five times what she was paid as a school-teacher. Word-of-mouth played a huge part in the success of Baby Einstein; moms kept telling other moms how much their children loved the videos.

The birth of Baby Einstein coincided with a huge wave of time-poor wealthy older parents splurging on products they felt would give their children a headstart in life. Aigner-Clark is careful to avoid saying that her videos make children smart, preferring to describe them as simply "engaging" for children. "Do I think (Baby Einstein products) will get (kids) into Harvard? No. But I do think they give children exposure to great and beautiful things," she says.

Independent retailers helped Baby Einstein find a market, but to reach bigger markets, Aigner-Clark knew that the company needed a large distribution partner. They formed an ill-fated partnership with an entertainment company that resulted in a substantial mass-market distribution strategy that included product tie-ins with Huggies diapers, Chlorox bleach, and Cheerios cereal, and Baby Einstein presence within stores such as Target and Wal-Mart. Within eighteen months, 2.5 million Baby Einstein videos were sold in the U.S. But this alliance was not a happy one for Aigner-Clark. "The partnership was a terrible choice for us," she says. She alleges that the entertainment company misrepresented to Aigner-Clark the number of units sold. "We lost a huge amount of money on that deal, and the stress of that relationship was incredibly difficult."

Disney first approached Aigner-Clark to discuss a book license for a series of Baby Einstein books. She was attracted to the idea of building the brand. At first the relationship was just for books, but Disney then offered to buy the company outright. It was a difficult decision but Aigner-Clark felt that the market was changing, there was more competition, and taking the business to the next level needed more time than she could give it. "We were spending less and less time with out kids and hated that," she says. "Bill and I decided on how much money would be enough for us to be able to walk away completely happy, gave that number to Disney, and they agreed. We have no regrets," she says. "I sold my baby . . . and all the rights and I'm okay with that."

When Aigner-Clark and Clark sold the company to Disney, sales had reached $20 million. Disney has pushed the brand into another league with sales in 2003 of $165 million. There are now more than seventy Baby Einstein products on the market. "That's always where we hoped the brand would go but didn't have the ability to take it," says Aigner-Clark. In hindsight, she believes that Disney paid a bargain price for her business but she is happy with her deal.

Aigner-Clark is still a consultant to Disney on the Baby Einstein brand. Bill and Julie are now working on two new start-ups, Aigner-Clark Creative and Memory Lane Media, developing media products on safety for children and for Alzheimer's patients, respectively. Aigner-Clark happily calls herself a "serial entrepreneur."

In 2004 Aigner-Clark was diagnosed and successfully treated for breast cancer. Bill, Julie, and their family live in Colorado. After homeschooling for several years, the children now attend a school for gifted children. Maybe the Baby Einstein videos will get them into Harvard after all.

NOTES

"Crack cocaine . . ." Talaga, Tanya. "Baby Einstein's Creator is a Genius," *Toronto Star*, 1.3.05, p. E01.

"I am a full-time mom . . ." Guida, Tony. "Baby Einstein Company Founder & CEO," CNNFN, 1.14.00.

"I charged up . . ." Seitz, Patrick. "Julie Clark's Eureka Moment." Section Leaders and Success; National Edition, *Investors Business Daily*, 8.20.04, p. A03.

"We would manage our time..." Clark, Bill. "Doing it the All-Cash Way," *Entreworld.org*, September, 2001,
http://entreworld.org/content/entrebyline.cfm?columnid=326.

"Do I think . . ." Deam, Jenny. "The Quest for a Brilliant Baby," SCN, *Denver Post*, 5.28.02, p. F01.

"That's always where . . ." Milstead, David. "Disney Buys Little Bundle of Energy," Business, *Rocky Mountain News*, 11.7.01, p. 2B.

REFERENCES

Advertising Age, Denver Post, Internet Wire, Investors Business Daily

Callaway

How Big Bertha made a fortune

IN 1982 ELY CALLAWAY, THEN SIXTY-THREE, WAS PUTTERING about a pro shop at a golf course called the Vintage Club in Palm Springs. As he waited for service, he noticed an unusual club for sale. Unlike the modern clubs around it, it had an old-fashioned wooden shaft, like the ones he had used as a teenager. Yet it wasn't an old club, it was actually the product of a new Californian business called Hickory Stick.

Callaway had recently sold a winery for $14 million—raising more than enough cash to live on comfortably for the rest of his life. A dapper man, he loved Cuban cigars, Brioni suits, Turnbull & Asser shirts, lunch at the Four Seasons, and his Rolls Royce. He had been married four times and had had three children. (His son Nicholas runs a book company called Callaway Arts and Entertainment, best known for publishing the Miss Spider series of children's books, as well as Madonna's children's books.)

But he wasn't quite ready to retire. Intrigued by the odd golf club, which actually employed modern technology in the form of a hidden metal shaft beneath the hickory, he called the company and discovered that its owners, Richard Parente and Dick de la Cruz, were desperately looking for growth capital. It was a tiny company, but it was trying to do something different, which appealed to Callaway. And as a life-long fanatical golfer, he could think of worse things to do with his money than invest it in golf, so he bought the business and in 1985 relocated the factory from Cathedral City, California to Carlsbad, just north of San Diego, and renamed it Callaway Golf.

He dropped the hickory line, concentrating instead on drivers and in 1991 introduced the club with the least forgettable name in golfing history. Big Bertha had an oversized, inelegant metal head and made an unappealing "clank" sound when you hit the ball, but it was easier to hit with and gave you more distance off the tee than any other driver...at least, that was what many golfers came to believe. To the typical hack golfer desperate for any assistance, Big Bertha was an instant fix—the Holy Grail of amateur golf. By 1992, golfers were on waiting lists of weeks, even months, for the club, which retailed at $250, twice the price of a normal driver.

By 1996, Callaway was the world's largest manufacturer of golfing equipment. By 1997, revenues were close to $850 million. It created multimillionaires of its company officers, and millionaires of those lucky enough to buy stock when the company floated in 1992 (it split several times). It turned the sleepy town of Carlsbad (pop. 78,000) into the world capital of golfing equipment, with several other major manufacturers attracted there by Callaway's presence. It almost certainly improved the game of some five million golfers around the world, and was at least partly responsible for the boom in golf in the 1990s. Its success even brought it into bitter conflict with the highest authorities in golf, and made it a target for counterfeiters and thieves, who targeted numerous sports stores, taking only Big Berthas.

The man who stirred up all this chaos in the erstwhile deathly stead world of golf, Ely Callaway, was born in 1919 in LaGrange,

Georgia. He had a privileged childhood: his family ran eight cotton mills and his parents were members of the Highland Country Club, where Callaway excelled on the fairway, winning the club championship from 1936 to 1939. "My mother always said it was the beauty of Ely's golf swing that made her fall in love with him," Nicholas said in 2001.

When World War II broke out, Callaway joined the army, becoming the chief procurement officer for cotton goods. After the war, he stayed in cotton, joining Deering-Milliken, selling cloth to the companies he had ordered uniforms from, turning his network of suppliers into customers. He was affable, refined, and easy to get along with, developing friendships in all sorts of useful places. But Callaway also had an entrepreneurial streak and a flair for marketing. In his youth, he sold magazine subscriptions, was the business manager of his high school newspaper, and once made $750 profit from investing in a peach orchard. At Deering-Milliken, he came up with an unforgettable stunt to demonstrate the water resistant properties of a new polyester-wool blend called Viracle. He invited staffers from *Life* magazine to lunch at a country club, where he had dressed models in the new fabric. Just before lunch began, he soaked the models with a hosepipe; by the time the *Life* staffers had finished their meal the models were bone dry.

Callaway moved to Burlington Industries, where he became president at forty-eight, but, after he was passed over for CEO, he quit in 1973 to work full-time at a winery he had bought outside San Diego, the Callaway Vineyard and Winery in Temecula. It had been an usual place to start a winery: conventional wisdom in the industry declared the location too hot and too southern to make good wine. But Callaway called on expert advice and by 1974 was producing excellent vintages including a Riesling that was served to the queen of England at a bicentennial dinner in New York in 1976. A friend had helped Callaway get the wine on the menu, but the queen liked it so much she ordered a second glass and asked to meet its maker. Thanks in part to the royal seal of approval, Callaway sold the winery in 1981 for $14 million.

The other major player at Callaway was a former pool hustler called Dick Helmstetter, who had parlayed a risky career playing the game with the likes of Minnesota Fats into a business making pool cues. In 1968, he went to Japan to find out how they were exporting cues to the United States so cheaply, and ended up moving his businesses there. Helmstetter lived in Japan for eighteen years and raised a family, but by the early 1980s was planning to return to the United States so his two boys could attend college.

By chance, on a visit to California he played a round of golf at the Vintage Club in a foursome that happened to include Ely Callaway. Something about Helmstetter impressed Callaway, who wooed him to come and work for him despite his lack of experience in the golf industry. In 1985, Helmstetter not only accepted Callaway's offer, he invested $52,000 in the business. Moving from cues to clubs was "surprisingly easy," Helmstetter says today. "Both are 'stick and ball' games and flex, torque, and spin play a key role in both."

The new chief club designer got to work on a range of metal woods, producing a terrific three wood and a mediocre driver. Puzzled, Helmstetter gave the University of California-San Diego engineering department a research grant to find out what made the clubs so different. The findings suggested a bigger head would produce better shots, so Helmstetter developed metal technology that would allow them to make a bigger club that was still playably light. "A sort of tipping point of various factors suddenly occurred to make it obvious what needed to be done," Helmstetter says. "I just happened to be first."

Callaway's first successful club was a metal wood called the S2H2, which Callaway had financed by persuading the General Electric Pension Fund to invest $10 million. The S2H2 doubled

Callaway's sales in two years; by 1990, the year before Big Bertha's launch, the company was worth $23 million.

Dick Helmstetter hated the name from the get-go. "The name was Ely's idea and I was absolutely against it," he said in 2004. "I thought it was sexist and demeaning. I thought no woman would ever buy it and no woman would let her husband buy it, either."

But he also recalls the day he and Callaway tested one of the prototypes. "One afternoon Ely Callaway and I went out to the driving range of a local club and hit the BB-3 prototype and neither of us could do anything but hit it great. We just sort of looked at each other and said, 'wow, we'll never be able to make enough.'"

Ely Callaway knew just how to sell it, with an animated campaign that appealed to amateurs: an early advertisement showed a caricature of Isaac Newton with the words "you can't argue with physics." Named after an enormous cannon that the Germans used to terrorize Paris in World War I, Big Bertha was a terrific name: memorable, different, and a bit of fun in comparison to the po-faced competition.

Callaway also knew the value of professional endorsement: he once targeted professionals appearing at a trade show by taking out an ad in the Wall Street Journal, then having a copy delivered to every hotel room in the area.

Word quickly spread: pro golfers got more distance, weekend hackers found they were suddenly hitting the ball better. "Up until 1991, what was wrong with drivers is that everybody hated them," Ely Callaway said in 1999, two years before his death. "The driver was the least favored club in the bag, or the most feared. They bought them but they didn't like them. Big Bertha changed the attitude of the masses from one of fear about the driver to one of affection."

By 1992, demand was so strong for the $250 club that golfers were on waiting lists of weeks, even months. In February 1992, Callaway floated on Wall Street, making multimillionaires out of company officers, one of whom bought a Porsche Turbo with the license plate "THXELY" (thanks Ely).

Satisfied customers included President George Bush, who endorsed Big Bertha on national TV, President Bill Clinton, and Prince Andrew. Callaway also persuaded a bizarre range of celebrity golfers to appear in advertisements for the club, including singer Celine Dion, rocker Alice Cooper, and Microsoft Chairman Bill Gates, who had lunch with Callaway one day and agreed to do a spot that was filmed by the director of *The Natural* and *The Right Stuff*. (More traditionally, Callaway also sponsored PGA players such as John Daly and LPGA star Annika Sorenstam.)

Not everybody loved Big Bertha. Traditionalists argued that amateur golfers should practice more, not depend on a fancy club to improve their game. The U.S. Golf Association was concerned that big-headed clubs acted like trampolines—as the metal faces tend to be springier—introducing a test in 1998 that it could use to ban nonconforming clubs from regulation competition. Ely Callaway took out full-page advertisements in the *New York Times* urging golfers to protest against what he claimed was a conservative backlash against the growing interest in golf among ordinary Americans. In 2000, the association finally did ban a Callaway club, the $1000 ERC (named after Ely's initials), though it was still legal in Europe, where *The Scotsman* newspaper conducted a test where five delighted volunteers all added between twenty-five and fifty yards to their drives.

By the end of the 1990s, Callaway was losing a little of the market share it had gained so quickly as competitors caught up and the Asian economic crisis cooled demand a little. The company had attempted to expand into websites, publishing, and expensive swing analysis centers, all of which lost money, prompting Ely Callaway, who had retired in 1996, to return as CEO in 1998, cut seven hundred from the workforce and close down the ancillary businesses. He still showed up at work at 7:45 a.m. each day for three more years, until his death from pancreatic cancer at age eighty-two, on July 5, 2001.

Without Ely, Callaway is no longer quite the sensation it once was. Rather, it is settling down into middle age—as merely a major force in golf, a public company with millions of shareholders to please, three thousand employees, sales of close to $1 billion a year, and forever on the lookout for the next Big Bertha.

NOTES

"The name was Ely's. . . ." A'Amato, Gary. "Wisconsin Inventor Makes Big Impact," *Milwaukee Journal Sentinel*, 2.29.04, p. 05S.

"My mother always said . . ." Freeman, Mike. "Golf World Celebrates Man Who Revolutionized Industry," *Copley News Service*, 7.25.01.

"Up until 1991, what was wrong with drivers . . ." Williams, Jeff. "Out of the Woods," *Cigar Aficionado*, November/December 1999.

REFERENCES

ABC Business World, Brandweek, BusinessWeek, Cigar Aficionado, Copley News Service, Financial Times, Fortune, Golf Digest, Golf Online, Golfspan Online, The Independent, Milwaukee Journal Sentinel, New York Times, The Scotsman, USA Today, Washington Post

Barbie

When it comes to business, it is always nice to be able to say "I told you so"

"THEY DIDN'T THINK THAT THE PUBLIC WOULD ACCEPT A doll with breasts for children. I knew they were wrong," said the creator of the Barbie doll, the late Ruth Handler. If ever anyone had the right to say "I told you so" to her doubters, it was Ruth Handler. Ever since the launch of the blonde, blue-eyed "Barbie Teen-Age Fashion Model" at the New York Toy Fair in 1959, Barbie has been a toy phenomenon. The $3 doll with her zebra-print swimsuit, eyeliner, and beauty-queen hair was an instant hit, selling 351,000 in the first year of production. It took three years for manufacturer Mattel to catch up with consumer demand. Since then, more than one billion Barbies have been sold around the world, generating an estimated $2.2 billion in revenue for Mattel. According to Mattel, 172,800 Barbie dolls are now bought every day and the typical American girl under ten owns eight Barbies.

The youngest of ten children, Ruth went to Hollywood at the age of nineteen, leaving behind her life in Denver, Colorado. Her parents were Polish immigrants who had arrived in America on a steamship.

Handler and her husband, Elliott, had been running an industrial design business since the late 1930s, when Elliott had set up a workshop and created a successful line of plastic homewares. In 1944, the Handlers joined up with fellow industrial designer Harold Matson and created the Mattel Corporation. The team began making picture frames and, ever resourceful, spun off a business making dollhouse furniture out of the picture frame off-cuts. After Handler attended the New York Toy Fair, they saw an untapped market for new toys and developed a range of novelty toys including a pint-sized ukulele and a popular burp gun. In 1955, Mattel was the first company to line up a tie-in deal with a children's television program (*The Mickey Mouse Club*) to sell a range of complementary toys and became the first company to advertise toys on television. In effect, Handler bet the whole company on the Mickey Mouse Club deal, investing $500,000. This deal tripled sales for Mattel and provided the capital for Ruth to develop the toy that would turn into a global sensation.

The idea for Barbie bubbled around in Handler's head for almost a decade. In 1951, she noticed that her daughter Barbara (nicknamed Barbie) preferred adult paper dolls to childlike, prepubescent dolls. "I realized that if we could 'three dimensionalize' the adult paper dolls, we'd meet a very basic play need," she said. During a trip to Europe in 1956, she came across a rather saucy German pin-up-style plastic doll called Lilli in a shop in Lucerne, Switzerland. Lilli was not made for little girls to play out their dreams for the future, but was more of a novelty doll with her 38-21-33 measurements.

(Lilli was based on a bawdy German newspaper comic strip created by Ralf Hausser. Hausser only discovered Barbie in the early 1960s, and was paid an undisclosed sum by Mattel when he pointed out the similarities between Lilli and Barbie.)

Despite her seedy background, Lilli came home in Handler's suitcase, and back in California, Handler began working on a slightly more innocent prototype that would become Barbie (more Southern-belle hair, a little less eyeliner, but essentially the same controversial, top-heavy figure). Real dresses with zips and buttons were commissioned, the hair was sourced, and a Japanese manufacturer was found to make the dolls.

But Handler's husband Elliott and business partner Matson weren't convinced. Elliott was busy developing a talking doll and he and Matson believed Barbie would be too risky and expensive to manufacture. Handler persevered with her doll, however, getting the prototype and ever-important first outfit right, and Barbie was launched in 1959. The doll made a profit in its first year of production.

Wanting to keep the momentum up, Handler devised a heavy marketing and advertising schedule that has been a part of the Barbie sales strategy ever since. Advertisements have been continuously on air, updating little girls on the latest developments in Barbie paraphernalia including new members of Barbie's family (initially all named after Handler's children and grandchildren). Handler wanted to make sure Barbie fans were never bored and proceeded to roll out all manner of Barbie scenarios, initially sticking to old-fashioned stereotypes involving pool parties, town houses, and campervans, but eventually allowing Barbie to take on more politically correct roles as the President and an astronaut. (The hugely successful supermodel and Totally Hair Barbies outsell the politically correct dolls, hands down.) By 1965, Mattel sales had reached $200 million. On a sad note, in 2004, Ken and Barbie officially split up in a failed marketing attempt to boost sales following an 18 percent slump in quarterly Barbie sales following the rise of the Bratz doll.

Barbie has copped enormous flak from feminists, but an unperturbed Handler always insisted that her breakthrough doll with breasts was an important educational experience for girls, which allowed them to anticipate and play out their future as women, and encouraged girls to plan to have a career like she herself had achieved. (Ironically, one of Handler's granddaughters, Stacey, whom Handler named a Mattel doll after, wrote a book about her eating disorders and complexes associated with unrealistic body image.)

Another casualty of the Barbie phenomenon was Lilli's creator Ralf Hausser, whose undisclosed lump-sum compensation for his original idea is rumored to have been a pittance. Handler herself was a casualty of the Barbie success: Mattel kept growing and diversifying, and, as new management joined the company, Handler was sidelined and kept out of important decision-making.

By the 1970s, Mattel had annual revenues of $300 million but a string of management decisions following a strike and factory fire in 1968, just before Christmas deliveries, were calamitous, causing major cash flow problems and financial losses that were then covered up by management. Mattel subsequently reported its first losses, battering the share price. Ruth Handler was forced to leave the corporation in 1975 when news broke that she had been charged with stock manipulation, relating to the company's financial accounts between 1968 and 1974. Handler did not contest the charges (though she claims she was not kept informed of financial matters in the company) and was fined a record $57,000 and sentenced to 2,500 hours of community service. Mattel shareholders were also compensated, with the Handlers selling half of their stake in the company to raise $2.5 million towards the payout.

Handler was going through a very rough patch, also recovering from breast cancer and a mastectomy. After being appalled at the prosthetics available, she began developing a new range of prosthetic breasts called Nearly Me. Ever the entrepreneur, the product was a hit and she sold the company for $1 million before her death in 2002 at the age of eighty-five.

Today, the $8.3 billion Mattel is the number one toy company in the world, incorporating toy giants including Fisher-Price and Hot Wheels. One of the original Barbies from the first New York Toy Fair in good condition is worth around $5,000.

NOTES

"**I realized that if...**" Handler, Ruth and Jacqueline Shannon. *Dream Doll: the Ruth Handler Story*. Longmeadow Press, 1994.

"**They didn't think...**" Handler, Ruth and Jacqueline Shannon. *Dream Doll: The Ruth Handler Story*. Longmeadow Press, 1994.

REFERENCES

Brand Strategy, BusinessWeek, Financial Times, Fortune, Los Angeles Times, Marketing, The Economist, The Guardian, The Independent, The Observer, The Times, USA Today, Washington Post

Hallmark Cards

Folksy pansy greeting cards are more popular than you might think

———

THE CREATOR OF THE HALLMARK GREETING CARD EMPIRE, Joyce C. Hall, was already earning money to survive by the time he was eight in the small town of David City, Nebraska. His father, a true cad, left his wife and three children when Joyce was just seven. For Hall, hunger was a great motivator to make money. He dreamt of being able to eat a baked potato with three pieces of butter every day.

At sixteen Hall and his two brothers, Rollie and Bill, started an imported postcard business. Despite postcards being all the rage at the time, the business was not a great success. Hall knew he needed to find bigger markets than a tiny Midwestern town.

At the age of eighteen, in 1910, Hall caught a train to Kansas City with two shoeboxes full of postcards and started his own card company. He sold postcards to local shops and also started a mail order business from his single bed in the Kansas City YMCA. He sent packages of postcards to towns in the Midwest. Simply addressed to "The Leading Postcard Dealer," he relied on the post offices in each district to know which dry goods store to deliver the cards to. Some stores sent the cards back, some sold the cards but didn't send back the money, but enough stores sent back the proceeds and ordered more postcards. Soon Hall was asked to leave the YMCA due to his excessive volumes of mail. Things weren't so bad; he now had $200 in the bank.

Hall found new premises and, when his brother Rollie joined him in the big smoke, the pair formed their company called Hall Brothers. It was around this time (1911) that Hall noticed the postcard's popularity waning and he had an inkling of what could replace it: a missive that was the perfect balance between letter and postcard—the greeting card, a more personal method of communication. As an added attraction for less articulate people, his cards would contain a heartfelt message. In 1915, the Hall brothers began making their own greeting cards, unlocking a previously untapped revenue stream that today delivers more than $4 billion in sales annually to the company.

In 1915, a fire destroyed all of the Hall Brothers' stock, but the pair refinanced, bought an engraving business, hired an illustrator, and introduced the lucrative Hall Brothers Christmas cards. In 1921, Hall's other brother, William, joined the business. They started printing "Hallmark" on the back of each greeting card in 1928, but the Hall brothers did not officially change the company name to Hallmark Cards until 1954.

Today, the company churns out more than 23,000 new and redesigned cards each year, with the bestseller remaining a folksy pansy card first printed in 1941. It has sold more than 30 million copies.

Under JC, as Joyce was known, Hallmark introduced groundbreaking staff policies such as holiday pay, life insurance, and even paid bonuses to long-serving staff. Today, the company remains privately owned. JC is remembered as a marketing genius for his constant monitoring of card sales performance and his fascination with the behavior of customers.

A third generation of the Hall family is running Hallmark today with annual sales of more than $4 billion. The family still owns two-thirds of the company stock, and Donald Joyce Hall Jr. is the current CEO. JC died in 1982 at age ninety-one, leaving his property to his children and more than $100 million to charity. "Work is how I have fun," he said.

NOTES

"Work is how I . . ." *United Press International*, "Hallmark Founder's Estate Said to Be $100 Million," 11.2.82.

REFERENCES

Advertising Age, Associated Press, Brandweek, BusinessWeek, Businesswire, Chicago Sun-Times, CNN, *Financial Times, The Guardian*, Hallmark.com, Hoover's Company Capsules, *Inc, Investors Business Daily, Kansas City Star, New Yorker, New York Times, Philadelphia Inquirer, PR Newswire, Washington Post, Washington Times*

Section 2

THANKS FOR THE IDEA

Red Bull

Taste doesn't always matter

A FIZZY ENERGY DRINK IN A SLIMLINE CAN HAS JUGGERNAUTED its way to beverage superstardom. Launched in 1987 in Austria, Red Bull now sells more than 1.9 million cans of sweet, caffeine-packed energy drink in over seventy countries around the world each year. Red Bull is enjoying up to 90 percent share of the energy drink market in countries where it is sold.

The man behind the brand is tan, tall, and media-shy Austrian billionaire Dietrich Mateschitz—a former toothpaste salesman and marketing executive for German company Blendax, later acquired by multinational food company Proctor & Gamble. It was Mateschitz who took a Thai drink favored by blue-collar workers, students, and drivers and turned it into a global phenomenon.

While working in Asia, Mateschitz came across caffeine-filled energy drinks on sale throughout the region. Often foul-tasting, the drinks typically contained exotic ingredients that promised to remedy ailments from flu to impotency. They were sold at a premium price in tiny bottles or vials. According to company history, Mateschitz got the idea for his business while sitting in the Mandarin Hotel in Hong Kong in 1982, sipping on such a drink.

Mateschitz started investigating the potential for energy drinks and began hearing about the fortunes being made from selling them locally. He set about finding a formula he could take back to Austria. The answer was Krating Daeng, Thai for "red water buffalo." The Thai version of Red Bull is a non-fizzy drink containing synthetic taurine (an amino acid), caffeine, sugar, and glucuronolactone, a substance that is claimed to give its drinkers increased stamina, enhanced mental alertness, and physical endurance. Krating Daeng had been created by Thai Chaleo Yoovidhya's TC Pharmaceutical Company in 1978. Chaleo Yoovidhya happened to be a Blendax licensee in Thailand, and met with Mateschitz in Bangkok and struck a deal so that Mateschitz could license the drink in Austria. "I eventually managed to convince him," says Mateschitz. Both Yoovidhya and Mateschitz own 49 percent of Red Bull, and Yoovidhya's son has the other 2 percent. They each initially invested $500,000 of savings in the deal.

Mateschitz then spent three years analyzing the market, working on the new formula, developing a marketing strategy, and finalizing the design of the can (smaller than a Coke can but more expensive for consumers to buy) before he finally got approval from Austria's Ministry of Health. Mateschitz founded Red Bull GmbH in 1987 in Fuschl, Austria, near Salzburg. Mateschitz says he spent millions developing the product for the western market but won't disclose where he found his backers.

Mateschitz took a health tonic, made it less syrupy, gave it more fizz, put it into a sleek, slim can, and turned it into a "smart drink" that claims to enhance performance. He was not deterred by terrible market research that told him his drink was truly disgusting. It is made primarily from synthetic ingredients, many of which are supplied by pharmaceutical companies. The debut of Red Bull in 1987 was an enticing market proposition at a time when a new wave of sports drinks were taking off in the Western market.

Red Bull had a positive response from the market. It was first launched outside Austria in Hungary and then gradually throughout Europe. Red Bull took on the U.S. market in 2001 and, after a slow start, sales are now booming. "When we first started, we said there is no existing market for Red Bull. But Red Bull will create it. And that is what finally became true," says Mateschitz.

Part of Mateschitz's genius is how he has positioned Red Bull in the marketplace. He built Red Bull's reputation away from the mainstream, connecting the drink to a world far from ordinary, to extreme sports, the hippest bars, vintage airplanes, and aerobatics teams, to every kind of motor racing and adventure, to Flugtag (a daredevil competition where people build their own flying machines), and even to a wacky cartoon version of Leonardo da Vinci, who stars in many of Red Bull's advertising campaigns.

Mateschitz puts the success of Red Bull down to marketing: "It is essential that one develops a unique communication and advertising strategy, above and below the line, a campaign that combines body and mind in a very non-conformist way. The image of Red Bull is definitely nothing to do with any food product, but has a luxury, lifestyle identification."

The brand is all about mystique (and you thought it was just a drink). The company devised tactics such as recruiting teams of cool college students to act as "consumer educators." They take cases of Red Bull to the "right" parties to create a buzz about it, rather than trying to promote the product through traditional channels. Red Bull has fleets of custom-built cars driving around city streets promoting the brand, and then there has been the supporting role of celebrities such as Madonna, Britney Spears, and Demi Moore, snapped by paparazzi drinking their afternoon Red Bull pick-me-up as part of their so-called normal daily lives. Through these channels, the company has created a brand associated with a life less ordinary—a world away from the other type of Red Bull drinkers: those working away in a call center, office, or study, needing a kick-start.

The Red Bull marketing campaign has not been cheap to pull off. *Sports Illustrated* magazine estimates that, in 2002, Red Bull spent $80 million on sponsoring extreme sports events such as the Flugtag human flying competitions and kite-boarding from Miami to the Cuban coastline (without shark nets). Red Bull sponsors up to five hundred extreme athletes and has a motor racing academy in Austria for studying and developing the athletic potential of motor racers. The greatest publicity triumph so far has been a Red Bull-sponsored crossing of the English Channel by Austrian Felix Baumgartner, who jumped from a plane 9,000 meters above Dover and glided across the Channel aided only by carbon-fiber fixed wings, to land in Calais six minutes later. Mateschitz also has a Formula One racing team. Overall, an estimated 30 percent of revenue is spent on marketing the product.

The real threat to the continued success of Red Bull is from a health perspective. Critics argue that Red Bull has introduced a new generation to caffeine addiction. The drink has already been banned in Canada, Denmark, Norway, and France. The company itself recommends drinking no more than eight cans per day.

Mateschitz shies away from the media, preferring the brand to take center stage. He is known as a bit of a playboy, likes extreme sports, and owns a Fijian island. He has built an office in Fuschl in the shape of two volcanos. With an estimated fortune of $2 billion, he can easily afford an aircraft hangar that houses his collection of sixteen priceless aircraft. Mateschitz is also building a motor sport and aviation theme park in Austria. Mateschitz has no plans at this stage to sell the business that he sees is still all about reaching new markets. Sales have already reached $2 billion and the company is now looking to Mexico, Russia, and the Middle East to start drinking the sugary, caffeinated Red Bull. Mateschitz can be confident that a few more priceless airplanes are not going to break his bank.

NOTES

"When we first started..." Gschwandtner. "The Powerful Sales Strategy behind Red Bull," *Selling Power*, p. 60, 9.04.

"I eventually managed . . ." Kositchotethana, Boonsong. "Austrian Marketing Mogul Puts Stamp on Thailand's Original Red Bull Drink," Marketing section, *Bangkok Post*, 8.29.03.

"It is essential that . . ." Kositchotethana, Boonsong. "Austrian Marketing Mogul Puts Stamp on Thailand's Original Red Bull Drink," Marketing section, *Bangkok Post*, 8.29.03.

REFERENCES

Australian Financial Review, Brandweek, BRW, Business Times Singapore, Fast Company, Financial Times, Forbes, Guardian, Jerusalem Post, Montreal Mirror, The Nation, Outside, San Francisco Chronicle, Selling Power, Sports Illustrated, Sunday Times, The Times

Sony Walkman

Make it pocket-size

APPLE MAY HAVE BROUGHT US THE IPOD, BUT IT WAS SONY who came up with the original template some two decades earlier. That was, of course, the Walkman, the portable cassette player that laid the foundations for every handheld entertainment device since, right up to the iPod and Sony's own multimedia portable PlayStation PSP. The Walkman—and its modern incarnations—is such a daily necessity for millions (if not billions) of people that it's impossible to imagine a world without it. Yet it nearly never happened: it underwent no market research, there was no obvious demand for it, even its name was nonsense.

Sony went ahead with the Walkman anyway, on the orders of its maverick cofounder Akio Morita, and for the first month after it went on sale in July 1979, it looked like the omens had been correct: only 3,000 of the first batch of 30,000 units sold.

Then, somehow, it started to catch on. Most likely because anybody who actually tried the Walkman was amazed by the unexpectedly high-quality stereo sound. A press demonstration was held in a park where journalists could try it out on the move and observe active young people enjoying it while they rode bicycles. Sony even took the unusual step of hiring demonstrators to walk the streets and persuade passersby to have a listen. Suddenly the Walkman crossed a word-of-mouth threshold and retailers in

Japan had trouble keeping any in stock. Sony had to double its production run every month.

Word spread overseas when tourists bought them in Japan and raved about them back home, and initial plans to modestly launch the device under several region-specific names (including Soundabout in the United States, Stowaway in the United Kingdom, and Freestyle in Sweden) were shelved. Everybody wanted this new "Walkman"—a word that instantly entered the vernacular. In 1986 the name was even included in the Oxford English Dictionary. Other manufacturers rapidly produced their own versions, but whatever they called them, to the buying public they were all Walkmans.

Stories vary as to how the Walkman actually came about, but Akio Morita was certainly its champion. In one account, Morita wanted to listen to music while he played tennis. In another, he observed cofounder Masaru Ibuka staggering around with a conventional tape recorder and wanted to do him a favor. In yet another, he wanted to give the device to his children so he would not have to listen to their rock music. According to Sony's official history, Ibuka was about to travel overseas and wanted to listen to music while on the plane, so Sony's engineers whipped something up in four days, converting an existing player called the Pressman, which used special batteries that disappointingly ran out during Ibuka's trip (and were not easily replaceable). Whatever actually inspired the Walkman is irrelevant—because it served all of these purposes and many more besides.

Technically, the Walkman was nothing special. The first model was built in such a hurry—four months, for a summer launch—there was no choice but to fling it together from pieces cannibalized from existing products with some canny modifications suggested by Morita, including twin headphone jacks for shared music and a "talk" button that muted the sound so you could have a conversation with someone. Many years later, in fact, a German inventor attempted to sue Sony for patent infringement, claiming he had come up with the idea in 1972 while on a skiing trip, but the British patent court found that the idea was technologically "obvious" and therefore did not amount to an "invention."

It was Morita, however, who was the first to exploit the commercial potential in this "obvious" device. "Our plan is to lead the public with new products rather than ask them what kind of products they want," he said in his autobiography. "The public do not know what is possible but we do."

Many thought the first Walkman needed a recording function: Morita alone disagreed. Neither was he overly concerned with its looks. Above all, it had to be reliable, or it would flop. Later models were prettier, most notably the stunning (for its time) Walkman II, which was the size of a cassette case. Morita also insisted on new, lightweight headphones.

Above all, as John Nathan points out in his comprehensive history of the company, *Sony: The Private Life* (HarperCollinsBusiness, 1999), the Walkman existed solely because of Morita's instinct and determination that it should.

Perhaps the Walkman was so successful because it provided much more than music: with its headphones it was an insular, cocooning experience that provided a little bubble of privacy, even on a crowded commuter train. Its relative cheapness (launched at a modest $280) and compact size also meant anybody could now enjoy the quality of stereo sound previously available only to those who could afford expensive hi-fi equipment. It was also remarkable that Morita, in his sixties, and Ibuka, in his seventies, had such a strong instinct for what would sell to consumers in their teens and early twenties.

Akio Morita and Masaru Ibuka met in the Japanese navy during World War II when they were working on a research project into heat-seeking weapons. In 1946, Ibuka set up a company that converted AM radios into shortwave radio receivers, and soon Morita joined him. Their company was initially called Tokyo Tsushin, or Tokyo Telecommunications Research Institute, and their factory was on the third floor of a bombed department store. Their main focus was radios, but in need of cash they quickly turned out some cheap consumer goods including a rice cooker that tended to burn the rice and an electrically heated cushion that caught fire and burned people's bottoms.

They had more success with more complicated technology, producing Japan's first reel-to-reel tape recorder (the G-type), then, in 1955, Japan's first transistor radio, after Ibuka, on his first trip to the United States in 1952, negotiated the rights to license the transistor technology, which had been invented in Bell Laboratories in 1948, for $25,000 from Bell's parent company, Western Electric.

Ibuka handled technology development while Morita showed a knack for marketing. In 1957, Sony claimed it had built the world's first pocket-sized radio, the TR-63; when it turned out to be slightly larger than most pockets, Morita simply had his salesmen demonstrate it using shirts with slightly larger pockets. More importantly, this was the first Japanese transistor radio to be exported, and it met with great success.

In 1958, they changed the name of the company to Sony, a made-up word they believed suggested youthfulness. More importantly, it was a word that was easily pronounced everywhere, especially as it was written in Roman characters, an unusual step at the time for a Japanese company. Morita also showed an early penchant for travel and an ability to charm, both of which were important in breaking into overseas markets. His visit to the Dutch electronics giant Philips in 1953 convinced him Sony should seek a global market. So, in 1963, he moved his family to New York for a year and became a hit on the social scene, entertaining the likes of Henry Kissinger. With his distinctive mop of white hair and outspoken views—particularly for a Japanese businessman—he became the global face both of Sony and Japanese manufacturing. In the early 1970s, he grew his hair long because, he told a group of executives, the company should be a trendsetter and he did not want to fall behind the times either.

Under Ibuka's guidance, Sony established itself as a technological pioneer, including among its successes the Trinitron television (a new format that set the standard for decades to come), the PlayStation in all its forms, the first videocassette recorder designed for home use, and, with Philips, compact disc technology.

But Morita understood that branding and salesmanship were just as important as products. Early on, he turned down an order for 100,000 radios from the American company Bulova because they had to carry Bulova's logo; despite the financial cost, he always said that was the best decision he ever made. Sony's logo dates back to 1973, and is almost identical to the one designed in 1957. There has been constant emphasis on making the design of all Sony products as uniform as possible, so that each is instantly recognizable as "a Sony." According to company history, in 1983 Morita himself thought up one of Sony's most effective advertising campaigns with the classic catchphrase: "It's a Sony!"

This blend of constant research and unchanging brand values gave the Sony name such cachet that for many years it was able to charge 20 to 30 percent more than its rivals for similar products. That margin has eroded recently as Sony struggled to compete in plasma screens and computers, but the company—now headed by non-Japanese-speaking, Welsh-born Howard Stringer—is still viewed by many consumers as the premium Japanese brand of electronics, particularly following the success of its market-dominating PlayStation and PlayStation Portable video game systems.

NOTES
"Our plan is . . ." Morita, Akio. *Made in Japan,* E.P. Dutton, 1986.

REFERENCES
Morita, Akio. *Made in Japan,* E.P. Dutton, 1986.
Nathan, John. *Sony: the Private Life,* Houghton Mifflin, 1999.

BusinessWeek, Daily Mail, Financial Times, Fortune, The Guardian, The Independent, The Independent on Sunday, Los Angeles Times, New York Times, Sony company history

Section 3

THE LONG AND WINDING ROAD

Liquid Paper

From little things big things grow

BORN IN 1924, TEXAN BETTE NESMITH GRAHAM WAS A single mother who wanted to be an artist, but in order to support her young son Michael she had to settle for life as a secretary. She began work for the Texas Bank & Trust in 1951 and, despite her poor typing skills, Graham did well, becoming an executive secretary for the chairman of the board. In the 1950s this was about as high as women could expect to climb on the corporate ladder.

Around the same time, the electric typewriter was gradually making its way into American offices. It proved an enormous headache for Graham as the carbon-film ribbons in the machines could be extremely messy. It was impossible to get rid of mistakes (which she made all the time) without leaving blotches of ink behind.

Graham came up with the idea for Liquid Paper when workers were painting the bank windows for the holiday season. When a mistake was made on the window decorations it was simply painted over with white paint. Now, why couldn't Graham do that when she was typing?

She began to use white, water-based tempera paint and a thin paintbrush to cover her typing errors, calling it "Mistake Out." She mixed the Mistake Out in her kitchen, using her artistic skills to blend the paint to match the exact shade of paper. Her boss never noticed the paint on his documents and for five years she kept her product secret. Eventually, though, her colleagues found out about it and wanted Graham to share her secret weapon against typos. She sold the first bottle of Mistake Out in 1956.

The recipe for Mistake Out evolved over time as Graham always wanted to improve the product to be thicker and faster drying. Unable to afford the services of a real chemist, the resourceful Graham recruited an office supplier, a school chemistry teacher, and a friend from a paint company to help her perfect her product. As Mistake Out became increasingly popular, her son and his friends helped fill bottles with the white mixture in Graham's garage.

Graham had a good product, which she renamed Liquid Paper in 1958, but it was certainly no overnight success. She continued to work in the bank, managing her business after hours, making batches in her kitchen and packing and distributing from the garage. By 1957, she was selling around one hundred bottles a month. Good press coverage in an office supply magazine increased turnover fivefold and the business begn to show real potential. Graham began researching how to develop her business further and promote her product, and would often cold-call office suppliers.

In 1958, Graham was fired from the bank for using its letterhead on one of her Liquid Paper deals, but by then she could just about afford to devote her time to the Liquid Paper business as orders kept increasing.

She hired part-time help, but it was not until 1961, thirteen years after she first created the correction fluid, that Graham took on her first full-time employee. In 1964, Liquid Paper headquarters moved to a purpose-built shed in her backyard. In 1968, the company was big enough to invest in a factory and a grown-up head office. Annual sales had reached $1 million. Liquid Paper headquarters was built in Dallas and, under Graham's instructions, included a childcare center and a library. Throughout the sixties, demand for Liquid Paper soared and by 1969, the company was producing one million bottles each year. By 1972, five million bottles were sold annually and sales only continued to increase.

Graham retired from the company in 1975 to concentrate on philanthropy, charitable work for women's welfare, and the arts. She died in 1980, at age fifty-six, just six months after selling her corporation for $47.5 million to Gillette, leaving a fortune and royalties to her only son (a member of the pop band The Monkees) and to the charities she established. Liquid Paper is now owned by Newell Rubbermaid.

A Christian Scientist, Graham is remembered as a feminist whose invention showed people what women could do in a time when they were not often seen beyond the role of the housewife.

REFERENCES

Albuquerque Journal, *Chicago Sun-Times*, *The Guardian*, *Houston Chronicle*, Ideafinder.com, *Insight on the News*, Inventors.About.com, Massachusetts Institute of Technology Inventor Archive, *New York Times*, *Washington Post*

Dyson

Suck it and see

———

JAMES DYSON WOULD HATE THIS, BUT HIS GREATEST ACHIEVEMENT was to turn the vacuum cleaner into a status symbol—a desirable, covetable object that people were prepared to pay top dollar to own. Dyson, an engineer and inventor, would no doubt prefer to think that the public appreciates the technical brilliance behind his invention and believes as obsessively as he does that rival vacuums are so inferior as to be worthless. He is that kind of guy. Either way, his "dual cyclone" became the best-selling upright model in America (in dollar terms), has appeared on *Friends*, and has been handed out in gift bags to presenters at the Oscars.

Dyson was born in England in 1947; his father died when he was just nine. He thought he might be an actor, but then studied art and design at the British Royal College of the Arts. With little formal technical training, he went to work for a friend who ran an engineering company, recognized Dyson's talent for invention, and set him to work inventing a new kind of flat-hulled boat called the Sea Truck. Dyson added the art of salesmanship to his talent as a designer and could have worked there forever, but left out of a desire to go it alone.

He started up a company building a contraption called the Ball-barrow, a plastic wheelbarrow that used a pneumatic ball instead of a traditional wheel, minimizing damage to lawns and rolling through sticky mud with impunity. Through small ads in newspaper supplements, Dyson advertised it at three times the price of conventional barrows, and although it soon took the bulk of the British domestic market, it was only moderately successful. "The problem," he says, "was that the wheelbarrow market wasn't very big. It was a great idea but never made any money."

In 1978, he turned his attention to another mundane household object, the vacuum cleaner, in a fit of irritation when his ancient Hoover wouldn't pick up enough dirt. Dyson surmised that as the bag filled with fluff, the motor lost its ability to suck, as the particles blocked the tiny holes in the paper that drew the air through. Instead of just buying a newer, more powerful model like anyone else might have done, Dyson set about rethinking the fundamentals of vacuum design. After observing how a local sawmill used an enormous cyclone system to separate out sawdust, he figured a similar technology could work in vacuums. He made a basic cyclone out of cardboard, stuck it onto his Hoover instead of the bag, and was amazed to discover it worked. But it needed finessing. At the age of thirty, and married with children, Dyson raised $80,000 by selling a block of land and borrowing some money from a friend, and devoted the next three and a half years to building prototypes—he built 5,127 in all—living on his wife Deirdre's teacher's salary, and penny-pinching around the home.

"I had lots of doubts," he now admits. But he eventually produced a design he called a "dual cyclone," achieving his goal of a machine that used a twisting torrent of air to throw dust into a canister instead of through a traditional bag, leaving its ability to suck uncompromised by a build-up of dust (it's difficult to visualize the process without a diagram; for a full technical explanation go to www.dyson.com).

That should have been the end of the story—great invention, swift success. But when Dyson took his prototype on the road to the major British and European manufacturers, nobody wanted it, largely, Dyson believes, because its existence mocked their expertise—if there was a better way of designing a vacuum cleaner, why had nobody at their company done it already? He also wondered, were they in the vacuum cleaner business, or the business of selling vacuum bags?

Potential success with an American firm turned to disaster when they reneged on the deal and simply "borrowed" the design, but Dyson eventually licensed the technology to a Japanese company who built it in pink and sold it locally as the G-Force for the equivalent of $2,000, creating a sensation as a tech-fashion statement in 1986. Dyson then negotiated a series of near-fatal licensing deals with American companies, which left him mired in expensive legal battles, but eventually enough versions of his machine made it to market that he was able to survive until, with tooling financed by Lloyds Bank and from sales of the G-Force in Japan, he started building and selling his machines under his own name in Britain.

He launched the first model under his own name, the Dyson DC-01, in January 1993. It looked radically different from anything else on the market, with Dyson's technology enveloped in a grey and yellow body with a clear plastic cylinder you could watch filling up with dust. People thought he was mad on several counts. His bagless idea was batty. His plan to take on the multinationals with his own factory was ludicrous. Marketing types who saw the machine in operation swore customers would be revolted by the sight of swirling grime. And the price, close to $350—more than twice the price of a conventional model—was ridiculous. But Dyson believed people would be happy to pay for a superior product and was proved right when, after a low-key introduction that lasted two nail-biting years, he convinced major retailers to stock his baby, and in February 1995 the Dyson became the best-selling vacuum cleaner in Britain. With its flamboyant looks it was, well, sexier than anything else on the market. Its innovative approach pushed the right buttons in an increasingly tech-aware marketplace, for the first time making the banal household appliance attractive to men. And the visible dirt was not a turnoff after all: in fact, customers loved seeing the results of their labors. You could actually see it removing dirt from the carpet. Not that the marketing campaign was particularly sophisticated—for all the machine's advantages, the line taken in advertisements was simply that it did not have a bag. "You can't sell more than one message at a time, or you lose the belief of the consumer," Dyson explains in his autobiography, *Against the Odds*: "We had to establish, beyond all question, that our machine overcame a problem that all other systems suffered from."

Suddenly the choice for vacuum buyers was the old-fashioned or the radical—and consumers knew what they preferred. In 1996, a Dyson was even featured on BBC news as the cleaner used to vacuum the steps outside the Prime Minister's residence at 10 Downing Street in preparation for a visit by French President François Mitterrand. A range of models followed, in a variety of bright colors, building an annual profit of $173 million by 2005.

James Dyson is now one of the richest men in Britain, worth upwards of $1.1 billion. In 2003, he bought a $35 million Georgian estate. He and wife Deirdre have three children: Jacob, an engineer; Emily, who started a bedding company; and Sam, a musician. Dyson has been invited to join numerous design boards and was recently appointed as a government adviser on manufacturing, despite a scandal over his decision to move his manufacturing to Malaysia, costing eight hundred jobs. "That was slightly upsetting," he says of the move. "It was an unhappy moment to have to make people redundant."

He owns 100 percent of the business and refuses to sell any shares, saying the risk keeps him on his toes. An uncompromising character who banned suits and ties in his company (believing they stifled creativity), he has fought a string of legal battles to defend his patents.

He is now, after all his troubles, in a position to run his business his way. The office canteen is actually a delicatessen. There are no internal walls and no pieces of furniture higher than three feet. Memos are banned in favor of conversation. "We try to get people to do things in a different way," says Dyson, whose preferred employees are those who come, unsullied, straight out of design school.

He claims his new range of washing machines (called the Counter-rotator) is as revolutionary as his dual cyclone vacuum cleaner, and has priced them accordingly. There are plans for a robotic vacuum cleaner, which has been widely publicized but not yet put on the market due to delays—an early model would have cost $2,700 in the shops, so Dyson ordered it reengineered to make it more affordable. And rather than contract out the robotics technology, Dyson hired graduates to develop their own systems. There are some 1,000 Dyson patents and countless other designs under consideration (and under wraps).

The plan is to make Dyson a global brand, synonymous with innovative, premium-priced products. Stage one, the British market, is complete. Stage two, conquering the United States, is firmly under way with strong sales of vacuums since 2002, and Dyson has been a hit in Australia and France. Stage three, to make Dyson a household name worldwide, looks like it's only a matter of time.

REFERENCES

BBC, *BusinessWeek, Daily Telegraph, Forbes, The Guardian, The Independent on Sunday, Los Angeles Times, Mail on Sunday, Sunday Telegraph, Sunday Times*

The Kellogg Company

Big brother bullies don't always win

———————

THE CREATION OF CORN FLAKES WAS AN ACCIDENT. IN THE 1890s, brothers Dr. John Kellogg and William Kellogg, sons of a broom maker, were working at America's most prestigious sanatorium, known as "the San," in Battle Creek, Michigan. The likes of Henry Ford, Thomas Edison, Amelia Earhart, George Bernard Shaw, as well as socialites and former presidents, came to the San to eat a vegetarian diet, perform rigorous calisthenics, and abstain from drinking, smoking, and the evils of sexual activity.

The five-foot-four Dr. John headed up the San and was, by all accounts, an overbearing leader. A bona fide celebrity, Dr. John was always dressed in white and often seen with a cockatoo on his shoulder. William played second fiddle and was Dr. John's bookkeeper, business manager, and lapdog. Dr. John had been given a scholarship to study medicine by the founder of the Battle Creek sanatorium, but William was not so lucky. He left school after grade six, failed as a broom salesman, and was expected to call his brother "Dr. Kellogg," even giving him a shave or a shoeshine when requested.

John and William were always experimenting with cereals, trying to come up with palatable new foods for the San guests who, as part of their health regime, would eat dried, ground-up bread for breakfast. These early versions of breakfast cereal were so tough that patients were in danger of breaking teeth trying to eat their breakfast.

One day in 1894, John and William were preparing boiled wheat that they would put through rollers to form long, flat sheets of dough for breakfast. John was called off to see a patient and the sheets were left to dry out for two days. The brothers then put the dry wheat dough through the roller again and, instead of one sheet of wheat, it broke into little flakes. So they baked the flakes until they became crunchy and served them with milk to patients. The patients loved the cereal, which the brothers called Granose. When patients left the San, they would mail order stocks of the cereal and other San health foods, such as a coffee substitute. John was initially appalled by the idea of lending the Kellogg name to any commercial enterprise but he allowed the mail-order business, called the Sanitas Nut Food Company, to develop slowly. After John patented their cereal-making process, William was left to run the concern.

Meanwhile, a booming industry of health food copycat companies was sprouting up in the area. Former San patient Charles Post formed the successful C.W. Post Company, selling coffee substitutes and a cereal called Grape Nuts. His company would later become part of General Foods, and Post is credited with kicking off the commercialization of wheat flakes.

William continued experimenting with the flake process and by 1898 he had replaced the wheat with corn hearts and added malt flavoring. With his now well-honed business skills, William approached former patients at the clinic and managed to raise $200,000. In exchange for stock in the company, John gave William his cereal patents, and when John frittered away his stock by giving it to his sanatorium staff in lieu of pay raises, William proceeded to buy the shares back from the staff.

By 1906, William had the majority of shares and became general manager of the Sanitas Nut Food Company. He changed the company name to the Battle Creek Toasted Corn Flakes Company, betting on the success of his breakfast cereal. He started putting his signature on each cereal box, to further differentiate his Corn Flakes from other health food products. Soon he had three hundred employees producing 4,000 boxes of Corn Flakes a day. "I am not interested in selling Corn Flakes by mail," William said in 1905. "I want to sell them by the car load."

By 1914, Corn Flakes were being sold in Canada and the UK followed in 1922—the same year the company was renamed the Kellogg Company. In 1924, the first Kellogg's factory in Australia was opened. There are now Kellogg's factories in nineteen countries, including Japan, Latvia, India, China, and Mexico.

As well as paying above-award wages to his workforce (thus avoiding industrial trouble), William spent as much as he could afford on advertising, educating American women in magazines such as *Ladies' Home Journal* on the benefits of a cereal-based breakfast. According to Kellogg's records, sales leapt from thirty-three to 2,900 cases per day after the ads were published in 1910.

William planned quirky marketing stunts, such as the risqué 'Wednesday is Wink Day' campaign, promising housewives a free sample of Kellogg's cereal if they winked at their grocer. In another stunt, housewives were offered a year's supply of Corn Flakes if they convinced their grocer to stock the cereal. William also began placing trinkets in the cereal as an added incentive to buy Corn Flakes and he employed a dietician to develop recipes using Corn Flakes.

Kellogg's continued to advertise heavily during the Depression, kept sales high, and was even able to increase production despite the struggling economy.

William Kellogg amassed a fortune, much of which he gave away or invested in Battle Creek schools and other local facilities. In 1930, he used $47 million to establish the Kellogg Foundation, which still owns 31 percent of the Kellogg Company. William died in 1951 at the age of 91.

The Kellogg Company remains the world's biggest cereal producer, with around 25,000 employees. It has approximately one-third of the cereal market. Its products, including William's other creations—All-Bran, Special K, and Rice Krispies—are sold in 160 countries, with annual sales in 2004 of $9.6 billion.

The most radical recent changes at Kellogg's have been Corn Flakes' new foil wrapping in some markets, and experiments with a new box shape to further seal in the cereal's freshness. Some analysts believe these changes are a response to Kellogg's having lately lost market share to arch rival Weetabix.

Battle Creek remains the center of the Kellogg's empire, with pretty much the whole town named after the cereal company. The popular tours of the plant have stopped, though, due to paranoia about competitors poaching company information.

The product that started out as a health food for "overweight women and overworked men" is no longer considered a health food at all—it's become more mainstream than Dr. John could ever have imagined with literally billions of bowls of the cereal eaten every year. Kellogg's has been forced to alter the original recipe, cutting the salt content of Corn Flakes due to increasing concerns that salt levels are too high. Despite the changes, a bowl of Corn Flakes still contains more salt that a standard bag of potato chips.

NOTES

"I am not interested in selling . . ."   Zacharias, Patricia. "Snap, Crackle and Profit," *Michigan History Magazine*, 8.7.99.

REFERENCES

Gould, William. *VGM's Business Portraits: Kellogg's*, NTC Publishing Group, McGraw Hill, 1997.

Adweek, Associated Press, BusinessWeek, Business Wire, Daily Mail, Evening Standard, Hoover's Company Records, *Investor's Business Daily,* Kellogg.com, *Michigan History Magazine, New York Times, Palm Beach Daily Business Review, Seattle Times, Toronto Star*

3M and the Post-it Note

Developing new products is a sticky business

THE POST-IT NOTE WAS NOT INVENTED IN A SHED BY AN aspiring inventor who was then able to single-handedly get the product to market. Its success is credited to two salary men, Art Fry and Spence Silver, who worked as research scientists at diversified technology company 3M.

Silver invented the not-so-sticky glue on the Post-it Note in 1968 while he was experimenting with glues to use with adhesive tape. Silver's adhesive was revolutionary because it could stick and come unstuck without ruining the surface it touched. He couldn't find a real use for the adhesive, but he kept plugging away, promoting his "low-tack" adhesive to other researchers within 3M, hoping to spark some interest.

It was another scientist, Art Fry, who, after attending one of Silver's presentations, came to see a commercial use for the glue. During a church choir rehearsal, Fry became irritated when the paper markers he used to mark pages in his hymn book kept falling out. He realized that if he used Silver's adhesive on the paper notes, he could mark the pages with sticky bookmarks without damaging the book. Bingo.

But the development of this practical, original product was a slow process. Even five years after Silver created his adhesive, commercialization of the Post-it Note was barely plodding along. Some 3M executives thought the Post-it Note would be competing with scrap paper and therefore people would never pay for the 3M alternative.

Nonetheless, Fry kept working on his pet project, setting up a machine in his basement that could apply the sticky adhesive to rolls of paper. Fry has always maintained that problems are par for the course in the innovation process. "A lot of my type of folks just love problems that have stumped others or that have not even been recognized by others as a problem," he said. "People just love to create things and they tend to love and nourish what they create."

The first market tests of the product in 1977 were not encouraging. But 3M did its own in-house trials and found that the staff was beginning to use Post-it Notes as a new way of communicating, leaving them as reminders here, there, and everywhere. The company was still in two minds when a 3M executive arranged to have Post-its (then known as "Press and Peel" notes) tested in a town called Boise in Virginia to see if people would buy them, but the response was overwhelmingly positive, and the Post-it Note was saved from extinction.

When the Post-it Note was finally launched in 1980, it was an instant success. There are now more than 1,000 varieties of Post-it Notes on the market. Fry stayed with 3M, rising up through the ranks and winning international awards, until his retirement after forty years with the company.

3M has a track record for clever inventions, from disposable diaper closure tape and CFC-free inhalers to fiber-optic network connections and Scotch Magic Tape. The company has interests in the industrial, consumer, transportation, and healthcare sectors, has developed the careers of more than 7,000 scientists, and registers hundreds of patents each year. It also has a policy of allowing scientists to spend a proportion of their work time on personal scientific projects.

As a publicly listed company, 3M needs to continue to generate serious revenue from its ideas. In 2004, 3M had sales of more than $20 billion and several hundred million of that figure can be attributed to the Post-it Note. The hope for the scientists and the long-term bottom line of the company is that staff will continue to have time to develop their ideas. Perhaps 3M management should heed Art Fry's words: "If we discover something, we have a chance to stop and look at it. This is very important because lots of things are discovered and passed by because everybody's too busy."

NOTES

"A lot of my type . . ." O'Leary, Christopher K. "The Pain Papers Newsletter #6," The Power of Pain.com, 8.31.01.

"People just love . . ." O'Leary, Christopher K. "The Pain Papers Newsletter #6," The Power of Pain.com, 8.31.01.

"If we discover . . ." Bob Black, Great Ideas for Living, GreatIdeasforLiving.com.

REFERENCES

SAM Advance Management Journal, vol. 52 number 3, summer 1987.

3M.com, *BBC News*, *BusinessWeek*, *The Guardian*, Hoovers Company Capsules, *The Independent*, Inventors.About.com, Massachusetts Institute of Technology School of Engineering, *New York Times, Washington Post*

Section 4

DO WHAT YOU LOVE

Weight Watchers

Stop eating chocolate cookies, start building a business

I N 1961, New York housewife Jean Nidetch was thirty-eight, weighed 195 pounds, and described herself, her bus-driver husband, her two sons, her poodle, and most of her friends as overweight. A "When are you due?" question tipped Nidetch over the edge and she decided to do something about her ballooning weight. She began her battle to overcome an addiction to chocolate cookies, which she would eat by the packet, and took herself to the New York City Department of Health obesity clinic for a diet plan.

Months later, Nidetch invited a group of six "fat friends" around for coffee and announced that she had lost forty pounds, challenging them to get with her program. The group began meeting regularly: Nidetch would hand out diet sheets and everyone would assess their weekly progress. Two months later, they all chipped in and bought some scales. "We weren't going to blame our genes, our hormones, or our mothers anymore," says Nidetch. Demand was huge. Soon there weren't enough chairs or space in her apartment.

Al Lippert, an overweight buyer for a coat company, and his wife, Felice, heard about Nidetch's meetings and invited her to their home for a meeting. As well as quickly starting to lose weight (one of the Lipperts' sons had described his parents as being "like two beach balls"), the Lipperts immediately saw the business potential in these meetings.

Nidetch and the Lipperts hatched a plan at the Lipperts' kitchen table for an enterprise they called Weight Watchers. They would run weekly motivational, empathetic meetings and charge a fee. The biggest risk was a month's rent on a space above a cinema in Little Neck, Queens. Being a woman, Nidetch could not sign the lease, so her husband (whom she later divorced) had to sign it.

The first commercial Weight Watchers meeting was held in 1963. The company charged $2 per person, per session, the same price as a movie ticket at the time. After the first meeting, Nidetch recalls stuffing more money than she had ever seen in her life into her bags. Within a year they were selling Weight Watchers franchises. The business expanded through a system where franchisees paid a few thousand dollars for a license and agreed to pay 10 percent of their revenues back to Nidetch and the Lipperts. Within three years turnover reached $160,000, and by 1970 turnover was $8 million.

With the combination of Al Lippert's business administration and marketing prowess, Felice's writing and support skills, and Nidetch's natural leadership, motivation, and speaking skills, Weight Watchers was the perfect way to make money at a time when the post-war generations were packing on the pounds. Nidetch was the "Energizer bunny," Al was the marketing genius, and Felice the creative force.

In 1978, the Lipperts and Nidetch sold the company to H.J. Heinz for $72 million. The deal was so smooth, Al Lippert has boasted that lawyers and accountants were not involved in the process. Heinz sold the business to European investment firm Artal Luxembourg in 1999, and today the company is worth $4.8 billion. There are more than 46,000 weekly Weight Watchers meetings in thirty countries around the world, with sixty million people attending meetings in 2004. Until 1997, the Weight Watchers regime had been based on a simple points system, but now two different food plans are available. One plan involves points; the other doesn't. Meetings cost more than a movie ticket these days, but the results of Weight Watchers programs speak for themselves—an estimated 78 percent of people who regularly attend Weight Watchers keep the weight off. Attendances continue to rise as the obesity epidemic continues to spread across the Western world, with more than one billion people around the world now considered to be overweight.

Al Lippert died in South Africa in 1998, after a day of golf. Felice Lippert died of lung cancer in 2003. Nidetch lives in Las Vegas and is a generous philanthropist. Nidetch says that once she learned how to stop eating chocolate cookies, she could set her mind to achieving anything. For the once overweight housewife, the business was never about the money: "I'd do this for nothing on a street corner," she once declared.

NOTES

"We weren't going to . . ." Smith, Lyrysa. "Weight Watchers Turns 40," *The Times Union*, 4.29.03, p. D1.
"Like two beach balls . . ." Lippert, Felice. Obituaries, *The Express*, 4.1.04, p. 34.
"Energizer bunny . . ." Sajbel, Maureen. "Been There, Ate That," *InStyle*, 6.97, p. 170.
"I'd do this for . . ." *PR Newswire*, 8.18.81 p 1.

REFERENCES

The Australian, CBS News: *The Osgood File, Chattanooga Times Free Press, Chicago Sun-Times, Chicago Tribune, Courier-Mail, Daily Record, Daily Telegraph, The Guardian, Herald-Sun*, Hoover's Company Capsules, *Houston Chronicle, The Independent, Mail on Sunday, Men's Fitness, New York Times, Newsday, Newsweek, The Observer, Ottawa Citizen, Sacramento Bee, Star Tribune, Sunday Age, Time, Times Union, USA Today, Vancouver Sun, Washington Post*

Quiksilver

Don't underestimate surfer dudes

O
NCE UPON A TIME IN THE LATE 1960s, TWO SURFER DUDES
were living the good life around the legendary surf spot
Bells Beach near Torquay in southern Australia. In
between surfing sessions, beers, and tins of baked beans, Alan

Green and John Law began making board shorts. They wanted to rid their lives of the uncomfortable, impractical surfing shorts available at the time. The business was funded with a $1,900 loan from Green's father. Word of mouth grew about these boardies and their little concern gained momentum. The pair also created sheepskin boots they called Ugg Boots (nice to wear after a surf in freezing conditions) and began selling those.

Green and Law got their timing right, arriving in the marketplace just as surfing culture was getting widespread mainstream attention. Following on from the 1959 movie *Gidget* and films such as *The Endless Summer* promoted the sun, sand, surf, and sex lifestyle, and a growing army of wannabes wanted to feel a part of this exclusive club, regardless of whether or not they surfed. Equipment and fashion for this market was primitive, so there was plenty of scope for new products and fashion. Quiksilver had a good idea of what their customers wanted because Green and Law wanted it too—a better wetsuit, a better surfboard, boardshorts with maximum movement, and a cool sweatshirt to wear after a surf.

In 1973, the company became known as Quiksilver, a business that has become the biggest surfwear brand in the world, valued at close to $1.5 billion. For three decades the company has enjoyed annual growth of 25 percent.

A big key to the success of Quiksilver has been its roots in surf culture and its sponsorships of top surfers, snowboarders, skateboarders, and surfing events. Quiksilver has the likes of world-champion surfer Kelly Slater and skateboarder Tony Hawk on its sponsorship books. The company has also cleverly gone to great lengths to distance itself from mainstream retailing and advertising campaigns.

Initially, Quiksilver sold its products locally, then to surf shops in other parts of Australia. As the company grew, Quiksilver sold licenses to other parts of the world. In 1976, Quiksilver launched overseas when champion surfer Jeff Hakman took twenty pairs of boardshorts back to the United States to sell. Hakman was so keen to get the U.S. license for Quiksilver he is reported to have eaten a paper doily, at Green's request, during a 1976 drinking-session dare in Torquay. He ate the doily and got the license. Hakman brought in his friend and fellow surfer Rob "Buzz" McKnight, now chairman of Quiksilver. "When Greenie first gave us the right to do Quiksilver in America, it was really just meant to be a summer project," says McKnight. "Live near the beach, chase girls, surf, have some fun. We didn't have a business plan, we didn't have this whole thing outlined and projected. We just took it as it came."

But is building a business that easy? You get the feeling that this laid-back ethos is an essential part of the brand strategy of a surfwear company. Surfers understand the importance of timing, patience, strategy, competition, and personal performance, but they tend to talk more about the metaphysical aspects of surfing than about the aggression, adrenaline, and multi-skilling needed to be a good surfer. Their natural competitiveness has surely been a part of the growth of the businesses, but the company spin is all about having board meetings on catamarans in exotic locations, opening hip new stores in Times Square with Malibu surfboards all over the ceilings.

Quiksilver listed on the New York Stock Exchange in 1986 and forged ahead. Green and Law keep their hand in the Australian operations, introducing hit lines such as Roxy, until 2002 when they sold the last of their rights to the Quiksilver name for $125 million to the U.S. operations Quiksilver International, now based in Huntington Beach, California. Law and Green still retain a 6 percent share in the company and have profit share agreements in place.

Law and Green still live in Australia's surfing capital Torquay, at least for part of the year, when they are not off skiing or surfing around the world. At every stage, they have been quick to promote the fact that surfing still takes priority over work and, now that they are in their sixties, they are living every baby boomer's dream: surfing and skiing around the world with a combined fortune of more than $400 million. Alan and John are still regularly seen at the Torquay Hotel sinking beers, thirty years later. "My first passion is not working," says Green. "You are a long time dead, and I don't want to spend my life waiting for it." They can afford to relax—owning 6 percent of a company worth nearly $1.5 billion leaves a person with plenty of options.

NOTES

"When Greenie first gave us . . ." Collins, Luke. "True Blue," *Australian Financial Review*, 3.28.03.

"My first passion . . ." Stewart, Cameron. "The Beach Boys," *The Australian Magazine*, 8.17.02, p. 1.

REFERENCES

The Age, The Australian, Australian Financial Review, BRW, Courier Mail, Herald Sun, Hobart Mercury, Hoover's Company Capsules, *New York Times, Sunday Age, Sydney Morning Herald, Weekend Australian*

Kate and Andy Spade

It's amazing what you can do with some Scotch tape and white drawing paper

———

THE KATE SPADE COMPANY, WHICH NOW ENJOYS ANNUAL SALES of more than $125 million, started with a dare at dinner. In 1991, Andy Spade and his girlfriend Kate Brosnahan were eating out in New York City. At the time, Kate was accessories editor for *Mademoiselle* magazine and was far from inspired in her $14,500 a year job. Why not start something together, suggested Andy—with his vision, her innate sense of style and attention to detail they could make something work. The couple talked about what Kate could do. Andy suggested handbags. After all, she adored them and knew the product extremely well. "How hard could it be?" said Andy.

Kate Spade arrived in New York City in 1986 with $7 in her pocket. She grew up in Kansas City, the fifth of six children. Her father ran a construction company. Kate studied journalism and met skateboarder and advertising whiz kid Andy Spade at Arizona State University. He grew up in Birmingham, Michigan.

Despite saying to Andy, "You don't just start [a business]," Kate took up Andy's dare, quit her job, and started designing handbags in their tiny apartment on the Upper West Side. The Kate Spade bag concept began with white drawing paper and Scotch tape. Kate painstakingly put together six prototypes and had samples made up in satin-finished nylon rather than leather. She found suppliers through *Women's Wear Daily* classifieds and they launched in January 1993. "Everyone said we'd be out of business in a year because we had no experience," says Andy. Kate and Andy called the company Kate Spade. The brand name was Andy's idea. "Andy kept saying 'Kate Spade, Kate Spade.' And he wasn't proposing," says Kate. (That would happen a few years down the track.)

Kate Spade started attending accessories trade shows in 1993 to spruik her wares. The night before one of the early shows, Kate was inspired to unpick all the Kate Spade labels sewn inside the bags and reattach them to the outside of the bag—and the signature Kate Spade bag was born. While the first few trade shows did not generate enough orders to cover exhibition costs, they received small orders from prestigious retailers such as Bergdorf Goodman, Barney's, and Fred Segal, a clear sign that Kate's bags were getting noticed by the fashion crowd. The Kate Spade brand was fresh, quirky, and accessible yet still stylish. Her stands always stood out, not just for the bags. Because she couldn't afford to hire the trade show furniture, Kate would set her stand up with flea market chairs and tables that she collected, adding an extra style dimension to her stands. The bags sold brilliantly and word began to spread about this 5'2" girl from Kansas City. To cope with demand, Kate invited two friends, Pamela Bell and, later, Elyce Arons, to join the business. Instead of salaries they were offered equity in the company. (She broke all those golden rules about working with friends and lovers.) Both are still principals with the company.

Kate never had the fever for conventional handbag brands—hot one minute, relegated to the back of the closet the next. She preferred vintage, having no desire to repeat what was already out there. Her range of bags was quirkier, with plaids, herringbone, bold stripes, bright linings, and a classic, uncomplicated, slightly unconventional character. After all, this was a girl known to carry raffia bags in NYC in the middle of winter. The Spades cleverly pitched their brand at the more affordable price point of $100-$500. All those girls who couldn't afford Hermes and Gucci now had a new, distinct brand of their own. They also had a new style icon in Kate, with her bold accessories, quirky bags, etiquette, midwestern charm, and a love of elegance. (After more than a decade in New York, taxi drivers mistake Kate for a tourist because she is too polite to be a local.)

Rather than have two collections of bags each year, Kate chose to offer her clients five. She playfully designed bags with a personal touch—her favorite greens, yellows, checks, even a favored wallpaper pattern could end up incorporated into a new bag. The new product lines were about that Kate wanted to do next. "One idea just leads to another," she says.

In 1993, the business had sales of a respectable $100,000. By 1995, revenues had tipped $1.5 million. The fashion press was closely following Kate's every move, the best retailers were stocking the bags, and the explosive growth of the company had begun. Andy Spade knew that he could afford to quit his day job in advertising when he started being offered lots of money for stakes in the business. He left his advertising job in 1996 and became president and creative director.

The Spades estimate that it cost $35,000 to get the business off the ground. Both loathe borrowing money, so they cashed in their savings, lived off Andy's salary from the advertising agencies he worked at, and ploughed every cent they could back into the business. There were no salaries at Kate Spade until 1996, the year Kate received an award for Best New Fashion Talent from the Council of Fashion Designers of America for her accessories.

In 1997, Kate Spade launched its leather handbag range, there were overseas licensing deals, an ad campaign, the launch of Kate Spade eyewear, and the opening of two new retail stores. This incessant growth, while exciting, created huge pressures on the business. By this stage, the Spades' home had become a giant storeroom of boxes. Neither of the Spades were prepared or interested in logistics, distribution, and other back-end aspects of the business. Andy was the marketing guru, the "brand visionary"—Kate implemented the big ideas, designed, and kept her eye on the product details.

The Spades appointed experienced fashion executive Robin Marino as president of Kate Spade in 1999. She had worked with Burberry, Ralph Lauren, and Donna Karan and brought to the company the skills it needed to expand, particularly in terms of operations and licensing deals. Later in 1999, the Spades sold a 56 percent stake in the business to prestigious retailer Neiman Marcus for $33.6 million. Now there was the cash to fuel further growth, allowing the brand to move into more categories such as stationery, footwear, beauty, accessories, and homewares. The next five years would see retail expansion, offshore expansion, particularly in Japan, and moves into homewares, luggage, textiles, wallpaper, and the Jack Spade label for men. There have been fluctuations in sales and, more recently, questions as to whether Kate Spade is continuing to develop must-have products for its customers. Not that the Kate Spade business is showing any signs of slowing down. There are plans for fifty more stores in the next three years.

From its inception, Andy Spade's marketing strategy for the brand has been brilliant, always a little offbeat, fresh, and fun, from books about what people keep in their handbags, to Kate's books on manners and entertaining, to ten-page advertisements celebrating ten years of Kate Spade that documented the dizzy soiree Kate and Andy hosted. It's all so carefully orchestrated, keeping an edge of mystery about what the pair will do next.

In October 2004, Andy announced that he would be stepping down as chief executive of Kate Spade. He is expected to launch a brand consultancy. Added to his previous experience managing accounts for companies including Pepsi and Coach, he should be very highly sought after.

Today, the pair live on the Upper East Side, surrounded by their contemporary art collection, flea market finds, Kate-designed wallpapers, flatware, glassware, and the honeysuckle perfume that is Kate's signature scent. The latest addition to the household is their daughter Frances Beatrix Spade, born in February 2005. In September 2005, the *New York Times* reported that Kate Spade is considering putting the business on the market, or selling off further stakes in the business to finance growth. Thirty new retail stores is not a cheap exercise.

NOTES
"How hard could it be . . ." The *Tulsa World*, 1.15.1998.

"You don't just start . . ." Tischler, Linda. "Kate Spade," *Fast Company*, 3.05.

"Everyone said . . ." Walton, A Scott. "A Clothing Line Not in the Cards," *The Atlanta Journal and Constitution*, 10.26.03.

"Andy kept saying..." McCauley, Lucy. "Next Stop the 21st Century," *Fast Company*, 9.99.

"One idea . . ." White, Jackie. "Kate Spade: the Woman and the Brand Share a Flexible Nature," *The Kansas City Star*, 9.10.02.

REFERENCES
Atlanta Journal and Constitution, CNN, *Footwear News*, *Forbes Small Business*, *InStyle*, *New York Times*, *Town & Country*, *USA Today*, *Vanity Fair*, *Vogue*, *W* magazine, *WWD*, *Washington Post*

Nobu

Sushi with a twist

————

HOW THE SON OF A TOKYO TIMBER MERCHANT CAME TO BE running one of the world's most fashionable restaurant chains is a lesson in making the most of opportunities and talent—and riding out bad luck.

Nobuyuki "Nobu" Matsuhisa is the chef-entrepreneur behind Nobu, the Japanese-influenced restaurant that first opened in New York and now has some eleven sister establishments as far afield as London and Tokyo.

Born in 1949, Matsuhisa lost his father in a traffic accident when he was seven. At eight, his elder brother took him to a sushi restaurant where he was so fascinated by the ritual that he remembers deciding he would make it his career. He left school at seventeen and took a live-in apprenticeship at a Tokyo sushi restaurant where he slept on the floor. The art of sushi is taken so seriously Matsuhisa was not allowed to make sushi for his first three years; instead he spent his time fetching fish, cleaning, and washing plates.

Once behind the counter, however, he made friends with a Peruvian of Japanese descent, who persuaded Matsuhisa, then twenty-four, to go to Peru to open a restaurant in the capital, Lima. The local fish was excellent, the restaurant excelled, and Matsuhisa began to add South American flavors and techniques to his repertoire—influences that would later launch him as a major culinary force.

After three years, Matsuhisa fell out with his partners over food costs—a common chef/owner dispute—and moved to Argentina where he struggled in another restaurant for a year before returning to Japan with his wife and young daughter. Life was difficult in a cramped Tokyo apartment so in 1977 they moved again, this time to Anchorage, Alaska, where Matsuhisa borrowed money to open a restaurant. When the uninsured restaurant burned down, he was left deeply in debt and reportedly feeling suicidal. He spent the next nine years recovering, and in 1987 managed to raise the funds to open a little forty-seat restaurant in Beverly Hills, Los Angeles, which he called Matsuhisa.

The quality of his produce and skill as a chef attracted a fashionable crowd, among them actor Robert De Niro, who approached Matsuhisa to open a restaurant with him and restaurateur Drew Nieporent (president of the Myriad Restaurant Group) in New York. Matsuhisa demurred for four years, but De Niro kept his offer open and in 1994 Nobu opened in New York, while Matsuhisa retained his original restaurant in Beverly Hills.

The combination of De Niro's celebrity, Nieporent's ability to create a buzz, and Matsuhisa's innovative food was irresistible. In New York, there's a longstanding joke that it is so difficult to get a booking that staff answer the phone, "Hello, No . . ." instead of "Hello, Nobu."

Nobu opened in London in 1997, immediately becoming popular with the A-list and gaining worldwide notoriety in 1999 when it was revealed that tennis player Boris Becker had fathered a child there, during a brief after-dinner tryst in a linen cupboard with a Russian model.

Nobu London created a model for expansion that requires the close supervision of Matsuhisa himself. (Tokyo followed in 1998, then a joint venture with Giorgio Armani in Milan in 2000.) A typical two-week stretch for Matsuhisa might go like this: Los Angeles, New York, Miami, then a single day in Japan, back to Los Angeles, on to London, Paris, Tokyo, back to Los Angeles, then Miami again, New York again, then Tokyo. Though, of course these days, he travels first-class.

REFERENCES
CNN, *Daily Telegraph*, *Evening Standard*, *Financial Times*, *The Guardian*, *Korea Herald*, *Korea Times*, *New York Magazine*, *New York Post*, *New Yorker*, *Observer*, *Salon*

Wolfgang Puck

You can get a lot done when you only need two hours of sleep

WHEN THE CLASSICALLY TRAINED CHEF WOLFGANG PUCK came to LA in 1975, he started cooking at one of the city's most exclusive French restaurants, Ma Maison. Puck quickly earned himself a reputation for his thick Austrian accent, fiery temper, and food that thrilled the hard-to-please Hollywood set. The restaurant, which had been on the verge of bankruptcy, began to thrive. Puck put in eighteen-hour days in the kitchen and lived in a retirement village close by. He would often forget to cash his salary check. After all, what did he need money for? He was busy feeding lobster salad and warm salad of preserved duck to the likes of Gene Kelly, Orson Welles, Cary Grant, and Sylvester Stallone.

It was not long before talk turned to Puck opening his own restaurant. His idea was along the lines of an Italian eatery with checkered tablecloths and a Mt. Vesuvius mural on the wall, hardly the stuff of empires. He could have been just another talented chef with dreams of his own restaurant. But Puck was different thanks to the beautiful, glamorous, entrepreneurial, and pushy Barbara Lazaroff. They met in 1982 in a Hollywood nightclub and married in 1983. Lazaroff urged Puck to demand a payrise at Ma Maison and get serious about his future. They started planning a new restaurant in West Hollywood, with Lazaroff playing the role of designer and project manager. (She ditched the checked table-cloth idea fast.) The place would be called Spago, slang for spaghetti in Italian. A consortium of twenty investors put up $70,000 capital for the venture, which opened in 1982 above a car rental business on Sunset. Lazaroff came up with the idea of an open kitchen so that diners could watch the theatre of Wolfgang Puck at work as they ate.

On opening night, Spago ran out of food. Hollywood society began fighting ferociously for one of Spago's window tables. The restaurant declined three hundred restaurant reservations a day. "Spago barely acknowledged average people, who were escorted to the back room, if they were lucky," reported the *New York Times*. Spago was not as snooty as Ma Maison (which had an unlisted phone number) but the general public would typically wait three months for a Spago table. Puck learned to cater to this notorious-ly needy, fickle celebrity clientele, keeping a private menu for reg-ulars, ever mindful that they always need to feel special and be in the limelight.

The pug-nosed Wolfgang Puck was born in in 1949 in St. Viet an der Glan in Austria. His father was a coal miner and his mother cooked in a restaurant. He was sent to work in the kitchen as an apprentice at the age of fourteen. After eighteen years of classical training, Puck came to the U.S. in 1973 by way of France where he worked in Paris, Monaco, and Provence, a region that would great-ly inspire his cooking style. He cooked in New York and Indianapolis before his arrival in Los Angeles.

The Puck/Lazaroff partnership was a formidable one: the combination of Puck's food and Lazaroff's drive, dealmaking, and organizational abilities came at a time when a wave of culi-nary change was sweeping California. Puck was one of a handful of chefs moving away from laborious, overly rich, formal, and fussy food, opting instead for new, fresher flavors that showcased the produce of the area. This more informal approach inspired dishes such as Puck's "Jewish" pizza (smoked salmon, crème fraiche, chives, red onion, and a dollop of caviar), Sonoma baby lamb with braised greens and rosemary, and grilled Californian goat cheese salad. Investors clamored to be a part of future Puck projects.

A second restaurant, Chinois, followed a year later, an East-meets-West fusion restaurant serving raw fish, wontons, and Szechuan flavors complete with Lazaroff's dramatic, extravagant interiors, fine art, antiques, custom-made light fittings, and carpets. Again Puck and Lazaroff triumphed (and inspired countless copycat restaurants around the world). As word spread, opportunities to extend Puck's name into a brand went way beyond best-selling cookbooks—there were plenty of other high-margin ways to turn Wolfgang Puck into a household name.

By the early 1990s, there were four restaurants grossing $25 million a year, a $10 million packaged foods deal, and a series of pizza-cafes in the planning. Lazaroff was extremely savvy about forging relationships with appliance makers, for example, promising them editorial coverage in the lifestyle magazines that loved to write about Puck for their patronage. In years to come, Puck would become as famous as many of the people he cooked for and amass a $300 million fortune from fine dining, cafes, frozen pizzas, tinned soups, blended coffees, saucepans, cutlery, cookbooks, syndicated columns, and television programs. He has designed food for airlines, has more than forty restaurants, a catering business that handles functions for the White House's Governors Ball, rock stars, royalty, and Swifty Lazar's Oscar night dinner.

On the surface, his personality was not really suited to schmoozing. He was shy and prone to screaming in the kitchen (that would have been fun to watch), but he got over his aversion to coming out and pressing the flesh.

In 1997, Space Beverly Hills opened as their flagship restaurant with an indoor garden, mahogany and Italian marbles, fountains, and Lazaroff's quirky color palette. The original Spago suffered, closing in 2001, the same year Puck signed an estimated $20 million deal with ConAgra, the second largest retail food supplier in the U.S., to license Wolfgang Puck food products.

Puck has always been frank about his lack of financial skills, claiming to fall asleep at the accountant. He deals with money pressures by gaining weight. (He put on twenty-five pounds in the lead-up to Spago opening.) Not every Wolfgang Puck venture has worked. A frozen dessert venture flopped, a Malibu restaurant could not survive seasonal fluctuations, and Puck and Lazaroff divorced amicably in 2002. Lazaroff once described their partnership as Puck being able to "laugh and play but I'm the one that takes the shit." Puck remains the president and CEO of Wolfgang Puck worldwide. Lazaroff remains on the board of directors.

An estimated 500,000 people eat Puck's food in some shape or form every month. Wolfgang Express cafes can be found in airports around the country. Puck's move into the mainstream can be credited to the late Johnny Carson, who used to order up stacks of Puck's woodfired pizzas, stick them in the freezer and reheat them after his show. More than 5 million Wolfgang Puck pizzas are sold each year.

One thing has remained consistent throughout his career besides his duck sausage pizza—a monumental workload. He upholds the theory that people who only work twelve hours a day can never be successful. Puck's ex-wife Barbara Lazaroff told *New York Times* food critic Ruth Reichl: "He thinks I don't work hard because I need more than two hours sleep."

NOTES

"Spago barely acknowledged . . ." Weinraub, Bernard. "For the Old Hollywood, Last Suppers at Spago," *New York Times*, 3.29.01, p.14.

"Laugh and play" Reichl, Ruth. *Comfort Me with Apples*, Random House, 2001.
"He thinks I . . ." Reichl, Ruth. *Comfort Me with Apples*, Random House, 2001.

REFERENCES

Reichl, Ruth. *Comfort Me with Apples*. Random House, 2001.

Associated Press, BusinessWeek, Chicago Tribune, Florida Times, Los Angeles Times, New York Times, Seattle Post-Intelligencer, USA Today, Variety

THANKS FOR NOTHING: THE FOUNDERS WHO MISSED OUT ON THE BILLIONS

Chanel No. 5

If you believe in your product, don't give away the profits to the people who "help" you

T HE SIGNATURE FRAGRANCE OF THE FASHION WORLD'S TRUE renegade, the anti-corset, tomboy, bobbed-haired style icon Gabrielle 'Coco' Chanel, remains the world's best-selling perfume more than eighty years after its creation, reigning over the $15 billion global perfume market. It's a pity the visionary Coco herself never enjoyed more than 10 percent of the royalties.

In 1921, eleven years after she opened her first millinery shop in Paris, Coco Chanel became the first fashion designer to launch a scent. She worked with one of the best noses in France, Ernest Beaux, to come up with a perfume quite unlike the frilly, tizzy floral scents popular at the time. Of the series of sample fragrances Beaux concocted, Coco chose number five. While typical perfumers of the day only evoked the scent of one flower, number five was a combination of flowers including jasmine, tuberose, and May roses. The perfume was tested in her boutiques and given to her favorite clients. It was a smashing success.

Chanel No. 5 came to life with the help of Theophile Bader, owner of department store Galeries Lafayette. He advised Chanel on how to develop her fragrance business and introduced her to Pierre Wertheimer, from the family that built the Bourjois cosmetics house in France in the late 1800s. The Wertheimers had the infrastructure to produce large volumes of the perfume for mass distribution, so if she wanted her perfume to be widely sold, Coco had no choice but to do a deal.

La Société des Parfums Chanel was established in 1924. Chanel was to receive just 10 percent of profits, the Wertheimers 70 percent and Bader 20 percent. Chanel No. 5 hit the mass market in 1924 and was an instant hit.

During World War II, the Wertheimers fled France but wanted to keep the Chanel No. 5 deal, protecting the perfume recipe and future profits. Coco wanted to take back her fragrance, but the Wertheimers prevailed due to Coco's connection to a Nazi officer, which saw her briefly exiled to Switzerland. After the war, Coco renegotiated her deal with the Wertheimers, this time securing just 2 percent of royalties from sales of the perfume worldwide.

Chanel had closed her business during the war, and in 1954 the Wertheimers funded her return to fashion. In return for funding her lifestyle and business ventures, they received her name, brand, fashion designs, and her perfume. Upon her death, the Wertheimers would be entitled to the entire Chanel empire, having bought out Galeries Lafayette's Bader's 20 percent stake in Les Parfums Chanel.

The Wertheimer dynasty continues today with Pierre's grand-sons Alain and Gerard running the business. *Forbes* estimates the Wertheimer fortune is $4.8 billion.

REFERENCES

Madsen, Axel. *Chanel: A Woman of her Own*. Henry Holt & Company, 1991.
Wallis, Jeremy. *Coco Chanel*. Heinemann Library, 2001.
Charles-Roux, Edmonde. *Chanel and Her World*. Rizzoli, 1981.

Boston Globe, Financial Times, Forbes, Fortune, The Independent, Mail on Sunday, New York Times, Newsweek, The Times, Washington Post, Washington Times, Women's Wear Daily

The Coca-Cola Company

Develop a mystique

———————

OCA-COLA WENT ON SALE AT JACOB'S PHARMACY IN Atlanta, Georgia, in 1886, the same year that the city became a dry area. The drink was not an instant hit, although the real cocaine in the drink would surely have given consumers a buzz. It sold for five cents a glass, roughly one dollar in today's money. In the early stages, the most glasses of Coca-Cola sold in a day was thirteen—a long way from the 12,600 Coca-Cola drinks sold every second today.

According to legend, doctor, pharmacist, and wannabe entrepreneur John Stith Pemberton brewed the first batch of Coca-Cola in a three-legged brass kettle over a fire. It sounds romantic but the potion was actually made in Pemberton's modest Atlanta laboratory where he had also created hair dyes and liver pills. The recipe included coca leaves (that originally provided the cocaine in the concoction), kola nuts supplemented with exhausted tea leaves (for the caffeine kick), sugar to mask the bitter taste, and a little alcohol. It was sold both as a medicine and a refreshing drink.

Coca-Cola was invented in an era when all manner of tonics and potions were available. They were often laced with dangerous amounts of alcohol, and narcotics—even poisons—were common ingredients. These profitable drinks were making people very rich and Pemberton wanted to be a part of the action.

In the first year of Coca-Cola's life, sales raised a measly $50, with marketing and advertising costs blowing out to $73.96. Pemberton knew he had a good product but he was no good at marketing, and it was only being sold locally. So he embarked on a very messy trail of deals to try to finance his business. He was dying of cancer, and was also nursing a morphine habit, a substance he first encountered after being wounded as a Confederate officer during the Civil War. One of the people who put up money to fund the business was an ambitious pharmacist named Asa Griggs Candler. In early 1888, Candler acquired a share of Coca-Cola for $1,200.

Pemberton died in August 1888 at age fifty-five. Candler was a pallbearer at the funeral, and two weeks after Pemberton's death, Candler bought out the rest of the company for a total of $2,300.

In 1892, Candler and a consortium formed the Coca-Cola Company. Candler knew he had a good idea to turn into a business and decided that he needed an aggressive sales and marketing strategy. Candler registered the Coca-Cola logo in 1893, began offering free samples, and developed a range of branded products including clocks, calendars, and pharmacy scales with the signature Coca-Cola logo. He also invested heavily in advertising. Some early advertisements featured glamorous opera singers posing beside a five-cent Coca-Cola bottle. This "beautiful people" advertising strategy continues today with the Coca-Cola Company spending an estimated $1 billion per year on advertising.

Candler's strategy worked, and by 1895, there were Coca-Cola syrup plants in Chicago, Dallas, and Los Angeles and the drink was available in every U.S. state. The Coca-Cola syrup was mixed with soda water in drugstores. Around the same time, Mississippi businessman Joseph Biedenharn became the first person to put Coca-Cola in a bottle. He bottled the drink at the back of his drugstore, but Candler was not excited by the concept of bottling Coca-Cola. Biedenharn did not develop the bottling idea further than his local area and never realized the potential of his backyard enterprise.

In 1899, Candler was approached by Benjamin Thomas and Joseph Whitehead, two lawyers from Chattanooga. They nutted out a deal whereby the lawyers could buy Coca-Cola syrup for $1 per gallon and they would do the bottling. The deal was the start of the real expansion of the Coca-Cola Company, based on shipping the secret syrup to bottling plants, controlling the advertising and marketing, and safeguarding the brand. Bottling plants were to play by the company's rules in order to enjoy advertising support and Coca-Cola's business. According to author and Coca-Cola historian Mark Pendergrast, this actually turned out to be a terrible deal for the company. "In fact," he says, "Candler gave away the bottling rights, thinking nothing would come of it, and this caused much conflict and many lawsuits throughout the years."

Candler still became a very wealthy man. In 1916 he was devastated to learn that his wife had breast cancer. He was made an offer of $25 million for his company but he declined, deciding instead to give the company to his children at that time, giving comfort to his wife that his fortune would not go to anyone outside the family without his consent. Candler's children then sold the company in 1919 for $25 million to a consortium lead by Ernest Woodruff, a banker notorious for his corporate raiding practices. Candler allegedly learned of the sale by reading about it in the newspaper. Woodruff went on to lead the company for thirty-two years.

The Coca-Cola formula remains in a bank vault in Atlanta.

REFERENCES

Hays, Constance L. *The Real Thing, Truth and Power at the Coca-Cola Company*. Random House, 2004.

Pendergrast, Mark. *For God, Country & Coca-Cola*. 2nd ed. Basic Books, 2000.

Witzel, Michael Karl and Gyvel Young-Witzel. *The Sparkling Story of Coca-Cola*, Voyageur Press, 2002.

Albuquerque Journal, BusinessWeek, Chattanooga Times, Chicago Sun-Times, Courier-Mail, Daily Mail, Evening News, The Express, Financial Times, The Guardian, Houston Chronicle, The Independent, Irish Times, Marketing, The Mirror, Newsweek, Seattle Times, Sunday Age, Sunday Times, Toronto Star, The Washington Post

Clarence Birdseye

Some people just can't stop inventing

THE IDEA FOR WHAT IS NOW A $30 BILLION INDUSTRY CAME to Brooklyn-born Clarence Birdseye during a stint working in the Arctic Circle as a field naturalist for the U.S. Biological Survey. From 1912 to 1916 he was working in Labrador, in Canada's northeast, observing the local people, the Inuits. During fishing trips, he noticed that fish caught would freeze almost immediately on the ice due to the arctic temperatures and icy winds. In this state, the fish would keep almost indefinitely and when cooked have a similar flavor and texture to when they were fresh.

Birdseye began experimenting with fresh cabbage and salt water to see if the same could be done with vegetables. It could. When he returned to the U.S. he continued his experiments. Without the help of the arctic climate, he needed to create an artificial snap-frozen process, experimenting with ice blocks, dry ice, and an electric fan. He also put fish in candy boxes with dry ice. Birdseye's daughter Ruth remembers their bathtub was often filled with ice and fish.

Birdseye knew that there was great potential in frozen food. But he had his work cut out for him to turn his idea into a viable business. Not only did he need to get the technology right, there was absolutely no infrastructure to support his product, no refrigerated vans or train carriages, no supermarket freezers, and consumers' homes could barely keep fresh food cold for a day in their iceboxes, let alone keep frozen food frozen. It was a big job, but he had the attitude that "just because something has always been done in a certain way is never a sufficient reason for continuing to do it that way."

Birdseye was born in 1886. As a child, his hobbies were all about animals, dead or alive. They included taxidermy, selling frogs to the New York Zoo to feed to the reptile population, selling rats to research laboratories, and even selling coyote skins. He is said to have eaten skunk, mice, chipmunks, and gophers.

Birdseye went on to study biology, but dropped out of college, citing financial difficulties, and began working for the U.S. Biological Survey where he saw a future in freezing fish.

He patented his first freezing technique in 1921. The following year, he established Birdseye Sea Foods, near New York's Fulton Street Fish Market. Concentrating on fish fillets, Birdseye continued trying to improve the way he could freeze food. His next breakthrough was flat freezing, where food was frozen between two heavy refrigerated plates. Despite this breakthrough his company struggled financially. His idea faced opposition from butchers, consumers (who were ill-informed and thought frozen food was unhealthy), and the icebox itself, as it was just not capable of keeping food frozen.

Around that time, wealthy heiress Marjorie Merriweather Post enjoyed a goose dinner on her luxury yacht. The goose had been bought frozen by the chef, a fact that intrigued this businesswoman, a child who had inherited her father's Postum Food company. She immediately saw the potential in frozen food, found out about this experimental Clarence Birdseye, and expressed interest in buying the Birdseye business. She could have bought the business for $2 million, but her board of directors was not confident about the investment. She kept working on the board, and four years later, in 1929, she bought the company with a consortium of investors for $22 million. After this acquisition, the new venture had the funds to properly launch Birds Eye Foods in the marketplace.

By 1930, frozen food was ready to revolutionize American eating habits. In a test of consumer interest, twenty-six different types of frozen food including fish and vegetables were sold in ten supermarkets in Springfield, Massachusetts. Back then, no one had a freezer, so goods were just taken home and thawed for eating that night. It was a big step up from canned everything and salt pork.

The frozen product was problematically thawing out in the supermarket, and Birdseye, now a consultant to the company, set about solving this. He struck a deal with American Radiator Corporation to manufacture deep freezes. Within four years, he had an irresistible offer for supermarkets—a gleaming new freezer unit to rent for $8 a month. Birdseye also worked on the introduction of insulated railway cars to distribute Birdseye foods around the country, which proved the real start of the moneymaking. By the 1950s, annual sales had tipped $1 billion.

Frozen food is by no means Birdseye's only claim to fame. He registered more than 250 patents in his lifetime and is credited with the invention of the infrared lamp and a recoilless harpoon gun.

Birdseye died in 1956. "I am best described as just a guy with (a lot) of curiosity and a gambling instinct," he said. "Any youth who makes security his main goal shackles himself at the very start of life's race."

NOTES

"I am best described . . ." Krause, Reinhardt, "He Had an Eye for Innovation," *Investors Business Daily*, 2.14.02, p. 3.

"Just because . . ." Krause, Reinhardt, "He Had an Eye for Innovation," *Investors Business Daily*, 2.14.02, p. 3.

REFERENCES

Albuquerque Journal, Bookrags.com, *Daily Mail*, *Daily Telegraph*, *The Economist*, *Fortune*, *New York Times*, *Sunday Business*, *Time*, *The Times*, *Toronto Star*, *USA Today*, *Washington Post*

Section 6

EXTREME MAKEOVERS

Nokia

"Be adaptable to survive"

A DECADE AGO, NOKIA WAS AN UNKNOWN COMPANY IN A TINY country on the edge of the Arctic Circle. So little was known about it, in fact, that until recently most people assumed it must be Japanese.

Today, the Finland-based firm makes three out of every ten mobile phones sold around the world, convincingly trumping electronics giants such as Motorola and Ericsson. Its brand was rated the sixth most valuable by Interbrand in 2005, just behind Microsoft and Coca-Cola. It is Finland's largest exporter, has inspired a technology boom around the capital, Helsinki, and its shares have created thousands of Finnish millionaires. Mobile phones are so commonplace in Finland today (seven hundred per one thousand people) that teenagers call them kännykkä, or känny, which means "an extension of the hand."

Bold leadership, inspired hiring decisions, good timing, and an element of national character all played a role in Nokia's success.

The company dates back to 1865, when it ran a lumber mill in the southern Finnish town of Nokia. It expanded slowly into rubber, making boots, cables, and phone lines. In the early 1960s, thanks to its telecom connections, it began to dabble in early radio telephones. Sparsely populated Scandinavia was a natural market, and when the region launched a basic cellular network in 1981, Nokia ran a small factory to supply the early phones, such as a ten-kilogram car phone.

If that was where the company's future lay, though, it was far from obvious. Nokia diversified into televisions and computers without much success. By the mid-1980s, the company's main achievements were as the chief supplier of toilet paper to Ireland and the world's only manufacturer of studded winter bicycle tires. In 1987, Nokia's fledgling mobile phone business started losing money. Under the direction of CEO Kari Kairamo, Nokia started looking for a Japanese partner to help it build a consumer electronics brand, but, as negotiations were under way in 1988, Kairamo committed suicide after battling depression. In 1991, the Soviet Union, Finland's main trading partner, collapsed, and Nokia's traditional businesses started struggling too.

With shareholders complaining, Nokia management considered selling off the mobile phone interests to cut costs. First, though, they turned to a young executive called Jorma Ollila to see if the mobile phone division could be turned around.

Ollila, who had joined the company in 1985, was always a bright prospect. Although born and schooled in Finland, at the age of seventeen he gained a scholarship to attend Atlantic College, an idealistic boarding school in Wales designed to bring together future leaders. After graduating, he studied for an MBA at the London School of Economics and worked at Citibank's London office, where he was given the Nokia account to look after.

Within a year of joining Nokia, he was appointed head of finance. In 1990, he was made head of the mobile phone division and was given six months to decide whether to sell up or keep it. After four months, he replied: keep it. He had visited the factory in Salo, about an hour from Helsinki, where he learned the company was struggling to prepare for the new European mobile digital standard, GSM (Global System for Mobile Communications). "The GSM project was in disarray," Ollila recalled in 2001. "There was a lot of disillusionment with the spec and the difficulty of the technology." He streamlined the process so successfully—the first GSM call was made in 1991 by the Prime Minister of Finland on a Nokia mobile—that in 1992 Ollila was named CEO.

Ollila was not the only smart newcomer Nokia had hired in the 1980s. In 1989, it had sent Matti Alahuhta, a young manager, on a sabbatical to a Swiss business school to ponder the company's future: particularly, how it could overtake its rivals from such a small base. He concluded that what Nokia needed was a technological shift, something Nokia could grasp first and use to gain an advantage.

Ollila could see that shift occurring. In 1991, with his right-hand man, CFO Olli-Pekka Kallasvuo, he decided on a new mantra: "telecom-oriented, focus, global, value-added." In a nutshell, that meant mobile phones. Ollila believed mobiles, at that stage still expensive and cumbersome business equipment, would become ubiquitous—important enough to bet the company on.

Investors liked the new approach enough that Nokia was able to raise cash in the United States and the company set about ditching the rest of its businesses (today Nokia rubber boots are considered collectors' items).

Nokia had gambled correctly on digital, manufacturing the first digital phone, and GSM, which was to become the dominant world standard. But technology was only part of the equation: Ollila knew he had to build Nokia into a brand.

The company had previously sold mobiles under several names, including RadioShack; now it would only sell under its own name. Just as important was a uniform look to the company's products, so they were recognizable even before you saw the brand.

Ollila contracted a Los Angeles designer called Frank Nuovo to work on the first of the new line of phones. Nuovo sculpted a smoothly rounded form with a big screen and intuitive keys, a quantum leap from its sharp-edged predecessors. Nokia hoped to sell 400,000 of the model, launched in 2004 under the name 2100. It sold more than 20 million.

Nuovo joined the company as chief designer in 1995, which was when Nokia began implementing the second pivotal phase of its branding strategy: differentiation.

Up until now, it had been enough for a phone to be small and cute. But now that more and more people owned one, Nokia realized it could sell different kinds of phones to different people. Nokia folklore has it that its engineers started painting their phones with car paint so they would recognize them on the bar of the local watering hole.

So, under the guidance of Frank Nuovo, Nokia started making phones in different colors. Then, phones with interchangeable faceplates and phones with dozens of different ring tones. Then came the phone as fashion statement: shiny, tiny, high-status phones. Its competitors, particularly Ericsson and Motorola, could not keep up. By 1998, Nokia was the world's number one cell phone manufacturer. In five years its stock had risen almost 2,000 percent.

It was not just about fashion, though: during the 1990s Nokia had developed a corporate culture that it says allows departments to do their own thing and for ideas to bubble up from anywhere in the organization, whether in Finland or at any of a growing number of factories, offices, and design labs around the world. Keeping what Ollila calls a "meritocracy" under control is a tight-knit management team—mostly Finns—who act as gatekeepers: Frank Nuovo, for example, signs off every design decision.

It is a resilient structure that in recent history has weathered severe stock market volatility. As a company, Nokia has already survived much worse, including the Bolshevik revolution, a civil war, and the death of its CEO in 1988.

Ollila believes Nokia is well-placed for the so-called third generation of phones, which will put the Internet in everybody's pocket. The new phones use Internet-style data transmission, which means Nokia is facing competition from phone makers such as Asian makers Samsung and LG and a revitalized Sony-Ericsson partnership, but also from computer firms such as Palm (who make electronic personal assistants) and even Microsoft, who can see endless possibilities in software applications. As a result, Nokia's market share slipped from 38 percent of the world market in 2004 to 30 percent by the end of 2005, resulting in another savaging of the historically volatile share price, though its market share appears to have stabilized since. In 2005, Nokia announced a new device called the 770 Internet Tablet— not a phone, but a book-sized web browser you could use in Wi-Fi hot spots instead of a full-blown laptop, for around $350 (or less as part of a phone-style connection deal).

Nokia argues that as the dominant brand, with the highest volumes in the industry, it is in the best position to exploit the new technology, wherever it leads. "We can jump on it and adapt," says Ollila. "Finns live in a cold climate: we have to be adaptable to survive."

NOTES
"The GSM project . . ." Silberman, Steve. "Just Say Nokia," *Wired*, 9.99.
"We can jump . . ." *The Economist*, "A Finnish Fable," 10.14.00.

REFERENCES
BusinessWeek, CNN, *Daily Mail, Economist, Financial Times, Fortune, Korea Herald, New Media Age, New York Times, New Yorker, Pittsburgh-Post Gazette, Scotland on Sunday, The Times, Utopian Studies*

Avon

Reinvention can happen to even the oldest brands

Mrs. P.F.E. Albee of Winchester, New Hampshire, sold her neighbor some perfumes in 1886 and has gone down in history as the very first Avon lady. David McConnell established the California Perfume Company with a view to sell fragrance through a network of representatives rather than through a store. He kept himself busy developing affordable new cosmetic luxuries, and Mrs. Albee kept selling. In just twenty years, McConnell had 10,000 women around the country selling 117 different products. The company became Avon in 1928, and today there are 4.9 million Avon representatives in 143 countries, generating 98 percent of Avon's global sales of $7.7 billion. In Brazil, there are more women in Avon than in the country's army and navy.

When McConnell died in 1937, he left the business to his eldest son. The company enjoyed steady growth, expanding into international markets and developing new product ranges, but the business never reached its potential. Fast forward to 1990 when the company was not in good shape. The "ding dong" Avon lady and her catalog (introduced in 1906) needed a serious makeover. Avon was being run by former mailroom clerk Dave Mitchell. It was fighting off hostile takeovers, sales were down, there had been some disastrous acquisitions, and the company clearly had an image problem.

Around the same time, a young Andrea Jung was learning the ropes of retailing. Andrea was born in Canada in 1959 and raised in Wellesley, Massachusetts by a Shanghai-born mother and Hong Kong-born father who wanted the best for their daughter, a Mandarin speaking, Princeton University graduate and accomplished pianist.

Andrea surprised her parents by taking a job in a management training program at the department store Bloomingdale's, while still planning to go back to study law. She never returned, as she loved retail and the psychology of inspiring customers to spend. She worked for several major department stores before beginning consulting work with Avon in 1993. Jung instantly became enamored with the company, its culture, and its opportunities. She officially joined the marketing team in 1994, became CEO in 1999, and was elected chairman in 2001.

When Jung and her signature double-strand pearl chokers arrived at Avon, no one, she says, believed that the company was capable of growing.

Jung's makeover strategy involved rethinking the entire organization, from suppliers to the way products were distributed, ordered, and delivered, product development time cycles, and slashing costs. There needed to be new product lines, more glamorous, glossy advertising campaigns, and definitely no more "ding dong, Avon calling" catchphrases. Jung had to lead the company's total change of heart. "You have to be bold, thoughtful, and calculated so the financial markets remain calm. But I think you have got to drive enough change to unleash that kind of growth," she says. Ironically, Jung was raised, she says, "to be submissive, caring, and averse to conflict," but she says she has learned how to be empathetic and make tough decisions.

Jung's plans to transform the brand and deliver double-digit growth were deadly serious. She was in a hurry, too. The original revitalization plan was scheduled to take three years, but Jung did it in eighteen months, earning her the title "the mistress of the turnaround."

"The beauty model that will dominate is the one that reinvents itself first. Brand reinvention can happen to even the oldest brands with the greatest image issues. And if we can do it, you can do it, anybody can do it," she says.

Avon introduced a new range of skincare called Anew that is selling well, particularly in the U.S., a new range for teenagers, sold by teenagers, called Mark, and there is a Fifth Avenue flagship spa in New York City.

Avon is also focused on expansion in China. After a 1998 ruling banning door-to-door sales in China, Avon began selling in beauty salons. The network has now expanded to more than 6,300 outlets throughout the country. It has even cleverly set up franchise shops with China Post. Avon is also targeting such far-flung frontiers as Tibet and Kazakhstan. Although, in late 2005 the company has faced, for the first time in Jung's tenure, a lowering of earnings expectations following slower-than-expected growth in its emerging markets such as China.

Meanwhile, the Avon share price is at an all all-time high, up 165 percent since she took over, with the market acknowledging that Jung and her team know how to chase future markets and future revenue. She regularly calls her top twenty sales performers in each region together and grills them on ways she can improve the product and its delivery. "Tell us the good, the bad, and the ugly," she says. This is a phrase she repeats to a CEO advisory council that helps keep her connected to the company. Jung has also introduced serious succession planning. Two years ago, 15 percent of the top 100 jobs could be filled from within if someone left; now it's 87 percent. The top 400 staff also receive individual coaching and emotional intelligence training (pioneered by Daniel Goleman, it argues that people have an emotional as well as an intelligence quotient). "The good news is that all of this can be done; the bad news is that it all has to be done at once," she likes to say.

Jung is now one of just eight female chief executives heading Fortune 500 companies, and she joined the board of the New York Stock Exchange. She keeps a cushion in her Manhattan office that reads: "If you are not the lead dog, the view never changes."

NOTES

"You have to be bold . . ." Jung's Keynote Address, *Women's Wear Daily* Beauty CEO summit, 2002.

"To be submissive . . ." Jung, Andrea. "Seeking Frank Feedback," *Harvard Business Review*, 1.04, p. 31.

"The mistress of the turnaround . . ." Foster, Lauren and Andrea Jung. "Mistress of the Turnaround Answers Avon's Calling," *Financial Times*, 11.6 03, p. 14.

"The beauty model . . ." Jung's Keynote Address, *Women's Wear Daily* Beauty CEO summit, 2002.

"Tell us the good, the bad . . ." Jung, Andrea. "Seeking Frank Feedback," *Harvard Business Review*, 1.04, p. 31.

"If you are not the lead . . ." Foster, Lauren and Andrea Jung. "Mistress of the Turnaround Answers Avon's Calling," *Financial Times*, 11.6 03, p. 14.

REFERENCES

AdAge.com, *BusinessWeek*, CBS *Market Watch*, ChiefExecutive.net, CNN, *Economist*, *Fortune*, GaleGroup.com, Goldsea.com, *The Industry Standard*, TheStreet.com, *That Money Show* (PBS), *Time*, *USA Today*, Wharton Business School, *Women's Wear Daily*

LVMH

Keep control of the brand

THE POLITE, GENTEEL WORLD OF LUXURY GOODS HAS BEEN turned on its head by Frenchman Bernard Arnault. The *New York Times* describes him as a man who has "built an empire out of companies he pried, for the most part, from the resistant grasps of others, one by one."

Born in Roubaix in northern France in 1949, Arnault attended the prestigious École Polytechnique and earned a reputation for being studious rather than social. He was raised by his strict Catholic grandmother and worked in the family property and construction business, including stints selling real estate on the French Riviera and in Florida. At twenty-five he was CEO of a company with one thousand staff members. Arnault was influenced by the American can-do approach to business, a far cry from the more conservative French approach.

He is now the richest man in France and among the top-ten richest people in the world, with an estimated fortune of $20 billion. According to *Forbes* magazine estimates, his net worth will triple between 2003 and 2005. His family now owns 48 percent of Louis Vuitton Möet Hennessy. He presides over a $40.5 billion empire of the world's most prestigious brands, including Louis Vuitton (the most profitable luxury brand in the world), Christian Dior, Guerlain, Givenchy, and Möet et Chandon, with interests in wine, fashion, retail, jewelry, leather goods, perfume, and beauty products. In 2004 the group had sales of more than $15.1 billion.

In 1984, the former property developer entered the luxury goods business when he invested $15 million of family money in buying a bankrupt textile company called Boussac, as part of an $80 million deal with a consortium of investors. The portfolio included the unprofitable Christian Dior brand and a diaper company called Peaudouce. Arnault believed that Dior was worth salvaging. He sold off most of the Boussac companies, unceremoniously culled half of the company's sixteen-thousand-strong workforce and began building his empire, one brand at a time. Arnault was cashed up, thanks to the sale of the diaper business, which netted $400 million. He set his sights on the French bastion of luxury, Louis Vuitton Möet Hennessy, executing a hostile takeover in 1988 that cemented his reputation as the "wolf in cashmere clothing." His takeover style involved his holding companies buying up stock and then, with 45 to 60 percent of the company equity, taking over. Then it was on to the next acquisition.

When Arnault took over LVMH, the group controlled ten luxury brands; now it owns more than fifty, including Chateau d'Yquem, Celine, Christian Lacroix, Dom Perignon, Bon Marché, TAG Heuer, Domaine Chandon, Hennessy Cognac, St. Emilion, and Glenmorangie. LVMH is also involved in joint ventures with DeBeers and DFS duty-free stores.

Arnault calls his company a "federation" of brands. He has built his luxury goods empire on his two favorite things: creative force and hard-nosed business, principles he calls "the artist's vision and the logic of worldwide marketing."

Arnault buys the history, tradition, prestige, and recognition of a brand and takes it from there. He reinvigorates each brand, not just the products themselves but the business from end to end, the design, the manufacturing (all brought back in-house to maintain quality control), the distribution (no licensing, all in-house) and sales, all with the help of impossibly glamorous, high-end advertising campaigns and the right celebrity endorsements. The transformation must also include tight cost controlling for higher profit margins.

Under Arnault, every stage of the manufacturing of a purse is meticulously planned for high productivity. "If you control your factories, you control your quality: if you control your distribution, you control your image," he says. Each business is kept separate and independent, but there is synergy between them. If one knows of good leather supplies, or a better way to make a product, then there is cross-pollination and all the little brands add up to a superpower.

In more recent times, Arnault has talked publicly about his "star brands" theory, explaining how they take time to grow, how they need heritage. Arnault estimates that it takes a decade to build or rebuild a brand into what he calls a "star brand," that is, a brand that is "timeless, modern, fast-growing, and highly profitable."

Arnault describes the compelling offer to customers of his star brands: "You feel you must buy it, in fact, or else you won't be in the moment. You will be left behind." He argues that the history and tradition of a brand are not enough. Aristocratic links and status certainly help a brand, but they do not guarantee a star brand that makes products that people have to have now, right now.

For his brands to move out of their comfort zones, Arnault had to do things differently. He removed the almost sacred designer Hubert de Givenchy from Givenchy and brought in twenty-seven-year-old Saville Row tailor and British bad boy Alexander McQueen. Similarly he hired British fashion devil John Galliano to take over as chief designer at Dior. Arnault says he is only interested in the youngest, brightest, and the most talented. Since Galliano came on board, he may have presented some outrageous collections—one inspired by the homeless of Paris, another with a 1950s-meets-ancient-Egypt theme—but Dior sales have quadrupled under Galliano's creative direction. "I don't care what they do as long as it's on the front page," says Arnault, who has had the Dior haute couture shows rescheduled to the afternoon so the show's images can make the evening news and the next day's newspapers. Arnault estimates that it took six years to transform the Dior brand "from a fashion dowager duchess to a young hipster."

To keep the LVMH juggernaut firing, Arnault has surrounded himself not with fashion sycophants but with experienced executives from multinationals who understand the business world outside fashion realms. Though when he interviews senior executives for roles in his companies, he is said to set out one hundred ties and asks candidates to choose ten. If they pick bad ties, they must go on to the scarf test. If they choose badly again, there is little chance of them getting a job. Arnault wants staff with the business skills and good taste to help sell a dream to the world. No one needs a $5,000 hand-stitched purse, but for many across all races and demographics, it is an object of enormous desire. And creating desire is what luxury goods retailers must do. Says Arnault: "Our products are about making people dream. We take it really seriously."

NOTES

"**Built an empire . . .**" Steinhauer, Jennifer. "The King of Posh," *New York Times*, 8.17.97, section 3, p. 1.

"**If you control . . .**" "Protecting the Exclusivity of Luxury Brands through Retailing," *Brand Strategy*, 6.20.97.

"**Star brands . . .**" Givhan, Robin. "The French Connection," *Washington Post*, 4.28.02, p. F01.

"**Star brand . . .**" Wetlaufer, Suzy. "The Perfect Paradox of Star Brands: an Interview with Bernard Arnault of LVMH," *Harvard Business Review*, 10.01.

"**You feel you must buy it . . .**" Johnson, Jo. "Arnault Defers Decision on Sale," *Financial Times*, 3.7.03, p. 26.

"**I don't care what they do . . .**" *The Economist*, "The Cashmere Revolutionary," 7.15.00.

"**From a fashion dowager . . .**" Menkes, Susy. "LVMH Chief Sees a Very Good Year for Luxury," *International Herald Tribune*, 2.12.04, p. 15.

"**Our products are about . . .**" Steinhauer, Jennifer. "The King of Posh," *New York Times*, 8.17.97, section 3, p. 1.

REFERENCES

The Australian, Australian Financial Review, BusinessWeek, The Economist, Evening Standard, Financial Times, Forbes, Fortune, Hoover's Company Capsules, *Independent on Sunday, International Herald Tribune, Le Figaro, New York Observer, New York Post, New Yorker, Sydney Morning Herald, Time, The Times, Vanity Fair, Washington Post, Women's Wear Daily*

Gap

Stick to your game

WHAT WOULD YOU BUY? THAT BASIC, RELIABLE PAIR OF khaki pants that will still look fine, if boring, in five years? Or low-cut, hip-hugger jeans that show off your figure, but will no doubt look terribly out of date in six months?

Gap has never quite been sure which pair of pants suits it best. It made its name selling chinos and plain cotton T-shirts, but every few years it has given in to the temptation to update its image and appeal to younger, more fashion-conscious shoppers—usually with disastrous results.

Occasionally, Gap has found itself enjoying the best of both worlds, like the time in 1991 when *Vogue* put ten supermodels on its cover, each dressed in all-white Gap outfits, to celebrate the magazine's one-hundredth anniversary. But, in recent years, it has either been criticized for being too dull, for selling clothes your parents would buy—or for being too edgy and alienating its traditional customers. "I don't like fashion," Gap's most successful CEO, Millard "Mickey" Drexler, once said. You can understand why.

Gap started life as a hippie-style jeans store in San Francisco. Founder Donald Fisher went to exchange a pair of Levi's he'd bought at a department store that turned out to be an inch too short, but was told he could not. He decided there was a need for a store that stocked a comprehensive range of sizes, so in 1969 he and his wife Doris opened a place they called Gap, after the generation gap (this was the hippie era, after all), advertising "four tons of Levi's." By the end of 1970, there were six Gap stores in California, and, in 1976, the company went public though it immediately found itself in a price war with competitors slashing their margins on Levi's. Gap, in the first of its many boom-bust crises, responded by diversifying into more directional lines under such house-brand labels as Foxtails and Fashion Pioneers. But poor fashion sense saw it forced to sell too much stock at a discount, and Gap began to smell suspiciously like a bargain basement.

In 1983, Fisher hired Mickey Drexler, a New York retailing whiz who had just revamped Ann Taylor, another clothing company that had been in similar trouble.

Drexler's vision was single-minded: at meetings with Gap executives, he handed around plaques with just one word on them: "Simplify." Like any experienced spring cleaner, his first move was to eliminate all the "junk" —the cheap-looking clothes stacked ten deep across the stores.

In its place, he emphasized "essentials": good-quality jeans and T-shirts in a wide range of sizes and colors, designed and manufactured by Gap so it could boost quality while keeping costs low.

Under Drexler's hands-on approach, stores were redesigned to emphasize space and light—the beginning of what would become Gap's trademark look of elegant shelves, polished timber floors, and white walls. Drexler, who became company president in 1987, put new styles on tables in the center of the store, where customers were encouraged to pick them up and try them on, and he developed a list of directives that made sure his sleek, streamlined stores stayed that way. At the top of the list of priorities, as anybody who has worked at Gap will testify, was constant refolding of clothes the customers had messed up. Drexler was often found popping unannounced into stores to see how well the assistants remembered the code.

As Gap jettisoned other brands to focus on its own single house label (a range of upmarket basics that appealed to middle-class buyers reminiscing about the preppie look of their college days), Drexler and Fisher built lines of distribution that enabled stores to react almost daily to fluctuations in demand, which gave them the flexibility to pull items that weren't selling well. It also meant stores could carry less floor stock: if shoppers saw just two or three sweaters in the same style, they carried an air of exclusivity—even though there were thousands more just a phone call away.

Gap used a similar technique in its advertising to make its basics seem more exclusive. In 1988 it ran a campaign called "Individuals of Style," a series shot in black and white featuring celebrities wearing their favorite Gap piece. Dizzy Gillespie transformed a basic black turtleneck into the epitome of cool. It was such a successful campaign Gap has relied on carefully chosen celebrities, from actress Kim Basinger to Madonna, to "individualize" its mass-market clothing ever since.

By 1990, Gap had 965 stores, including GapKids, BabyGap, and Banana Republic, making it the second-largest clothing retailer in the United States, behind Levi Strauss. In 1993 Drexler successfully flirted with more fashionable lines to combat complaints that Gap was becoming boring, and also to fend off competitors who were now copying its line of basics.

When Gap launched another brand, Old Navy, in 1994, Drexler reworked the old formula once again, this time offering a line of simplified cotton classics to the masses, often in warehouse-style stores in working class neighborhoods. Old Navy, named after a sign on the side of a building in Paris, became the first retail chain to reach $1 billion in sales in the first four years of operation.

Gap continued to expand throughout the next decade, when it became not only the default choice for smart casual clothing, but also for workers embracing the dressing-down trend inspired by the dot-com boom. While the geeks in Silicon Valley turned up to work in Nikes and ponytails, elsewhere chinos and polo shirts became an acceptable alternative to suits. In a 1997 stunt, Gap sponsored the first "casual day" at the New York Stock Exchange, dressing 3,500 traders in khakis and white button-down shirts. That year, Robert

Fisher (son of the founders, who still own some 25 percent of Gap), joined Gap as president.

Mickey Drexler's vision was certainly inspired, and more often than not his gut instinct was right. But critics feared his hands-on style was inappropriate, even risky, for a company that had grown as big as Gap, now with close to 4,000 stores.

In 2001, with the dot-com boom foundering and demand for khakis becoming erratic, Drexler steered Gap and Banana Republic towards younger fashions, competing with fast-moving rivals for a fickle teen market. He failed to attract new customers but succeeded in alienating old ones. He later admitted: "When we get tricky, when we get young, when we get gimmicky at the Gap, we kind of lose it."

In 2001 he ditched the teenybopper wear and aimed instead at fashion-conscious twenty-somethings, carrying fewer of the traditional classic lines. Again, a wrong move. Executives told *BusinessWeek* magazine off the record that Drexler's short attention span, decisions based on gut feelings, and "impulsive flip-flopping" had created a culture of uncertainty. In 2001, Gap suffered what Drexler described as its "most difficult year ever:" it had made $877 million profit in 2000, but actually lost $7.7 million in 2001, prompting Drexler and Fisher to write in the annual report that Gap had forgotten one of its basic maxims: always keep it simple. The following year, Drexler attempted to spark some of the old magic, once again hiring stars, including Dennis Hopper and Christina Ricci, to promote denim and khaki. Sales lifted a little, but the company had lost its confidence in Drexler, and he stepped down.

Gap's new CEO, Armani-wearing Paul Pressler, was a more traditional choice. Hired from Disney, where he ran the theme park business, he was to be a CEO whose experience lay in management, not ideas for new T-shirts. He announced plans to step up consumer research and leave specific decisions about garments to the brand managers. Initially he concentrated on cost-cutting and improving marketing and operations across the 3,000-plus Gap, Old Navy, and Banana Republic stores. Employee numbers have dropped under his charge but profits doubled between 2002 ($476 million) and 2004 ($1.1 billion). He has continued Drexler's lead in hiring celebrities to promote the product, including Missy Elliot and Madonna, though he raised eyebrows when Gap replaced *Sex and the City* star Sarah Jessica Parker in 2005 (who was about to turn forty) with teen songstress Joss Stone: which age group was Gap actually aiming at? Meanwhile Pressler announced a new brand called Forth & Towne that aimed at the thirty-five-plus customer; its name, Pressler said, evoked a sense of place. Sooner or later, though, he will need to replace Drexler's vision with a new one and, eventually, confront Gap's demon: fashion.

NOTES

"I don't like fashion . . ." Bechett, Andy. "How We Fell into the Gap," *The Independent*, 11.28.93.

"When we get tricky . . ." Seals, Kimberley Lanise. "Mind the Gap," Business, *The Independent*, 8.16.00, p. 1.

"Most difficult . . ." *Retail Week*, "Gap Rethinks Management," 3.8.02, p. 6.

REFERENCES

BusinessWeek, Display and Design Ideas, Financial Times, Forbes, Fortune, New York Times, The Record, Rocky Mountain News, San Francisco Chronicle, San Jose Mercury News, Time, Toronto Star, Vogue

Samsung

It's never too late to fix your brand

———

WHEN KOREAN ELECTRONICS GIANT SAMSUNG LAUNCHED AN Internet-ready fridge in 2002, it was more an attention-seeking exercise than anything else. Did anybody really want a fridge with a computer screen stuck on the front? It didn't matter—the Internet fridge appeared in ads and magazine stories the world over and made everybody ask, Samsung? What is Samsung?

Not long ago, the answer would have been: a no-name manufacturer of commodity-class microwaves and cheap TVs, the brand you bought when you couldn't afford anything better.

Today, Samsung has successfully repositioned itself as a prestige brand with a flood of desirable products backed by clever, focused marketing campaigns. In the United States, it is now the top seller of television sets over $3,000. It leads the market in sales of flat-panel computer displays, and is a whisker behind Motorola and Nokia in mobile phones. And as the Internet fridge suggested, Samsung is not just after its share of the present—it wants a big piece of the future, too. The fridge was just a taste for the global market. In Seoul, Samsung has fitted out a whole apartment complex with "smart" appliances, allowing 3,000 families to control washing machines, dim the lights, open the blinds, adjust the air-conditioning, and even wake up to freshly brewed coffee from a single remote control—a bold, even unlikely vision. But Samsung's claim that it would soon be a world leader in electronics, which once would have sounded absurd, is rapidly coming true.

The company, one of Korea's vast, family-controlled conglomerates known as chaebol, started life in 1938 as a trading operation, sending dried fish and fruit to Japanese-occupied Manchuria. Its founder, Lee Byung-Chul, was a regular visitor to Tokyo. A keen student of Japanese management practices, Lee made human resources a priority and claimed he spent 80 percent of his time hiring and cultivating good talent. After World War II and the Korean War, Samsung benefited from government rebuilding programs and under Lee's leadership the firm diversified rapidly into ship-building, petrochemicals, and aircraft maintenance. By the time Lee died in 1987, handing the company over to his son Lee Kun-Hee (the company's chairman today), Samsung had dozens of separate businesses including semiconductors, financial services, watches, and even a baseball team. While Samsung Electronics was its largest division, the company as a whole was still a vast and unwieldy conglomerate when the Asian economic crisis struck in 1997. Samsung had also started building a massive auto plant that was on target to be producing 500,000 cars a year by 2002. Had it continued down that path it is all too possible it would have encountered the same vast losses as the other Korean car-makers, which all but bankrupted Daewoo and Ssangyong.

The Korean economic crisis forced a swift rethink of Samsung's expansion plans. By the middle of 1998, Samsung Electronics, the Samsung Group's cash cow, was rapidly heading backwards. In response, Samsung Electronics CEO, Yun Jong-yong, pledged to cut costs by 30 percent in five months or resign. Yun's measures were drastic, cutting 20,000 jobs and ending the policy of lifetime employment. He reportedly turned down the heating in the head office so low workers had to wear thermal underwear, and cancelled executive perks such as golf club memberships. By 2000, Yun had wiped out $10 billion in debt, and Samsung Electronics was profitable. It was also now the group's core business—Lee Kun-Hee having decided to sell off many of the less profitable arms, including watches and medical equipment, and phase out low-end products such as electric fans and radios.

Since 1983, Samsung had invested heavily in semiconductors, particularly memory chips, which are essential to most electronic devices. By the late 1990s, though, prices for memory chips had reached commodity levels and many players decided to get out of the business. When the market for chips rebounded at the end of the 1990s Samsung was the dominant manufacturer, and, thanks to its investment in research and development, was able to command premium prices.

The healthy cash flow from chip sales to companies including Sony now allowed Yun Jong-yong to pursue the next stage of Samsung's revitalization: its transformation into a premier consumer brand. Why just sell chips to others when it could use them to power its own products? Samsung's diversity, once seen as a liability, now became an asset. Already manufacturing everything from mobile phones to televisions, Samsung was perfectly placed to take advantage of the increasing interest in digital convergence. Korea, which had embraced the Internet with the highest uptake of broadband in the world, was a perfect test market for products such as video-capable mobile phones.

What Samsung, best known to Western consumers as a manufacturer of microwave ovens, did not have was brand cachet. But as companies such as Levi's, Nike, and even Sony have discovered in recent years, brands are no longer immutable.

It fell to Eric Kim, headhunted in 1999 to become head of global marketing operations, to make Samsung desirable.

Kim hired hundreds of designers to crank out cool-looking products and spent close to $1 billion advertising them—2001's DigitALL campaign reportedly cost $400 million alone—to change customer perceptions. In July 2003, the global consulting firm Interbrand declared Samsung the world's fastest growing brand.

A blizzard of products created some major hits, among them a gorgeous Porsche-designed flat-screen computer monitor and a mobile phone widely embraced by U.S. networks.

Kim said the focus fell on three qualities: "wow," simplicity, and exclusivity. Each department has a quota for how many 'wow' products it must create each year. Samsung does not expect everything to succeed, but such devices as the Internet fridge and a robot vacuum cleaner create a halo effect for the more mundane products.

"It normally takes decades to grow a brand," said Kim. "We achieved tremendous success in coming from nowhere to be one of the top contenders, but in some ways that was the easier challenge. To be truly number one, you have not simply to be known. You have to be loved."

Superficially, Samsung, which accounts for 20 percent of Korea's exports, now appears to be a multinational corporation like any other. However, Samsung's corporate governance structure is still that of a chaebol; it is a public company, but the Lee family owns a controlling interest. Group Chairman Lee Kun-Hee, sixty-one, is the wealthiest person in Korea with assets worth around $2.8 billion. He demands absolute loyalty from employees, and, in the best tradition of chaebol, his rule has been tainted by charges of bribing politicians and subsidizing weaker companies.

Analysts complain that family control makes Samsung's finances murky: in 2001 Korean courts found evidence of internal corruption and fined company executives. And despite his progressive attitudes about recruitment, Lee still plans to hand the company on to his Harvard-educated son, Lee Jae yong, recently promoted, at age thirty-five, to vice president of Samsung Electronics.

NOTES

"It normally takes decades to grow a brand . . ." Pesola, Maija. "From Microwaves to the Matrix," *Financial Times*, 9.11.03, p. 8.

REFERENCES

Advertising Age, Adweek, AFP, Asiaweek, Business Times (Singapore), *BusinessWeek, Edmonton Journal, Financial Times, Forbes, Fortune, Korea Herald, Korea Times, Philippine Daily Inquirer, Time, Times of India, Toronto Star, Twice*

Guinness

The birth of the widget

T RADITIONALLY, GUINNESS IS A DRAUGHT BEER, POURED slowly from taps in pubs with a technique that produces a creamy foam sitting on top of the dark brown ale beneath. It has been loyally enjoyed since 1759—so imagine the frustration of Guinness executives as they watched other brewers making fortunes from canned beer, while theirs was only available in pubs, or bottles that delivered a vastly inferior version. Guinness could not follow suit because, poured from a regular can or bottle, Guinness failed to get that magical foamy surface—so to sell it in a can would be like selling a cappuccino without the froth.

Guinness is less fizzy than regular lager-style beers because it contains less carbon dioxide; instead, it contains a shot of nitrogen, which produces tinier bubbles, resulting in a creamier, thicker froth. The nice head is formed in pubs because it is poured slowly from a specially designed tap, which agitates the nitrogen as it passes into the glass. Pouring it from a regular can or bottle does not agitate the gas sufficiently.

How to get the same effect from a can? It took Guinness five years to come up with the answer, during which time it tried virtually any method it could think of, including pouring beer through nylon stockings, and through a spout lined with sandpaper.

The answer was a device costing only a few cents to produce: a plastic "widget" created by two Guinness researchers, Alan Forage and William Byrne, which liberated Guinness from pubs and into cans around the world. Forage and Byrne's patented solution, also called a "smoothifier," was a little hollow plastic cylinder with a tiny hole in it, which was placed at the bottom of the can. When the can was then filled with beer and pressurized, beer was forced though the tiny hole and into the widget. Opening the can, though, instantly returned the beer to atmospheric pressure—apart from the beer stuck inside the widget, which then spurted out through the hole and into the main body of the can so forcefully it injected millions of nitrogen and carbon dioxide bubbles into the rest of the beer. That produced an effect Guinness called "the surge," and formed the trademark creamy head once the beer was poured into a glass.

Guinness launched the new cans nationally in Britain in 1989, selling 49 million in the first year and making it Britain's sixth most popular take-home beer brand by 1991. After three years on the market the product had sold 200 million units and become a bestseller in numerous overseas markets including the United States.

Subsequent improvements to the widget resulted in today's free-floating version, a plastic ball not unlike a Ping-Pong ball with a tiny hole in the side, which can be heard rattling about inside the can. The company now makes around 338 million can widgets a year, and another 78 million bottle widgets.

For the brand's next trick, Diageo, which now owns Guinness, is attempting to crack the Japanese bar market with a gizmo called the Surger. Japanese bars often don't have enough room to install the usual equipment required to pour draft Guinness. So now they can pour the beer from a regular tap, then place it on a bar-top device that uses ultrasound to stir up the bubbles in a pint of Guinness and create the much-desired creamy head before the customer's very eyes. So far, Diageo has installed Surgers in 6,000 outlets, claiming a threefold increase in the amount of beer sold as a result, and is now considering "surging" into other markets.

REFERENCES

Beverage World, Birmingham Post, Brandweek, Campaign, Daily Mail, The Economist, Fast Company, The Grocer, The Guardian, The Independent, New Scientist, Off License News, The Scotsman, Sunday Times, USA Today, Windsor Star

Adidas

Never give up on an aging champ

B ack in the early 1930s, in a tiny German town with a hard-to-pronounce name, a young man called Adolph Dassler heard about a brilliant American sprinter, Jesse Owens, who was coming to compete in the Berlin Olympics.

Dassler, who preferred to be known as Adi, and his brother, Rudolph, made sports shoes in their little workshop in Herzogenaurach in Middle Franconia.

Dassler experimented with new materials including shark skin and kangaroo leather for his running shoes, and would later accumulate hundreds of patents. He approached Owens and offered to make him a special pair of running shoes to compete in. This being long before the days of celebrity endorsements and lucrative contracts, Owens happily accepted his free shoes and went on to win four gold medals in Berlin in 1936, annoying Hitler to no end and giving the Dassler brothers an idea that was to prove the foundation of what became the world's biggest sportswear company: get athletes to wear your shoes and other people will pay for them.

They managed to survive the war but not each other: in 1948 Adi and Rudolph had a famous falling out—some say it was about Nazism, others claim it was over a girl—and never spoke again. Rudolph took half the shoe-making machines and set up a new business on the other side of the river Aurach, calling the venture Puma. Adi called his business Adidas (from "Adi" and "Das"—not, sadly, an acronym for "All Day I Dream About Sex," as the rumor used to go) and a year later incorporated the three stripe trademark. Unlike Nike's swoosh, which was dreamed up by a design student, Adidas's three stripes originally had a practical purpose, helping to support the arch of the foot.

Both brothers pursued athletes to wear their shoes, an increasingly successful strategy as events began to be televised, but Adi pulled ahead decisively in 1954 when he outfitted the West German World Cup soccer team with new cleats that had replaceable screw-in studs instead of the standard molded pattern. The final was on a wet day, giving the cleat-wearing Germans an advantage over Hungary and their first World Cup victory.

Dassler had another secret weapon: his son, Horst. Dassler had five children—four daughters and one son—and encouraged them all to join the business. His wife, Kathe, also worked at headquarters and after Dassler's death in 1978 ran the business herself. But Horst was something else—according to one report, when he was sent by his father to hand out shoes at the 1954 Melbourne Olympics, he bribed workers at the docks to stop Puma equipment being unloaded.

By 1960, Adidas had a lock on the Olympics, with 75 percent of track and field athletes wearing Adidas shoes; at the 1972 Munich Olympics, every official wore Adidas and the majority of the athletes did too. The roster of Adidas-backed stars grew to include high jumper Dick Fosbury, gymnast Nadia Comaneci, and Muhammad Ali and Jo Frazier, who faced each other in 1971, both wearing Adidas.

Adidas was the premium brand of its day, so most athletes would have worn its products willingly. But Dassler knew how to cultivate contacts and built relationships with the International Olympic Committee that guaranteed its status as the official supplier (which it is to the National Olympic Committee in China in 2008). When Dassler died in 1978, age seventy-eight and yet to retire, Horst, who had opened his own branch of the firm in France, cemented his position as a sports "godfather." He had developed enormous influence across the various sporting bodies, particularly as he helped them to maximize their commercial opportunities through a marketing company he had cofounded.

Horst took complete control of Adidas in 1985, but died two years later, at age fifty-one. After Horst's death, his sisters squabbled over the direction of the company and it lost market share—from an all-time high of 70 percent of the U.S. sports shoe market, Adidas rapidly hit a low of under 3 percent, attacked largely by Nike but also by the swathe of other brands that erupted during that decade's sportswear boom.

In 1989, a swashbuckling French business-rescue specialist called Bernard Tapie stepped in and seduced the sisters into parting with Adidas for what was regarded as a bargain $320 million. Tapie, who became France's Urban Affairs Minister, was spread too thinly to manage the company properly and soon found he could not pay the interest in his loans (he later went bankrupt and spent six months in jail after a match-fixing scandal). In 1992, a French bank found another buyer for Adidas, now losing more than $100 million a year.

Even the otherwise relentlessly upbeat official company history refers to the early 1990s as "a difficult transition period." But the new buyer, a Harvard MBA called Robert Louis-Dreyfus, had a strong track record of successfully rescuing moribund firms. He struck an incredible deal with the bank, buying a 15 percent stake in Adidas with a partner for an initial stake reported to be just $10,000 each, with the banks and other investors providing the rest of the capital. He sacked most of the senior management, slashed costs, and doubled marketing spending.

In the United States, Adidas bought a Portland-based sports marketing company called Sports Inc. and turned it into Adidas America in 1993. It was headed by two former Nike executives, Peter Moore and Rob Strasser, who had been instrumental in projects such as the Air Jordan and the "Just Do It" marketing campaign. Unfortunately, Strasser died of a heart attack shortly after the buyout, but he had time enough to persuade Adidas to set up its U.S. operations in Nike's home turf, which proved an enormous stimulus to the brand, criticized in the past for being out of touch.

Luck also played a part: with retro a major trend in the mid 1990s, Adidas rereleased a line of classic "old-school" sneakers that was an enormous hit and most likely a complete surprise to Nike, then focused on high-tech innovation.

Adidas went public in 1995 and has slowly clawed back market share. Louis-Dreyfus has reportedly turned his initial $10,000 investment into a stake worth some $390 million.

In 1998, Nike, keen to boost its sales of soccer cleats, sponsored the Brazilian team in the World Cup, backed by an enormous global advertising campaign. But it was France, wearing new Adidas "Predator" cleats, who took home the trophy. The war continued off the field: Nike signed the Manchester United soccer team; Adidas signed its star player, David Beckham. Nike recently claimed to have edged out Adidas as the top supplier of soccer footwear in Europe, but Adidas is still ahead globally, and supplies more balls and apparel.

Off the field, Adidas is still playing the retro card with its line of originals, backed by a marketing campaign that draws on the brand's historical connections with popular culture, particularly hip-hop (Run-DMC, one of the first mainstream hip-hop acts, were Adidas fans, and even had a hit single in 1986 called *My Adidas*). In 2004, the sky-blue 1976 model Sl76 was re-released after starring in the remake of *Starsky and Hutch*, and the recent rerelease of the old school "Superstar" sneaker generated queues in front of sneaker stores around the world.

Adidas has also, however, reinvested in technology, taking on Nike at its own game. In 2000, Australian swimmer Ian Thorpe won three gold medals at the Sydney Olympics wearing a bizarre full-body suit made by Adidas; more recently, the company introduced Adidas 1, a $250 computerized shoe that responds electronically to provide different levels of cushioning, and a custom fitting service that measures your feet as you run on a treadmill and sends the details to the factory called Mi Adidas.

More significantly, in mid-2005 it announced plans to buy and merge with Reebok, which meant that the number two- and three-placed brands were joining forces against number one, Nike.

The company is also expanding its retail presence, opening large stores in New York, London, and, more significantly, China, where CEO Herbert Hainer announced plans to open forty stores per month for forty months, on top of the existing five hundred outlets—just in time for the 2008 Olympic Games.

REFERENCES

The Advertiser, Brand Week, The Business, BusinessWeek, Calgary Herald, Courier Mail, Economic Times of India, Economist, Financial Times, Fortune, The Independent, Montreal Gazette, The Observer, Newsweek, New York Times, Sunday Telegraph, Toronto Financial Post, USA Today

THE REVOLUTIONARIES

IKEA

Attack your competitors with innovation; reward your customers with value

A N ENTREPRENEURIAL STREAK WAS PULSING THROUGH THE veins of Ingvar Kamprad from an early age. At five, he was selling matchboxes door-to-door. By seventeen, dyslexic Kamprad was selling pencils, an enterprise that developed into a mail-order business also selling soap, seeds, and stockings. This venture was so successful that Kamprad registered the company name IKEA: an acronym where I stands for Ingvar, K for Kamprad, E for Elmtaryd (the name of the farm Kamprad grew up on), and A for Agunnaryd (the Swedish village he grew up in). IKEA started in a shed that had been used for storing milk churns. His strategy was to seriously undercut his competitors, and by twenty-three, after serving a carpenter's apprenticeship, he had turned his attentions to a furniture business. He had very big plans.

Today, IKEA has 225 stores in more than thirty countries, an annual turnover of more than $17 billion, and 90,000 employees. Kamprad is one of the richest men in the world with a personal fortune of $18.5 billion. Kamprad revolutionized furniture retailing by making what was once a luxury more accessible to more consumers. Now, instead of spending many years' salary to furnish a home, IKEA customers can deck out their homes with only a few months' salary.

In 1953, the first IKEA showroom opened in Almhult, a railway town in Sweden. The first showroom was a huge success, leaving other Swedish furniture retailers particularly unhappy with Kamprad's ability to undercut competitors. When the Swedish

National Association of Furniture Dealers boycotted him, Kamprad was forced to look outside the country for suppliers and to design pieces in-house.

Around the same time, Kamprad stumbled on the idea of flat-packing furniture when a coworker took the legs off a table for easier transport. Bingo. Because of the boycott, IKEA began manufacturing in Poland and, to save on shipping and storage costs, designed pieces that could be flat-packed for delivery back to Sweden. Instead of assembling the furniture once it arrived, Kamprad sold it from the warehouse straight to customers, who could easily take the flat packs home in their cars and assemble it themselves. The concept for what is now the world's largest furniture retailer was born.

Other IKEA stores appeared throughout Sweden with the flagship store in Stockholm opening in 1965. Other megastores followed in Norway, Denmark, Germany, Australia, Canada, the Netherlands, Britain, and the United States.

The company, where titles and suits and ties are rare, remains privately owned through a web of private trusts and charitable foundations. Profits have never been revealed, but Swedish analysts estimate that IKEA's profits are around 6 to 7 percent of total sales. The company ethos encourages its more than 90,000 staff to be known as coworkers, and all must follow Kamprad's nine commandments that center on themes of enthusiasm, humbleness, questioning the status quo, responsibility, self-analysis, simplicity, and thrift. (For more on Kamprad's doctrine, read his 1976 *The Testament of a Furniture Dealer*—the retailer's answer to Chairman Mao's *Red Book*.) Company policy also extends to a blanket ban on extravagance, favoring economy class airfares and public transport rather than taxis. Waste is a mortal sin to Kamprad, from leaving the lights on to time-wasting. He recommends dividing the day into ten-minute blocks.

Throughout the evolution of the IKEA store, Kamprad has been obsessive about market research. A former group chief executive,

Anders Moberg, remembers Kamprad spending a seven-hour train trip to France asking passengers what they thought of his company. "He was unstoppable," he said. This focus on customer needs dates back to the 1950s. After noticing that customers were leaving his Stockholm store around lunchtime because they were hungry, Kamprad introduced an inexpensive café to keep his customers in the store. Similarly, he introduced childcare and play areas to attract young families.

According to *Forbes* magazine, Kamprad is one of the ten richest people in the world. He moved into tax exile in Switzerland in 1974, and IKEA is owned by Kamprad's charitable foundation, Stichting Ingka Foundation, based in the Netherlands. His business empire is a complex one, with accounts being lodged in Ireland, Luxembourg, and the Netherlands, according to Swedish economist Stellan Bjork.

A confessed alcoholic for thirty years (Kamprad says he learned to consume copious quantities of vodka during Polish business trips), he now regularly attends Swedish health farms to dry out. His darkest hour was in the late 1990s when he confessed to being a Nazi sympathizer in his adolescence, something he deeply regrets.

Looking ahead, IKEA is hoping that an aggressive rollout of stores in Asia, particularly in China and Japan, and also its Russian store rollout will continue to boost annual sales above the current $17 billion.

Kamprad has been gradually toning down his input in day-to-day operations since 1986 and there is much speculation as to his succession plans, with all three sons, Peter, Jonas, and Mathias, involved in the running of the company and already established on the board of IKEA. Kamprad's official title with the company now is senior adviser.

Despite Kamprad's fortune, he eschews luxury. He still flies economy, drives a non-descript Volvo, never wears suits and catches public transport. Legend has it that Kamprad waits until closing time at his local market in Lausanne in order to drive hard bargains with stallholders. But Kamprad is not completely obsessed with savings in his old age. The billionaire admits: "From time to time, I like to buy a nice shirt and cravat—and eat Swedish fish roe."

NOTES

"He was unstoppable . . ." Heller, Richard. "The Billionaire Next Door," *Forbes*, 8.7.00, reprinted in *BRW*, 8.25.00, p. 84.

"From time to time . . ." Brown-Humes, Christopher. "The Bolt That Holds the IKEA Empire Together," *Financial Times*, 8.12.02, p. 11.

REFERENCES

Torekull, Bertil. *Leading by Design: The Ikea Story.* HarperCollins, 1999.

The Age, Australian Financial Review, BRW, BusinessWeek, Daily Telegraph, The Economist, Fast Company, Financial Times, Forbes, The Guardian, New York Times, The Observer, Sunday Times, Sydney Morning Herald

RE/MAX

Dogged determination is a great asset

I T IS VERY POSSIBLE THAT BILLIONAIRE DAVE LINIGER IS THE SORT OF person who would have been successful at whatever he did; he knew from when he was a little boy growing up in Marion, Indiana, mowing lawns for twenty-five cents an hour that he wanted to get rich. He dropped out of college, married young, served in the Vietnam War, and, after successfully buying and selling "fixer-uppers," he fell into a career in real estate. After failing to sell a single house in his first six months on the job, a motivational talk shifted the mindset of this short, square-shouldered man. With newfound confidence, Liniger started selling houses like no one's business. He even brokered a deal on the way home from that very seminar when he went to buy some milk. He soon left behind the clapped out Volkswagen (with no air conditioning) he was driving around Phoenix, Arizona, and moved to Denver, Colorado. Liniger was such a gun salesman that he interviewed the best agents in the city to see which one he would like to work for, not the other way around. Not content with being a top agent at blue-chip realtor Van Schaack, Liniger began to resent the system that allowed Van Schaack to earn 50 percent sales commission on every sale he made while doing next to nothing for him. The more his sales grew, the more he hated the system. He figured that the top 20 percent of sales people were generating 80 percent of the business and carrying all the non-performers as well. Instead of being looked after, developed, and trained further, the top agents were pretty much ignored, expected to keep bringing home the bacon.

Liniger thought about his ideal agency where the best salespeople in the business paid a flat fee for office space and other services and did not pay commission on their sales. (50 percent was a high price to pay for a safety net they didn't need, right?) The agents, in effect, worked for themselves. This idea was not original. Liniger had worked in a no-split commission agency in Phoenix, but it was by no means a blue-chip agency. He was convinced this concept could work at the top end of the market. He would sell RE/MAX as an "everybody wins" business. The idea for RE/MAX was born, a real estate agent business as opposed to a real estate business.

He took his pitch to Van Schaak management, but they were not interested in changing the rules—things were too comfy the way they were. After just twelve months at Van Schaack, Liniger quit in 1973 and started to look for someone who might believe in his business idea. He managed to find investors in a group of real estate developers who were willing to put in $400,000 seed funding. The name RE/MAX, short for Real Estate Maximums, was hatched at a late-night tequila session. Unfortunately, the backers only ended up giving Liniger $15,000 due to their own financial troubles, but that

$15,000 was enough to rent office space and employ one Gail Main (now Gail Liniger), the cofounder of RE/MAX. She ran the office, and he concentrated on recruiting new agents.

The early years were extremely tough. He thought he would be starting the business with funds behind him. "Everything we earned went to pay the debt," he says. "It was a lousy way to fund a business." Top sales people in the blue-chip realtors were not prepared to take the risk to join this fledgling business. He remembers out of 1,000 inquiries, only four people were prepared to join the company. Three of the four were women who were, in those days, traditionally cut out of the real estate jobs despite their knowledge of what people look for in real estate. "We were different and we were ostracized," he says. "We were so different and so dangerous because we were changing the business model."

Liniger has said on many occasions that RE/MAX was built to a large extent by women. He realized early on that their potential to be great at selling houses was being overlooked. He made the most of that. It was not until 1977 that top male agents would defect to RE/MAX, with two hundred joining up en masse.

Liniger started the business with insufficient capital and no management skills and was up against an industry very set in its ways. But what Liniger lacked in experience and finances, he made up for in resourcefulness: his ability to talk his way out of any situation and a dogged determination to operate the biggest real estate network in the world. There were times when they simply couldn't pay the bills, telephones were cut off, the IRS came knocking for unpaid taxes, branch managers nearly revolted, and, when the original investors in RE/MAX went bankrupt, Liniger ended up saddled with their debt. Even when the front page of the local business papers reported that RE/MAX was bankrupt, Liniger and Main never gave up. They lived on credit cards, did not draw salaries, and always found a way to keep going. Main would always have some clever payment plan or strategy to keep the creditors at bay, explaining to the debt collectors why the business had to the potential to survive and pay its debts. Liniger started out young and naïve, "but the naïve part disappeared after being in the furnace of a new business."

Within twelve months there were eight RE/MAX offices. In order to keep the company afloat and fund growth, Liniger reluctantly started selling RE/MAX franchises after agents inquired about owning their offices and collecting the office fees themselves. The first franchises sold were in Denver and Kansas City in 1975. Franchises originally cost $3000–4000. Liniger realized that a franchise model would be critical to the sustained growth of RE/MAX. All franchisors pay around 15 percent of the fees they collect to the parent company owned by the Linigers. While this money helped keep the business running, it was not growing fast enough to keep ahead of the business costs. Luckily, Liniger sold franchises to a number of Canadian regions in 1977 where RE/MAX took off. Canadian RE/MAX was soon recruiting record amounts of new RE/MAX agents. These fees kept the business alive whilst the U.S. operations slowly grew.

Despite the constant squeeze, Liniger and Main were absolutely confident that RE/MAX could work. It was only a matter of time. Main, to this day, says she is surprised that the explosive growth didn't happen sooner. The business became profitable in 1978, five years after starting out.

RE/MAX really was built inch by inch, agent by agent. In the first ten years, RE/MAX recruited 5,000 agents, many of whom Liniger describes as "malcontents, people who weren't happy with the powers that be." Growth exploded in the next decade with 35,000 RE/MAX agents on board by 1993, and 50,000 by 1998. Liniger says that in all this time, the core goals of the business never changed; the management team stayed the same. This exponential growth didn't happen overnight, but it did happen. His pitch remained the same: "Promote yourself. Advertise as much as you want. Negotiate your own commissions. Decide your own deals. Grow your business the way you know how to grow it."

Every morning, Liniger receives a print out of how many agents RE/MAX has around the world. Liniger can always quote these figures off the top of his head. The focus remains the same decades on.

The high brand awareness of RE/MAX, particularly in North America, is closely linked to the RE/MAX balloon fleet. Originally Liniger didn't like the idea of a hot-air balloon to sell the brand, but the first RE/MAX balloon's maiden voyage at a balloon fair in New Mexico resulted in extensive television exposure and Liniger changed his tune. There is now a fleet of more than one hundred RE/MAX balloons around the world, the balloon synonymous with the brand.

There are now more than 108,000 RE/MAX agents working in more than fifty-six countries. While many agents keep 100 percent of their sales commissions, others prefer to work on 95/5, 90/10, and 85/15 systems.

As RE/MAX started to make serious money, Liniger was able to put money into giving agents the things he knew would motivate them to be more successful. Obsessed with continuous improvement, he started offering courses and seminars to help agents reach their potential. Liniger held huge conferences and conventions, spreading the RE/MAX gospel (and cheekily charging RE/MAX agents a fee to hear him talk). RE/MAX became the first real estate organization to offer a satellite television network with a crammed schedule of classes, seminars, and speakers to help people maximize sales. Again, agents paid to enroll in the courses. "It takes a great deal of time to develop proper business judgement," says Liniger. "It does not come in one week or one year; it is a continual learning process."

With the wave of fees rolling in, Liniger and Main became rich— very rich. They married in their RE/MAX office 1984 after Main had recovered from a seaplane accident in Canada that had left her partially paralyzed. They still run the company with Dave Liniger spending an average of 270 nights on the road for RE/MAX (although it's a little easier now that he flies in a corporate jet). The Linigers have been able to indulge in their passions for NASCAR racing, wildlife, Arabian horses, and hot air ballooning. They also own their own private golf course. Dave has also joined the trend for entrepreneurs to indulge in high-risk record-breaking pursuits. His took the form of trying to travel around the world in a helium balloon. After nine months of planning, Dave ended up in the middle of the Australian desert waiting for take-off. After nine weeks of failed attempts, the mission was aborted due to bad weather. Typically, Dave saw the $8 million venture as a success because of enormous media exposure the RE/MAX balloon had in the lead-up to the event.

RE/MAX, for now, remains a privately held company with the Linigers owning 90 percent of the business. Talk of going public is never far off, but for now, and the Linigers are happy with the way things are. An IPO will happen to avoid estate taxes. "Everything goes to charity," he says. At the time of publication, RE/MAX has recorded 360 months of consecutive growth, and the Linigers will be happy their goal of RE/MAX world domination is on track. For Liniger, there is no way that the growth will stop. If it does, he swears, "I am going to jump off the twelfth story of the building."

Despite the jets, NASCAR teams, scuba diving trips, and private jet travel, Liniger stresses that wealth does not mean a great deal to him. He likes the adventure of it all. "I have had zillions of adventures, but the biggest adventure has been building this company."

NOTES
"Promote yourself . . ." Harkins, Phil and Keith Hollihan. *Everybody Wins*. John Wiley & Sons, 2004.

REFERENCES
Business Wire, CBS News, *CBS This Morning*, *Courier-Mail*, *Denver Post*, *The Financial Post* (Canada), *The Guardian*, *Inc*, *Rocky Mountain News*, *Seattle Post-Intelligencer*, *USA Today*

JD Power

People will pay dearly for the right information

I T WASN'T AS IF THE CAR COMPANIES COULDN'T HAVE DONE IT themselves. They could have easily asked their customers what they liked and disliked about the cars they sold, then used the information to make their cars better. But back in the 1960s—and in some cases for decades beyond that—car makers didn't really want to know what their customers thought.

For James David Power III, an MBA hired by Ford as a researcher in 1959, that arrogance and myopia was, at first, enormously frustrating. Then he realized it was also a great business opportunity.

Power, born in Worcester, Massachusetts in 1931, spent four years in the coast guard, including a stint in Antarctica, before returning to study for his MBA at Wharton School of Business at the University of Pennsylvania. He moved to Detroit to work for Ford, then at another research firm doing work for Buick. In those days, he says, his reports were routinely tidied up to please higher-ups, masking his real findings. Not all companies were resistant, though: when Power reported his customer research to a maker of chain saws, they not only acted on his recommendations (to make the saws lighter and cheaper) but hired him as director of corporate planning. Sales soared.

Now convinced of the value of his consumer research, Power struck out solo in April 1968, assisted by his wife, Julie. His scheme was straightforward: circulate surveys to customers, analyze the results around his kitchen table, and sell the information back to the companies who sold the products. Unlike, say, Ralph Nader, Power was not primarily a consumer crusader. His goal, he has often said, was to give car makers information they could use to improve their product—and a direct connection between his research and their bottom line was something he could charge for.

"When I started the company, I wasn't considering myself an entrepreneur," he said in 2004. "I just wanted to start a company that would do things the way I wanted to."

Unsurprisingly, the U.S. car makers were not initially interested in his idea. Why would an outsider know better than them? It was Toyota that was willing to try something new to boost sales of its Corona model in the early 1970s.

Power cold-called the importer when he heard it had set up an office nearby, and first convinced it to let him survey owners of Toyota forklifts. (When Toyota's executives suggested they meet Power at his offices, he had to run out and rent some space.) Power then analyzed the Corona, Toyota's attempt at a breakthrough model after an earlier failure, suggesting mechanical improvements.

Toyota's willingness to listen to its customers and to act on the faults they discovered eventually propelled it to the top of the JD Power customer satisfaction survey. But it was another importer's lack of interest that made Power's reputation. In 1973, Power bought a list of Mazda owners from another market researcher. Julie was reading through their responses to a survey when she noticed several owners reporting problems with the "O" rings in their engines. Neither she nor Power knew what an "O" ring did, but they knew it meant major engine trouble.

The Detroit office of the *Wall Street Journal* heard about his report and called, asking Power to confirm his findings. He typed up a press release and within days his finding had made news around the world. He had been calling Mazda for a year without success; after the "O" ring fiasco they called him.

Today, Power releases a basic account of his reports to the public, for free, simply revealing which cars top his various categories, such as the initial quality survey, where 100,000 owners report their opinions after three months of ownership (Power surveys some 4 million customers a year). Car makers who pay for results get a three-hour head start on reporters to prepare statements and detailed findings into all models on the market. For an additional fee of up to $100,000, they can use Power's findings in their advertising.

Power grew the business slowly, living frugally and reinvesting his profits rather than borrowing heavily. He diversified into survey-ing other consumer products such as computers and insurance and by the mid-1980s the business was growing at 25 percent a year, with half of his revenue from auto surveys. By 2005, when Power sold his firm to the publisher McGraw-Hill for an undisclosed sum, he had some 600 employees and annual revenues around $150 million.

NOTES
"When I started the company . . ." Macchiarella, Gretchen. "A Man of Clout and Respect," Business, *Ventura County Star*, 7.9.04, p. 1.

REFERENCES
Advertising Age, Adweek, Automotive News, BusinessWeek, Los Angeles Times, New York Times, St. Petersburg Times, The Record, Venture County Star, Virginian-Pilot

Mark Burnett

Only results count

————

MARK BURNETT, THE MAN WHO BROUGHT US *SURVIVOR* AND *The Apprentice*, did not begin life with particularly high expectations. He grew up in East London, England, where his parents worked in factories, his father at Ford and his mother filling car batteries. Burnett obviously wanted a little more excitement out of life than a factory job, coming home one day at age eighteen and announcing to his father, Archie, that he had joined the paratroopers. He saw active service in Northern Ireland

and then in 1981 was shipped to the south Atlantic to fight in the Falklands War, where twenty-four men from his regiment were killed in action.

He returned to Britain where he quit the army and left the country, departing for Los Angeles in 1982 with the vague notion of traveling onwards to South America to work as a "military advisor."

Landing in LA with $600 in his pocket, he heard about a job from a friend—as a nanny in Beverly Hills. In the first of what became many convincing sales pitches in Burnett's career, he told the couple that while he had never been a nanny, his military training made him ideal: they were not just hiring a child minder, but a bodyguard, too, and he had parade-ground standards of cleanliness.

He successfully worked as a carer for several families and then for a time supplemented his income selling T-shirts off the sidewalk at Venice Beach, buying seconds for $2 and selling them for $20. He initially regretted paying $1,500 monthly rent for a piece of fence, but his instinct paid off and he expanded his business to five stands and parlayed some of the profits into a real estate deal that netted him a quick $75,000.

No wonder Burnett is such a believer in the American dream.

By the age of thirty-two he was earning good money in a marketing job and was about to marry his fiancée, Dianne, when, in 1991 he had what his friends thought was an early midlife crisis.

Burnett came across an article about an extreme cross-country race called the Raid Gauloises, in which teams hike, climb, and kayak their way across rugged terrain. That, Burnett thought, would make a great television show. To find out what it entailed he set about putting a team together to enter a race himself.

Through his race partner he then got a meeting with Doug Herzog, chief programmer at MTV. Despite his complete lack of experience in television, he somehow convinced Herzog he could create and produce a show around a new event he would call Eco

Challenge. Herzog later told the *New York Times*, "It was clear this was a guy who could climb a mountain."

After convincing television crews to tag along while he competed in two of the Raid races, Burnett organized his first Eco Challenge in 1995, a race through the wilds of Utah. It first screened on MTV and in later seasons, on the Discovery Channel.

In 1995, Burnett was at Fox Studios talking about Eco Challenge when an executive mentioned another idea that had been floating about—a reality show where you trapped a bunch of people on a desert island. An English producer called Charlie Parsons and musician, entrepreneur, and humanitarian Sir Bob Geldof had come up with the idea as far back as 1988, but had been unable to convince anybody to make the show.

Enter Burnett, with a big pitch. He struck a deal with Parsons for the U.S. rights to the show in 1998, and, after tortuous meetings all over Los Angeles, successfully pitched it to CBS after turning down an offer from a smaller network that he felt would not have the resources to produce the show properly.

To Charlie Parsons' original idea, Burnett added what would become signature touches: *Survivor*'s dramatic tribal council ceremonies, elaborate physical challenges, and stunning photography. At the start of the first series, he had twenty-three cameras trained on the castaways as they sailed to their island, Pulau Tiga in Borneo, aboard a native sailing vessel, before taking what they needed and jumping overboard at their destination. His attention to detail is apparent to anybody who has watched the show. "I tweak and tune until the moment filming begins, making sure everything is just right," he says in his entertaining autobiography *Jump In!* "I'm not afraid to look stupid and admit that I was originally wrong. The bottom line is that only results count. How you arrive at them does not."

Survivor rated so highly so quickly—attracting 51 million viewers for the first season—that it was credited with revitalizing CBS. It certainly created a new brand: Burnett, who was soon comparing himself with such legendary producers as Aaron Spelling.

According to Burnett, CBS accepted the show on condition Burnett brought advertisers to the party. In return, Burnett has said, he won a share of the advertising stream, a deal that reportedly netted him some $100 million on the first series alone. Whatever the true figure, CBS was certainly very happy with Burnett, sending him a champagne Mercedes 500SL sports car as a token of their appreciation, the ultimate token of Hollywood success.

In 2002 Burnett was at New York's Wollman ice skating rink shooting the finale of *Survivor Marquesas*. He saw Donald Trump, who had refurbished the rink, and introduced himself, telling Trump he had read his book *The Art of the Deal* while selling T-shirts at Venice Beach and had been inspired. Would Trump be interested in an idea he had for a show? Trump had turned down numerous pitches to participate in reality shows, but he met Burnett and liked the educational aspect of *The Apprentice*. The show, which won the highest ratings of any new U.S. series in 2003–2004, also shamelessly promoted Trump's businesses, and Trump later (unsuccessfully) tried to trademark the phrase "You're fired"—the catchphrase he used to eliminate unsuccessful contestants.

Survivor continued to rate in the top ten shows even into its eighth season, and, by 2004, Burnett had top-rated shows on three of the four U.S. networks (an uncomfortable ABC, which originally passed on *Survivor*, was the odd one out). In 2004, *Time* magazine named Burnett in its list of the world's 100 most powerful people.

Why are his shows so successful? Perhaps because Burnett was relatively naïve, his production standards were unprecedented. A single episode of *Survivor* required a crew of 400 (Burnett has some 1,500 staff in total). He built strong teams (staff from the early shows went on to run other successful franchises such as *The Apprentice*), cast participants brilliantly, and innately understands the elements of captivating drama. Burnett also believes that what viewers want is not voyeurism but human drama, so while *Survivor* is cast with a certain babe factor, there are surprisingly few lingering shots on contestants' bodies. And while most "reality" shows depend on humiliating their participants, Burnett's shows prefer to create audience interest by developing characters, as you would in a scripted drama. Participants do, invariably, humiliate themselves in *Survivor* and *The Apprentice*, but it's their own doing.

Burnett is unashamedly commercial—he has said he wouldn't have an issue if Microsoft, for example, took naming rights over the Microsoft Grand Canyon National Park, if it was paying for its upkeep. In *Survivor,* he had the brainwave of making contestants sweat though a hideous challenge to win cans of Mountain Dew and Doritos corn chips. The brands had paid for the in-show exposure and for traditional thirty-second spots during the episode. It's a revenue stream that could become increasingly significant as viewers using TiVo and similar recording devices screen out traditional commercial breaks.

Burnett's strike rate has been high, but not perfect. His most ambitious show, to send a reality contestant into space—*Destination Mir*—crashed when the Russian space station fell out of orbit. And he has struggled with scripted drama, despite numerous attempts—a comedy called *Are We There Yet*, about an American family road-trip, never made it to air, nor did *Commando Nanny*, a sitcom based on Burnett's own experiences. He is still dreaming of making a movie.

In the meantime, he is growing ever more imaginative commercially. For his boxing reality series *The Contender*, he cooked up a deal with equipment manufacturer Everlast to promote their iconic products. Everlast, a tiny operation, could never have afforded the now-usual hefty cost of a Burnett product placement; instead, Burnett and his partners negotiated for 5 percent of Everlast's stock per season. *Fortune* magazine also revealed that while negotiating behind the scenes with Martha Stewart to star in her version of *The Apprentice*, he made a deal with her company that saw him given warrants to buy 2.5 million shares of stock, which almost tripled in value—to $50 million—when he eventually revealed the show would go into production.

Now a motivational speaker and the author of several self-help-style memoirs, Burnett is eager to pass on his wisdom. Unfortunately, while his life story is inspirational, his "tips" usually boil down to fairly obvious advice such as work hard and take risks. The real key to his success is better explained by Jeff Probst, the long-serving host of the *Survivor* series. "He gets people to do things they really don't want to do," Probst told CBS in 2005. "He gets guys to leave their families for longer than they probably should to go out in the middle of nowhere, to live in a tent with rats crawling all over them, scorpions crawling all over them. I'm not kidding."

NOTES

"It was clear this was a guy who could climb a mountain . . ." Carter, Bill. "Survival of the Pushiest," *New York Times,* 1.28.01, p. 22.

"I tweak and tune . . ." Burnett, Mark. *Jump In!* Random House, 2005, p. 98.

"He gets people to do things they really don't want to do . . ." *CNN People in the News*, "Profiles of Donald Trump, Mark Burnett, Simon Cowell, Kyra Phillips, Carol Lin, Paula Zahn," 5.21.05.

REFERENCES

Advertising Age, CNN, *Entertainment Weekly, Evening Standard, Financial Times, Fortune, New York Times, Newsweek, The Oprah Winfrey Show, The Times, USA Today*

Howard Schultz, Starbucks

"With a growth company, you can't play catch up."

OWARD SCHULTZ GREW UP IN THE BROOKLYN PROJECTS IN the 1950s. He always wanted to escape the life his parents endured—dead-end jobs, bad pay, no health benefits, no security, let alone any job satisfaction. Schultz is very frank about the influence his father's professional frustration had on his own life and career and the $23.4 billion company he nurtured from its early years. Young Howard had paper routes, worked in canteens and knitting factories, and even stretched animal skins for a Manhattan furrier. "I always wanted to escape. I always wanted to improve my standing," he says. Thanks to a sports scholarship, practically the only way to escape the projects, he attended Northern Michigan University. He wasn't as good at football as he'd hoped to be, so after graduation he began working at Xerox, known for its excellent management training programs. Schultz proved to be adept at sales and by his early twenties was earning good money working for Swedish housewares company Hammarplast in New York City.

At Hammarplast, Schultz noticed one of his clients, a small coffee bean retailer in Seattle called Starbucks, was purchasing high volumes of drip brewing thermoses. He decided to investigate this little coffee shop, and, in 1981, he flew down to windy Seattle.

The first Starbucks Coffee, Tea, and Spice store had opened in 1971, selling freshly roasted whole and ground coffee beans. To begin with it was a coffee store rather than a café, founded by business bohemians Gerald Baldwin, Zev Siegl, and Gordon Bowker. For Schultz, it was love at first sight, although he had nothing to do with the business officially until 1982, after he had spent twelve months convincing the Starbucks owners that he could do wonders for the sales and marketing side of the business. Schultz was so enamored with the business that he left his well-to-do Manhattan life and relocated to Seattle. He took a pay cut and was offered a small amount of equity in the company in lieu of a big salary.

Schultz had great expectations for Starbucks, though this enthusiasm was something that irked the owners who were passionate about their business but not about growth or change—two of Schultz's favorite things in life. The business would plod along for years until the coffee-in-a-cup aspect of Starbucks would be realized.

Schultz hatched the concept for the Starbucks café after a visit to Italy in 1983. He liked the romantic, feelgood communal aspects of the Italian cafes, the barristas greeting regulars and deftly serving up coffees, a sentiment he has milked ever since. Schultz quickly picked up on the importance of the ritual of it all. It was not just about the cup of coffee. "Everything matters" became his motto, and it remains so today. He recognized that customers have many different motives to come back to a café, from the handsome man in the corner, to the music, to the convenience. It is not just about a caffeine fix. He realized that Starbucks had been missing the point.

Schultz thought that America was ready for this café concept and was itching to reconfigure the Starbucks stores. Not so fast Howard, said his bosses who had just spent all their cash buying out several other coffee stores. There was simply no money to develop the cafés, and Schultz had to sit back while his great epiphany of an idea bubbled away in his mind. So frustrated was Schultz that he decided to quit Starbucks. He raised $3.8 million through a group of investors (he didn't have any of his own capital) and launched a new coffee chain, Il Giornale, in 1987. That same year, just as the Il Giornale business was getting off the ground, Starbucks' owners decided to sell up. Schultz saw his chance to be reunited with his beloved Starbucks, and he went ahead and relentlessly raised $4 million and took over the company in 1987. With a sales background, Schultz was able to deliver a compelling pitch to potential investors. Even with the gift of the gab, he estimates that out of the hundreds of pitches he made, only a fraction of the meetings resulted in funding. Those who did invest would become part of the most profitable businesses in the world during the 1990s.

Now that Schultz was finally captain of the Starbucks ship, he set about changing the business. He kept the great coffee scouts, the bean roasters, purists, and team players, but he added to the mix high-calibre executives from more mainstream businesses working there such as Wendy's and Taco Bell. He wanted the right people for the business before he needed them. "With a growth company, you can't play catch up," he says.

His new executive team would help Schultz realize his ambitious plans to build Starbucks. In four years, business went from $4 million to $273 million when it first floated on the NASDAQ in 1992. The stock has risen 3,098 percent since its debut. From 1987 to 1997, Starbucks went from six stores to 1,300 stores. Today there are more than 8,500 stores around the world, and sales in 2003 were $5.3 billion. Currently, the company has a cash surplus and is virtually debt-free. It is one of the busiest retailers in the world with an estimated 25 million customers each week and 74,000 employees. Regulars visit Starbucks a phenomenal 216 times a year.

Schultz became a pin-up CEO for his progressive human resource and environmental policies, paying coffee suppliers well, offering healthcare and stock options (even for part-time workers) and high levels of training for his employees (who Schultz prefers to call "partners").

The color-schemed stores, perky barristas, piped Kenny G music, and not-too-strong coffee hit the spot with American consumers. While the stores started out being very traditional about the coffees they served, Schultz eventually realized that introducing nonfat milk, frappes, and other coffee drinks for non-purists would deliver bigger profits.

As much as Schultz loves to sing the praises of the whole Starbucks experience, that is not the real reason why so many people visit Starbucks every day. They do so because the Starbucks real estate division has been ruthless in tracking down the best retail sites and driving out competitors. "The real estate business in America is a very, very tough game. It's not for the faint of heart," says Schultz. Starbucks likes to saturate an area with its stores. This may seem like cannibalism, but it effectively drives out competition so people have to buy their coffee at Starbucks. Schultz has also fostered customer loyalty through credit card programs, CDs, and souvenirs. "Retail is detail," he says.

After more than twenty years of double-digit growth, Starbucks began to look offshore to sustain its growth levels. In order to minimize risk and contain costs, Starbucks has entered into several franchising and partnership deals to ensure a fast pace of expansion. Franchising is something Schultz strenuously avoided during the early days of the company. Today, around one third of Starbucks stores outside the U.S. are owned by the company, and it licenses 20 percent of its U.S. stores.

Starbucks is rolling out stores in thirty-four countries including Britain, Spain, Hong Kong, Mexico, Chile, Peru, France, China, and Brazil. One of the great challenges the company faces is the perception of its coffee. When Starbucks opened in 1970s America, the only competition was from nasty, brewed coffee, not from espresso machines. And Starbucks, that started out as a quirky, edgy company, is now one of the most recognizable brands in the world. The whole concept is perceived, particularly by older generations as very yuppie, its coffee weak, pricey, and American style.

While Starbucks in America started with no competitors, in Europe, there is stiff competition for the retailer. Where Starbucks arrived in America when people were looking a more sophisticated lifestyle, Europeans already have strong culinary and coffee traditions.

Schultz, who stepped down as chief executive in 2000, is currently chairman and chief global strategist of the company. He remains typically optimistic about Starbucks' future. He argues that the company still only has such a small slice of beverage market in the U.S., let alone offshore, that all he can see is potential. He has set his sights on 30,000 Starbucks stores around the world with an average of four opening every day. He has 8,500 so far and is fond of saying, "We're building a brand, not a fad."

NOTES

"With a growth company . . ." Schultz, Howard. *Pour Your Heart into It.* Hyperion Press, 1999.

"I always wanted to . . ." *The Business,* "A Latte to Go and a $4 billion Turnover S'il Vous Plait," 1.25.04, p. 1.

"The real estate business . . ." *BusinessWeek,* "Planet Starbucks, Stanley Holmes, Drake Bennett, Kate Carlisle, Chester Dawson," 11.9.02, p. 100.

"Retail is detail . . ." Witchel, Alex. "Coffee Talk With: Howard Schultz," *New York Times,* 12.14.94, p. C1.

REFERENCES

Brandweek, BusinessWeek, CNNMoney, Fast Company, Financial Times, Fortune, The Guardian, The Independent, New York Times, The Observer, The Times

Section 8

IT DIDN'T HAPPEN OVERNIGHT, BUT IT DID HAPPEN

Amazon

Think biggest

A MAZON IS ONE OF THE BEST-KNOWN INTERNET START-UPS, with a share price that soared so high in 1999 that *Forbes* valued its founder, Jeff Bezos, at over $10 billion.

When the dot-com bubble burst, many expected Amazon, which had spent billions without showing a profit, to implode and become an Internet morality tale. The man *Time* magazine named its person of the year in 1999 was surely about to look pretty dumb (and poor).

Except Bezos is neither. While the share price was certainly unsustainable, the business plan was not, and Amazon emerged from the crash in stronger shape than ever.

Jeff Bezos was always a smart kid. At eight, a test confirmed he was especially bright and his parents—mother Jackie and stepfather Miguel—enrolled him in a program for gifted children in Houston. He earned a degree in electrical engineering and computer science from Princeton, where in 1985 he was one of the first people outside the military to encounter the Internet.

Early in his career, Bezos demonstrated an unusual ability for marrying technology with business, at twenty-six becoming the youngest-ever vice president at Bankers Trust. He then joined the hedge fund DE Shaw and Co., one of the first companies to use computers to predict stock prices.

In 1994, Bezos famously came across a startling statistic: Internet usage was now growing at 2,300 percent a year. That, Bezos decided, represented a hell of a growing market. After looking closely at five different kinds of product, including CDs, he decided that books were the way to go. "Books are incredibly unusual," he said in 1999. "There are so many of them you can build a store online that simply couldn't exist any other way." (His favorite novel, incidentally, is *The Remains of the Day*.) Bezos hurriedly visited a booksellers' convention in Los Angeles to absorb the basics of the business and, according to *Time* magazine, persuaded his parents to lend him $300,000 they had saved for their retirement.

Bezos rented a house in suburban Seattle, which was both an IT hub and close to major book distributors. Working from his garage with four employees, Bezos, then age thirty, launched the Amazon.com website in July 1995, and in his first week of business took orders for $12,438 worth of books. By September, he had sales of $20,000 a week.

Then things went completely crazy. *Time* magazine named Amazon one of its ten best sites of 1996. On May 15, 1997, Amazon stock floated at $18, raising $54 million. An Internet company based on an easily understood idea that was actually bringing in cash, Amazon.com was irresistible to investors. At its peak in 1999, one share was worth $113. Bezos soon realized Amazon needed its own warehouses so it could control the whole transaction. It would no longer be a middleman, but a proper retailer that carried stock (even if it had no physical shops). Bezos expanded, both virtually and physically, swallowing up some other dot-coms and building eight warehouses capable of carrying three million books each.

The share price did not survive the dot-com crash, at one point hitting $5.97 in 2001 and wiping seven billion dollars off Bezos's paper worth, and he was forced to close down two warehouses and lay off 15 percent of his employees to reduce costs.

One of Bezos's favorite nicknames for the company was Amazon.org (the Internet suffix for a non-profit organization). Amazon accumulated enormous long-term debt (carrying $2.1 billion by the end of 2001), though it finally made its first—world famous—quarterly profit in the fourth (Christmas) quarter of 2001. It posted its first full-year profit in 2003 (of just $35 million), then made a more reassuring $588 million profit in 2004 and has begun to pay back its long-term debt, though, with turnover close to $7 billion, the profit margin is still small. (Bezos, who owns around a quarter of the company, is now worth some $4 billion.)

Today, constant improvements to the computer-run warehouses, a policy of savage discounting (which Bezos prefers to advertising) and discounted shipping have increased Amazon's operating profit to around 5 percent.

A growing proportion of its income comes from partnerships with companies such as Toys "R" Us, uses Amazon as its online portal. While still primarily a bookseller, Amazon now carries an enormous number of DVDs and CDs, plus a department-store-sized selection of clothes, toys, and electronics. Eventually, Bezos says, Amazon will offer just about anything that can be mailed.

NOTES

"Books are incredibly . . ." *Business Wire*, Transcript of Sam Donaldson interview with Amazon.com's Jeff Bezos, 12.21.99.

REFERENCES

Ad Age Global, BusinessWeek, Business Wire, Fortune, The Guardian, The Independent, Maclean's, Observer Life Magazine, Seattle Post-Intelligencer

Columbia Sportswear

Never underestimate a stay-at-home mom's potential

G ERT "MA" BOYLE IS LIVING PROOF THAT A HOUSEWIFE AND mother of three with no formal business experience can take over a company and lead the transformation of it from an almost worthless, debt-laden business into a billion-dollar company. Columbia Sportswear was founded by Gert's father, Paul Lamfrom, in 1938, in Portland, Oregon after the family fled Nazi Germany, where Gert's father had run one of the country's largest shirt factories. It started as a small wholesale hat company, the Rosenfeld Hat Co. It did not start making outdoor gear for hunters, skiers, and fisherman until the 1950s when the popularity of hats was on the wane.

The wisecracking Gert was born in Augsburg, Germany, in 1924. She never had any plans to go into business. She studied sociology at the University of Arizona and married Neal Boyle, who took over the family company in 1964. Despite never liking housework or cooking, Gert did what women were expected to do at the time, staying at home to raise her three children. Beyond tinkering with the designs of the clothing, adding extra pockets to a fishing vest for example, she did not have a formal role in the company.

All that changed when Gert's husband died suddenly of a heart attack in December 1970. Gert discovered that the business was in bad shape. Neal had, just months earlier, taken out a $150,000 loan to keep the business afloat, using their home, their beach house, and her mother's property as collateral. The company's lawyers and advisors urged Gert to sell up. They didn't want a housewife running the business. Gert has likened the next few months to the Hitchcock horror film *The Birds*. In the next twelve months, sales slumped 25 percent to $600,000 and Gert reluctantly agreed to sell the business. Gert was literally holding the pen, ready to sign the papers when the buyer lowered the price to a paltry $1,400 and her stubbornness kicked in. For so little money, she might as well run the business into the ground herself. After all, she had next to nothing to lose. "I figured I was going to be poor one way or the other, and I decided to fight for it," she says.

Growing up in a family that ran a manufacturing business, Gert says she learned to listen a lot and ask lots of questions. "People don't get ahead in business unless they ask questions," she says. Her parents also taught her the importance of having a forward-looking strategy. "Looking ahead and running an enterprise is more than an occupation, it is a way of life."

It was time for a clean sweep. The bankers gave Gert and her son Tim six months, and they moved ahead. The lawyers and advisors were fired, along with many staff members not prepared to move forward with Gert. She put together an informal board of new advisors that resulted in the company cutting its product range, getting rid of the dead wood, and concentrating on the products with the most potential. Columbia started manufacturing for other outdoor brands to boost turnover. A new team was assembled, who were all instilled with Gert's frugal mindset. Tim left behind his plans to become a lawyer or journalist and joined his mother full-time. It has been an enduring partnership with Tim taking on the day-to-day running and Gert in charge of marketing.

Gert and Tim's foray into outdoor wear was well timed. In the 1970s, outdoor wear became fashionable, it became more functional, and new products and materials, such as lightweight, waterproof, and breathable Gore-Tex, became available and sent every outdoorsmen into the stores wanting to update their casual wear. Columbia was the first to use Gore-Tex in its outerwear clothing.

Columbia Sportswear designed the innovative Bugaboo, a two-jacket-in-one parka with a waterproof outer shell with a fleecy jacket layer underneath. Skiiers loved it, sales were in the millions, and the company's fortunes were reversed.

With stronger sales, there were now funds available for advertising, one of the key ingredients, believes Gert, in the success of Columbia Sportswear. She often cites a saying she heard as a child, "Early to bed, early to rise, work like hell and advertise." Initially Columbia could only afford specialized niche publications. Brand awareness skyrocketed after Gert was persuaded to star in a series of advertisements as "one tough mother," making son Tim test out Columbia gear with the catchphrase: "Before it passes Mother Nature, it has to pass Mother Boyle." Gert has been putting her face out there ever since. She likes it that way, not in the least because the company doesn't have to pay anyone else to do it.

The public could not get enough of Gert. And their campaign offered a real point of difference. Ma Boyle, with her fake "Born to Nag" tattoos, has a reputation for not suffering fools gladly (she has turned down three invitations to the White House so far).

Like fellow Portland business Nike, Columbia began outsourcing production to Asia, chasing bigger margins and keeping its pricing at the lower end of the scale. The range expanded with the top range of gear sold to specialist stores, less rugged gear at department stores aimed at the clientele who tend to wear their outdoor gear at the mall rather than on a mountain. Sales moved from $13 million in 1984 to $1.1 billion in 2004. The company successfully floated on the NASDAQ in 1998 with the Boyle family retaining 65 percent of the stock. Growth is still on the cards through offshore expansion, acquisitions, and improved domestic retail strategy. Gert's recipe for success, which she delivers in her autobiography *One Tough Mother*, is simple. Don't give up. Be prepared to change strategy. Tap into the wisdom and experience of others who know about what you are trying to do. Listen to your customers. Be a team player. Focus on what makes you unique. Don't spend money you don't have. Walk before you run. Always tell the truth. Do your best every day.

"We are in the business of making products that our customers need and want," she says. "And when you make the right product and deliver it at the right price they come back asking for more. That is how you build a company bigger and better."

Gert has an estimated personal fortune of more than $300 million. Despite her age, there are no retirement plans. Gert is still in at the office every weekday and personally signs every check for the company. ("I know what comes in. I want to know what goes out. If you know that your boss is going to look at your expenses, then you're going to be a little more careful.") This approach is a long way from her housewife days when she had a monthly ritual of taking all the household bills and throwing them against the wall. The one that flew the furthest, she would pay.

The big question remains: What will Columbia Sportswear do without Gert Boyle? Says her son Tim, "We'll just have her stuffed."

NOTES

"I figured . . ." "Talking with One Tough Mother," Small business section, *BusinessWeek*, 4.7.05.

"I know what comes in . . ." Jung, Helen. "The Monday Profile Portland's First Citizen Gert Boyle," *The Oregonian*, 3.28.05, p. A01.

"We'll just have her stuffed . . ." Holmes, Stanley. "Gert Gets the Last Laugh," *BusinessWeek*, 6.10.02, p. 100.

REFERENCES

Boyle, Gertrude with Kerry Tymchuk. *One Tough Mother: Success in Life, Business and Apple Pies*. WestWinds Press, 2005.

Associated Press, Bloomberg, BusinessWeek, The Columbian, Fortune Small Business, The Oregonian, People, Sunday Pregonian, Women's Wear Daily

Nutrimetics

Major success is made up of many small successes

———————

S ELLING TELEVISION LAMPS DOES NOT SOUND LIKE A VERY glamorous start to a $364 million fortune, but that's how young Bill and Imelda Roche started out in the direct selling business.

The couple met in an Australian supermarket in 1956. Bill, who was working for Kellogg's, was organizing a Corn Flakes display, and Imelda, who worked for a cash register company, was doing an on-site display. They began dating, but did not have the means to get married and set up house until 1961. Dollars had always been scarce in both Bill and Imelda's families so the couple hatched a plan to change that. "When we grew up we were prepared to do any-thing to make money to get married and have a family," says Imelda. "People are a bit more selective about what they want to do today. They miss a lot of opportunities."

Bill and Imelda's courtship coincided with the introduction of television in Australia. At the time, it was recommended that peo-ple watch television in a dark room to protect their eyes, with just a lamp above the television for additional lighting. Bill and Imelda invested in some wire lamp frames, enlisted family members to help make plastic and raffia shades, and began selling their TV lamps directly to the public. For the next four decades, the Roches would stick with the business of direct selling—first lamps, then women's clothing, then cosmetics.

Imelda had been hunting around for other direct sales opportu-nities when, in 1968, the couple responded to an advertisement seeking local representatives for a Los Angeles-based cosmetics company. The brand, Nutrimetics, sold only through direct sales, offered a range of skincare and makeup of comparable quality to high-end mainstream brands. The Roches received no response for months, until the phone rang one day when Imelda was getting the children ready for school. She learned that a deal had fallen through with an Australian distributor and a shipment of Nutrimetics products was stuck on the wharf. "We became intensely interested," says Imelda. The Roches paid less than $1,000 to release the stock and began selling Nutrimetics on a commission basis. Their lamp and clothing business was to be run by Bill's brothers while he and Imelda concentrated on Nutrimetics.

"From day one I had the feeling," says Imelda, "that this had the potential to be anything we wanted to make it."

The Roches established Nutrimetics by building up their sales force, using the rather obvious equation that more consultants equaled more sales. Their aggressive drive to recruit new sales consultants (anywhere, anytime) counteracted the inevitable churn rate in the industry: to the Roches' credit, Nutrimetics had a consultant turnover of just 20 percent, against the industry average of 70 percent. After beginning with just five consultants, in the first twelve months, the Roches recruited 1,200 Nutrimetics representatives.

Imelda, who turned seventy in 2004, is one of the few business-women of her generation to have spoken out about the challenges women face trying to break into the male-dominated business world. Part of her initial attraction to Nutrimetics was that it would be a business built by women for women.

The Roche direct-selling approach also centers on not trying to sell too many products at once. Nutrimetics has stuck to selling cosmetics and toiletries, allowing consultants and customers to avoid confusion about the products. "It is very difficult to train tens of thousands of people to understand and be able to sell a lot of different products. It is much smarter to stick to a narrow range and train your people thoroughly," says Imelda.

Capitalizing on their Australian success, the Roches bought out 20 percent of the parent company in the mid-1970s. They then took Nutrimetics to Asia and bought out 100 percent of the Australian and international Nutrimetics business in 1991. By then, there were 270,000 Nutrimetics consultants in twenty countries, and the company had an estimated annual turnover of $250 million. The Roches kept building the business, planning to pass it on to their four children; but in 1997, after pursuing the Roches for three years, the Sara Lee Corporation offered to buy out the business, with Imelda staying on as chairman. They accepted the undisclosed offer. By then, sales for the company had reached $300 million, with 90,000 representatives in Australia alone.

Imelda says she has been the "nuts and bolts" of the Roche enterprises, while Bill has been the "visionary." "Bill is more interested in planning, backroom management, whereas my eyes glaze over the third time I see a set of plans," she says. "I get more involved in the people and personal issues." She is quick to emphasize her business partnership with her husband: "Everything has been with Bill."

When the Roches moved out of operational roles at Nutrimetics, they began expanding their portfolio of property investment and development. The Roche Group now oversees a property portfolio that includes whole suburb developments, ranches, wineries, a luxury lodge, and significant commercial property. Far from retiring, the Roches' grandest project to date is the $80 million Hunter Valley Gardens venture in New South Wales near Sydney. It encompasses more than three hundred hectares, two hundred staff, a man-made waterfall, 34,000 roses, 1,000 fruit trees, and extensive formal gardens. "It is our gift to the state, to the nation," Imelda says.

"There's a great deal of expectation today," says Imelda. "I don't think people are prepared to be as patient as we had to be a few generations ago. You were grateful for small rewards and you grew and developed those. Today, unless something has enormous potential, people wait around until that comes and quite often it never does."

Despite her trademark coiffed hair, impressive displays of jewelry and a conservatively estimated shared fortune of $364 million, the former bookkeeper and grandmother of twelve considers herself a "very ordinary woman who has had some extraordinary opportunities and fortunately on many occasions, I have been in the right place at the right time." To Imelda, a major success is "made up of many, many small successes." Imelda credits her grandmother with giving her a strong sense of confidence. "She gave me a confidence that I could do anything I wanted in life, to never be intimidated by any single person or any circumstance."

NOTES

"When we grew up . . ." Crisp, Lyndall. "Paradise Costs: Bill and Imelda Build a Garden in a Million," *Australian Financial Review*, 9.20.03, p. 24.

"It is very difficult . . ." Shoebridge, Neil. "Money Is Not the Main Motivator," *BRW*, 9.1.97, p. 42.

"There's a great deal of expectation . . ." Crisp, Lyndall. "Paradise Costs: Bill and Imelda Build a Garden in a Million," *Australian Financial Review*, 9.20.03, p. 24.

REFERENCES

The Age, The Australian, Australian Financial Review, Australian Women's Weekly, BRW, Canberra Times, Courier Mail, Daily Telegraph, Gold Coast Bulletin, Illawarra Mercury, Ita Magazine, Newcastle Herald, Sun Herald, Sunday Telegraph, The Sunday Times, Sydney Morning Herald, The Weekend Australian

THAT'S WHAT I WANTED, I JUST DIDN'T KNOW IT

Cirque du Soleil

Joining the circus can be a smart business decision

O NE OF THE MORE UNUSUAL DEBUT ENTRIES IN *FORBES* magazine's annual list of the world's richest people in 2004 was a trained fire-eater and juggler by the name of Guy Laliberté.

A founding member of the Cirque du Soleil theater group, Laliberté steered the company from near-bankruptcy in its infancy to become a billion-dollar international corporation—and along the way outmaneuvered his original partners to become its sole owner.

Laliberté grew up in Montreal, the son of an Alcan aluminum executive and a nurse. He has said his childhood was completely normal, yet he evidently had wanderlust, organizing a school trip to Louisiana at sixteen, reportedly leaving a note for his mother that quoted Kahlil Gibran's *The Prophet*: "Your children are not your children. They are the sons and daughters of Life's call to Life."

At eighteen he headed off again, this time to Europe, where he spent his first night in London on a bench at a corner of Hyde Park. He lived on the streets for a year in the company of other buskers, learning to juggle, breath fire, and engage passersby with sleight-of-hand.

By 1979, in his early twenties, he was back in Canada, working as a theater producer at a youth center in Baie-St-Paul, a small town northeast of Quebec City. It was there in 1979 Laliberté met Gilles St. Croix, a fellow youth worker and stilt walker. With another theatrical type, Daniel Gauthier, they started a ragtag troupe called

Club des Talons Hauts (the High Heels Club) to tour the region's summer festivals in 1982. Then, in 1984, the provincial government announced it was offering cultural grants to celebrate the 450th anniversary of the discovery of Canada by Europeans. Laliberté and his partners received funding to tour with an avant-garde show they named Cirque du Soleil. While ostensibly a circus, it had no animals and little of the hokiness of traditional companies; rather, it took street entertainment and turned it into a slick, ironic, acrobatic show aimed at adults.

Cirque toured eleven cities in eleven weeks, charging $2 for adults and $1 for children. It was a sell-out. Their success encouraged them to take the show further afield, to English-speaking Toronto, where they were billed as the "Sun Circus." Unfortunately, something was lost in the translation, with members of the audience demanding their money back when Cirque's animal-free, artistic performance did not live up to their expectations of a "real" circus. Worse was to come when they took the show south to Niagara Falls to cash in on the thousands of tourists who visited daily; it turned out the tourists wanted to see the falls, not clowns, and Cirque ended up playing to fifteen people a night.

The troupe struggled on until 1987, when Laliberté saw an opportunity for one more shot at the big time. The Quebec delegation in Los Angeles convinced one of the organizers of the highbrow Los Angeles Arts Festival to see the show in Quebec City; the organizer saw it four times, then gave Cirque top billing at the Los Angeles Festival's opening night. It was a risky move by the organizers to open with a circus, riskier still for Laliberté, who agreed to do the show for no upfront fee—just the promise of an audience filled with celebrities and the box office takings, if there were any. He claims the company did not even have the gas money to return home when they arrived in Los Angeles. According to one newspaper report, a local entrepreneur even offered $1 million to buy the circus, which Laliberté flatly turned down. They were invited to appear on the *Johnny Carson Show* and stories began to appear in the national press. (Cirque, which soon began charging rather more than traditional circuses, was eventually even parodied on *The Simpsons*, as "that $80 circus.")

The first Los Angeles season was eventually profitable—Cirque ended its season with more than $40,000 in the bank—and in 1986 Laliberté had another brain wave: instead of running one troupe all year, closing down periodically to plan new shows, he suggested they start a second company that would operate in parallel, so there was always money coming in. Many of the original performers opposed the idea, arguing it compromised their artistic integrity, but Laliberté won out. "The idea was to create a self-feeding circle," he said.

By 1988, Cirque was drawing close to $10 million in corporate sponsorship. In 1991, it struck a $6 million deal with the Japanese television network Fuji to perform one hundred shows in eight Japanese cities. Then, in 1992, it found a permanent home in Las Vegas with a show called Mystère, which had a guaranteed run of ten years. Cirque expanded to offer several touring shows and shows at permanent sites, including one at Disney World in Orlando, Florida, with a show called La Nouba, a deal in which Disney provided a $52 million theater, Cirque performed the show 450 times a year, and split the profits from tickets costing $100 with Disney.

As you would expect, money and success—or, rather, what to do about them—became a major source of conflict among Cirque's original founders. Run by a threesome comprising Laliberté, Gauthier, and Normand Latourelle, there was a showdown over taking the company public in 1989, resulting in Latourelle's departure and Laliberté and Gauthier taking over as a partnership, keeping the company in private hands. They were to remain close for the next eleven years. In 2001, though, Laliberté bought out Gauthier for a reported $483 million to become Cirque's sole owner and a billionaire in his own right, ranked 548 on the *Forbes* list of the world's richest people in 2005 with $1.2 billion.

Laliberté spends part of the year at Cirque's high-tech headquarters in Montreal, and the rest on the road between the various shows and the company's other offices in Amsterdam, Singapore, and Melbourne, traveling with his girlfriend, three children, and two cousins who work as nannies. Laliberté may not have been, according to Gauthier, the business brain, but he has yet to trip up.

NOTES

"The idea was to create . . ." McCarroll, Jo. "Business Lord of the Rings," *Sunday Star Times*, 1.21.01, p. 9.

REFERENCES

Associated Press, Australian Financial Review, Brisbane Courier Mail, BusinessWeek, Canada AM, Canadian Business, Financial Times, Gold Coast Bulletin, The Independent, MacLean's, Montreal Gazette, National Post (Canada), *New Statesman, New York Times, Newshour with Jim Lehrer, Newsweek, The Observer, Ottawa Citizen, Profit, Stage, The Times, CNNFN, USA Today, Washington Times*

Rollerblade

Live your product

THE STORY OF ROLLERBLADE, THE COMPANY THAT PIONEERED one of the world's most popular sports, is an object lesson in how entrepreneurs can trip up with even the most successful ventures.

Rollerblade began when Scott Olson, a young hockey enthusiast from Minneapolis, started looking for a way to train in the off season. Olson lived across the road from an ice rink and had fallen in love with the sport, becoming an all-state goalie in high school and eventually landing a professional contract with a minor league team, Winnipeg Jets. At a local sports store, he found the answer—a basic in-line roller skate called the Super Street Skate, which looked like an ice skate but had wheels instead of a blade.

In-line skates were hardly a new invention. They had been around since the Dutch experimented with wooden versions in the 1700s; an American inventor called AJ Gibson had patented a three-wheel version as early as 1869; numerous other variations followed in the early 1900s. The Super Street Skate, however, was probably the first to look like the modern in-line skate, with the front and rear wheels protruding beyond the base of the boot, giving the user more stability than earlier attempts. Invented by hockey team owner Maury Silver as a training aid, it was patented in 1975 as the Tandem Roller Hockey Skate. Silver went into business with Ralph Backstrom, an LA Kings player, to sell it. Hockey players bought them, but they couldn't get backing from a major manufacturer, so the idea languished. "I think we were just ten years ahead of our time," Backstrom said recently. "Sometimes I wonder if we gave up too soon."

Scott Olson saw the skates' potential, however, using his pair to commute from home to Minneapolis—a thirty-mile round trip. Olson was a decent hockey player but, it turned out, a better entrepreneur. When his fellow hockey players wanted the skates too, Olson reportedly borrowed cash from his dad and bought the sports store's entire stock to sell on to his friends. He negotiated the local distribution rights for the Super Street Skate with Silver and Backstrom, and started looking for ways to improve the design, experimenting in his parents' basement with his younger brother Brennan, then fourteen. They started out selling just the skate assembly, which they fitted to old boots hockey players brought in, for $50, offering a five-day money-back guarantee. "Never happened," says Olson.

They then ditched the leather boot of the original design, using a plastic style more like a ski boot, and replaced the hard rubber wheels with colorful polyurethane ones, such as those developed for skateboards, which offered better grip.

When Olson discovered some of their innovations were covered by an old patent held by the Chicago Roller Skate Company, he hitch-hiked to the Windy City and negotiated to buy the rights, calling his new skate the Rollerblade. While Brennan Olson was happy to remain tinkering in the basement, Scott Olson took the skates to the streets, literally skating everywhere he could, even when he went to take his future wife, nightclub singer Kerry Ciardelli, out on their first date. *Newsweek* later reported when he once showed up in court to fight a disorderly conduct charge and the judge expressed surprise at seeing him on roller skates, Olson replied, "Geez, your honor, these aren't roller skates. These are Rollerblades." When he did drive, it was in a car that had an enormous wooden skate on the roof. He ran roller hockey and roller tennis tournaments, and held long-distance skateathons that raised money for Ronald McDonald House and generated publicity for the product in local papers.

By 1984, Olson was doing well, with some fifteen employees, a warehouse, and sales of $300,000 a year. Then, Olson has recounted, he discovered one of his employees had embezzled around $100,000 and created a tax crisis that threatened the company with bankruptcy.

Enter Robert Sturgis, a former entertainment manager, and Robert Nagele Jr., who had made a fortune from billboard advertising. Olson invited them in to save the business, which they did, but the result was that Olson lost control of the company. Olson says he was initially offered $3 million for half the company, but eventually agreed to sell 95 percent of the company for just a few thousand upfront and an annual royalty of 1 percent until 1997. (He later won another royalty payment for $4.8 million for overseas sales.) Olson later told the press he had been outfoxed by his investors. They, in turn, claimed they had saved the business from extinction. "He needed money and he had to make a deal with the Devil to get it," Robert Sturgis told *Newsweek* bluntly in 1994. A year later, Sturgis told another publication, "He felt like he got screwed. But the company could have gone bankrupt. And as it is now, as the company grew, he kept making more and more money. So I don't feel sorry for him."

Olson quit the company he had started at the age of just twenty-six. After his departure Rollerblade embarked on a strategy of increasing the appeal of the skate beyond hockey players and athletes, which included sponsoring a skating federation and skating events. By 1990, Rollerblades had become a fitness phenomenon and the company was having trouble meeting demand, a situation that was enviable, but also opened the door slightly for competitors: customers would walk into skate shops asking for a pair of Rollerblades, then buy another brand when there were none of the original versions available.

In 1991, Nordica, a subsidiary of the Italian giant Benetton, bought 50 percent of the shares in Rollerblade, then paid Nagele another $150 million in 1995 for the remaining shares. (Nordica later sold to another Italian, Technica, in 2003.)

The trend continued to grow. In 1995 New York's Central Park would host up to 50,000 skaters on a warm day; in 2000 Paris introduced something called "Friday Night Fever," where streets were closed to allow some 20,000 skaters free passage. By 1997, according to Rollerblade, 20 percent of American households had a pair of in-line skates; a survey taken in 1998 found 32 million Americans over the age of six had tried in-line skating at least once that year.

All thanks, of course, to Scott Olson, who did make a small fortune from the skates, but it was nothing compared to the large fortune he would have made had he been able to stay in charge of the company. After leaving Rollerblade, he continued to innovate. He tried his luck with a skate that converted from wheels to an ice blade, then sold life-size penguins as lawn ornaments, then developed the Rowbike, a bicycle you row instead of pedal. "The jury's still out on the Rowbike," he says, although he continues to market it as passionately (and physically) as he did Rollerblades. Olson now lives in a barn he is remodeling outside Minnesota while dreaming up his next big idea. "I want another hit and I'm working hard at doing that," he says. "I don't like it when people introduce me as 'the Rollerblade guy.'"

NOTES

"I think we were just ten years ahead of our time . . ." Peif, Sherrie. "From In-line Skates to Ab Rollers . . . This Windsor Man Has Found Success," *Greely Tribune* online, 3.25.05.

"Geez, your honor . . ." Marin, Rick and T. Trent Gegax. "Blading on Thin Ice," *Newsweek*, 12.12.94, p. 64.

"He needed money . . ." Marin, Rick and T. Trent Gegax. "Blading on Thin Ice," *Newsweek*, 12.12.94, p. 64.

"He felt like he got screwed . . ." Thomson, Ellen. "The Rollerblade Boy," Express section, *Saint Paul Pioneer Press*, 3.12.95, p. 1g.

REFERENCES

AdWeek, BusinessWeek, CNNFN *Business Unusual, The Guardian, The Independent, National Law Journal, New York Times, Newsweek, Saint Paul Pioneer Press, San Francisco Chronicle, Star Tribune, Sunday Times,* United States Patent Office, *Washington Post*

Websense

So that's how you make money out of the Internet

———

IN 1993, A THIRTY-YEAR-OLD SAN DIEGAN CALLED PHIL TRUBEY had a revelation about the still-embryonic Internet: it was going to be a mighty big time-waster. Trubey was then working as a "systems integrator," somebody who puts together computer networks for businesses. More and more often as he went about his work he heard company managers worrying, if they gave their employees Internet access, would they spend all day surfing porn sites instead of working?

Trubey had seen an early Internet browser (a forerunner to those such as Yahoo or Google) in action and figured, yes, employees would probably spend a lot of time looking at porn sites (or sports sites, or shopping sites, or anything that wasn't actually work). To their bosses, that would mean lost time and lost money. And if companies were losing money, Trubey figured, they would most likely pay him to make the problem go away.

He quit his day job, borrowed $8,000 on his credit card and set up a business eventually named Netpartners Internet Solutions in his spare room at home. He started out a little obliquely, as a reseller for a Canadian company that made firewall software, which companies install to protect their networks from viruses and hackers. By the end of 1995, though, Trubey had made enough cash to develop the product he had envisioned all along, a system of monitoring and blocking Internet connections he later called Websense.

Other people had had similar ideas for the home market, using software installed on individual computers to block children from accessing sites where banned words—such as "sex"—appeared. But they tended to block sites indiscriminately—a site for nursing mothers might be blocked because it contained the word "nipple."

Websense was far more labor intensive. Instead of looking for suspect words, Trubey's employees surfed the Internet to build a database of sites managers did not want staff browsing during work time, divided into categories such as gambling and pornography. By 1998, they had found more than 275,000 suspect sites. The database has since grown to over 10 million sites, and, according to Websense, the company searches another 35 million a day looking for malicious code, such as spyware and phishing (where criminals attempt to find out your bank account passwords and other personal details by pretending to be the organization you trust).

The system was designed to live in the central computer server of companies (or government departments or schools) where it monitored how everybody within the organization accessed the

Internet. Employers who bought the software could nominate to restrict access to categories of sites, or they could leave the connections open and opt to spy on their staff instead, generating reports that showed them if individual employees had accessed any of the sites on the Websense database.

Trubey launched Websense in 1996, charging organizations for the software installation and then an annual subscription fee of around $10 for every employee being monitored. In 1998, Trubey successfully solicited $6 million in venture capital from Morgan Stanley Venture Partners and Edelson Technology Partners, which he largely used to market Websense. But it also cost him his position as CEO four months later when the venture capitalists came to the conclusion that Netpartners had outgrown his abilities. After a brief wrestle for the helm, Trubey departed, but he and his wife, Janet McVeigh, retained a large stake in the company.

The new CEO, John Carrington, took the company public in March 2000 under the name Websense. After some early losses it began to post solid earnings towards the end of 2001 and now has earnings of over $100 million annually.

Websense now works with 24,000 organizations worldwide, including over half the Fortune 500 companies, and monitors 20 million users. Most clients pay their subscription fees—now around $15 per seat at the 1,000-user level—upfront, with an average contract around $8,000.

It owes much of its success to savvy marketing that has cemented the Websense brand as the market leader in the media. The company has funded numerous surveys and productivity summits that highlight losses from employee websurfing. In 2002, for example, the *New York Times* reported that a survey carried out by Harris Interactive for Websense had discovered that 25 percent of the 305 employees polled were "addicted" to the Internet. It has also exploited one-off opportunities to dramatize the so-called dangers of browsing, in 2000 warning that employees watching *Big Brother* could potentially waste millions of dollars in lost time, and before the 2000 Victoria's Secret lingerie webcast it warned clients that they had the ability to block the show, warning it could bring their networks to a standstill.

Despite its enthusiastic marketing of the problem and the solution, Websense has neatly passed ethical responsibility for its product to its clients. While most companies use the software to block sites and remove their staff from temptation, those who use Websense's ability to monitor individual usage and effectively spy on their employees' Internet habit are usually quite within their rights to do so. Websense had also made some unusual clients. In 2000, Britain's *Guardian* newspaper revealed that the Saudi Arabian government was using Websense to censor the Internet usage of the entire country, where the only legal Internet connection is funneled through a government department. The United States military has also bought Websense, in 2001 spending $1.8 million to install it at over one hundred military posts around the world to block some 200,000 soldiers from accessing pornography and gambling sites.

REFERENCES

Associated Press, BusinessWeek, CNBC *Dow Jones Business Video,* CNN *Money Washington Post,* CNNFN *Market Coverage, Computerworld, The Guardian, Inc Magazine, Industry Standard, Investors Business Daily, IPO Report, IPO Reporter, New York Times, San Diego MIT Enterprise Forum, San Diego Union-Tribune, Washington Times*

Craigslist

Who needs bells and whistles?

H OW MUCH IS ENOUGH? FOR CRAIG NEWMARK, FOUNDER OF the classified advertising website Craigslist, enough means a nice house with off-street parking, a Toyota Prius hybrid car, a healthy salary (*Fortune* magazine estimates it at around $200,000), and a job he loves. He likes babies, dogs, Thai food, and walks everywhere with a pedometer: his goal is 8,250 steps a day. He could probably sell his stake in Craigslist for tens, if not hundreds, of millions of dollars, but, to date at least, he has resisted the temptation to cash in. Why? Because money was never the point. "If you're living comfortably, how much do you need?" he asks.

Craigslist, if somehow it hasn't crossed your consciousness, is a local service in dozens of cities across the country (and around the world) where people can advertise stuff for free. Unlike eBay, which is a global garage sale, Craigslist is purely local, helping people to find apartments, sell unwanted Christmas gifts, hook up with members of the opposite sex, advertise their community events, complain about a coworker's romantic overtures, or give kittens away to good homes. It started in San Francisco, and it has a distinct type-only home page that hasn't changed much in five, even ten, years. It is one of the most-visited sites on the Internet, yet it makes relatively little money as it charges for nothing except job advertisements in San Francisco, New York, and Los Angeles. A private company, its revenues are confidential, but they are estimated at around $10 million, more than enough to clothe and feed its eighteen staff as overheads are minimal, but a tiny sum given the site's commercial potential.

Craig Newmark spent his first fifty years in anonymity. Born in Morristown, New Jersey, on December 6, 1952, to a salesman father and book keeper mother, he grew up—as he is fond of recounting—a nerd with pocket protectors and glasses held together with tape. He studied computer science at Case Western Reserve University in Cleveland, then worked for IBM for seventeen years as a systems engineer, consulting with customers, until he was caught in a wave of downsizing. He had previously survived cutbacks by scratching around for another position within the company, but this time he decided to get out, and head for San Francisco and a job with the brokerage firm Charles Schwab. "I just wanted a change from the east coast," he says.

He arrived in 1993: single, new to the city, and with time on his hands. Interested in the connections between technology and art, he began to hang out at gallery openings, particularly parties and events held by Joe's Digital Diner and a group called Anon Salon, which, according to its website, "teases technology, embraces the arts, and flirts with the unknown."

In 1995, Newmark started an email mailing list to alert his growing group of friends to interesting arts happenings. It was popular enough that six months later he had 240 names, enough to cause him problems with his email. His solution, in late 1995, was to turn the list into a web page, and he wrote a neat little piece of software that took incoming emails and put them onto his new website, which meant postings happened automatically, without somebody having to type them in manually.

Newmark first wanted to call it "sf-events" but was persuaded by his friends—despite his modesty—to call it what they did: Craigslist. Then, a weird thing happened: instead of just posting information about upcoming arts events, people started sending notes to Craigslist when they needed a roommate, or had an old TV to sell, or if they needed work. Like the window of a neighborhood Laundromat, only much bigger. Newmark monitored the ads, encouraging users to write them in a natural voice rather than faux sales speak. Craigslist, it says on the website, "is about giving each other a break, getting the word out about everyday, real-world stuff."

By 1997, the site was clocking a million page views per month and Newmark was suddenly wondering what he should do with his ever-expanding creation—how about something good? With philanthropy in mind, he brought on board three associates to help him run the new venture. Nancy Melone, a senior manager of electronic commerce at KPMG, came on as Craigslist CEO, with web developer Weezy Muth, and career consultant Christina Murphy. They launched an organization they called the Craig's List Foundation, canvassing projects such as mentoring programs, sponsoring technical training, and running networking events. The List Foundation launched a website that was similar in appearance to the regular Craigslist site, with the expectation that regular users would migrate over to the new portal.

Around that time, Newmark, now spending around eight hours a week running the listings, was approached by Microsoft Sidewalk to discuss running lucrative banner ads. He declined. "I wasn't terribly fond of banner ads," he says.

As the media became aware of this quirky little website, it began to grow exponentially, and, in February 1999, Newmark quit his day job—as a contract programmer—to run it full-time.

In August 1999, Melone left abruptly to start her own website, Metrovox, another listing service, run from her bedroom. She also took with her the List Foundation web domain, which she used as a host for the new site. Users who logged on to www.listfoundation.org, listfoundation.com, and listfoundation.net—all of which used to lead to Craigslist—suddenly found themselves at Metrovox.

Reaction from the Craigslist community, who fired off hundreds of complaints, soon prompted Melone to display a prominent notice stating that the new site was not Craigslist, with a link to the real Craigslist. She also posted a plea: "Despite the rumors, we're not heading for an IPO, staging a corporate takeover, or swimming in venture capital. We're five people trying to take the Listfoundation.org URL and make it even better." Metrovox was not a non-profit organization, she wrote; instead, it would donate 30 percent of its profits to community projects.

Attorneys were hired, there was talk of injunctions and arbitration, but, as time passed, legal action became moot: after an initial drop-off in traffic, Craigslist prospered at the original web address www.craigslist.org; Metrovox is not longer in existence (though it later morphed into, among other things, a site called www.powerstatus.org, which predicted power outages).

Craig Newmark's next partnership was more successful, in 1999 hiring Jim Buckmaster, first as chief programmer, then CEO, after spotting his résumé on—yep—Craigslist. Newmark remained as "customer service rep and founder," which means he spends much of his time hunting spammers and dealing with complaints. Buckmaster grew the organization from its current home, on a single computer, to a multiserver environment, and then, in 2003, expanded internationally with sites in London and Tokyo. Some view the appearance of Craigslist in a city as a sign that the inhabitants have reached the information age; today it has footholds in cities as diverse as St. Petersburg, El Paso, Shanghai, Milan, and Cardiff. Not all are prospering (yet), but as the listings happen automatically, neither do they cost much to run—"essentially nothing," says Newmark.

The company's hand-off approach to the ads has occasionally caused problems. Buckmaster introduced a system where users could "flag" offensive material to have it removed, but there are still plenty of unsavory postings you would not want your twelve-year-old to come across, particularly in the personals section.

The flip side of the laissez-faire approach is the random postings where people aren't trying to buy or sell anything; they just want to vent some steam about an issue, and many are very well written.

(Find these in the forum Best of Craigslist.) Newmark has plans to build on this base of community writers to create a forum for community journalism, following an extremely successful model in South Korea, where broadband Internet usage is commonplace.

By mid-2005, Craigslist was registering five million new classified ads each month—a figure to put the fear of God into newspaper executives (one analyst estimated Craigslist was costing newspapers over $50 million in lost revenue in San Francisco alone).

Figures like that also make Craigslist an attractive takeover target for other media companies. Indeed, in 2004 eBay bought a 25 percent stake in Craigslist when a former employee sold his share for $12 million. The founder of eBay, Pierre Omidyar, now sits on the Craigslist board, but Newmark insists the relationship is two-way—eBay approached Craigslist about the purchase first to see if it would be mutually beneficial. eBay wants to learn about the organic community of Craigslist; Craigslist learns anti-spamming methods and the hurdles of international expansion, particularly launching sites in other languages. Besides, says Newmark, he and Omidyar—a philanthropist who is giving away his billions—share similar values. At Craigslist, Newmark says, "Just following our collective moral compass, we've established a community of trust, of goodwill."

REFERENCES

Boston Globe, CIO Insight, CNN, *Economist, The Independent, National Post, New York Times, PC Magazine, USA Today, Washington Post*

MTV

Who on earth would want to watch music television?

H ERE IS A BUSINESS IDEA. CREATE A LOW-COST CABLE television channel that will reach one billion cool twelve-to thirty-four-year-olds, get record companies to pay for all the content, and make a ton off advertising revenue and sub-scriber fees. Make the station so influential that not only will it make or break artists, but politicians will clamor to get on air, and presidents will even try and play the sax on it. The channel will grow to have double the viewers of CNN and become a global brand alongside heavyweights such as Coke, Nike, and Levi's.

Back in 1981, a new cable channel appeared in the United States. Everything about it was deliberately different, from its in-your-face logo, thrashing theme songs and frenetic style through to its con-tent—wall-to-wall music. MTV changed cable television, and it altered the course of the music industry. It ushered in an era where music fans would watch a song as opposed to simply listening to it. From the very first clip it played, the prophetic "Video Killed the Radio Star," MTV was on to something. "Not since silent films gave way to talkies has such substantial change been forced upon performing artists so quickly," says *New York Times* chief film critic Janet Maslin.

The previous generation was lucky to watch an hour or two of their favorite musicians on Ed Sullivan or *Top of the Pops*. Considering how popular these programs were and how hot a com-modity rock'n'roll was, it is quite baffling as to why no one had thought of music television before. When MTV launched, rock videos were in their infancy, with pioneers such as ABBA (who worked with renowned Swedish director Lasse Hallström on their clips because the band was sick of touring) and Queen. These bands were trailblazers, leading their onslaught with dry ice, kaleidoscope camera work, tight pants, and very rudimentary styling.

"When we first introduced the idea of MTV, no one in the entertainment industry thought it would succeed because the programming was too narrow," says Robert Pittman, a top rating disc jockey turned radio programmer from Mississippi who would become one of the fathers of MTV along with David Horowitz, John Skyes, and John Lack.

Pittman (or "Pitchman") is the son of a Methodist minister. By the age of twenty-one he was the highest paid radio programmer in the U.S. Pittman began researching the potential for an all-music channel for cable television in 1980 despite the fact that his critics said music should be heard and not seen. He was backed by the Warner Amex Satellite Entertainment Company. In August 1981, MTV went live through 300 cable networks. It was Pittman who is credited with the "I want my MTV" moniker as part of a campaign to get more cable companies signing on for MTV. Pittman had David Bowie and Mick Jagger, for example, telling viewers to tell their cable company, "I Want My MTV." Of course Bowie and Jagger helped out the cause, wanting to keep their videos on high rotation.

Pittman's strategy has always been content driven, with a strong emphasis on brand-building. He wanted his audience to immediately recognize that MTV was something different. From there, advertisers could be inspired to tailor campaigns specifically to this demographic. Within two years 1,775 cable companies were airing MTV. Pittman left MTV in 1987 after a failed management buyout. He had risen from program director to CEO, had launched channels such as VH-1, Nickelodeon and Nick at Nite, and Court TV, and presided over its Initial Public Offering. Pittman then started his own company, Quantum Media, the beginning of an eclectic phase in his career that included stints running Century 21 Real Estate, the Six Flags Theme Parks, and AOL. He left AOL, a Time Warner company, in 2002 to concentrate on his investment vehicle The Pilot Group. He has always been modest about his MTV years, but clearly they have taken a toll on him. "I never want to build another brand as long as I live. It takes about a billion dollars of marketing and five to ten years," he said.

MTV now reaches subscribers in 166 countries. As MTV has grown and found new markets, it has been careful to feed local audiences 70 percent local content, with local veejays. New Yorkers don't necessarily love the same music as Parisians.

MTV is not sitting back enjoying its success, either. No only does it have to deal with increasingly conservative censorship laws (described by some analysts as cable TV getting its mouth washed out); it has to contend with Rupert Murdoch's Sky Channel, which is gaining ground, particularly in Europe, and the challenges of digital technology, which create whole new opportunities for delivering content. The key to its growth is not in broadcasting its music videos, but in coming up with innovative programs, such as stunt crazy *Jackass*, that are helping the station to build its audience as well as develop in international markets. It is also devising new stations and interactive components as part of its expansion. Its research department is so obsessed with its precious teenage audience that it now employs people who track trends, to the point where they are happy to look in adolescent boys' smelly bedrooms to see what posters are on their walls to see what makes them tick, the shoes they wear, and the tracks they want to download for their iPods. MTV tapped into the lucrative youth market, and it can't afford to lose touch with the people that bring home the bacon.

Pittman told *Harvard Business Review* in 2005 that the best advice he ever got is to "ignore conventional wisdom." While developing MTV he was told time and time again that "music was meant to be heard, not seen." Says Pittman: "Imagine if we had listened."

NOTES

"Not since silent films . . ." Maslin, Janet. "A Song Is No Longer Strictly a Song, Now It's a Video," section 2, *New York Times,* 1.23.83, p. 23.

"When we first introduced . . ." *Advertising Age,* "Pittman Gets Physical with Six Flags," 6.1.92, p. 47.

"I never want to build . . ." Kornblum, Janet. *CNET News,* 4.21.97.

"Ignore conventional . . ." *Harvard Business Review* "The Best Advice I Ever Got," 1.05.

REFERENCES

Advertising Age, AdWeek, Business 2.0, BusinessWeek, CNN, *Columbia Journalism Review, Daily Variety, Financial Times, The Guardian, The Hollywood Reporter,* Hoover's Company Capsules, *Red Herring, Salon, Telegraph, Wall Street Journal, Washington Post, Washington Times*

TiVo

Let me into your home

Y OU HAVE A TRULY AMAZING PRODUCT. A DEVICE SO IMMEDIATELY essential that its users cannot believe they once lived without it. Surely that's enough to guarantee success? Not in the case of TiVo, the next-generation video recorder that has the potential to change everything about the way the world watches television, if only we'd give it a chance.

TiVo's creators, Michael Ramsay and Jim Barton, started their own company in Sunnyvale, California, on August 4, 1997. They had both worked for years in tech firms, Ramsay at Silicon Graphics and Barton at a company called Network Age Software, where he gathered the initial ideas for TiVo, though he had also worked previously on a joint venture between Silicon Graphics and AT&T to launch a small-scale interactive television system in Florida.

Their first business idea was home networking, using the Internet to link household appliances, but they couldn't crystallize why anyone would actually need it. Then they thought about television and about how a typical American cable subscriber had to wade through literally hundreds of channels to find the shows they wanted to watch, and if they wanted to record something on their VCR they usually botched the programming.

The solution was TiVo, a video-sized box that uses a computer-style hard drive instead of a video tape, and marries it by a phone connection to a TV guide.

Launched in March 1999, TiVo's technology allows its subscribers to record shows by scrolling through a menu of titles and clicking on the ones they want—with no tricky programming. But it can also do things like remember to record every upcoming episode of a favorite show (even skipping the repeats), or seek out every movie starring Julia Roberts on any channel you have connected, ad infinitum. Because hard drives store information in a different way from tapes, TiVo can also do things such as allow the user to watch last night's episode of *Commander in Chief* while simultaneously recording *The Sopranos*. Or let the user start watching a show fifteen minutes after it starts, skipping through all the ads. Or pause and rewind live TV, as 400,000 TiVo users did when Janet Jackson revealed her sunburst nipple ring at the 2004 Superbowl.

TiVo is available as a stand-alone box sold in electronics shops, but Barton and Ramsay have always focused on licensing their technology to other companies that can build their own TiVo-powered boxes or incorporate TiVo functions into other consumer products such as DVD players and recorders.

TiVo did not, however, take off as quickly as expected for a product so clever. It took over four years to sign up 1 million subscribers, the number at which it expected to start making money. To get to that point, it had amassed up an accumulated deficit of over $560 million—borrowed from venture capitalists—and was forced to lay off eighty of its 350 employees in April 2001.

The problem, it seemed, was the difficulty in explaining what TiVo could do, and why people needed it. They initially sold TiVo as "your own personal TV network," meaning users could program it to deliver a whole season tailored around their preferences. But people who didn't understand how TiVo worked didn't get what the slogan meant. TiVo has now fallen back on the description "digital video recorder," which carries a reminder of a product most people hated, but is more easily understood.

In the early days after the launch TiVo spent millions on TV advertising campaigns that were clever but did not explain TiVo's features. Then it took a different approach: convincing celebrities to try TiVo and hopefully spread good word-of-mouth. It worked: David Letterman sang TiVo's praises on his show, and TiVo was written into the scripts of *Friends* and *Sex and the City*. Through alliances with satellite television provider DirecTV and licensing deals with manufacturers including Sony and Pioneer, subscriptions grew to three million by early 2005—creditable, but still a long way from setting the standard for this new technology.

The people who buy TiVo love it. According to the company, 97 percent of users tell their friends to buy one, and virtually none cancel their subscriptions once signed up. Michael Powell, chairman of the U.S. Federal Communications Commission, described it as "God's machine."

The danger for TiVo is that the market is becoming increasingly flooded with similar products, including personal hard disk recorders packaged into cable set top boxes and DVD recorders, though none so far has managed to blend the technology with such a user-friendly package, which is surely the point of it in the first place. In the meantime, TiVo is transforming itself from a technology company to an information company. Just as one of

TiVo's features is its ability to learn its owner's preferences, TiVo knows exactly which shows its customers watch, how often they skip through the ads (around 80 percent of the time) and has partnered with ratings giant Nielsen to explore how this information can be best used. Then there's targeted advertising. The trouble with most ads, Ramsay and Barton argue, is that they are broadcast scattergun style. Using subscriber information collected by TiVo, they say, advertisers could target viewers far more accurately—perhaps by sending custom ads to groups of one hundred viewers, or even, in theory, to individuals. Presently, viewers can choose to request more information from advertisers.

The search engine Google has already shown that ads tied to specific interests are far more effective. In the future, TiVo viewers may be able to push a button for more information on the hemorrhoid cream or four-wheel drive that takes their fancy, and even make the purchase via their TV.

TiVo stands to make billions from its technology but its first, fundamental challenge remains—getting enough of its boxes into homes.

REFERENCES

American Spectator, BusinessWeek, CNBC, *Contra Costa Times, Edinburgh Evening News, Electronic Media, Financial Times, The Guardian, Hollywood Reporter, Los Angeles Times, Monterey County Herald, New York Times, Newsday, Newsweek, Online Reporter,* Salon.com, *San Francisco Chronicle, United Press International, USA Today, Variety*

Hooters

Even a little bit of sex sells

HOOTERS, THE RESTAURANT CHAIN FAMOUS FOR ITS SCANTILY clad waitresses, was started in 1983 in Clearwater, Florida, by six friends who clubbed together $140,000 to open a place they couldn't be thrown out of. L.D. Stewart, Ken Wimmer, and Dennis Johnson were tradesmen, Ed Droste a real-estate executive, Gil DiGiannantonio a liquor salesman, and William Ranieri a retired service station owner. With no previous experience of running a restaurant, they designed the place to suit themselves, which meant comfort food such as fried chicken wings, sports on the TV, and attractive waitresses. They hired their first "Hooters Girl," Lynne Austin, after spotting her at a bikini contest on the beach. She was later featured in *Playboy* magazine.

In 1984, restaurant executive Hugh Connerty walked in, thought the place had potential, and struck a deal with the founders to franchise their male-fantasy-come-true. He negotiated to pay them $50,000 up front and a percentage of future profits, while they kept ownership of the trademark and the right to run Hooters restaurants in Chicago and Tampa Bay.

Like McDonald's, the Hooters founders rigidly standardized their operating procedure in a detailed manual: "Socks are to be white," "The shirt must fit with no bagginess," "Under no circumstances should bra straps ever show," and so on. In 2001, the founders sold the trademark to current chairman Robert Brooks for $60 million and the headquarters moved to Atlanta. Today the chain has four hundred outlets worldwide and revenues over $800 million annually.

You might attribute Hooters' success to hiring young women and dressing them in a uniform of a tight tank top, orange shorts, and sneakers, but there are numerous establishments that cater for men who want to look at women in various states of undress. What Hooters offers its customers, 70 percent of whom are men, is a sexually titillating experience that is made socially acceptable through innuendo (the chain's logo is an owl—get it?) and a jokey atmosphere. In return for flirting with the customers, Hooters waitresses can make hundreds of dollars a day in tips. "Even if you're not funny, we'll still laugh," promises one of the numerous "funny" signs around the restaurant.

In 2003, Hooters of America, the parent company, launched Hooters Air (using two chartered 737s, operated by Pace Airlines), sending two Hooters girls aloft on each flight alongside regular flight attendants. By June 2005, there were several Hooters planes in service, flying to eleven destinations from its base in Myrtle Beach, South Carolina, and generating enormous publicity for the chain.

The chain has fought battles with the Equal Opportunity Commission for refusing to hire male waitstaff (a sexual discrimination complaint was filed in 1991, and the matter was eventually dropped). Local residents have protested when a new Hooters was planned for their neighborhood, but Hooters has responded to negative publicity by using increasing awareness of political correctness to its advantage, claiming to offer men a haven from a confusing world. Hooters has even expanded internationally, including opening a store in Shanghai in October 2004, where the regulation "sporty" uniform had the effect of making its staff of slim, elegant Chinese girls look like they belonged to a softball team.

REFERENCES

Atlanta Journal and Constitution, Charlotte Observer, Denver Post, Fortune, Legal Intelligencer, Record, Restaurant Business, South China Morning Post, St. Louis Post-Dispatch, St. Petersburg Times, Tampa Tribune, Washington Post, Washington Times

Liz Lange Maternity

Block out the noise around you and forge ahead

I N THE MID-1990S, LIZ LANGE WAS WORKING IN A TINY FASHION business in New York City when she had an "a-ha moment." She kept meeting all these well-heeded pregnant women who kept complaining that they had nothing to wear. They would come into her studio and try to squeeze into normal ranges, exasperated that they could choose to burst out of non-pregnancy clothes or wear the traditional maternity gear—tent-like dresses, dungarees, and other frumpy styles. Lange knew maternity wear was a fashion wasteland and that there were plenty of women prepared to pay handsomely to look stylish, whatever the trimester.

Traditionally, the rag trade, particularly the big brands, has not seen maternity wear as a potentially profitable area, reasoning that women aren't prepared to spend money on clothes they can only wear for a few months. Liz's extensive customer experience told her that there was an opportunity here that no one could really see. She knew there were all these doctors, lawyers, and stay-at-home moms with nothing to wear and she knew what they needed.

Born in 1967, Liz Lange is an Upper East Side girl through and through. The daughter of a wealthy business owner, she grew up in the finest blocks of New York City and was educated at private schools and prestigious Brown University, where she studied comparative literature. She had a summer internship at auctioneers Sotheby's and worked at *Vogue* magazine. Her life was on track to marry well, start a family, and become a lady who lunches. But Lange chose a very different path. "Always an achiever," she admits her life took a different path when she fell in love with Jeffrey Lange. He grew up in less privileged circumstances. His success came through a series of scholarships to Stanford and Yale and he now runs a company that designs mathematical models for trading derivatives. He made her think differently about her future—to make bolder plans.

At age twenty-four, while working at *Vogue*, Lange met struggling young designer Stephen DiGeronimo, who was producing a small sportswear range in the garment district. Lange became his "sort of apprentice" and ended up revamping the brand and working alongside DiGeronimo. "That's where I learned the business," says Lange, who has never formally studied design. The label Geronimo was "somewhat successful." Lange worked there for several years during which time she met and married Jeffrey Lange. "Things started to shift in me, in my expectations of life," she says.

When Lange mentioned her maternity line idea to DiGeronimo he was not keen. Maternity was boring, right? She had to get used to pretty much everyone telling her that her business idea would never work. "I ignored all the outside advice and listened to my instincts," she says. Jeffrey Lange advised her to "block out the noise around you and just forge ahead." Lange wanted to create a fashion label like any other high-end brand, it just happened to be for pregnant women.

"It got to the point where if I didn't do it, I would always regret it," says Lange, who quit Geronimo in late 1996 and launched Liz Lange Maternity in late 1997 with no business plan and no brand strategy. During that period, she remembers spending many days curled up in her bed wondering what she was doing. She kept going because she realized that "customers and investors will never have your vision for the product because they can't touch it and feel it in advance. It's your job to follow your instincts, prop yourself up, and trust that if you build it, they will come."

The business started out with a small range of cashmere twin sets, stretchy knits, and smart separates. She sold through appointment-only in a tiny first-floor office on East 61st Street. There was a phone, a fax, and a rack of clothes. The rent was $1,500 a month. Orders took two weeks to fill, with the range being made up by a small factory on 8th Avenue. One of the biggest myths about Liz Lange Maternity is that Lange started it because she herself was pregnant and couldn't find anything to wear. This is not true. Although she has a son and a daughter now, she believed that if she had been pregnant at the time she started she would have been too "bogged down in the mechanics of pregnancy" to be thinking about making beautiful clothes.

The seed funding came from her father. Lange estimates that start-up costs were $50,000. The range sold from the very start, so sales easily covered the modest overheads. A year later she moved to larger premises on Lexington Avenue. The first-floor premises was always busy. By this stage, while the wives shopped, their husbands "were throwing their business cards at me," says Lange. They wanted to invest in the business. She partnered with two silent investors that remain on the board of the privately-held company. Their money funded new retail stores on Madison Avenue and in Beverly Hills.

Her fashion background helped Lange understand how a product gets exposure, the right editors to approach, and the people she needed to dress. "I was very pushy about that. I had to get over any shyness," she says. If a celebrity was pregnant, she would contact them or their people and invite them to have a Liz Lange pregnancy.

Having supermodel Cindy Crawford appearing on national television every week telling the audience she was wearing Liz Lange would always cause the phones to ring off the hook. The line appealed to fashion-forward women. She dared to dress her customers in fitted clothes, so radical at the time that the *New York Times* reported the trend. Other "yummy mommys" such as Catherine Zeta-Jones and Cate Blanchett were powerful ambassadors for the brand.

For a company with thirty-five employees and annual sales of around $10 million, it is no wonder that Lange jokes "the brand is bigger than we are." Licensing deals with Nike (2001) and Target (2002) to produce maternity ranges have given Lange national exposure (at no cost to the business). Lange remembers when she received the call from Nike. She was on vacation, and one of the female senior executives called her up. Lange assumed she was pregnant and wanted some clothes, but she wanted Lange to design a range for Nike.

Lange doesn't think her business would survive if she was starting out today. "Then, I was offering something that couldn't be found. It is different today." Customers wouldn't wait two weeks for their orders, and she would not be able to compete with more established maternity brands or afford to advertise.

Lange's success has inspired many competitors, and many well-resourced moms, to think about starting their own little range. What sets her apart from those start-ups is that her label filled a "genuine hole in the market. I had struck oil," she says. "It was one of those crazy things. I hit on something."

These days while Lange is juggling the business and a young family ("and that feeling that you are always in the wrong place"), she appears on cable television and has plans to open more stores. While the business is a success, "there are no plans to go out and buy a Gulfstream." There are no plans to sell up and become the Upper East Side wife either.

NOTES

"I ignored . . ." *Harvard Business Review*, "The Best Advice I Ever Got," 1.05.
"Block out the noise . . ." *Harvard Business Review*, "The Best Advice I Ever Got," 1.05.

REFERENCES

Crains New York Business, Fortune, Good Housekeeping, International Herald Tribune, Time, Mail on Sunday, New York Magazine, New York Times, USA Today, Vogue, Washington Post, Women's Wear Daily

Section 10

SURVIVAL OF THE FITTEST

Microsoft

Revenge of the nerds

———————

BILL GATES DID NOT BECOME THE WORLD'S RICHEST MAN BY making an amazing discovery or dreaming up an irresistible product. His skill lay in less tangible areas: an uncanny ability to anticipate what his customers would need in the future, recognizing opportunities, and harnessing the talents of people around him.

Gates, son of an attorney father and schoolteacher mother, had always been the archetypal computer nerd, writing commercial software from the age of thirteen while at school in Seattle.

He has always looked the part, too—unkempt hair, scruffy clothes, out-of-date glasses. His appearance and mannerisms have, if anything, worked to his advantage, catching others off guard. Behind the geeky façade lay a natural entrepreneur who combined knowledge of the law, business sense, and a love of computer technology in a formidable package.

His first opportunity presented itself when he was nineteen and a halfhearted accounting student at Harvard who spent most of his spare time fiddling about with computers. Paul Allen, a slightly older friend who shared his passion, came across the January 1975 issue of *Popular Electronics*, which featured on its cover the world's first personal computer, a machine called the Altair 8800.

Back then, computers cost hundreds of thousands of dollars. The Altair was laughably crude by today's standards but cost just $395 in part form. Instead of just wondering how they could get their hands on one, Allen and Gates wondered, did its makers need somebody to write software for it? A month later they had sold the makers of the Altair a computer language program called Basic.

The entrepreneur in Gates woke up, decided to drop out of Harvard and moved with Paul Allen to Albuquerque, New Mexico, of all places, where the Altair was built. They set up shop across the street from the Altair people in a business they called Micro-Soft (they later dropped the hyphen). After their success with the Altair, they began to make a name for themselves, attracting business from other hardware manufacturers, including Commodore, RadioShack, NCR, Texas Instruments, and even Apple, which bought a program called Applesoft Basic from them for a flat fee of $21,000. By the end of 1978 Gates and Allen had made sales of $1 million.

Towards the end of the 1970s, IBM, the market leader in commercial computers, decided it wanted in on the burgeoning personal computer market. Late to the party, it locked in a tight one-year schedule and decided it would be easiest to buy software rather than waste time developing it in-house.

In July 1980, a team of IBM executives headed by Jack Sams visited Gates and Allen at their new offices in Seattle. Gates was still only twenty-four years old and looked much younger. "I knew Bill was young, but I had never seen him before," Sams recalled of the meeting. "When someone came out to take us back to his office, I thought the guy who came out was the office boy. It was Bill. Well, I'll tell you or anybody else, that by the time you were with Bill for fifteen minutes, you no longer thought about how old he was or what he looked like. He had the most brilliant mind that I had ever dealt with."

Gates did not have an operating system he could sell to IBM. But he knew that another young programmer, who happened to be just down the road, had been selling a rudimentary program called QDOS (Quick and Dirty Operating System) for about a year. Gates hired its creator and renamed it MS-DOS. He and Allen fixed it up and, crucially, licensed it to IBM, rather than selling it outright. Instrumental in the deal was a man named Steve Ballmer, who had come on board as Microsoft employee number twenty-four and helped to negotiate both the purchase of the original software and the licensing deal with IBM.

By then Microsoft had grown from a tiny company with three employees (including Gates and Allen) and revenues of $16,500 to a small business with 128 employees and a turnover of $16 million.

IBM's decision to buy software rather than develop its own gave Gates a foot in the door. IBM's next decision, to allow other manufacturers to license its computer designs, was to make Gates's fortune. By allowing other companies to build what became known as "clones," IBM set the industry standard. It benefited by creating a large market, and initially taking a major share of it, but eventually the clones won out. IBM and clones alike required Bill Gates's software to make them do anything. By 1984, Gates was worth $100 million.

That was the year Apple launched the Macintosh, a personal computer that offered a point-and-click interface instead of the clunky command-based interface of MS-DOS. In terms of usability, the Macintosh was infinitely superior to the IBM-style computer—something Gates realized immediately.

His response, a program called Windows, did not work nearly as well as Apple's system and was not immediately successful. But Apple's reluctance to license its products to other manufacturers, as IBM had done, cost it the chance to make its superior system widespread. Microsoft persisted and, after two revamps, launched a version of Windows that, while still not as good as Macintosh's, worked well enough—and had enough momentum behind it—to become the world standard. It was a similar story with applications such as spreadsheets and word processors. Other companies had superior products, but eventually they slipped up—shipping a new version behind schedule, or overloading it with complicated features—and Microsoft was there to take their place, helped along by the dominance of its operating system.

In 1992 Microsoft's stock value overtook that of IBM. In 1995, when Microsoft launched Windows 95, it sold 11 million copies in the first five minutes. Today, over 90 percent of the world's personal computers run a version of Windows, and most are loaded with other Microsoft programs.

Microsoft, which reported a profit of $12 billion for the 2004–05 financial year, has revenues of $30 billion and has cash and other short-term reserves of around $50 billion.

Its dominance has mired it in antitrust litigation: to cut an extremely long story short, in 1998 the U.S. Justice Department filed antitrust charges against the company, which were eventually settled, though there were threats for some time that the company would be broken into two. Microsoft also faced actions from, and eventually reached agreements with, Netscape, Sun, and Novell.

Bill Gates stepped down as CEO of Microsoft in January 2000, creating a role for himself as chairman and chief software architect. Practically, that means he still spends much of his time supervising projects and looking for opportunities, ceding much of the day-to-day running of the business to CEO Steve Ballmer.

Personal time with Gates is judged to be so valuable Microsoft calls it "Bill Currency."

Gates spends his spare time with his wife, Melinda, and their three children, and administers a charitable foundation through which he has started giving away much of his fortune—last weighed in at around $46 billion—to causes such as the fight against AIDS. The Bill and Melinda Gates Foundation has an endowment of some $29 billion and by 2005 had given away close to $7.5 billion—impressive enough for Queen Elizabeth II to make Gates a knight of the realm (though, as he is not a British subject, he is not called "Sir").

Paul Allen, who left Microsoft in 1983 after being diagnosed with Hodgkin's Disease, made a full recovery—and his share holdings in Microsoft ensured he had the cash to enjoy life to the full. He now spends much of his time aboard the $200 million yacht

Octopus, which was until very recently the largest privately owned yacht in the world (and is still rather impressive by most people's standards), and he dabbles in spaceflight—in 2004 bankrolling the successful attempt by the privateer craft SpaceShipOne to become the first commercially-owned vehicle in space.

NOTES

"I knew Bill was young . . ." Tucker, William. "Open Season on Bill Gates," *The American Spectator*, 7.98.

REFERENCES

BusinessWeek, Forbes, The Economist, Fortune, The Guardian, Salon.com, *Seattle-Post Intelligencer, New York Times, Toronto Star, Washington Post*

Mars Inc.

The creators of chocolate empires are not necessarily sweet

———

T HERE HAVE BEEN MANY DESCRIPTIONS OF THE LATE FORREST Mars, the magnate who created the Mars family $10 billion fortune, but none of them are kind. He has been described as the Monster from Mars; a tyrant with a terrifying temper and a cold-hearted, cruel father; and regular humiliator of his staff. Forrest will go down in history as one of the toughest, most private, and single-minded entrepreneurs. His company is one of the most secretive in the world; it never releases financial information; photographs of the Mars family are not permitted; the staff are forbidden to talk about their workplace; interviews are never granted to the media; and information about the Mars product range is strictly on a need-to-know basis. Recipes for hit products such as Snickers, Milky Way, and Mars bars are kept in alarmed safes with staff only knowing specific parts of each recipe, never the entire process. The culture is more secretive than the CIA's, whose headquarters is just down the road from the Mars headquarters in Washington, D.C.

The business was started in 1911 by Forrest's father, Frank C. Mars, with a range of butter cream candies made in the family kitchen in Tacoma, Washington. Forrest's parents divorced soon after, and young Forrest (born in 1904) was shipped off to his maternal grandparents. While Forrest was growing up, his father's candy businesses went bankrupt twice. His fortunes changed around 1920 when Frank started the Mar-O-Bar Co. The business had its first breakthrough in early 1924 with a nougatty chocolate bar called Milky Way. (Forrest had suggested his father make a chocolate bar that tasted like a malted milkshake.)

Young Forrest ended up studying mining at the University of California, yet business was always foremost in his mind. During college he sold Camel cigarettes and ties, and he turned his job in the college cafeteria into a lucrative side business that earned him $100 a week (a fortune at the time). After graduating with a degree in industrial engineering from Yale in 1928, Forrest went to work with his father during which time they launched the Snickers bar (1930). His dad finally became the rich man he had always wanted to be. He started spending all the money he never had on Cadillacs, ranches, and an extravagant lifestyle. Forrest was drastically opposed to his father's excesses, believing it would be his ruin once again. Forrest wanted to put tighter controls on the company and expand operations into Canada, but Frank was not interested. He also rejected his son's requests for a one-third share of the business. When his father refused, Forrest said, "I told my dad to stick his business up his ass."

Forrest left for Europe in 1932 with a $50,000 payout and the European rights to Milky Way bars. He briefly ran a shoe tree business in Paris and worked with Nestlé in Switzerland before setting up in Slough, England, in 1933. He started his own chocolate company, releasing a sweeter version of the Milky Way bar called the Mars bar. The following year, he began manufacturing pet food that remains a core part of the Mars business. Forrest was always scouring trade journals looking for product innovation and new business ideas.

While Forrest was based in Europe, Frank Mars died, and Forrest's stepmother took control of the company. Forrest began fighting for control of his father's business but that would take thirty years to come to fruition. Meanwhile, Forrest had serious business plans. "I'm not a candy maker—I'm empire minded," he said.

His time in England was especially useful because it was there that he heard about Spanish soldiers who ate little sugar-coated pieces of chocolate that never melted despite the Mediterranean heat. In 1937, Rowntree Macintosh introduced a version of the chocolate drops in England, calling them Smarties. Forrest knew that these little chocolate spheres would work in America, so he bought the rights from Rowntree Macintosh and came back to America in 1939 to manufacture his own version of Smarties. To ensure a constant supply of chocolate during the second World War, Forrest partnered with Bruce Murrie, the son of Hershey's president, Milton Hershey, hence the name M&M, and the candies were released in 1941. They became staple rations for American soldiers for the rest of World War II.

His empire was well and truly establishing itself. Forrest introduced the Uncle Ben's range of parboiled rice and continued to expand M&Ms, introducing the peanut version and a string of new Mars products. The bitter feud over his father's business was not resolved until 1964 when Forrest finally took over his businesses. Frank got rid of the fancy executive rooms and brought in his austere culture. No more corporate helicopter or French chef. He introduced the five principles of Mars: quality, responsibility, mutuality, efficiency, and freedom.

Forrest did not believe in company cars, oak-paneled board-rooms, and executive offices. Staff are expected to answer their own phones, travel coach class, and be frugal where possible. This austerity was fundamental to how Forrest wanted to live and work and has resulted in a debt-free company with enormous cash reserves to invest back into the company, particularly in terms of state-of-the-art manufacturing equipment, marketing, advertising, and product development. No one was spared from his obsession with creating the Mars empire.

In the world of Mars Inc., a Snickers bar must contain exactly fifteen peanuts, an M&M must have the M&M logo perfectly positioned on the candy, and staff must accept a workplace where there is a genuine guillotine at the head office that reads: "Head on the block responsibility."

Forrest Mars had an extremely loyal, non-unionized workforce that was paid above award rates, could earn enormous bonuses if performance targets were met (up to fifteen times the normal salary), was given 10 percent bonuses if they arrived on time every day, and enjoyed profit share, health insurance, and a deliberate lack of hierarchy and bureaucracy. The business objective was simple: profit.

His sons, Forrest Jr. and John, were not spared their father's wrath. He did not want his sons to be idle playboys and made them work their tails off in the business. In 1973, Forrest Jr. and John took over the company, which by now was involved in a wide variety of products from breath mints to pet food, vending machines and automated payment systems. Forrest died in 1999 after living his final days in accommodation above one of his factories.

The company is now owned by his three children, John, Jacqueline, and Forrest Jr., who together are the 32nd richest people in the world with a fortune of $10.4 billion. The fourth generation of Mars is also working in the family company. Mars products are sold in one hundred countries around the world.

NOTES

"I told my dad . . ." Brenner, Joel Glenn. "Planet of the M&Ms," *Washington Post Magazine*, 12.4.92, p. W11.

"I am not a . . ." Brenner, Joel Glenn. "Planet of the M&Ms," *Washington Post Magazine*, 12.4.92, p. W11.

"Head on the block . . ." Brenner, Joel Glenn. "Planet of the M&Ms," *Washington Post Magazine*, 12.4.92, p. W11.

REFERENCES

Brenner, Joel Glenn. *The Emperors of Chocolate*, Random House, 1999.

Associated Press, BusinessWeek, Daily Mail, The Economist, Financial Times, Forbes, The Guardian, The Independent, Hoover's Company Capsules, *New York Times, Washington Post*

XM Satellite Radio

Some companies need a lot more than a kitchen table to get started

―――――――

A S A CONCEPT, XM SATELLITE RADIO IS BRILLIANT. PITCHED mainly at listeners in their cars, XM is the antidote to commercial radio's limited playlists and high ad ratios, and is a refuge from bad reception. With superb sound and more than 150 stations, XM offers everything from reggae to a Playboy channel and can be heard all over America. No more local, yokel stations. Sixty-five of XM's stations are commercial free too. All XM radio subscribers have to do is buy an XM radio for around $150 and then pay $12.95 a month for the service.

Developing satellite radio and bringing it to market is not the sort of business that can be hatched at the kitchen table and run on a shoestring. The idea for satellite radio came out of a business incubator organized by American Mobile Satellite. The company bought some bandwidth and wanted to see if it could be used for satellite radio. Once it was deemed a commercial opportunity, the idea was spun-off into American Mobile Radio Corporation (AMRC).

A promising young media executive from the Bronx, Hugh Panero was headhunted to join the venture. He came up with the name XM, moved into a windowless office in Washington DC, and set to work as one of the true pioneers of satellite radio. Panero started out as a journalist and studied his MBA at night school, never shy to ask people he admired for advice. He then worked at Time Warner Cable before running the cable television company Request Television. He earned himself a reputation as an open-style manager, very hands-on with high expectations of his staff, and someone who is relentless when it comes to getting things done.

Leading XM, Panero has had to be an aggressive capital raiser and satellite radio evangelist in order for the business to survive. Panero has serious time constraints. He has to try and make the business profitable before it runs out of cash and investors lose their nerve. Since the early days, XM has spent $2 billion trying to make the business work, investing in two satellites (named Rock and Roll) and repeater systems to boost the signal in urban areas, setting up sales and marketing teams, and building a *Star Trek*-esque Washington headquarters with eighty studios and a broadcasting studio in Nashville at the Country Music Hall of Fame.

XM Radio floated on the New York Stock Exchange in October 1999 at $12 a share. The shares have been volatile, reaching $60 and falling to $5 in early 2003. The shares have since settled at around $30, and the company has a market capitalization of $6.3 billion, buoyed by reports that satellite radio is being adopted faster than CD players were when first released. Competition from rival satellite broadcaster Sirius, which has around 2 million subscribers, has been fierce, but XM has built itself a healthy 70 percent marketshare.

XM Radio was launched on September 25, 2001, nearly two weeks late because an engineer halted the initial blast-off because he misread a message on one of his monitors. The first million sub-scribers took twenty-three months to procure. By late 2005, XM Radio had 577 staff, another fifty channels, and has secured 4.4 million subscribers. Sales surged in 2004 to $244 million, up from $91 million in 2003.

In the midst of all this intensity, Panero's wife, Mary Beth Durkin, was diagnosed with leukemia, so he has had to juggle his family life, two children, and a company that needed every minute of his time.

Despite all the drama, Panero is confident that the company is on track to make its first profits in 2008, and reach the 20 million-subscriber milestone by 2010. Already satellite radio is available in rental cars, on JetBlue flights, 120 different new car models, and will soon be available to 100 million America Online members in a partnership to form the largest digital radio network in the world. Says a stoic Panero: "We've answered the question, 'Will people pay for radio?'" Now he has to round these people up, and fast.

NOTES
"We've answered the . . ." Flynn, Laurie J. "Investors and Broadcasters Watch Growth of Satellite Radio," *New York Times*, 1.7.02, p. C7.

REFERENCES
Audio Week, Baltimore Sun, Billboard, Brandweek, Broadcasting & Cable, BusinessWeek, CBS Market Watch, Communications Daily, Daily Deal, Forbes Small Business, Fortune, Hollywood Reporter, Los Angeles Times, Mediaweek, New York Times, PR Newswire, San Francisco Chronicle, Satellite Week, USA Today, Variety, Washington Post, Washington Times

Section 11

BORN TO SELL

Ray Kroc, McDonald's

Any color you like, as long as it's brown

R AY KROC WAS A BORN SALESMAN WHO BELIEVED STRONGLY in persistence and determination, but it was not until the age of fifty-two that he finally got the break he needed.

Born in Chicago in 1902, he left school at fifteen to sell coffee beans door to door, and then signed up to drive an ambulance in World War I, though the Armistice was signed before his unit left America. He worked as a jazz pianist in the Prohibition era, then as a real estate salesman in Florida, selling land that was technically underwater, and as a salesman of paper cups. Life was a struggle for young Kroc. Then he got a job selling multimixer milk shake machines. It was a hard slog and not particularly lucrative, but it brought him in 1954 to the drive-in hamburger stand in San Bernardino, California, run by Richard and Maurice McDonald, who were bringing in some $350,000 a year. Kroc watched in awe as they mixed up forty shakes at a time for a stream of customers, but was particularly taken by the uniformly golden French fries, which, he later wrote, "would become almost sacrosanct to me, [their] preparation a ritual to be followed religiously."

Instinctively grasping the potential of the operation, which included a menu with just nine items, run with what the McDonald brothers called the "Speedee Service System," Kroc badgered the brothers until they agreed to let him franchise the operation. On April 15, 1955, Kroc had opened his own version of McDonald's, in Des Plaines, outside Chicago. By May 1959, Kroc had one hundred stores but was making relatively little money himself because of the original agreement with the McDonald brothers. In 1961, he convinced them to sell the business outright for $2.7 million—an enormous sum then, which Kroc had to get a crippling loan for. He got his payback in 1965 when the company floated and he was worth some $36 million. Kroc's restaurant chain went on to expand across the globe, having sold 35 billion hamburgers by 1980, and having 31,000 stores worldwide by 2005.

Kroc, who died in 1984, had two insights early on that were to prove the foundation of his fortune. The first was financial: the company leased or bought the land underneath many of the franchise's restaurants, then rented it back to them for a profit. According to analysts, the company owns 75 percent of the restaurant buildings and 40 percent of the land they stand on, making it as much a real estate developer as a hamburger peddler. Kroc's second flash of inspiration was children: in particular, Ronald McDonald, the clown created to attract children to the restaurants. In 1986, the company claimed 96 percent of children could recognize Ronald McDonald. McDonald's introduced the Happy Meal—a meal with a free toy—in 1979, further encouraging children to visit the restaurants. Today it even has a presence on the popular children's website Neopets, where children can visit a virtual McDonald's store. (McDonald's has also given away millions of plush Neopet toys with happy meals in a particularly successful cross-promotion.)

McDonald's prospered for almost five decades by doggedly following Kroc's obsession with uniformity. Like a Henry Ford of the food industry, Kroc applied the principles of the production line to his restaurants, giving customers fast, cheap, reliable food. Any color you like, as long as it's brown (or something like that). So what if the menu never changed? People liked it. It was straightforward, not like in those swanky restaurants where the waiters made you feel dumb. Kids liked it. It was cheap: this was a restaurant where ordinary families could dine out regularly. And it was reassuring—food that was exactly the same from one day to the next, wherever you ate it, ordered, paid for, and consumed it, with none of the fuss associated with normal restaurants. The restaurants' top-selling items are still the Big Mac, introduced in 1968, and the Quarter Pounder, first sold in 1971.

Kroc turned the preparation of food from something carried out by trained chefs into something that happened largely in factories. Fries arrived at the stores precut and deep-frozen, buns were precut, and frozen burgers were delivered ready to slap onto the hot plates. Instead of cooking individual burgers on demand, store managers estimated ahead of time how many would be ordered and had the sandwiches assembled and sitting under heat lamps before the customer had even handed over the money.

These systems, dictated in each store's company manual since Kroc first put it together in 1958, also allowed McDonald's to hire staff that might otherwise be considered too young or inexperienced to work in a kitchen or service industry. With a few hours of careful training, a teenager paid the minimum wage can make a Big Mac identical to one made by a manager of thirty years standing. It was estimated in 1992 that 7 percent of the American population had their first jobs at McDonald's.

McDonald's is a mix of company-run (9,000) and franchise stores. Franchise owners agree to operate under rigorous conditions that ensure they put the bulk of their efforts into running the one or two stores they are allotted. McDonald's dictates where they buy their ingredients, how they cook them, how they are advertised, and what they charge for them. The result is a company-controlled store that runs with the energy of a small business.

Ray Kroc's system surpassed any reasonable expectations, delivering constant growth for half a century despite a product line and advertising campaign that had changed little since Ronald McDonald made his first appearance on American television in 1963. The one flaw in the system, as in any totalitarian order, was its lack of flexibility: it works fine if all you want is to sell the same burgers from Guam to Azerbaijan, but it stumbles when somebody asks for theirs without the pickle. And by the end of the twentieth century, it seemed as if the world was finally sick of pickles.

In November 2002, following profit falls, McDonald's announced it was shutting down 175 restaurants around the world, withdrawing completely from three countries in Latin America. It ended the year posting its first ever quarterly loss. Financial analysts pointed to several factors behind the slide including a slump in the world economy, fierce competition in the U.S. domestic market, and Mad Cow Disease in Europe. Eric Schlosser, author of the best-selling exposé *Fast Food Nation* and a long-time McDonald's critic, saw the announcement as a symptom of the company's obsession with expansion. "I see this as another case of imperial over-reach," he said. "They got too big too fast and, like the British empire, their huge increase in size abroad really cloaked fundamental weaknesses."

The official line from McDonald's was that the closures were nothing more than an adjustment; the company still planned to open far more restaurants than it had shuttered. But the brand, too, was under attack. When McDonald's sued two British activists, Dave Morris and Helen Steel, in 1990 for handing out a leaflet that criticized the company's operations, it hoped to teach them a swift, unpleasant lesson that would end in an apology from the troublemakers. Instead, dozens of McDonald's employees, executives, and suppliers found themselves in the witness box giving excruciating evidence about their practices. The McLibel case, as it was called, was Britain's longest-ever court case, running for 313 days of evidence and submissions. It ended in an overall finding for the corporation, which won a damages claim and was initially awarded $100,000. But the judge, Justice Bell, found that some of the defendants' startling allegations were proven, namely that McDonald's did exploit children by targeting them in its advertising and was responsible for cruelty to the animals that were processed for its meals. Steel, a former gardener, and Morris, a single parent, claimed a moral victory, gained worldwide media exposure, and never paid McDonald's—which had spent millions on legal fees—a cent.

In France in 1999, farmer Jose Bove became a national hero when he trashed a half-built McDonald's restaurant in a protest against trade sanctions and the globalization of what he called "malbouffe" (bad food). Then an American filmmaker named Morgan Spurlock went on a McDonald's-only diet for a month and recorded the results, which included weight gain and ill health, for the documentary *Super Size Me*, which was a hit around the world.

Like a bull elephant that finally notices the spears sticking out of its back, McDonald's began to respond to the new world order. "The world has changed. Our customers have changed. We have to change too," declared chairman Jim Cantalupo in 2003, not long before he died unexpectedly at age sixty.

Following the lead of its competitor Subway, which had enormous success with a range of low-fat sandwiches, McDonald's is now rebranding itself as healthy, rolling out various low-fat alternatives, including (depending on where you live) yogurts, fresh fruit, light salads, and made-to-order sandwiches. Assisted by a worldwide ad campaign themed "I'm Lovin' It," mothers bringing their children in for Happy Meals, who once would have ordered just coffee, are now finding something "light" for themselves to eat—helping to lift the value of the average order. McDonald's has also moved into the made-to-order sandwich market to compete with Subway, and even ran a meal deal promoted by Oprah Winfrey's personal trainer that included a salad, a bottle of water, a book of walking tips, and a pedometer (which, sadly, wasn't yet available when poor Morgan Spurlock made his documentary).

It's not quite as simple as putting salads on the menu—do customers go to McDonald's for salads, or for a junk food fix? (The Big Mac—with thirty grams of fat—is still the best-selling item.) And new product lines, such as drive-though, made-to-order cappuccino and fresh sandwiches mean greater complexity and higher likelihood of system failures and food wastage. But McDonald's must have done something right: by the end of 2004 strong sales, with profits more than doubled since 2002, had vindicated the change in direction, and encouraged the company to experiment further.

After fifty years, it had finally shifted its focus away from the hamburger and the sky didn't fall down—quite the opposite—for McDonald's is not a hamburger company. It is a landowner, a real estate developer, a franchiser, a delivery system. It just happened to sell hamburgers because that, correctly, seemed to be the best bet in 1950s America. Its future rests on discovering what people want to eat in 2006 and beyond—it is now probably the world's biggest retailer of salads and yogurt. "Ray Kroc was once asked what sort of food McDonald's would make in the future," recalls McDonald's marketing executive Joe Talcott. "He replied, 'I don't know what we'll be selling, but we'll be selling more of it than anybody else.'"

NOTES

"Would become almost sacrosanct . . ." Kroc, Ray. *Grinding It Out: The Making of McDonald's*. St Martin's Press, 1997.

"I see this as . . ." Burkeman, Oliver. "Not So Big, Mac: All Is Not Well at McDonald's," *The Guardian*, 11.22.02.

"The world has changed . . ." *The Economist*, "Did somebody say a loss? But how?" 12.4.03.

REFERENCES

Schlosser, Eric. *Fast Food Nation*, HarperCollins, 2002.

Daily Mail, The Economist, Financial Times, The Guardian, Los Angeles Times, New York Times, New Yorker, The Observer, Scotsman, Sunday Age, Sunday Times

Dell

Celebrate for a nanosecond. Then move on.

SOME PEOPLE BUILD THEIR FORTUNES ON GREAT IDEAS. OTHERS, like Michael Dell, do very nicely by taking existing ideas and executing them better. Dell, the eleventh-richest man in America (at last count), has come to dominate an industry that worships innovation without really inventing anything himself.

That's not to say Dell, whose company now makes around 70,000 computers a day, isn't a smart, innovative guy. He's just more interested in making money now than dreaming up products that may or may not make money later. "If you invent something that no one wants to buy, I don't care," he said in 2003.

Dell was just eighteen when he saw the opportunity that was to make him (at thirty-one) the youngest-ever CEO to enter the ranks of the *Fortune* 500; that was when he started assembling computers from components in his room at the University of Texas and selling them by mail order. By the age of twenty-four, Dell had 1,600 employees and was worth an estimated $100 million.

Dell had actually been in business, after a fashion, since he took up stamp collecting as a twelve-year-old. As he observes in his autobiography, "Before long, my interest in stamps began to shift from the joy of collecting to the idea that there was something here that my mother, a stockbroker, would have termed 'a commercial opportunity.'" He set up his own mini-auction house, persuading collectors in his neighborhood to consign their stamps to him, which he then advertised in a journal under the name Dell's Stamps. He quickly made $2,000—a fortune for a kid barely into his teens.

He did a little stock and currency trading (as you do). Then at sixteen, he took a summer job selling subscriptions to the *Houston Post*. He soon noticed that the people most likely to buy subscriptions when he cold-called them were those who had either just moved or had just married. So he tracked down lists of recently issued marriage licenses and addresses of new homebuyers and targeted them directly with personalized letters, working after school and on the weekend.

"One day," he recalled, "my history and economics teacher assigned us a project for which we had to file our tax returns. Based on what I had made selling newspaper subscriptions, my income was about $18,000 that year. At first, my teacher corrected me, assuming I had missed the decimal place. When she realized I hadn't, she became even more dismayed. To her surprise, I had made more money that year than she had."

Dell's father wanted him to be a doctor, so Michael enrolled to study biology at the University of Texas as a precursor to medical school. But, once again, he sensed an opportunity that was too good to pass up. In 1980, fifteen-year-old Dell had bought an Apple II computer with money he made selling his stamps. He had taken it apart and discovered the components were made by companies other than Apple. He figured that if you knew where to buy the different bits, and how to put it together, you could make the computer yourself.

By 1983, IBM had launched its first personal computer and Dell could see a new market opening up. His first venture was based on simple supply and demand: he had heard local IBM dealers were overstocked, so with cash saved from earlier ventures he bought a batch of IBM PCs wholesale and sold them through the classifieds, undercutting the retail price by such a margin that he quickly made sales of $80,000. Adding extra components such as disk drives, he could soup up each computer to suit each customer, a service previously unheard of.

At first, he downplayed his business to his parents, hiding boxes of parts in the bathroom when they dropped by his dorm, but by the end of the first year, and with profits in excess of $50,000, he called an end to the bluff and dropped out of college altogether. "I just knew there was a huge business opportunity here, and I had to take it," he said. "If it had gone wrong, I could have gone back to medical school."

Dell's company, PCs Limited, moved into a shopfront in Austin, Texas, in 1984.That year he sold $6 million worth of hardware. The following year, Dell started building from scratch his own computer, which was custom-built for mail-order customers, and sales leapt to $34 million. An IBM clone called the Turbo PC, it was half the price of a comparable machine from IBM. Supplying direct to customers allowed Dell to cut out the middlemen and charge lower prices, and building directly to order for customers meant the company didn't have to carry much inventory, vital when the price of parts was falling constantly.

Dealing directly with customers also meant the company received instant updates on what was selling and what was slow: by 1987, it was receiving 2,500 calls a day in response to its advertisements in computer magazines.

Rapid growth meant Dell, still just twenty years old, had trouble meeting demand and the Texas Attorney General's consumer protection division was prompted to investigate complaints from customers about slow delivery. "I didn't know everything there was to know about running a large business like this," Dell said. "But I knew how to hire the people who did."

Perhaps prompted by these early glitches, he adopted what would become a Dell trademark: customer service that offered a thirty-day, money-back guarantee and unlimited telephone support. He also hired E. Lee Walker as president of the company in 1986. Walker, forty-five, had start-up experience and a no-nonsense style, firing or demoting most of Dell's senior staff immediately. In

1988, Dell floated the business and by 1990 was the sixth-largest manufacturer of computers in the United States.

The company is still based in Austin and still does pretty much what it did in 1984: it builds its own versions of IBM-style computers to order for its customers; though today, of course, they buy them over the Internet—from individuals at home to company-loads ordered by an IT department. Dell, barely forty, is worth $16 billion, and there's no great secret to his success: he was simply able to apply and continually refine his first principles as the business grew. Dell focused on areas of business most people find deathly boring: supply chains, operating margins, distribution, and customer feedback. Dell has over five hundred patents—but they are all for deeply unsexy business process ideas, such as a way to configure more efficient manufacturing stations.

The upshot is that Dell, which had sales of close to $55 billion in 2005, now takes around three hours to build a computer to order, with a cost structure that Michael Dell claims is half that of his competition.

Dell has convinced many of its suppliers to build factories nearby so it does not have to carry parts itself.

As a leader, Michael Dell is an odd mix of extrovert—to open a sales drive he once ran into a stadium filled with Dell employees carrying an Olympic-style torch—and introvert who loathes hype and fears hubris. A well-known Dell motto is "Celebrate for a nanosecond. Then move on." When in 2001 an internal review revealed employees found him impersonal and detached, he faced the criticism head-on, explaining in a videotape to the entire company that he was painfully shy but would work on becoming more approachable.

Michael Dell believes in a management style called "two-in-a-box," where executives are partnered with somebody who challenges and complements them. Dell himself has such a relationship with Kevin B. Rollins, who works in an adjoining office separated from Dell's by a sliding glass partition. Dell plays the visionary while Rollins, twelve years his senior, handles the day-to-day aspects of running the company. In March 2004, Dell announced Rollins would become CEO and that his own title would change from CEO to chairman.

Dell, who still owns around 10 percent of the company, is fond of Armani suits, sponsors a baseball stadium called the Dell Diamond, and is married to Susan, a fashion designer, with whom he has four children. In 1999, they established the Michael and Susan Dell Foundation, a children's charity, with an endowment of $1 billion.

NOTES

"Celebrate for a nanosecond . . ." Park, Andrew and Peter Burrows. "What You Don't Know about Dell." *BusinessWeek* online, 11.3.03.

"If you invent something . . ." Diaz, Sam. "Dell Succeeds by Breaking Silicon Valley Rules," *San Jose News Service*, 12.18.03.

"Before long, my interest . . ." Dell, Michael and Catherine Fredman. *Direct from Dell: Strategies That Revolutionized an Industry.* HarperBusiness, 2000.

"One day . . ." Dell, Michael and Catherine Fredman. *Direct from Dell: Strategies That Revolutionized an Industry.* HarperBusiness, 2000.

"I just knew . . ." Laurence, Charles. "My $16 billion? I don't think about it," *The Daily Telegraph*, 12.19.00, p. 16.

"If it had gone wrong . . ." Laurence, Charles. "My $16 billion? I don't think about it," *The Daily Telegraph*, 12.19.00, p. 16.

"I didn't know everything . . ." Bermant, Charles. "PC's Limited: Making Mail Order Pay Off," *InfoWorld*, 1.26.87, p. 1.

REFERENCES

Austin-American Statesman, The Australian, BusinessWeek, Computer Reseller News, Economist, eWeek.com, Financial Times, Fortune, Houston Chronicle, The Independent, Industry Week, Internet Week, Newsweek, San Jose Mercury News, Seattle Times, Sunday Telegraph, The Times, Vanity Fair

Arthur Blank and Bernie Marcus, The Home Depot

Getting sacked can be a beautiful thing

I N 1978, THE FIRST HOME DEPOT OPENED IN ATLANTA. ON grand opening day, despite the local newspaper forgetting to run the Home Depot advertisement, the store made so much money the bank where the proceeds were deposited was suspicious about this new business having so much cash (more than $10,000).

Founders Arthur Blank and Bernie Marcus turned hardware retailing upside down with their big-box concept. Instead of the traditional small, expensive hardware store with limited stock, Blank and Marcus came into the marketplace with 100,000-square-foot orange warehouses (roughly the size of three supermarkets), packed to the rafters with every conceivable hardware item. To top it off, because stock was coming straight from suppliers rather than through a wholesaler, Home Depot could offer everyday low prices with customers paying an average of 30 percent less for their hardware. They operated the stores with experienced builders and well-trained staff in their orange aprons, and staged DIY workshops—workshops that showed customers how to do their home projects rather than just selling them.

Blank and Marcus built a business culture where generous incentives, stock options, and extensive training helped create a workforce that would "bleed orange" for their bosses and go the extra mile on the shop floor. There were staff barbecues, rallies, hugs from the bosses, and Blank and Marcus made a point of spending 50 percent of their time in store, practicing what Marcus calls "ground-engaged management."

The model was so effective, Home Depot's store turnover was eight times greater than traditional hardware stores. Big profits fuelled aggressive growth and rapid introduction of new Home Depot stores. The company has grown to a 1,950-store powerhouse worth more than $87 billion. Blank and Marcus are billionaires and more than one thousand staff members also enjoy millionaire status thanks to their Home Depot stock.

Arthur Blank grew up in a New York City apartment and was never handy around the house. He did, however, show a flair for business. He studied accounting and had a string of little start-ups, including his own landscaping and laundry businesses. Blank's father, who died when Blank was fifteen, had a pharmaceutical supply business. Arthur's mother took over the business with her never-say-die attitude, a trait that he has cultivated throughout his career.

Bernie Marcus grew up in Newark, New Jersey. His parents ran a pharmacy in Queens. He had wanted to become a doctor, but his family could not afford the college fees. One of his early jobs was as a stand-up comedian, a skill he put to good use during his Home Depot years. Marcus told the jokes, and Blank laughed.

Blank and Marcus met in 1974 while they were working in senior roles at Handy Dans Home Improvement Centers, a chain based in California. Despite their age difference (charismatic Marcus is thirteen years older than Blank) they struck up an alliance. There is synergy between the two—Blank is more systematic, practical, and operational, while Marcus is an outgoing ideas man. Marcus is often described as the carrot, Blank the stick.

Blank and Marcus became involved in a union dispute in the company and were both fired from Handy Dan in 1978. Marcus and Blank decided they didn't want to work for anyone else again. Blank likens the lay-off to "being kicked in the ass with a golden horseshoe." Marcus and Blank wanted to stay in the industry and while Blank worked on the business model, Marcus went about raising funds to start Home Depot. They knew the industry was pricing goods too high. If they kept operational costs low, kept suppliers happy (they spent many a night at a local steakhouse entertaining them), offered best-practice training to staff, and kept administrative costs under control, they could shake things up. An investment group funded the venture.

Home Depot's arrival in the marketplace was brilliantly timed. The home improvement phenomenon was about to strike. Within a year, there were four Home Depots throughout Atlanta and three hundred staff members. The car parks were packed on weekends with customers wanting to make over their homes. In 1981, Home Depot went public with a starting price of $16 and the aggressive expansion began. By 1986, annual sales had hit $1 billion, and, soon after, Home Depot was the largest home repair company in the U.S. with 118 stores. Their revenge on Handy Dan was sweet, very sweet. Home Depot is the youngest retailer to reach $30 billion, $40 billion, $50 billion, and $60 billion in annual revenues.

For two decades, the profits just kept rolling in with Home Depot averaging profit growth of 35 percent each year during the 1990s. Its stock's value increased 3,700 percent during that decade reaching almost $60. This bull run did come to an end as competitors caught up, particularly the Lowes chain. The company was also scarred by a $104.5 million sex discrimination lawsuit that argued that women were not given the same job opportunities as men in the business, a decision that Marcus was particularly furious about.

In 1997, Marcus stepped down from his CEO role and Blank took his place, with Marcus staying on as chairman. Blank only stayed in the role until 2000 when Robert Nardelli, a top executive from General Electric, became Home Depot's CEO. Nardelli took the new role after finding out he would not be replacing GE leader Jack Welch. He didn't want to be number two anymore. Nardelli joined at a tough time in the company's history. The stock, after being the darling of Wall Street, had become one of the worst performers on the market. Offshore expansion into countries such as Chile had been disastrous. By early 2003, the stock price had almost halved. Says Nardelli: "Clearly our stores got old and stale. We got locked into a model that had served us well. It got us to around $40 billion [in revenues] but it wasn't going to get us to $100 billion."

Nardelli changed Home Depot's course. He slowed down new store openings and concentrated on upgrading existing stores and improving back-end efficiencies. Introductions have included a billion-dollar technology upgrade and signature GE cost-controlling programs throughout the business. In 2002, the year that Home Depot was the worst performing stock on the Standard & Poor's Index, Marcus gave Nardelli the role of chairman of the board, leaving more time for Marcus to concentrate on his philanthropic exploits. Marcus plans to give away much of his $2.4 billion within his lifetime. Blank has also been philanthropically active through his family's foundation, donating more than $120 million so far. In 2002, Blank spent $545 million acquiring the Atlanta Falcons.

Marcus and Blank remain on the board of Home Depot, still actively involved in the company and keeping an eye on their appointment. Living up to the expectations of these savvy gentlemen is not the thing that really worries Nardelli. He says: "The thing that keeps me awake in this business is the speed with which you have to move." Not even the most clever business can afford to rest on its laurels.

NOTES

"Kicked in the ass . . ." Skapinker, Michael. "When the Sack Is Not the End of the Story," *Financial Times*, 6.30.01, p. 11.

"Clearly our stores . . ." Sellers, Patricia and Julie Schlosser. "It's His Home Depot Now," *Fortune*, 9.13.04.

"The thing that keeps . . ." Insana, Ron. "Fixer-Uppers Spruce Up Profit at Home Depot," *USA Today*, 7.6.04, p. 4B.

REFERENCES

Marcus, Bernie and Arthur Blank with Bob Andelman. *Built from Scratch: How a Couple of Regular Guys Grew Home Depot from Nothing to $30 Billion*. Times Business, 1999.

Roush, Chris. *Inside Home Depot: How One Company Revolutionized an Industry through the Relentless Pursuit of Growth*. McGraw Hill, 1999.

Associated Press, Atlanta Journal-Constitution, BusinessWeek, CNN, *Financial Times, Forbes, Fortune,* Hoover's Company Records, *Investors Business Daily, New York Times, USA Today, Washington Post*

Mary Kay Ash, Mary Kay Cosmetics

Success is the best revenge

A S FAR AS ENTREPRENEURS GO, THE STORY OF TEXAN MARY Kathlyn Wagner is hard to beat. She built a billion-dollar direct-sales business from $5,000 in savings at a time when nice ladies stayed at home and looked after their husbands. A star saleswoman who used to write her sales targets in soap on her bathroom mirror, it is possible Mary Kay Ash would have kept working for other companies. But an experience in 1963 at World Gift, where she was a national director of sales, changed all that. Male colleagues she had trained were promoted above her on twice her salary. Mary Kay Ash had been a stellar performer there for eleven years. The reason? They wore a suit and tie, she wore a dress. After twenty-six years in sales, she retired.

Her direct sales cosmetics and skincare business, now among the largest in the world, came along at a time when the value of women outside the home was greatly discounted. Mary Kay Ash empowered hundreds and thousands of women to have lucrative careers and offered American women opportunities that didn't exist anywhere else. The business, says her son and business partner for almost three decades, Richard Rogers, was always about creating opportunities for women. "Cosmetics just happened to be the vehicle."

By 1963, she was so determined to start her own business that even the death of her second husband, George Hallenbeck, a month before Mary Kay was launched did not delay the opening of the business.

Mary Kay opened a storefront in Dallas in September 1963. "I was middle aged, had varicose veins, and I didn't have time to fool around," she said. The cornerstone of the original Mary Kay product range was a skin cream that had been devised by a hide tanner who had modified leather softener for human skin. Mary Kay had sampled it at one of her home parties and persuaded the Heath family to sell her the rights to the recipe for a reported $500. "The ace in the hole I had in starting was that I had spent twenty-five years in direct sales." Her team was comprised of nine consultants and her twenty-year-old son, Richard Rogers, who left his job as a financial administrator in an insurance company to help out. He leads the company today. Mary Kay was the undisputed leading lady of Mary Kay Cosmetics. "Her job description was to energize, recognize, teach, and motivate our independent sales force," says Rogers. "My job was everything else."

Wholesale sales for the first twelve months were a healthy $198,000. In 1964, Mary Kay held the first of what would become legendary get-togethers for two hundred. The ladies ate off paper plates. "Mother really did cook the chicken," says Richard Rogers. Over the next four decades, these events would become so huge that the company would become the largest annual user of the Dallas Convention Centre. Some 50,000 people would typically make the pilgrimage to Dallas to hear Mary Kay's motivational speeches. They came too for the awards nights where top salespeople shared in millions in prizes and got to wear crowns and sit on thrones. Mary Kay would arrive on stage in a horse-drawn carriage or Rolls-Royce, for example, and often leave through secret exits to avoid being mobbed. (This happened pretty much wherever she went around the country.) She became a cult figure and needed eleven secretaries to handle all the letters and gifts that arrived for her at the head office every day.

Mary Kay Ash knew what it felt like not to be recognized and rewarded for the work she did. She often said: "There are two things people want more than sex and money—recognition and praise."

Mary Kay based her business plan on the principles she had learned from decades in direct selling. That list of principles was so effective that in time this mother of three had the Harvard Business School and other academics attending her spectacular sales seminars to find out what this lady with the blonde wigs and pink mansion was doing in her business to make it perform so well.

Mary Kathlyn Wagner was born in 1918 in Hot Wells, Texas. By the age of seven she was caring for her invalid father, who suffered from tuberculosis, while her mother worked fourteen-hour days managing a restaurant. By seventeen, she was married and went on to have three children. Her first husband filed for divorce after he returned from serving in World War II (turns out he had been in a relationship with another woman), and Mary Kay was left a single mother with three children to support. She had wanted to study medicine but realized it was not possible with her responsibilities. She began selling child psychology books door to door, and her natural talent for sales blossomed. She then worked in direct sales for Stanley Home Products for eleven years (also a training ground for Brownie Wise, who would lead the Tupperware revolution).

At her company, recognition was a critical part of the success of the business. Her way of showing it was through pink Cadillacs, luxury holidays, and all manner of jewelry from diamond bumble-bee stick pins and little ladders through to flashy designer watches. She wanted her independent sales force to be the highest paid women in the U.S. Hundreds of Mary Kay representatives have earned commissions in excess of a million dollars. "She always focused on putting the honor in selling," says Rogers.

Mary Kay cosmetics appealed to the American heartland. Her product thrived in the conservative suburbs and country heartland of America. By 1966, sales had tipped $1 million. The company went public in 1968, raising funds for a new manufacturing plant in Dallas. Mary Kay was very good at creating a legend, with her coiffed blond wigs, diamonds, a thirty-room pink mansion and her signature pink Cadillac. She first drove a pink Cadillac in the 1960s in Dallas. It caused a sensation and was free advertising to boot. This reaction prompted Mary Kay to offer the ultimate incentive to her sales force—Mary Kay pink cadillacs. Through the Mary Kay Career Car Program, the very top sales people earned the use of a pink Cadillac. Typically, the recipient would receive a two-year lease on a Mary Kay pink Cadillac. When the lease would run out, the salesperson hopefully had performed so well they would be eligible for a newer model. This pink car program continues today with its salesforce of 1.5 million on five continents.

Growth continued until the 1980s when many Mary Kay representatives trailed off to pursue other career options and the brand became a little stale. In 1985, the family bought the company back in a leveraged buyout for $375 million, a state of play that suited the business. Without the short-term view of shareholders, the company could take a more long-term view and not worry about market reaction. The next five years saw sales increase by more than 95 percent to $487 million. During that time, Mary Kay resigned as chairman and took the title chairman emeritus. In 1987, Mary Kay's son Richard took the chairman's title. Consolidated retail sales topped $1 billion in 1991.

Mary Kay suffered a debilitating stroke in 1996. She struggled with poor health for the next five years, missing annual seminars for the first time in her career. She moved out of her pink mansion into a smaller home and she died on Thanksgiving Day in 2001 at age eighty-three.

Today the Mary Kay company is thriving with an annual wholesale turnover of more than $1.8 billion. The brand has had a renaissance in the past five years with an 80 percent increase in sales and 120 percent rise in the number of sales consultants. "I would say that we can't move any faster than our unique culture allows," says Rogers. "Where our corporate culture is understood and embraced, we do very well. It is as simple as that." Rogers is adamant that his mother would be very happy with the ways things have turned out. "Her dream that this business would transcend her life has been accomplished," he says. That Mary Kay sure showed her old bosses a thing or two.

NOTES

"I was middle-aged..." Nemy, Enid. "Mary Kay Ash, Builder of Beauty Empire, Dies at 83," *New York Times*, p 13, 11.24.01.

REFERENCES

Associated Press, BusinessWeek, CNN, *Daily Telegraph,* Hoover's Company Records, *Irish Times,* Mary Kay.com, *National Post, New Strait Times, New York Times, Texas Monthly, USA Today, Washington Post*

Simon Fuller

The Svengali of pop

WHEN BRITISH MUSIC ENTREPRENEUR SIMON FULLER pitched his *Idol* television idea to Los Angeles in early 2002, he was hoping for a chance to crack the tough U.S. market. His concept of a talent show where viewers control the voting was a smash hit in England, and he saw no reason why it wouldn't work in other countries. *Idol* judge Simon Cowell came over with Fuller, thinking pessimistically that a U.S. version of the show might only last a few weeks. "We'll have a nice holiday and go back to England," he said at the time.

Well, Cowell was wrong. *American Idol* has been a runaway success. More than 500 million people cast votes in the fourth season of *American Idol* in 2005, and 40 million viewers tuned in to the final. The program the *New York Times* describes as "Starsearch meets Gladiator" now has thirty-five different versions, including *Indian Idol*.

While much of the record industry is in a slump due to declining sales, Fuller rethought the way that artists could be marketed and built himself a $400 million empire. "The demand for music is intense," he says. "The problem facing the industry is how we turn that into business."

It is no accident that Fuller created a program such as *Idol,* as it perfectly reflects his strategy to make the artists he represents rich and famous (and himself even richer). Television was the perfect medium to market his talent. One television executive who worked with him at Thames Television on the *Pop Idol* format says, "His strength is that he does things on a very large scale. He's very ambitious, and he doesn't worry about obstacles or problems. Other people get distracted by reasons why you can't do something. Simon just goes for it, 100 percent." Rather than just seeing potential to find new artists and make money out of their records, Fuller orchestrates lucrative licensing and merchandise deals and revenue from voting—in short, a whole franchise of opportunities. Fans can buy *American Idol* varsity jackets, trading cards, an *American Idol* Gameboy game, and even a fragrance that promises to make its wearers "an instant hit."

Young Fuller started out running discos and arranging bands to play at his college in southern England. He moved to London to become a talent scout for Chrysalis Records. One of his early triumphs was to buy the rights to the song "Holiday," which would become Madonna's first big hit. After masterminding a number one song about the Vietnam War, "Nineteen," Fuller established his own management company called 19. Since its inception, Fuller's artists, including the Eurythmics and top songwriter Cathy Dennis (who wrote Britney Spears' "Toxic"), have recorded more than 106 number one songs and eighty-three number one albums. Fuller quickly became the most successful music executive in British history.

When Fuller took over the management of all-girl band The Spice Girls, he turned them into a brand, signed them up with Pepsi, stopped their squabbling temporarily, and helped them sell forty-six million records—not bad for a group of girls who answered to an advertisement: "no singing or dancing experience necessary." After eighteen months, the Spice Girls sacked him, wanting more control over their careers. Without Fuller, the band fell apart. He got on with his other projects.

Being sacked was something that Fuller never wanted to experience again and pushed him further toward his radical, all-controlling management style. His next band, S Club 7, was almost cartoon-like, superficial, and pure pop. They recorded a string of number one hits.

As his management company expanded into television, touring, sponsorship, and film, Fuller's overtly commercial style has earned him many critics who reject such a commodification of music. (It is hard to imagine Bruce Springsteen launching a fragrance.) Fuller does not care. He is the Svengali who constructs artists to find instant prime-time fame. "I don't want to be part of the establishment. I want to create my own establishment," he says.

In 2001, Fuller took his *Pop Idol* idea to Thames Television and struck a fifty-fifty deal with the network. It first aired in October 2001 and was an instant success. *Idol* winners Kelly Clarkson, Ruben Studdard, Fantasia Barrino, and runner-up Clay Aiken have racked up sales of more than $900 million among them. Without the Fuller machine behind them, the prime time audiences and careful management, it is safe to say that those young idols would never have found such success (or ever had the chance to be mentored by Sony BMG head Clive Davis). This is why Fuller is a very different kind of manager. Because of his expertise, his artists are expected to pay him more than the average 15–20 percent commission. He gets 25–50 percent or no deal. *Idol* artists have to sign these contracts in order to be on the program, so they really don't have much choice if they want to play in the big league.

In March 2005, Fuller sold his production company for $174 million to Robert FX Sillerman's CKX Inc., which also owns the rights to the Elvis Presley estate. Fuller's deal is valued at closer to $200 million because of his 4 percent stake in CKX. He will sit on the board of the company whose directors include Priscilla Presley.

Despite this windfall, Fuller has no plans to slow down. He is currently developing a theater show where the audience competes for prizes. He is working on I Love Music, a site that will sell downloadable songs for wireless services. He has launched a soccer academy in the U.S. and England with star footballer David Beckham, whom he also manages. Fuller divides his time between a manor house in Sussex, England, and homes in London, Los Angeles, and southern France. Needless to say, with his latest deal, he can more than afford the private jet and fast cars that he loves.

Fuller has cornered the market on instant pop with scores of artists having their fifteen minutes of fame under Fuller's stewardship; but these manufactured artists do not seem to last. Coldplay's Chris Martin was quoted in 2002 that Fuller should be melted down and turned into glue. But the clever thing about Fuller's plan is that the world is full of people who want to be famous and will do just about anything to achieve it. That's a big talent pool.

NOTES

"We'll have a nice . . ." CNN, "The Profiles of Donald Trump, Mark Burnett and Simon Cowell, Kyra Phillips, Colin Lin, Paula Zahn," 5.21.05.

"The demand . . ." Hay, Carla. "Shows's Founder Reveals Plans for 'Idol' Empire," *Billboard*, 6.28.03.

"His strength is that he . . ." Thomas, David. "The IOS Profile, Simon Fuller: The Three-Minute Wonder," *The Independent on Sunday*, 11.2.03.

"I don't want to be part . . ." Lieberman, David. "*American Idol* Zooms from Hit Show to Massive Business," *USA Today*, 3.30.05.

REFERENCES

Associated Press, Billboard, BusinessWeek, CNN, *The Guardian, The Independent, New York Times, USA Today, Washington Post*

Section 12

ME, MYSELF, AND I

Oprah Winfrey

The power of one

B E YOURSELF. BE ALL THAT YOU CAN BE. IF YOU ASKED OPRAH Winfrey for tips on running a business, it's likely you would get something inspiring along those lines.

It's the message she preaches on her daytime talk show and in her magazine. It's a message aimed at housewives caught in a rut, looking for inspiration or empathy. And it's a message that has made her America's richest entertainer, with a personal fortune of $1 billion, several homes (including 102 oceanfront acres on a Hawaiian island), and friends such as John Travolta, Brad Pitt, and Jennifer Aniston, who in 2004 helped her celebrate her fiftieth birthday.

But it's also a message Oprah has acted on herself ever since she became a television star in 1984. Today she is the owner and head of a company—Harpo—with an annual turnover of hundreds of millions of dollars, a company whose business, essentially, is Oprah. "Oprah reports to nobody but God," says one of her staff.

Her inspirational rise from poverty to success, her overcoming of such obstacles as teenage pregnancy and drug abuse, have allowed her viewers to feel they know her, and to feel she can relate to their problems. Oprah's drive and success is infectious, too, and while she freely admits she cannot so much as read a financial spreadsheet, she has been invited to sit on the boards of companies including Intel and Ralph Lauren (she declined).

Oprah has, though, taught a business course called "The Dynamics of Leadership" at the prestigious Northwestern University's Kellogg Graduate School of Management, where her ability to empathize and communicate were seen as valuable business tools (the text for Oprah's class was Stephen Covey's *Principle-Centered Leadership*). Oprah was also the subject of a course at the University of Illinois called "Oprah: the Tycoon"; she invited the class to come to a taping of her show and asked to see their essays about her.

Oprah was born in Kosciusko, Mississippi, on January 29, 1954. For her first six years she was largely raised by her paternal grandmother on a rural pig farm. Her parents couldn't even get her name right: they had meant to christen her Orpah, after the Old Testament figure from the book of Ruth, but spelled it wrong.

When her parents separated, she lived with her mother for a few years, during which time she was sexually abused by male family members and so-called friends. At thirteen, she ran away from home and narrowly avoided being locked up in a youth training center; instead, she was sent to live with her father, Vernon Winfrey. At fourteen she had a baby, who died soon after birth. Oprah says after that she realized she had been given a second chance to make a life for herself and, encouraged by her father, who demanded she read a book a week, became a good student.

Despite her troubled upbringing, Oprah retained an unusual spark; at sixteen, she became the first black Miss Fire Prevention for Nashville, a position that led to her being invited to read the news on a local radio station. She was voted Miss Black Tennessee, then gained a scholarship to Tennessee State University where she studied speech, drama, and English, landing a job age nineteen as coanchor on the television news program of the CBS affiliate station WVTF-TV. Three years later, at age twenty-two, she became the sole anchorwoman at a Baltimore station's news show, which proved to be both a disaster and the making of her. Inexperienced, she had a passion for ad-libbing that the station did not share. The station dropped Oprah from the news after a few months, deeming her more suitable for a morning chat show called *People Are Talking*.

Oprah had found her niche. She was confident, revelatory, and, best of all, she was somebody the viewers could relate to—black, down to earth, and not a stick-thin TV Barbie. She honed her skills for six years; then in 1983, at age twenty-nine, she headed to Chicago for an audition with the metropolitan station WLS-Ch.7.

It was obvious to the station managers that she was a major talent, and they gave her a job hosting a show called *AM Chicago*, on a salary of $230,000. Her success is legendary: within a month her ratings were higher than those of the incumbent number one, the veteran Phil Donahue. Two years later she went national with the show now called *The Oprah Winfrey Show*, and has held the number-one spot in her market sector ever since.

If Oprah was on her way to becoming an entertainer at age sixteen, she became a businesswoman in 1984 when she walked into the office of Chicago entertainment lawyer Jeff Jacobs seeking advice on her lucrative new contract. Jacobs evidently saw a big future for the young Oprah, suggesting she set up her own company. Two years later, they launched Harpo (Oprah spelled backwards).

Through her company, Oprah bought the rights to her show, which she now syndicates for around $140 million a year. Though the show is Harpo's cash cow, the company has diversified into television production, film, and magazines—all of which reflect Oprah and her philosophy of women's empowerment. Total income in 2003 was around $275 million.

Oprah has never married, but has for many years lived with her partner, Steadman Graham, a former male model and president of a North Carolina-based public relations firm, the Graham Williams group.

NOTES

"Oprah reports . . ." Jaggi, Maya. "The Power of One," *The Guardian Weekend*, 2.13.99, p. 10.

REFERENCES

The Australian, Black Enterprise, BRW, Charleston Gazette, Chicago Tribune, Chief Executive Magazine, Daily Telegraph, Entertainment Law Reporter, Forbes, Fortune, The Guardian, Inc, The Independent, Life, Los Angeles Times, The Nation, Newsday, Newsweek, Observer, Oprah Winfrey Show, Ottawa Citizen, Philadelphia Daily News, Success, Sunday Mail, Time, Toronto Star, USA Today

Sean Combs

"I wanted to make some good of my life."

B EST KNOWN AS A RAP ARTIST, RECORD PRODUCER, AND THE one-time boyfriend of actress Jennifer Lopez, Sean "Puffy" Combs does not, at first, appear to have much in common with Martha Stewart and Ralph Lauren—yet he once said he considered them his role models, at least in business.

For behind his streetwise façade, Combs, variously known as Puff Daddy, P. Diddy, and Diddy, is a hard-working businessman who has skillfully repackaged black urban culture for consumption in suburban malls, much as Stewart and Lauren did with their aspirational visions of upper-class America.

Initially successful in the music industry with his record label Bad Boy, in 1998 Combs launched the fashion brand Sean John. Revenues of his Bad Boy entertainment group, which today encompasses a restaurant chain, movie production, and an advertising company called Blue Flame, grew from an estimated $30 million in 1999 to $300 million today. Unlike rival clothing labels that leveraged hip-hop culture, Sean John has grown from the clichéd street-style T-shirts and baggy jeans into a sophisticated, tailored menswear label that shows its latest collections on high-fashion runways.

Combs was born in Harlem, New York, in 1970. From the age of two he was raised by his mother, Janice, after his father, Melvyn, a limousine driver, was shot dead in his car in Central Park in a drug-related incident. It was not the stereotypical life in the ghetto, though; Janice worked three jobs to give Combs and his sister Keisha a respectable lifestyle in aspirational Mount Vernon. "I wasn't going to allow myself to become homeless," she says. "I wasn't going to be on welfare, even if I had to work all day and all night. I wanted to be able to take my kids to plays and out to dinner. I wanted to be able to buy them decent school uniforms. I always used to emphasize the importance of education."

At twelve, Combs was inspired by a Martin Luther King Jr. speech. "I really wanted to make some good of my life," he said. "I wanted to make some history."

When Combs was thirteen he enrolled at Mount St. Michael's Academy, a private Catholic boys' school in the Bronx, and began to demonstrate an entrepreneurial flair, subcontracting out paper rounds to other children. Combs graduated and won a place at Howard University in Washington DC to study business management. He was more interested in the practice than the theory, though, and he reportedly made money running a shuttle service between the airport and the campus. Then, attracted by the burgeoning hip-hop music movement, he started organizing and promoting house parties.

Much to his mother's disappointment, Combs dropped out of school altogether to work at Uptown Records as an unpaid intern. He soon demonstrated an eye for talent, discovering such artists as Mary J. Blige, and at the age of nineteen was promoted by Uptown's owner, Andre Harrell, to vice president of promotion.

In 1993, Combs left Uptown to run his own label, Bad Boy, and gathered together a stable of artists, the most successful of whom was former drug dealer Biggie Smalls, known as the Notorious B.I.G. Combs was also gaining a reputation as a producer, working with artists such as Mariah Carey and Aretha Franklin.

In 1996, Tupac Shakur, a successful rapper on a rival record label, was killed in a drive-by shooting. The following year, the Notorious B.I.G. was shot dead while he was with Combs, in what many believed was a revenge killing for the death of Shakur. In response, Combs released an album of his own, *No Way Out*, which featured a song recorded with B.I.G.'s widow, Faith Evans. The track, "I'll Be Missing You," was criticized by rap aficionados for its reliance on a sample from The Police's "Every Breath You Take" but it became a number-one hit around the world. The album sold seven million copies. The posthumously released Biggie Smalls album, *Life After Death*, sold ten million copies.

In 1998, Combs bought a New York townhouse for $12 million; the following year, at age twenty-eight, Combs was included on the *Forbes* list of top 100 celebrities. Now a wealthy international celebrity, a position cemented by his relationship with the actress and singer Jennifer Lopez, Combs expanded his businesses into marketing, restaurants, and fashion. Yet he flirted with disaster. In 1999, he was arrested for allegedly beating a rival record company executive with a champagne bottle, but escaped with a fine and a day-long anger management course. Later that year, he and Lopez were arrested on much more serious charges after a shooting at a New York nightclub that left three people wounded. Combs went to trial in 2001 on charges of gun possession and bribery, which could have resulted in a fifteen-year jail term. After seven weeks of hearings, he was acquitted. Lopez and Combs parted company. The soft-spoken Combs later told the *New York Times* that his gangster persona was just an act.

Despite speculation the trial would damage his businesses, Combs survived relatively intact and today is responsible for a mini-empire with some six hundred employees, encompassing restaurants, advertising, marketing, and fashion, with 2004 revenue for the group estimated at $300 million. In 2005, he struck a deal with MTV to produce shows; the same year he announced a new scheme to sell music wirelessly via mobile phone downloads.

His personal ambitions extend beyond business. He ran the New York Marathon in 2003 and in 2004 starred in the Broadway musical *A Raisin in the Sun*. His personal income was such that he could afford to spend $350,000 turning a cargo van into a mobile office equipped with six plasma TVs, a wine cellar, and a handmade leather couch. In April 2005 a court ordered him to pay $21,000 a month in child support to an old girlfriend, celebrity stylist Misa Hylton-Brim, who has custody of Combs's eleven-year-old son Justin (after whom Combs named his restaurants).

Bad Boy records has experienced something of a downturn since the extraordinary sales of 1997, but Combs has had surprising success with his fashion label. Initially seen as a vanity venture, Sean John swiftly evolved from street-influenced casual wear into sophisticated menswear reminiscent of jazz-era Harlem, and broke into department stores across America. The Sean John collections occasionally lapsed into the flashy style popularized by rappers known as "ghetto chic," with a fondness for fur, but that only added a little big-city edginess to a range that was otherwise eminently wearable by thirty-something suburbanites.

Combs was even embraced by the likes of *Vogue* editor Anna Wintour, who enthused: "Puffy is so wonderfully over-the-top and flamboyant and, God, do we need that in our business."

NOTES

"I wasn't going . . ." Williams, Precious. "Who's a Mummy's Boy," *Mail on Sunday*, 2.16.03, p. 39.

"I really wanted to . . ." DeLuca, Dan. "The Black Sinatra," *The Philadelphia Inquirer*, 8.24.99.

"Puffy is so wonderfully . . ." Specter, Michael. "I am Fashion, Guess Who Puff Daddy Wants to Be?" *The New Yorker*, 11.9.02, p. 117.

REFERENCES

Black Enterprise, Chain Leader, Charlotte Observer, CNN *Daybreak, Crain's New York Business, Ebony, Hollywood Reporter, Houston Chronicle, New York Times, New Yorker, Newsweek, Observer, Ottawa Citizen, Philadelphia Inquirer, Pittsburgh Post-Gazette, Seattle Times, Sunday Telegraph, Sunday Telegraph* (Sydney Australia), *The Record* (Bergen County), *Vancouver Province*

Richard Branson

Hyperactivity helps

THERE HAVE BEEN ALL SORTS OF THINGS SAID ABOUT THIS lanky, ever-youthful man. He is greatly admired as Britain's most famous entrepreneur and equally loathed for his brassy, obstinate, underdog approach to business. No one could argue, though, about his survival skills, whether he finds himself in a business cash crisis, or ballooning in the jet stream at 180 mph without enough fuel tanks. "My interest in life comes from setting myself huge, apparently unachievable tasks and trying to rise above them," he says.

Born in 1950 in Blackheath, London, Branson excelled in athletics at school but was mildly dyslexic and struggled academically. "Who cared if I couldn't spell," was his attitude—until a knee injury took away that chance to be a sports star. He was relegated to spending much of his time in the library where he began to dream up business ideas (and write saucy tales of the sexual conquests of a guy with a knee injury).

Branson's first schemes, selling Christmas trees and budgerigars, failed. But then he came up with an idea that worked. While still struggling at school, Branson devised *Student* magazine. It was the 1960s, a time of heightened student awareness. In 1967, from the phone booth near his school, he sold enough advertising space to publish the first issue. He would have the phone operator connect him to potential clients, making it appear as if he had a secretary. He finished school and went to London, and the magazine became a hit, attracting cool interviews (Mick Jagger), contributors (James Baldwin), and cutting-edge illustrators and photographers. At the time Branson's headmaster predicted that he would either go to prison or become a millionaire.

Branson says he became an entrepreneur by default, out of a need to earn enough money to keep *Student* afloat. The seed capital from his mother, the princely sum of $7, had been used up. From his London squat-style headquarters, Branson hatched a plan to sell discount records via mail order through *Student*, spotting a potentially lucrative market in the music-mad youth of England. The venture was christened Virgin Mail Order, because it was to be run by "complete virgins at business," and the brand was born. Orders poured in and the record business started to look a lot more attractive than the magazine trade. At age twenty-one, he was arrested and briefly jailed for exporting records without paying purchase taxes. A deal was made with British Customs and no charges were laid but the experience was a sobering one.

The first Virgin record store followed soon after in 1971 in Oxford Street, London. Then a Virgin recording studio was built in Oxfordshire, and Virgin Records was launched in 1973. Over the next two decades, the label signed artists including Mike Oldfield (who made Branson his first million by recording "Tubular Bells"), the Sex Pistols, Phil Collins, Boy George, and Janet Jackson.

Throughout his career, Branson has always sought out more opportunities for Virgin to expand (and for him to dress up as a god, pilot, gal, etc.), particularly in areas where other businesses were seen as "fat and cosy"—areas where Virgin could move in and start discounting. Today there are an estimated 250 companies under the Virgin brand and they generate more than $8 billion in revenue annually. Mostly privately owned, the ventures include mobile phones, airlines, financial services, a modeling agency, wedding service, wine, cosmetics, cola, and music megastores. Branson works closely with seven lieutenants, at least one of whom sits on the board of each of Virgin's ventures. He has more than three hundred managing directors within the group and has fostered an internal promotions ethos. *Forbes* magazine has described Branson as a kind of venture capitalist, using funds from his existing companies to build new ones, taking advantage of the Virgin brand to kick-start the ventures.

Shoestring budgets are part and parcel of Virgin start-ups. Stinginess has often been a matter of survival. Branson says his only real extravagance is bringing his friends with him on holidays—up to two hundred at a time. To keep Virgin afloat, Branson has often had to sell off percentages of various Virgin businesses to keep the banker wolves from the door. Branson calls these experiences "close shaves." To hedge this risk, he has split up the businesses into largely separate entities so that if one fails it does not impact on other concerns.

A pattern of always looking ahead for new opportunities, while keeping existing businesses ticking over, has become a Virgin signature. "The most critical thing with any new venture is we must deliver a tremendous value to the consumer so that it enhances all the ventures we've done before," Branson says in his autobiography, *Losing My Virginity*.

Branson has never been one to walk past an opportunity. When an American lawyer came to him with the notion of starting a new airline in 1984, Branson's eyes lit up. His decision to set up Virgin Airlines has proved to be his riskiest and most lucrative business decision.

Branson is known to work from a hammock or a big, comfy chair—rarely from a desk. He keeps notes in little black diaries or on the back of his hand, rarely carries cash, is notorious for borrowing other people's mobile phones, and does not use computers. His assistants do his emailing for him. He calls people. He meets people. He usually works from home, which, depending on the time of year, could be Necker Island, Majorca, a South African game reserve, London, or Oxfordshire. "I don't think of work as work and play as play. It's all living."

Branson's glossy, entertaining autobiography is testimony to the Branson way. After a "close shave," he simply picks up the phone and gets to work again, walks away from the debris of a wrecked balloon, a failed business deal, a strained business relationship and gets on with it. The book paints the picture of a man with ridiculous drive, ambition, a love of risk, and a hunger to survive in business no matter how many banks are chasing him. Branson was knighted in 2000, the same year Virgin Mobile was launched and he lost the bid for the British National Lottery.

The telecommunications sector is now seen as the cash cow of the company with Branson having a 50 percent stake in Virgin Mobile in the U.S. (Sprint owns the other 50 percent). To keep things interesting, Branson is planning to launch a sub-orbital space travel business under the Virgin brand.

Today, Virgin employs more than 35,000 people in fifteen countries; annual turnover for the group is an estimated $8 billion, and Branson's personal fortune is an estimated $5.2 billion, kept in a labyrinth of offshore family trusts. He has two children and is still married to his second wife, despite quipping in *Esquire* magazine when asked his thoughts on monogamy, "What's that?" Despite his heavy media exposure and over-the-top promotions (television appearances with near-naked models painted as his Virgin credit card), his so-called accessibility and relaxed bedside manner, Branson remains an enigma, often slightly ill at ease in one-on-one interviews.

The great challenge for Branson, as he continues to expand, is to ensure that the Virgin brand keeps its customer focus. When he started out Branson always had his eye on enticing those customers. He says he used to count pedestrians passing by potential Virgin Music store sites to make sure there was enough passing trade. Branson had a natural instinct for finding customers, and he still does.

His life is now being made into a Miramax film with Branson pleased that Hollywood's leading men, including Brad Pitt, are up for the part. The movie will no doubt include footage of Branson doing deals on three continents from his hammock on his private island in the Caribbean (where, like everyone else, he pays $25,000 a day for the privilege). "Sometimes I do wake up in the morning and feel like I've just had the most incredible dream. I've just dreamt my life."

NOTES

"My interest in life . . ." Fussman, Carl. "Richard Branson," *Esquire*, 1.02.
"Complete virgins . . ." Branson, Richard. *Losing My Virginity*. Virgin Books, 1998.
"The most critical thing . . ." Branson, Richard. *Losing My Virginity*. Virgin Books, 1998.
"I don't think of work . . ." Morris, Betsy and Patricia Neering. "What a Life," *Fortune*, 10.6.03, p. 50.

REFERENCES

The Age, Australian Financial Review, BusinessWeek, Daily Mail, Daily Telegraph, The Economist, Evening Standard, Fast Company, Forbes, Fortune, The Guardian, Independent on Sunday, JohnShepler.com, *Management Today, The Observer, Sunday Business, Sunday Herald Sun, The Times*

Taschen

Trust your instincts, however bizarre

———

FINE ART. CHEAP HOTELS. CONTEMPORARY DESIGN. SUBVERSIVE sexuality. These are just some of the eclectic personal interests Benedikt Taschen has turned into a worldwide publishing empire with annual sales estimated at $100 million.

Taschen lives in the Los Angeles hills but was born in Cologne, Germany in 1961. He is one of those lucky people who always knew what he wanted to do—and what he wanted to do turned out to have enormous commercial potential. The key to his success appears to be his ability to make decisions, combined with a self-assured, if unorthodox, working style: he rises at noon and doesn't work long hours, but tries to be as effective as possible when he is in the office.

Taschen first dabbled in his chosen profession at age eight, when he set up a booth on the fringes of an art market to sell drawings he had made of vampires, netting a healthy $490. By thirteen, he had a mail-order business trading comic books. "You always come to the question where you have to decide whether to sell or collect," he recalls, "so I stopped collecting and became a dealer." At eighteen, he opened his own comic book shop in Cologne, helped by funding from his parents, both doctors.

Publishing followed: his first effort was a comic book called *Sally Forth*, whose cover featured a naked blonde surrounded by gnomes with bulging eyeballs. Then, in 1984, he played a hunch, borrowing money from his family to buy up 40,000 remaindered copies of an English-language book on the artist René Magritte, selling them for double the price back in Cologne. There was, Taschen had discovered, enormous demand for high-quality art books from the general public—the problem was most publishers printed them in small numbers and charged the earth for them.

Not Taschen, who entered fine art publishing with a book of Annie Leibovitz photographs, followed by a book on Salvador Dali that he sent to bookstores accompanied by a poster that depicted the artist looking shocked under the words: "A genius like me for only $6.99?"

His business methods were straightforward but totally unconventional. Unlike other publishers, he insisted on retaining the rights to all his publications, wherever they were printed and sold. He negotiated large upfront payments to contributors in lieu of the usual ongoing royalties and he refused to allow bookstores to return unsold books (if they ended up in bargain basements, he didn't care).

"What we always wanted to do was to make the books accessible and available and affordable for everyone who was interested," he said.

In 1993—now ensconced in a beautiful converted mansion in Cologne—Taschen ran an advertisement in the trade magazine *Publishers Weekly* that showed him fully dressed next to his former wife, Angelika, in the nude, with the words "Luxury for less." It caused a scandal in the staid world of books—which, of course, was the point. A book on Hitler's documentary-maker, Leni Riefenstahl, caused another stir.

Not all of Taschen's books are necessarily cheap or provocative, though: 2004's homage to Muhammad Ali was not only the heaviest book printed in living memory, but it cost $3,000 or $7,500 (depending on the edition), trumping the previous record-holder for price, an enormous monograph on the photographer Helmut Newton that came with its own coffee table for $1,500 (*Sumo*, now selling for $5,000)—another Taschen publication, naturally. Both sold well, proving Taschen could not only dominate the cheap end of the market, but the top too.

Today, with some fifteen million books sold annually, he has the means to indulge his passions, which include fogskin shoes, a French bulldog named Souci, and midcentury architecture. "I was very lucky," he says, "because I was able to make a living out of something I wanted to do anyhow."

NOTES

"**You always come . . .**" Feay, Suzi. "Publish and be Damned Rude," *The Independent, Sunday Review*, 10.29.95, p. 4.

"**What we always . . .**" Bernhard, Brendan. "Sex and Beauty, Art and Kitsch," *LA Weekly*, 9.13.02, p. 24.

"**I was very lucky . . .**" Tzortzis, Andreas. "Inspired and Made Rich by Art," *International Herald Tribune*, 10.24.05, Finance, p. 10.

REFERENCES

ABC, *Advertising Age, Business Week, Daily News Record, Daily Telegraph* (Sydney), *Evening Standard, Forbes, Fortune, Gap, The Guardian, The Independent, Interior Design, LA Weekly, Los Angeles Times, New York Times, The Observer, Publishers Weekly, San Francisco Chronicle, Sunday Age, Sunday Times, Time, The Times, WWD*

Danni Ashe

Beware the "geek with large breasts"

L IKE MANY ENTREPRENEURS, DANNI ASHE REALIZED EARLY IN her career she was never going to make much money selling her product to one customer at a time. Especially as that product was herself, a stripper paid by the hour.

The solution was the Internet: a way to sell herself to thousands of men simultaneously. In 1994, Ashe launched a website called Danni's Hard Drive and became one of the few women in the sex industry to head their own business.

The key to her success, though, was not starting a porn site— even in the early days of the Internet, pornography was every- where—but in grasping new technology that made her a pioneer in the Internet community at large. Today much of Ashe's business comes from consulting with straightlaced firms on streaming video, credit card security, and Internet marketing—technologies perfected by pornography companies.

Ashe, the daughter of a fireman and a real estate agent who later sold religious novelties on the Internet, started stripping at seven- teen, reportedly lured into the industry when two friends took jobs at a pole-dancing club in Seattle, where Ashe grew up. Ashe had once wanted to be a vet, but matured early and grew to be a very well-developed teenager (she says her bra size is now 34FF). The butt of jokes at school, she unsurprisingly found herself in high demand in the clubs. Stripping led to magazine modeling and eventually a career as a "feature dancer," touring the country making advertised performances at clubs to draw in customers.

Ashe has spoken of the early days as a dancer as liberating her from the sexual taunts of high school, of boosting her self-esteem. But she has also hinted at unpleasant experiences, including an incident in Florida when she had a run-in with local police at a local club, which prompted her to quit live appearances in late 1994.

Somewhere along the line, Ashe discovered a love for computers, spent $8,000 on equipment, and taught herself website programming skills. "I'm a geek with large breasts," she laughingly told the PBS *Frontline* show in May 2001. "I was obsessed with the computer. I thought, 'I want to become a computer programmer.' It was like the proverbial light bulb going off." But she did not exactly end up coding for Microsoft. While surfing the Internet she came across Usenet newsgroups where she discovered there was a large unofficial trade in Danni Ashe images, taken from magazines and publicity shoots from her stripping career. Other women may have baulked at the discovery, but Ashe saw an opportunity: here was a readymade fan base.

She launched her first website in 1995, encouraging the men she came across on Usenet to visit it. Unlike many of the sites launched during the dot-com boom, it had an instant revenue stream: subscribers paid $19.95 to access a library of images and personal information about Ashe and, later, other women. She has said that within a week her site had clocked a million hits; by 1999 she boasted 25,000 subscribers. By 2001—the year Ashe claimed to have become the world's "most downloaded" woman with a billion downloads—she was employing forty-five people and was making around $8 million profit a year.

Ashe, which is not her real name, met her husband Bert, a film producer, while working at a club. They worked together to handle traffic on the site, often till 3:00 a.m. "I prefer not to reveal my real name," Ashe says. "First, I've spent a lot of years promoting the name Danni Ashe and see no point in confusing people with a new name. Second, by using a pseudonym, I don't have to worry about the occasional obsessed fan looking up my home phone number!"

Ashe knew from the start how hard it was to get people to spend money online, particularly using credit cards on porn sites. So she kept costs down and focused on making cash, rather than waiting for an independent public offering or a buy-out. (She has taken meetings with numerous large companies tempted by her audience, but, as she told PBS, they inevitably bow out. "Somebody on the board says, 'oh no, you don't,' and the deal is dead. It happens all the time.")

One innovation Ashe and other porn sites developed was cooperatively sharing traffic: potential customers leaving Ashe's site would find themselves directed to another site they might like better, and vice versa, the idea being that of every thousand visitors shuffled back and forth, a few would stick at your site and subscribe.

Ashe also worked at improving the customer experience, through more personal content, such as real biographies alongside the models' images, and homegrown technology, such as her own streaming video, called DanniVision, which worked independently of any subsidiary technology. Ashe also developed better backroom systems such as search engine manipulation to direct more browsers to her sites, and credit card "scrubbing," a method of ensuring security. By 2001, she was in demand as a technology consultant, speaking at seminars as far afield as Hong Kong and Sydney, Australia.

As the Internet exploded, so did the competition, especially from free, amateur sites and from sites that offered more explicit images. Yet Ashe has kept her site strictly "softcore," which means no depictions of actual sex—in line with her own boundaries as a performer. "Danni's always tries to separate itself as the sought-after place to work for the best models and is constantly striving to create value for our customers," Ashe says. "Danni's Hard Drive lets customers be comfortable in their own surroundings and always get a great intimate experience. I learned that through stripping: to be successful, you have to emotionally connect while you are fulfilling highly personal fantasies."

She also espouses a kind of folksy feminism, saying she offers her models good career paths and a sense of identity as women on the site, rather than simply as sex objects. "If I had to start Danni's Hard Drive again, I'd try to keep emotions more separate from business decisions," Ashe says, referring to a split with a friend who used to work at Danni's Hard Drive but left to start her own business. "We were great friends but I knew in my heart that (she) was so smart and ambitious that she'd eventually need to strike out on her own. But because I loved her and wanted her with Danni's Hard Drive, I encouraged her to stay on too long, and ultimately our relationship waned. After a few years had elapsed, however, I got to see what (she) was truly capable of when given the chance to expand her talents independently—and I was amazed. Our friendship strengthened again and we swapped notes on how to be successful in this business. Now we're back together and I couldn't be happier."

One can almost imagine Ashe, in another life, ferociously selling Tupperware or starting a cookie business like Debbi Fields. But with her body, as she said in 2004, "I became a sexual object whether I wanted to be or not—I turned lemons into lemonade."

NOTES

"I'm a geek with large breasts . . ." PBS, *American Porn*, 2.7.02.
"Somebody on the board says . . ." PBS, *American Porn*, 2.7.02.
"I became a sexual object . . ." Nauman, Zoe. "Miss Hit," *Sunday Mirror*, 1.18.04, p. 38.

REFERENCES

The Australian, Charlotte Observer, Financial Times, The Guardian, Hollywood Reporter, Los Angeles New Times, New Media Age, Newsweek, PBS *Frontline, San Francisco Chronicle, San-Antonio Express-News, Sunday Mirror, USA Today, Variety*

I WANT TO BE ALONE: THE GRETA GARBOS OF BUSINESS

Oakley

Never stop innovating

J IM JANNARD WAS MEANT TO FOLLOW THE FAMILY TRADITION AND become a pharmacist. Instead, he created a billion-dollar company named after one of his dogs, Oakley. Oakley is now one of the biggest eyewear brands in the world, sold in seventy countries, and it employs 2,100. Oakleys are worn by soldiers, athletes, tough guys, and plenty of soft middle-aged ones (hence the huge sales figures). The company is now valued at $1 billion. It produces eyewear, shoes, accessories, clothing, and sports equipment.

Oakley takes the business of sunglasses very seriously. The hub of the company is the 500,000-square-foot, $40 million, fortress-like headquarters in Foothill Ranch, California, which *Fast Company* magazine likens to a bomb shelter. The reception area includes B-52 bomber ejector seats and a life-sized torpedo. The interior perfectly reflects the siege mentality of the brand: mess with us, steal our designs, dampen our sales, and we'll use everything we've got to take you on. Company advertising refers to sunglasses as "optical armor." The *Los Angeles Times* describes the company's sunglasses pitch as "a gated community for the eyes." Oakley has created sunglasses with bulletproof lenses, others worn by U.S. troops in Iraq offer laser protection, other frames come with eight different lenses for use in differing light conditions, and some frames are made from the same titanium as fighter aircraft.

Jannard, who still owns 63 percent of the company, is a secretive, elusive billionaire. He likes to play up his mad scientist persona and once turned up to a store opening wearing a gas mask. He is rarely photographed. This protective style extends to the patented designs of Oakley sunglasses. The company has sued major competitors Nike and Luxottica for allegedly stealing their designs.

Born in 1950, Jannard grew up in a family of pharmacists. Friends recall how he loved playing out Trojan war games and, with his fierce competitive streak, was fascinated with the aerodynamics of Frisbees. He studied hard so he could always beat his opponents with bizarre twists and turns of his Frisbee throws (a strategy he continues to use in business today).

Jannard dropped out of college, bummed around on his motorcycle for a time, and then began selling car and motorcycle parts in his home state of California. With a keen interest in motocross, Jannard, who always loved to invent things, came up with a motocross handlebar grip in 1975 that was perfectly shaped to fit the hand. Jannard's grip was four times more expensive than the plastic varieties available, but it was made of a tactile, flexible molding that was much more effective for the riders. Jannard would give these new grips to top riders to try out at races. They were well received, but the world-at-large did not notice Jannard's new product as riders' hands covered them as they raced. Jannard set his sights on an invention that would give his designs better exposure, in 1980 coming up with a pair of goggles with his "O" Oakley symbol prominently displayed. In 1984, he released the first Oakley sunglasses, with the signature wraparound look to fit the contours of the eyes.

Jannard had picked the perfect time to take on the sunglass market. In the 1980s, eyewear was becoming a serious growth area, with the market for $30-plus sunglasses just emerging, influenced by Tom Cruise's Ray Ban-wearing dance in *Risky Business* and *The Blues Brothers*.

Rather than courting movie stars, Oakley targeted cutting-edge athletes to promote his eyewear, realizing that this type of sponsorship was critical to build sales. Athletes including Michael Jordan (who sat on the board of the company for a period) and Lance Armstrong would become Oakley's stellar ambassadors.

Oakley sunglasses have continued to evolve. At the company headquarters, design teams spend months, even years, developing new eyewear technology. In addition to research and development, the headquarters also houses much of the company's manufacturing facilities (although footwear is now made in South Korea, after an expensive, disastrous attempt to produce shoes in the United States). Jannard has orchestrated the company so that there is a fast turnaround of each design once it has been perfected.

The company has always had to ride through peaks and troughs due to such variables as bad weather (fewer pairs of sunglasses sell when it is cloudy), economic slowdown, or a season of lackluster new products. In 1995, the company went public. Four years later, Jannard stepped down as chief executive, giving the top job to a former Gatorade executive, William Schmidt, who lasted less than six months in the role before Jannard came back to the helm. The company has survived board and senior executive reshuffles, downsizing, fights with key distributors, growth spurts, profit downgrades, and lawsuits, but sales are currently strong.

"In Oakley's twenty-seven-year history, I've learned that the best way to manage a company through difficult economic periods is to focus on the things we do best and position ourselves for the eventual recovery," said Jannard in 2002. His return to the top post has coincided with record sales for the company and the introduction of the world's first sunglasses with MP3 playing capabilities (Oakley Thump) and Oakley RazrWire sunglasses, which in conjunction with Motorola, feature a receiver with Bluetooth technology allowing the wearer to make cell-phone calls within close proximity to their mobile phone. But is Oakley too reliant on Jannard, who owns such a large slab of the company? After stepping down once to spend more time fishing on San Juan Island off Washington State, only to return to resume control, it is unlikely Jannard will be giving up his fight in the near future.

NOTES

"In Oakley's twenty-seven . . ." *Business Wire*, "Oakley Achieves Record Fourth Quarter and Full Year Sales in 2002," 2.12.03.

REFERENCES

BusinessWeek, CBS *Market Watch* , *Fast Company*, *FD Wire*, *Los Angeles Times*, *Newsweek*, *New York Times*, Oakley.com, *Orange County Register*, *San Francisco Chronicle*, *Seattle Weekly*, *Sunday Times*, *Vancouver Sun*, *Weekend Australian*, *Women's Wear Daily*

Revlon

No one said the beauty business was a pretty place to work

CHARLES REVSON, THE MAN CREDITED WITH DESCRIBING HIS trade as selling "hope in a jar," was the thorn in the side of Helena Rubinstein and Elizabeth Arden, the two pioneers of the modern-day beauty business: an industry today worth an excess of $10 billion. Before young Revson came along, these glamorous entrepreneurs reigned supreme with their beauty creams and salon treatments, but the Revlon brand changed the beauty landscape forever, adding new levels of sophistication to product development, marketing, advertising, and all-important brand strategy. Charles Revson, whom Rubinstein referred to as "that nail man," was a master at selling the beauty myth to women around the world and selling inexpensive-to-produce products at huge mark-ups.

In 1932, Revson was twenty-five years old, with a canny eye for color and a background in sales for a fabric and a manicure product company. He wanted to run his own business, and, at possibly the worst time in the twentieth century, Revson had the nerve to step out on his own. He started his manicure product business just before the Great Depression struck. He began selling a nail enamel made with pigments instead of dyes, which meant he had a much broader range of colors to market than the competition.

The Revlon Nail Enamel Company was a partnership between Revson, his brother Joseph Revson, and Charles Lachman. It's generally acknowledged that Charles Revson was the brains and brilliance behind Revlon's success, with the others just coming along for the ride. In 1939, a Revlon advertisement referred to Charles as the "spark plug" for the business. Charles Lachman did little more than add the "L" to the Revlon brand name and reclusive Joseph Revson sold his share in the business in 1955 to Charles and proceeded to live his life as a hermit.

Revson and his partners had just $300, no lines of credit, and no backers. Yet the company had something new for the women of the world that they didn't know they wanted yet—opaque nail enamel. At the time, polish was worn only by prostitutes; but Revson wanted to change all that and make it an essential fashion item.

Funds were desperately short in the early days and Revson relied on pawnbrokers to keep the business afloat, often paying 2 percent a month in interest. By 1933, sales were more than $11,000 with a modest profit of around $2,800 (not bad for Depression times). He began a series of ads promoting his glamorous product, making links to society women through his advertising copy. In 1939, Revlon introduced lipstick when he realized that there should be matching lips and fingertips available. By 1940, sales had increased to $2.8 million.

Revlon created not just a product, but a fantasy of an impossibly glamorous woman who wore Sun Rose on her nails and transcended the everyday. Perceptions of who wore nail polish were changed by Revson's advertising juggernaut. Revlon upped the stakes in its advertising campaigns and charged five times the price of other nail enamels for the privilege.

There are conflicting stories as to how Revson developed the nail enamel that would make the company viable. In her book *War Paint*, author Lindy Woodhead attributes the product to a man known simply as "Perrera," who would give manicures to society ladies in Venice, including the future *Vogue* editor Diana Vreeland, who took the polish back to New York and showed her manicurist, who happened to be dating Charles Revson.

Revlon's version of the opaque nail enamel was far from perfect in its early stages. Sometimes it would turn yellow, it took too long to dry, and did not last long. In an effort to improve his cornerstone product, Revson was indefatigable about personally following up all complaints and trying to iron out quality control problems. He also oversaw all aspects of product development.

Revson was also hands-on at cultivating his sales network of wholesale distributors and salons and department stores. He spread word-of-mouth about the nail enamel through beauty salons with the "ask your manicurist" tag line on many advertisements, thus giving it a sense of exclusivity.

With increasing competition in the marketplace, things got dirty. Revlon sales representatives were known to hide competitors' stock, offer "sell-up" bonuses to manicurists who sold Revlon product, and sabotage other firms' point-of-sale material. Revson tapped his staff's phones, eavesdropped on his competitors, and cultivated a culture of encouraging anything to beat off competitors (down to unscrewing tops of other nail polishes so they would dry out in the stores).

Revson drove his advertising agencies mad with his demands and copy rewrites. *Time* magazine describes Revson as a man who "simply worked too hard for the ad men to keep up." He went through account executives at a rate of knots. One of his former executives recalls Charles justifying his behavior: "Look kiddie, I built this business by being a bastard. I run it by being a bastard. I'll always be a bastard, and don't you ever try to change me."

Revson was notorious for holding impossibly long meetings, said to be because he was a lonely man. He was a hypochondriac known for his obsessive low-fat diets. He reportedly had his blood pressure measured in meetings, blaming his staff if it rose. Harvard Business School professor Richard S. Tedlow comments in his book *Giants of Enterprise* that Revlon was a malevolent dictatorship. "Every precept taught in America's business schools, every practice employed by its most admired companies, was violated by Revson," he says.

Revlon's 1952 "Fire and Ice" campaign is seen as pivotal in the history of cosmetics advertising. The Fire and Ice woman was awash with sexy contradictions and caused a sensation, with the advertisement asking American women a list of risqué questions ("Have you ever danced with your shoes off? Do you close your eyes when kissed?"). The campaign was backed up with heavy store display and point-of-sale promotion, and produced sales that blew competitors out of the water.

Following on from this marketing triumph, three years later, Revlon pushed cosmetics advertising into a new era with the sponsorship of the CBS top-rating program *The $64,000 Question*. Revlon purchased the show and paid for its production and prize money. The sponsorship equated to huge sales success for Revlon, recording increases of up to 500 percent with total turnover of $85 million. The program became caught up in scandal as the authenticity of the show and the contestants came under suspicion. Revlon was perceived to be vetting contestants, favoring attractive players and ultimately treating worthy winners unfairly. There was an inquiry and the question of the relationship between the producer and the sponsor was put in the spotlight to find out whether the show was fixed. The network itself came out the innocent party, with the producers and sponsors taking the blame. Regardless of the result, Revlon's sponsorship had been a brilliant idea. Revlon was now a household name.

In the same year, Revlon went public, with the share price quickly rising from $12 to $30. Revson became a very wealthy man and led an extravagant life, owning the third-largest yacht in the world at the time—so large that it would stretch a full city block. He also ended up buying his nemesis Helena Rubinstein's New York apartment after her death.

When Revson died on August 24, 1975, his company was valued at $988 million—not quite a billion, but a nice try. The mass-market company is now controlled by Ron Perelman, who bought the company in a leveraged buyout in 1985. The past two decades have been tough for Revlon: job losses, mergers, acquisitions, sell-offs, debt problems and stiff competition, but a range of new products and new executives have breathed life into the company. In 2005, the company reported its first profitable quarter in six years with analysts tipping that the company has reversed its fortunes and is heading into a period of strong growth. About time, is what Revson would be thinking.

NOTES

"Look kiddie . . ." Tedlow, Richard S. *Giants of Enterprise: Seven Business Innovators and the Empires they Built.* HarperBusiness, 2003.

REFERENCES

Tobias, Andrew. *Fire and Ice: The Story of Charles Revson, the Man Who Built the Revlon Empire.* William Morrow, 1976.

Woodhead, Lindy. *War Paint, Madame Helena Rubenstein and Miss Elizabeth Arden, their Lives, Their Times, Their Rivalry.* John Wiley & Sons, 2004.

Associated Press, Australian, Brandweek, BusinessWeek, CNN, Cosmetics, Daily Telegraph, The Economist, Financial Times, The Guardian, Hoover's Company Records, *Inc, Independent on Sunday, Mail on Sunday, Marketing News, New York Times, The Observer, Palm Beach Post, San Francisco Chronicle, Toronto Star, Washington Post, Weekend, Women's Wear Daily*

Luxottica

Never underestimate the influence of *The Blues Brothers*

———————

Leonardo Del Vecchio is referred to by his competitors as the "god" of the eyewear industry. His $9.4 billion Luxottica empire is ten times larger than any other optical group. Known for his bespoke suits and reclusive, hardline nature, Del Vecchio is rated the forty-third-richest man in the world by *Forbes* with an estimated personal fortune of $8.5 billion.

Born in 1935, Del Vecchio never knew his father, who died five months before his birth. Little Leonardo, one of five children, was reluctantly given to nuns at a Milanese orphanage by his single mother when he was just seven. As a young boy, he earned pocket money working for a medal engraver and quickly developed an appetite for long hours. Today, even pushing seventy, Del Vecchio still clocks up fourteen-hour days. "Work always came before everything," he says. "If I'd started selling fruit, I'd be passionate about fruit."

Del Vecchio took a design course, supporting himself as a workshop apprentice throughout his studies, and in 1958 he set up his own business in a single-roomed factory in Milan. The staff of twelve etched glasses for the spectacle companies in Belluno, a region in northern Italy known for spectacle making. The following year, he was offered land in Belluno. He bought it and founded Luxottica. It was the beginning of what Italians refer to as the miracle of the northeast. The region now produces two-thirds of the world's eyewear.

Del Vecchio began to forge relationships with designers to produce upmarket eyewear. Luxottica's company-making deal came with a partnership with fashion designer Giorgio Armani in 1988. Until 2002, when Armani severed business ties, Armani accounted for 7 percent of Luxottica's wholesale sales. Del Vecchio has also been successful in attracting the business of Prada, Versace, Chanel, and Bulgari, but his company began its real ascent after Tom Cruise in *Top Gun* and John Belushi and Dan Ackroyd in *The Blues Brothers* inspired the western world to wear designer shades. Del Vecchio was more than happy to supply them.

Another key to growth was Del Vecchio's retail strategy. He started to directly distribute Luxottica eyewear in the United States in 1982 when he bought out his U.S. distributor. From there he proceeded to squeeze out competitors and create stores that mainly stocked Luxottica brands. The 1990s saw Luxottica float on the New York Stock Exchange and acquire LensCrafters and the eyewear division of Bausch & Lomb (which makes Ray Bans and Revo brands). In 2001, Luxottica acquired the retail chain Sunglass Hut, which operates 1,900 stores around the world. More recently, Luxottica announced a merger agreement with 1,200-store, U.S. operation Cole National. That U.S. acquisition takes Luxottica's controlling stake in the global eyewear market to 24 percent.

Del Vecchio's company is now churning out 28 million pairs of glasses each year. There are 36,900 employees working in six factories in Italy and one in China, and in more than 3,000 retail stores. In 2004, the company's sales were $4.5 billion.

Signor Del Vecchio, as he is known, has announced plans to increase senior managers' stakes in Luxottica and has appointed a chief executive as part of his succession plans for the business. The plan is very much in its early stages, says a company spokesperson, so he is not giving it all away just yet. He still owns 69 percent of the business and is Italy's second richest man behind Silvio Berlusconi.

NOTES
"Work always came . . ." Kroll, Luisa. "Tough guy," *Forbes*, 2.4.02.

REFERENCES
The Age, The Australian, Australian Financial Review, Boston Globe, BusinessWeek, The Guardian, Financial Times, Forbes, Fortune, La Repubblica, New York Times, Sunday Express, Sunday Times, Sydney Morning Herald, Washington Post, Women's Wear Daily

AH, THAT'S HOW YOU DO IT

eBay

The global yard sale

ONE LONG WEEKEND IN 1995, PIERRE OMIDYAR, A YOUNG French-Iranian computer programmer, sat down in his San Jose home office and created the website that would shortly make him one of the richest men on the planet, worth $9.9 billion in 2005. His idea was eBay, or, as it started out, AuctionWeb: a website where people could post things they had for sale and other people could bid for them.

Paris-born Omidyar grew up in Maryland after his father moved there to take up a urology residence at the Johns Hopkins University Medical Center. Pierre demonstrated an early interest in computers, at one point writing a program for his school library, earning $6 an hour. He studied computing at Tufts University and then worked at several firms, including General Magic, a developer of mobile computing devices. In his spare time, he navigated the emerging Internet, where he encountered bulletin boards where people advertised their stuff for sale. Omidyar decided to start a site called AuctionWeb where items were bought and sold by auction. This project would improve his programming skills, and hopefully the site would sell an old laser printer he didn't want anymore.

By today's standards, AuctionWeb looked plainer than the classifieds page of a newspaper. There was no budget for graphic design or marketing. Omidyar was actually worried about paying his $30 monthly Internet bill. But the site was free, and slowly, through word of mouth, the listings began to build.

By February 1996, there was so much traffic on AuctionWeb that Omidyar's Internet service provider started charging him a commercial rate of $250 a month. Omidyar decided the only way he could justify keeping the fledgling site going was to pass some of the cost on to its users, and he started levying a commission on sales. He feared that would be the end of the experiment, but, to his amazement, sellers were happy to pay it. Unlike 99 percent of start-ups, Omidyar had discovered a straightforward revenue stream that actually covered his costs. He also gave his business a name: Echo Bay Technology Group, chosen because it sounded cool, but the closest domain name he could register was eBay.com.

In late 1995, Omidyar decided he needed a partner. He chose a young Canadian called Jeff Skoll. Skoll, a computer engineer and Stanford MBA graduate, had several assets including a head for business and a large living room in nearby Palo Alto, which became AuctionWeb's head office. Skoll wrote the firm's first business plan and became its first president, then its vice president of strategic planning and analysis. By June 1996 (nine months after the launch), revenues had doubled for the fourth consecutive month, bringing in enough money for them to quit their day jobs. So many checks were piling up at the door that Omidyar had to hire some-body to open them, he later recalled.

In 1997, the site changed its name to eBay. When eBay went pub-lic in September 1998, it was valued at $2 billion. By July 1999 Omidyar was worth $10.1 billion. Skoll's share made him Canada's fifth-richest man and a subject of some hilarity when, worth $4.8 bil-lion in mid-1999, it was revealed he was still living in a student share house. (Still worth some $3.7 billion—and ranked Canada's third-richest man in 2003–2004—Skoll left eBay in 2001 to start a charita-ble foundation and is now dabbling in movies, making films with a social justice bent with a vehicle called Participant Productions.)

Why was eBay so successful? Omidyar instinctively (or inadver-tently) made several great decisions in the site's first few years of life. His decision to run auctions, not just allowing people to post items with "for sale" signs on them, was made out of a libertarian desire to create a level playing field, but it had an unexpected side effect: people became addicted to the competitive nature of bidding. His decision, out of necessity, to charge a commission rather than, say, hoping to gain cash from banner ads, meant eBay became one of the rare Internet businesses that actually made a profit from the outset. Omidyar also kept a realistic focus on costs—employees assembled their own desks and Omidyar bought discounted cubicles from a warehouse.

When users suggested improvements to the site, Omidyar introduced them immediately. When he became swamped by emails, he added a bulletin board to the site where users could help each other out. Then he added the feedback rating system, which tackled the fundamental problem of trust. How do you know the seller will send you what you've paid for? Omidyar believed people were basically good and would generally do the right thing. But to encourage people to stick to the right path, he introduced feedback ratings that allowed users to police each other. Miscreants attracted black marks that warned other users to avoid them. To Omidyar's surprise, though, most feedback was enormously positive—people felt good about giving praise where it was due.

By encouraging eBay's users to manage their own affairs, Omidyar reduced the time he had to spend running the site and, later, the number of people he had to hire. It also fostered a sense of community that persisted as the site grew from the equivalent of a small village to the largest city in the world. Once the mechanics were in place, growth was exponential. As anybody who has devoted a few hours to browsing the site has discovered, eBay is addictive, combining the thrill of bargain hunting in the world's biggest yard sale with the frisson of auctions. "Where eBay departs the traditional pleasure of a flea market, though, is its sheer scale and its searchability," wrote author William Gibson, who became obsessed with eBay's watch auctions. "If you can think of a thing, you can search it on eBay. And, very probably, you can find it."

One of the best-known myths about eBay is that it was set up by Omidyar to help his girlfriend, Pam, sell her Pez dispensers. The press loved its rags-to-riches quirkiness, and, in 1998, hundreds of papers, including the *Wall Street Journal*, repeated the story, which was actually fabricated by a PR person, who admitted she used it to make eBay more interesting to reporters. (The story circulated now is that Omidyar used the embryonic eBay to sell an old laser printer, which sounds dull enough to be true.)

In mid-1997, Benchmark Capital, a venture capital firm, invested $5 million, which brought eBay a color website and a professional management team. In March 1998, Omidyar recruited Hasbro marketing executive Meg Whitman to become eBay's CEO. eBay was still a small start-up, but Whitman, a career manager with an economics degree from Princeton and an MBA from Harvard, had "an instinct that this could be big," as she told Oprah Winfrey in 2003. Others hadn't always seen the potential. In 2000, eBay had courted AOL and Yahoo over possibly selling them the business; both parties demurred. With a strong focus on cost management still alien to most Internet start-ups, Whitman took eBay public, growing the business from net income of $7.2 million in 1998 to $778 million in 2004, with 8,100 employees.

Along the way, she earned stock options that have made her a billionaire in her own right. In 2005 *Fortune* named her the most powerful woman in business. Omidyar stepped down from the day-to-day running of eBay in 1998. Today, he sits on the board of the Internet community classified website Craigslist, drives a Mini Cooper, and has pledged to give away most of his eBay billions through a foundation called the Omidyar Network.

There are still millions of little traders on eBay, but to make real money eBay has always aimed at higher-priced items. eBay is now the country's leading seller of used cars; sales of cars and parts now turn over some $8.7 billion. In 2001, eBay allowed sellers to open virtual storefronts on the site: in less than two years 30,000 "shopkeepers" signed up. By 2004, some 150,000 small business-people earned their living buying and selling on eBay, running eBay "shops"; more than 430,000 small businesses in the USA trade on eBay. And big business is experimenting with this brand new virtual economy too: Intel, Continental Airlines, and Cadbury Schweppes are among a growing number of corporations experimenting with business, eBay-style. In 2002, Nissan auctioned the first of its new 350Z sports cars on the site, making three times the sticker price and generating much free publicity along the way. The site is hoping cross-promotions with bricks-and-mortar businesses will further legitimize the online auction system.

As it grew, eBay required more complex governance. In the early days, users could buy or sell anything. Items put up for auction have included a seventeen-year-old Miami high school student's virginity (eBay cancelled the auction after bad publicity); a lunch date with investment guru Warren Buffett (sold for $202,000), a human soul (sold for $1,325 in March 2000 to a New York real estate agent); a Russian space shuttle prototype with a starting bid of $500,000 (no bids); and, in 2004, half of a grilled cheese sandwich that resembled the Virgin Mary (sold for $28,000).

Today, morally difficult items including guns, pornography, counterfeit designer handbags, and pirated software are banned, and listings are routinely scanned for contraband. Omidyar likens it to running the government of a small state. In fact, if eBay's community were a country, it would be the eleventh most populous—with 100 million users, it is larger than Great Britain or Mexico.

Its biggest challenge now is to expand and grow revenue while retaining its traditional users. eBay is much more than an auction house, wrote Michael S. Malone, a *Forbes* editor-at-large and one of eBay's first shareholders. "Once you realize that it becomes obvious that crucial to the company's long-term success is the ability to cultivate and nurture that community." He added a warning: "If eBay ever stops listening to its community it will wither and die."

Pierre Omidyar agrees: "If we lose that," he said in 2001,"we've pretty much lost everything."

NOTES

"Where eBay departs . . ." Gibson, William. "My Obsession," *Wired*, 1.99.

"An instinct that . . ." Whitman, Meg. *The Oprah Winfrey Show*, BNO, 10.17.03.

"Once you realize . . ." Malone, Michael S. "The eBay Elixir: Can the Website Keep Up Its Success?" ABCNews.com, 7.30.03.

REFERENCES

Cohen, Adam. *The Perfect Store: Inside eBay*, Little, Brown, 2002.

ABCNews.com, *Business2.0*, *BusinessWeek*, *Chicago Tribune*, *Fast Company*, *Forbes*, *Fortune*, *New York Magazine*, *New York Times*, *Observer*, SiliconValley.com, *Wired*

Limited Brands

Bigger is not necessarily better, better is better

———————

LESLIE WEXNER, A LAW SCHOOL DROPOUT AND WANNABE architect from Columbus, Ohio, had the nerve to tell his father, who ran a women's clothing store, that he was running his business all wrong. Wexner junior figured this out by delving into his dad's accounts when he went on holiday. He was curious as to what garments sold well and what didn't, a simple question his father had never thought to ask. Dresses and coats were doing disastrously but when Leslie asked his father what he thought were the bestsellers, his dad said dresses and coats. Says Wexner: "They worked eighty-hour weeks to scratch out a living, but they never made $10,000 a year."

Wexner, born in 1937, was probably earning more money than they were at the time, by selling T-shirts at college and from a lucrative summer landscaping job. His father, a Russian immigrant, was not interested in a young upstart with little retailing experience telling him how to run his business. To prove his point, Wexner borrowed $5,000 from an aunt and $5,000 from the bank and started his own clothes store, Leslie's Limited, in 1963. He stocked particular casual separates (the ones that sold well in his dad's store). The process was so stressful for Wexner that he had developed an ulcer by the time he was twenty-six. But the worry was unnecessary: in the first year, the business was more profitable than his parents' store had ever been, with turnover of $160,000. Sales tripled in the second year of trading. By the third year, his parents had started working for him after his father's store went bankrupt. Today, Wexner's retailing business, Limited Brands, has 115,300 staff and more than 3,775 stores around the United States, with an annual turnover of $9.4 billion. Wexner has continued to cleverly target America's middle market, estimated to have a disposable income of $3.5 trillion. This demographic is so enamored with particular brands that they will pay 200 percent more for their products than they would for so-called lesser brands.

Wexner opened a second Limited store a year after the first. By 1969, he had six stores, and by 1976 he had one hundred stores. Wexner funded the next stage of growth through an Ohio-only float in 1969. Shares in his company would rise 4,000 percent in the next two decades, making many local millionaires in the process. Wexner opened hundreds of stores throughout the 1970s, also developing a network of offshore suppliers who worked quickly to get trendy clothes onto Wexner's racks as quickly as possible. (Hit brands included labels with Italian-sounding brand names, all made in Asia.)

One city targeted in the expansion of the company was San Francisco, where Wexner came across Victoria's Secret, a four-store failing lingerie chain that he thought had potential. Its owner, Roy Raymond, did not want to sell but called Wexner months later as he was about to go bankrupt. Despite having no experience in the lingerie business, Wexner bought Victoria's Secret for $1 million in 1982. "It was a business on a g-string," says Wexner. Now the business is valued at $3.5 billion and continues to enjoy double-digit growth, largely due to Wexner's premise: "Women need underwear, but they *want* lingerie. I like to be in the 'want' business. The margins are better than in the 'need' business."

This was the beginning of the next stage in the growth of Wexner's business, developing a family of brands with the help of capital from Limited Brand's IPO on the New York Stock Exchange in 1982. Wexner bought Lane Bryant, Lerner New York, upmarket department store Henri Bendel, men's fashion labels, and teenage fashion labels. He bought preppy label Abercrombie & Fitch in 1988, turning it into a must-have teenage casual brand.

By the early 1990s, after three decades of expansion, Wexner's business was getting out of hand. Wexner felt he was losing control. "Every day I was coming to work and felt as though it was a zoo. All the cages were open and the animals were running around." Wexner sought advice from General Electric's Jack Welch, who told him to look after his talented staff. Wexner also consulted Harvard Business School professor Leonard Schlesinger and PepsiCo's Wayne Calloway. The company was reorganized before it was too late. "Before I could change my business model, I needed to change from sole inventor to the leader, the teacher, the coach," says Wexner. "It was the darkest time, but also enlightening."

Despite his reputation as a one-man band, Wexner radically changed his business model, making an effort to simplify The Limited's business structure. The finance and design teams were centralized, the quality of goods was improved, more talent was hired, and performance review processes were implemented. The stable of brands was rationalized and cut back from twelve brands to five. The new criterion was simple: if it isn't going to be a $1 billion stand-alone business in the U.S. market, Limited Brands shouldn't be involved in it. Wexner developed personal care businesses Bath & Body Works and the White Barn Candle Company with this ethos in mind.

The business became spread equally over three markets—clothing, personal care, and lingerie. This meant risk was hedged between several segments of retailing. More than 1,500 stores that were not reaching their targets were closed, and others were downsized. Wexner also changed his tune on the value of advertising, setting about creating a more savvy, slick, expensive sales and marketing strategy for each brand, particularly Victoria's Secret. Its advertising budget jumped from $5 million to $85 million in a matter of years to include diamond-encrusted bras worn by supermodels and million-dollar fashion parades (that jam the Internet when they are broadcast live). More than 365 million Victoria's Secret catalogs are distributed annually. With this more glamorous image, Wexner has been able to triple the average price of a Victoria's Secret bra to $30. In more recent times, Wexner has stated that Limited Brands' future lies in underwear and beauty products. A decade ago beauty products were only 4 percent of the business; now they are 30 percent. Underwear was 25 percent; now it is 41 percent. Clothing has slipped from 71 percent to 29 percent. Limited has also continued to employ a string of powerful players in retailing to continually keep his brands at their peak.

Today, the Wexner family owns 17 percent of Limited Brands. Wexner has a grand home in Aspen and a private estate in Columbus complete with $20 million mansion and a 316-foot super yacht named "Limitless." Despite having a relatively young family (he didn't marry until he was fifty), Wexner is working harder than ever. Since a near-fatal skiing accident in the 1980s, Wexner has also been one of America's most prolific philanthropists, setting up the Wexner Heritage Foundation and donating generously to Jewish causes in particular. In his hometown he has the status of the city's second mayor. The only blemish on his career has been his role on the board of publisher Hollinger International. Wexner, along with all the directors of the company including Henry Kissinger, were accused of being "totally quiescent" during Lord Conrad Black's behavior as he treated company funds as his own to fuel his extravagant lifestyle. The board was ordered to pay $50 million to shareholders, the cost covered by insurance.

The boy who has shoveled snow, mowed lawns, run day camps, and babysat is still really only interested in the next big thing in retailing. His business is cashed up and ready to roll. The most pressing question is whether Wexner will remain in the clothing business or leave that behind for his more profitable ventures. He has never been one for taking too many chances. "I don't believe bigger is better," he says. "Better is better."

NOTES

"They worked eighty-hour . . ." *FSB*, "Les Wexner: Limited Brands," 9.03, p. 40.

"It was a business . . ." Silverstein, Michael and Neil Fiske. "Trading Up, The New American Luxury," *Portfolio*, 2003.

"Women need underwear . . ." *Forbes*, "Shopping with Leslie Wexner, D.M," 6.5.95, p. 131.

"Every day I was coming . . ." *FSB*, "Les Wexner: Limited Brands," 9.03, p. 40.

"Before I could . . ." *FSB*, "Les Wexner: Limited Brands," 9.03, p. 40.

"I don't believe . . ." Michaels, Ed, Helen Handfield-Jones and Beth Axelrod. *The War for Talent*. Harvard Business School Press, 2001.

REFERENCES

CNNFN, *Catalog Age*, *Fast Company*, *Forbes*, Hoover's Company Capsules, *National Post*, *New York Post*, *The New Yorker*, *Retail Week*, *The Times*, *Women's Wear Daily*

L'Oréal

Foster a "cow and calf" culture

————

CHEMIST EUGENE SCHUELLER INVENTED A FORMULA FOR synthetic hair dye in 1907 in the bedroom of his Paris flat at the request of a hairdresser who knew how many women were desperate to be blonde without causing injury to their scalps. Schueller used hydrogen peroxide in his product and called it Aureole ("halo" in French). After two years of further experiments, he left his day job as a chemist and established the French Harmless Hair Coloring Co. with 800 French francs ($210). In 1911, he renamed the company L'Oréal. The following year, his products began to sell around Europe, and through agents and consignments L'Oréal started to make sales in the United States, South America, Russia, and Asia. By 1920, demand was so strong Schueller had three chemists working for him. Today, the $51 billion company has more than 2,800 scientists registering more than 500 patents each year. L'Oréal had annual sales of $17 billion in 2004 and its products are now sold in 130 countries.

The company has only had four leaders since its inception in 1911 and has a reputation for its aversion to debt, to external advisers, investment banks, and lawyers. The L'Oréal coffers have grown considerably since the appointment in 1988 of Welshman Sir Lindsay Owen-Jones as group chief executive and chairman. He has overseen two decades of double-digit growth.

Owen-Jones has fostered what he calls a "cow and calf" culture at L'Oréal. By that he means the company has to invest in not-yet-profitable ventures, to take controlled risk and invest in research and development, and to ensure profits in the future. "A herd only exists in the long term if it is producing calves and only a small proportion of the herd actually produces the milk. And instead of letting the accountants whittle down the herd to only the part that makes all the money, you have to be constantly investing long term in things that don't already do that." To prove Owen-Jones' point, fourteen of L'Oréal's twenty brands account for 92 percent of sales.

Owen-Jones pushed L'Oréal's expansion in the United States and Asia and into the lucrative ethnic beauty sector. The L'Oréal portfolio now includes Lancôme, Maybelline New York, Redken, Helena Rubinstein, Ralph Lauren, and Giorgio Armani Perfumes. More than 50 percent of its annual sales are made outside Europe, where L'Oréal is looking for growth, particularly in China and Japan.

The company's scientists are busy trying to develop products such as anti-aging pills, shampoos to stop hair from going gray, and others to promote hair growth. This tradition of innovation is combined with an aggressive sales and marketing strategy (it spends an estimated 30 percent of its revenue on advertising) to retain and increase its slice of the global beauty industry, currently growing at an estimated 5 percent per annum. Owen-Jones says "running L'Oréal is like steering a tanker as if it were a speedboat." In 2006 he plans to pass on the chief executive role to Jean-Paul Agon.

Schueller died in 1957. His only child, Liliane Bettencourt, inherited the majority of his estate, and today the intensely private Madame Bettencourt is officially the richest woman in the world.

Now in her eighties, she has an estimated fortune of $17.2 billion with the largest stake in the L'Oréal empire (more than 25 percent). She keeps a low profile and has had to weather the scandal of her father being linked with extreme right-wing groups. (These alliances are seen by Liliane as errors of youth.) Bettencourt has only one child, a daughter, Françoise, who also sits on the L'Oréal board.

Bettencourt's family owns the majority stake in the business, followed closely by Nestlé with 26.4 percent. For thirty years the two interests had a holding company that controlled L'Oréal, but recently that has been dissolved. A new arrangement allows Nestlé the first rights to buy the company if the Bettencourts decide to sell. Both have agreed to keep their shares for five years, and neither party will increase their stake while Liliane Bettencourt is alive.

NOTES

"Cow and calf . . ." Nisse, Jason. "The Lowdown: The Science That Means L'Oréal's Success Is More Than Skin Deep," *Independent on Sunday*, 6.15.03, p. 5.
"Running L'Oréal . . ." Nisse, Jason. "The Lowdown: The Science That Means L'Oréal's Success Is More Than Skin Deep," *Independent on Sunday*, 6.15.03, p. 5.

REFERENCES

The Australian, BusinessWeek, CNN, *Daily Deal, The Economist, Financial Times, Forbes, The Guardian,* Hoover's Company Capsule, *The Independent, Sunday Express, Le Figaro, Management Today, New York Times, The Observer, San-Antonio Express-News, Scripps Howard News Service, The Times*

BlackBerry

A strange fruit indeed

THE BLACKBERRY IS SUCH A STRAIGHTFORWARD DEVICE IT'S incredible somebody didn't think of it sooner. An inexpensive little gadget the size of a personal organizer, it allows you to access your email anywhere, and send new emails using the clever little thumb-operated keyboard on the front. It's always connected to the network, so new emails arrive as effortlessly as they would on your office computer. Its simplicity is the key: you can check your emails discreetly, anywhere—even in meetings, where using a mobile phone would be impolite.

Bill Gates swears by his. Michael Dell carries his everywhere. David and Victoria Beckham wear theirs as fashion accessories. In November 2000, Al Gore was about to concede the election to George W. Bush when he received a message on his BlackBerry from his campaign manager telling him to hold off, there was still hope—the result dragged on for another month. In the UK, the speaker of the House of Commons was forced to ban BlackBerrying in the house, threatening to remove any member of Parliament caught in the act. And Oprah Winfrey declared hers had "literally changed my life" on the annual "My Favorite Things" episode of her show in 2003.

The telling thing about BlackBerry, though, is that it was developed by a Canadian company that nobody had heard of—most people still haven't—called Research in Motion, founded by the son of Greek immigrants in the small Canadian town of Waterloo.

Naysayers have assumed either a major competitor would swamp it with a copycat product, or that BlackBerry would fail to convince people of its usefulness. Yet to date none of the big companies such as Motorola, Treo, Nokia, or even Microsoft has been able to come up with a compellingly decent competitor. There are personal organizers and mobile phones that send emails—but none has had the userfriendliness of the BlackBerry, a feature that has made it so addictive to its subscribers it's been dubbed "CrackBerry."

Since its launch in 1999, BlackBerry has collected over three million subscribers worldwide—"six million thumbs and counting"—most of them signed up through their employers. As mobile telephone networks have improved their ability to transmit data, they have in turn promoted BlackBerry, which makes money for them. And as data transmission prices fall, BlackBerry could eventually become a mass-market phenomenon spurred on by celebrity recommendations.

Research in Motion's founder, Mike Lazaridis, reportedly built a record player from Lego when he was four, a radio when he was five, a personal computer from scratch in high school, and went on to study electrical engineering and computer science at Waterloo University in Ontario, Canada.

Lazaridis left the university during his final term in 1984 to start Research in Motion with his best friend and fellow ham radio enthusiast, Doug Fregin, after they won a $300,000 contract from General Motors to design and build an industrial display system that could display messages on assembly lines.

They worked on several computer-related projects, including a device that read the bar codes on movie film, which won the company an Oscar for technical achievement.

In 1987, Lazaridis was approached to write software for an early wireless data network, at that stage just a jumble of wires and boxes, called Mobitex. That was when he had the idea for what he eventually realized as the BlackBerry twelve years later. It was a perfect opportunity, he said later: "Something people don't understand with lots of inefficiency and problems to solve." His approach was to model the device on pagers. "We discovered the essence of paging," he said. "We took that essence—wearable, unobtrusive, real-time, always on, always connected, low cost, and brought it to the future." (The name came from a California firm called Lexicon Branding, who initially came up with the functional but dull "PocketLink," then toyed with Strawberry, because the device looked a bit like one, but that sounded too sedate, and ended up with the friendly-yet-snappy BlackBerry.)

In 1992, Lazaridis hired chartered accountant and MBA Jim Balsillie to join him in the unusual role of co-CEO; Balsillie, who handles finances, is a friend of Malcolm Gladwell (author of *The Tipping Point*) but prefers his motivational reading a little more obscure, with Marcus Aurelius a favorite. In 1996, they developed an interactive pager that could send messages as well as receive them. Research in Motion went public in 1997, then enjoyed the benefits of dot-com market enthusiasm with a rising share price making multimillionaires of the partners to the extent that Lazaridis could afford to donate $85 million to found the Perimeter Institute for Theoretical Physics in Waterloo, Canada, among other donations aimed at improving educational opportunities. Lazaridis is also chancellor of his old college, the University of Waterloo, where he has founded an institute for quantum computing. The company's share price plunged after the dot-com bubble burst, but it quickly soared again on the strength of BlackBerry sales. More threatening has been a patent battle with a small U.S.-based patent holding company called NTP that threatened to see the device banned from sale in the United States if the companies could not agree on a settlement; by November 2005, legal wrangles had reached the U.S. Supreme Court. Nevertheless, Research in Motion had settled down into healthy growth with annual revenue predicted to reach $2.1 billion in fiscal 2006. Lazaridis is now a multimillionaire, not that he checks his daily worth: employees caught watching the stock price while at work have to buy doughnuts for everybody (it's not a joke: one employee was caught in 2002 and had to fork out for 1,000 doughnuts).

NOTES

"Something people . . ." Scott, Sarah, Brad Faught, and John Guise, "The Innovators," *National Post*, 8.1.02, p. 44.

"We discovered the . . ." Anderson, Mark. "High Wireless Act," *National Post Business*, 7.1.00, p. 48.

REFERENCES

The Australian, BusinessWeek, The Gazette (Montreal), *National Post* (Canada), *Profit, The Record* (Kitchener-Ontario), *Toronto Star*

Wal-Mart

World domination, one store at a time

E VEN WELL INTO HIS FORTIES SAM WALTON WAS OUTWARDLY no different from any other moderately successful business-man. As a youngster he had worked stacking shelves for J.C. Penney, learned to manage small stores, and then owned and oper-ated a chain of fifteen variety stores of his own across Arkansas, Missouri, and Oklahoma—typical businesses with typical margins.

Then, in 1962, it was as if a discount bug went around like the flu and everybody caught it. Kmart, Woolco (Woolworths), and Target all opened vast, warehouse-style general-merchandise stores that profited from low margins and high turnover. Sam Walton may have been a small operator from Hicksville, but he knew a good idea when he saw it. In fact, for Walton, discovering discounting was akin to a religious conversion. He opened his first Wal-Mart outside Rogers, Arkansas, in 1962, and was to spend the rest of his life devot-ed to his creed: "Everyday low prices."

Wal-Mart is one of the world's biggest corporations; it is certain-ly the world's biggest retailer with 5,200 stores worldwide.

By 2005 it had 1.7 million employees worldwide, making it the world's biggest private employer. Its sales on a good day are bigger than the gross domestic products of thirty-six countries (by 2005 sales had hit $285 billion a year). It is the biggest seller of just about any consumer product you can think of, from DVDs to dog food (where it has market share of some 36 percent nationally). Wal-Mart is China's eighth-largest trading partner. Economists have said Wal-Mart's low prices are responsible for reducing America's rate of infla-tion. If Wal-Mart continues its present rate of growth, it is possible that by the end of the decade it will become the world's first trillion-dollar corporation and the largest company in United States history as a proportion of GDP. By 2005, the Walton family (Sam Walton's widow, Helen; sons Jim, Rob, and John, who died in a plane crash in mid-2005; and daughter Alice) were the richest family in the United States with 39 percent of Wal-Mart stock worth some $90 billion.

Unlike the dot-com boom that produced billionaires overnight, Sam Walton's success came one store at a time. Born in 1918, it took Walton so long to become a billionaire that he was still virtually unknown in 1985 when *Forbes* magazine calculated that his stock ownership in Wal-Mart made him the richest man in America. Walton—or "Mr. Sam," as he liked to be called—enjoyed his anonymity; he created quite a persona as the good ol' boy who drove an old pick-up truck and held picnics for employees on his front lawn.

He may have been socking away billions of dollars in family trusts, but he genuinely had a common touch. He understood the advantages of a workplace that created a family atmosphere. He understood the importance of information that percolated up from the shop floor. He understood the effect he had on the workforce when he just dropped in, unannounced, and took morning tea in the back of the store just like a regular guy. "Nothing else can quite substitute for a few well-chosen, well-timed, sincere words of praise," Walton once said. "They are absolutely free and worth a fortune."

He offered small but significant benefits, such as a share plan for long-term employees. He also hated unions.

Walton had the imagination to see very early on that there was enormous potential for growth in rural America. He flew his light plane across the countryside, buying up chunks of farmland at the crossroads between small towns where he would build his stores. He was literally flying under the radar: even as late as the 1980s, the likes of Kmart could not understand how this company based in the rural south could pose much of a threat. Employees still gather together every Friday morning to yell out the ritual Wal-Mart cheer, which starts, "Give me a W!" and ends, "Who's number one?" Answer: "The customer!"

Behind the hokey façade, though, Wal-Mart is a technological innovator. As early as 1966, Sam Walton visited an IBM training school with the purpose of hiring somebody to computerize his operation. Today, not only is all stock tracked from factory to purchase, enabling managers to instantly rank the popularity of any item in any store, Wal-Mart is happy to share its information with its suppliers, who can keep tabs on their product through a system called RetailLink. Allowing suppliers to see for themselves how their products fare, hour-by-hour, encourages them to think proactively rather than just waiting to fill orders. After the Pentagon's, Wal-Mart's computer system is the largest in the country.

It is not unusual for a single Wal-Mart buyer earning $50,000 a year to handle $1 billion worth of business, which helps to explain why around 200 major suppliers have built their own offices in Bentonville and companies such as Newell Rubbermaid rarely launch a new product line without consulting a Wal-Mart buyer first.

As a mechanism for delivering cheap consumer goods, Wal-Mart is unparalleled. It has driven out of business the traditional mom and pop store and regional chains and now has the national brands such as Kmart and Target on the ropes. Even the Toys"R"Us chain, which has itself killed off countless smaller toy chains, suffered at the hands of Wal-Mart, which has the flexibility to shrink or expand its stock of toys with the seasons, while Toys"R"Us was stuck with aisles of Barbies and Legos year-round.

When Sam Walton died in 1992, some commentators believed Wal-Mart would lose its drive, but Walton had groomed his successor, David Glass, well. Glass may not have had Walton's down-home charisma, but he built on the company's strong foundations and expanded the chain's reach dramatically. A decade ago, pundits scoffed when Wal-Mart started selling food. Now, it is the biggest grocer in the country. Glass took Wal-Mart's revenues from $16 billion in 1987 to some $165 billion in 1999; in 2000, he was succeeded by chief operating officer Lee Scott, a twenty-year Wal-Mart veteran who stepped into the role of weekly cheerleader with barely a hiccup—"Give me a W! . . ."

Some analysts believe there is room for another 2,000 more stores by 2011. Wal-Mart also has operations in eight other countries, including ownership of the British supermarket chain Asda and a large stake in a Japanese chain. It is the largest retailer in both Mexico and Canada.

Enormous growth has not come without its hiccups, though. Attempts to export the Wal-Mart culture wholesale into Germany in 1997 lost the company money, thanks to uncooperative suppliers and unions. Back home, some employees complain that the old-time family atmosphere, which relied on managers' occasional goodwill, has eroded since Sam Walton's death and the introduction of twenty-four-hour trading. Some towns, particularly in the northeast and California, have fought hard against Wal-Mart opening nearby, fearing it will suck the life out of their commercial centers. Anti-globalization campaigners have criticized the chain for buying goods made cheaply in developing nations. In 2001, six current and former employees filed a sex-discrimination lawsuit against the company, which became a class action in 2004, alleging that Wal-Mart paid its female employees less than males ones and promoted them less often. In 2004, Wal-Mart ran a series of ads designed to combat its eroding public image after unsavory revelations about its labor practices and immigration raids that uncovered hundreds of illegal employees. It has been mercilessly lampooned on both *The Simpsons* (where Homer gets a job as a lowly paid greeter) and *South Park*. Despite its history of technological prowess, Wal-Mart's online presence is not yet a patch on that of Amazon.com, which can also afford to cut prices since it has no stores to run, and is way ahead in the experience it offers online shoppers.

It's unlikely any of these issues will make much of a dent in the bottom line, though. All empires crumble eventually. But, if you are one of Wal-Mart's competitors, that's not much consolation.

NOTES

"Nothing else can quite . . ." Neuborne, Ellen. "Sam's Rules: Listen, Share, Control Expenses," Money, *USA Today*, 7.16.92, p. 18.

REFERENCES

The Business 2.0, *BusinessWeek*, *Daily Telegraph*, *Economist*, *Fast Company*, *Financial Times*, *Fortune*, Slate.com, *Sunday Telegraph*, *Telegraph*, *Time*, *USA Today*

Warren Buffett, Berkshire Hathaway

"Price is what you pay, value is what you get"

T HE ANNUAL GENERAL MEETING OF WARREN BUFFETT'S company, Berkshire Hathaway, each spring in Omaha, Nebraska, is unofficially known as Woodstock for capitalists. Here, up to 15,000 investors in Buffett's $129 billion company come to pay homage to the man they call the Oracle of Omaha and listen to his thoughts on investment. His lengthy speeches are typically injected with his ideas on everything from the evils of corporate greed to the worthlessness of dot-coms and the wisdom of Dolly Parton ("If you want the rainbow, you gotta put up with the rain"). To many, he is more than the world's greatest investor; he is a folk hero.

There is good reason for the rapt attention. Buffett is unquestionably the most influential investor in the world. A $10,000 investment in the Buffett Partnership in 1956 which was then reinvested in

Berkshire Hathaway at the termination of the partnership, would be worth more than $350 million today. Original shareholders have seen their investment increase by more than 200,000 percent. A single share in Warren Buffett's company in late 2005 cost around $90,400, with an average annual return of 24 percent since 1965. Despite his performance as a chief executive, Buffett still only pays himself $100,000 per year (plus expenses) and has had no pay raise for twenty-two years. He is the lowest-paid chief executive of the largest two hundred companies in the United States.

The son of a small-time broker, born in 1930, Buffett has an estimated fortune of $44 billion. His success boils down to his uncanny ability to spot undervalued companies and stocks.

In his youth, Buffett always had a head for business, whether it was selling golf balls, pin-ball machines, dividing up six-packs of Coca-Cola and reselling individual cans for a profit, studying investment guides, or plotting his path to true wealth. His childhood bedroom was crammed with copies of the *Wall Street Journal*, annual reports, and stock analyzes: reading them was one of his favorite hobbies. Buffett and his sister Doris bought their first share parcel when Buffett was just eleven years old, in a company called Cities Service. He bought three shares at $38 each. After surviving a dip in price, he sold them for $40 a share, and then watched as the share price soared to $200. It was a good lesson in patience that he preaches to this day. He was a committed saver and managed his own tax returns diligently. At thirteen, he had five paper routes, delivering 500 newspapers before school, and his gross earnings were that of a full-time adult worker. By the age of fifteen, he had accumulated $1,200 cash to buy his first farm property. See a pattern here? He was generating cashflow to reinvest in undervalued investments.

After watching his family struggle to support themselves, Buffett wanted to be rich. "I wanted enough money so I could do what I wanted," he says. When he was nineteen, Buffett read a book that would change his life, Benjamin Graham's *The Intelligent*

Investor. "That was my Ten Commandments," he says. "It gave me the framework for thinking about business and investments."

In 1956 after completing university studies (he was rejected by Harvard Business School), he established an investment fund, the Buffett Partnership, promising his clients that there would be no fees for his services unless he returned at least 6 percent annually. If he did, clients would pay him 25 percent of the return above 6 percent. He was just twenty-five.

In 1962, Buffett started buying shares in a struggling textile company called Berkshire Hathaway. The 2,000 shares in his first parcel cost him $7.50 each. He took over the company in 1965 and began diversifying, particularly investing in insurance businesses. In insurance, the customers pay up front and the company pays out later, if at all—that meant Buffett now had a regular stream of capital to invest in other projects. He closed his investment fund in 1969 (after clocking up average annual returns of 32 percent) to concentrate on Berkshire Hathaway, a company that would become the world's largest public investment pool. He still owns 34 percent of the company and has never sold a share.

Berkshire Hathaway bought a string of cash-rich companies, reinvesting the cash in stocks and bonds. Today, Berkshire Hathaway has more than forty subsidiaries including GEICO (a car insurer), General Re (a reinsurer), companies that manufacture shoes, clothing, carpets, and building products, plus interests in financial services, private jet services, energy producers, real estate, homewares, jewelry, and major share-holdings in companies including American Express, the *Washington Post*, and Coca-Cola. It also has more than $40 billion in cash that it uses for new investments.

He has turned picking undervalued companies, particularly those with relatively good management in place, into a multibillion-dollar art form. Rather than collecting great art, he collects great companies. His strategies include avoiding short-term trends (he never touched dot-coms, although Berkshire Hathaway has bought bonds in online book retailer Amazon) and targeting undervalued companies with low overheads, potential for growth, and low price-to-earning ratios. "Great investment opportunities come around when excellent companies are surrounded by unusual circumstances that cause the stock to be misappraised," says Buffett. "The dumbest reason to buy a stock is because it is going up."

Robert Miles, author of one of many books about Buffett, estimates that Buffett has around $150 million to invest each week from a pool of more than $43 billion in cash. These days, the Berkshire Hathway portfolio includes considerable investments in cash and bonds, even international investments, because of the scarcity of good undervalued stocks locally.

In his 2004 statement to shareholders, Buffett reminded his audience that it is all very well to study what he has done in the past, but that does not mean they should overlook what he is doing today. "When analyzing Berkshire, be sure to remember that the company should be viewed as an unfolding movie, not as a still photograph. Those who are focused in the past on only a snapshot of the day sometimes reach erroneous conclusions."

His no-frills approach permeates his entire empire, from the very basic Berkshire Hathaway website, to his simple tastes for bridge, burgers, chocolates (from Berkshire Hathaway-owned See's Candies), and cherry Coke (he owns a $13 billion stake in the company). Buffett has lived in the same nondescript house in Omaha since 1958. He continues to work with his fellow Omaha buddy Charles Munger, also his business partner. His one confessed extravagance is a private jet he named "The Indefensible."

The big question now is how long can Buffett, renowned for his stamina, keep it up. Now in his mid-seventies (he was born in 1930), Berkshire Hathaway has a significant Buffett premium built into the price. The outspoken critic of poor corporate governance is not giving much away about his succession plans despite Buffett and Munger's increasing years. This has resulted in a series of downgrades from investment houses. Reportedly, Buffett has a list with three possible Berkshire Hathaway chief executive names on it. "Retirement plans? About five to ten years after I die," he says.

Buffett's wife, Susan, from whom he had been amicably separated for more than twenty-five years, died in 2004. Bill Gates has taken her seat on the Berkshire Hathaway board. "On the death of the last of the two of us—and maybe sooner—it will all go to a foundation. That will be it." Now that it's settled, the family charity will instantly become one of the biggest foundations in history with an endowment of more than $40 billion.

NOTES

"Price is what . . ." Hanley, William. "Weekend at Warren's," *The Financial Post*, 5.10.97, p. 6.

"I wanted enough money . . ." Lawson, Dominic. "This Man Is Worth $35 Billion," *The Mirror*, 5.13.03, p. 18.

"That was my Ten . . ." Lawson, Dominic. "This Man Is Worth $35 Billion," *The Mirror*, 5.13.03, p. 18.

"Great investment opportunities . . ." Lowe, Janet. "The Sayings of Chairman Buffett," *Investment News*, 7.12.99, p. 7.

"The dumbest reason . . ." Der Hovanesian, Mara. "The Worst May Not Be Over," *BusinessWeek*, 10.8.01, p. 74.

"When analyzing Berkshire . . ." Buffett, Warren. 2004 letter to shareholders, www.berkshirehathaway.com.

"Retirement plans? . . ." *Forbes*, 10.19.92

"On the deah..." Lawson, Dominic. "Warren's World," *Sunday Telegraph*, 5.11.03, p.1.

Roberts, Paul Craig. "Building Fortunes the American Way," *Washington Times*, 12.5.97, p. A20.

REFERENCES

Hagstrom, Robert G. *The Warren Buffett Way: Investment Strategies of the World's Greatest Investor*. John Wiley & Sons, 1997.

Lowe, Janet. *Warren Buffett Speaks: Wit and Wisdom From the World's Greatest Investor*. John Wiley & Sons, 1999.

Lowenstein, Roger. *Buffett: The Making of an American Capitalist*. Main Street Books, 1996.

Miles, Robert. *Warren Buffett Wealth: Principles and Practical Methods Used by the World's Greatest Investor*. John Wiley & Sons, 2004.

The Intelligent Investor: the Classic Bestseller on Value Investing, Benjamin Graham, 4th Edition, HarperBusiness, 1986.

The Australian, Australian Financial Review, BBC News, Berkshire Hathaway.com, *Bloomberg Markets, BusinessWeek, Financial Times, Forbes,* Hoover's Company Capsules, *The Independent, National Business Review, Omaha World Herald, Salon, Sun Herald, Sunday Telegraph, The Times, Washington Post*

NetJets

The "affordable" corporate jet

FEW COMPANIES IN THESE POST-ENRON DAYS CAN COMFORTABLY justify having their own corporate jet sitting out there on the tarmac waiting to whisk its executives wherever they feel like going. They may make noises about efficiency, but how many executives can really justify the expense of running a jet? It can easily run into the tens of millions a year—and that's before you start serving lobster and champagne en route.

But what if you could still use a plane whenever you needed it, at a fraction of the cost of owning your own jet? You still get to avoid the lines at check-in but suddenly you don't look quite so extravagant to your shareholders. And if you actually have to travel around the clock to make your living—maybe you're a professional golfer or tennis player—it can actually become cost-effective.

That was the thinking of a trained mathematician named Richard J. Santulli, who had bought a moribund jet charter business in 1984 and was looking for ways to turn it around. His solution, a fractional ownership program called NetJets, was to prove that out-of-the-box thinking can create new opportunities even in established industries.

Born in 1944, Santulli grew up in Brooklyn and attended Brooklyn's Polytechnic University, where he studied applied mathematics, later joining the faculty while he studied for his PhD. He then worked at Goldman Sachs, writing programs for computer modeling in investment banking, then running the company's leasing business. After quitting Goldman Sachs in 1979, Santulli started his own leasing company, RTS Capital Services, which specialized in helicopter leases. Then, in 1984, he bought an ailing aircraft charter firm called Executive Jet Aviation, or EJA, a firm with a colorful history. Founded by a group of retired Airforce generals, it had actor Jimmy Stewart on its board and the pilot who dropped the atomic bomb on Hiroshima, General Paul Tibbets, as its president.

Santulli had once considered buying his own jet, but realized he could not justify the expense, and that even sharing it with friends wouldn't work as their schedules would clash.

But what if his nominal shared ownership of one jet allowed him access to a whole fleet?

After examining the historical records of EJA flights, Santulli spent five months building a mathematical model that proved fractional ownership would be possible—that with a correctly managed fleet EJA would be able to guarantee a plane to any one of its customers within four to six hours at an airport of their choice. The key, of course, was that unlike a time-share holiday apartment, which could only be occupied by one of the owners at a time, EJA shared and shuffled its whole fleet among its owners to make the system work. It seems mind-boggling—which is why it took a mathematical genius to work out how to do it. "I spent months doing the mathematics," Santulli recalled in 2004. "People thought I was crazy and the competition thought they could copy it. But they didn't understand the mathematical heart of the model."

Santulli launched the program under the name NetJets in 1986, and, after a shaky start—customers were skeptical despite Santulli's money-back guarantee, and because of the 1990 recession—NetJets not only revived EJA but pioneered a new industry. Initially it offered a share arrangement, where customers would, for instance, buy one-eighth of a mid-size six-to-eight passenger jet for $1.5 million plus $15,000 a month in management fees and an additional $2,000 for every hour in the air. Later, NetJets partnered with another company to offer the option of the Marquis card, which allowed customers to bypass the whole fractional business and simply purchase air time in twenty-five-hour chunks, like a very expensive phone card (try $299,900 for twenty-five hours in a Gulfstream).

In 1998, Santulli sold EJA to one of his long-term customers, Warren Buffett. Buffett, who incidentally, named his own personal jet The Indefensible, argued that he wanted to conduct business on his own schedule, not somebody else's. "There's a reason people would rather hail a cab than wait for a bus," he told the *International Herald Tribune* in 2004. "NetJets has replicated that on-demand service—and a luxurious one at that—and just moved it 45,000 feet above ground."

Buffett retained Santulli as chairman and CEO of NetJets, and today the Berkshire Hathaway company has some 570 aircraft and 2,800 pilots, underpinned by a computer system that juggles schedules, bookings, pilots, and even meal and drink preferences.

NOTES

"I spent months doing the mathematics . . ." Kane, Frank. "Mammon: Has the Sage found an Heir?" *The Observer*, 11.7.04, p. 20.

"There's a reason people . . ." Phillips, Don. "Part of a Plane, None of the Hassles," *International Herald Tribune*, 11.13.04, p.11.

REFERENCES

Business and Commercial Aviation, BusinessWeek, eWeek, Financial Times, International Herald Tribune, New York Times, Washington Post, The Weekly of Business Aviation

IMAGE IS EVERYTHING

Nike

The art of selling air

N IKE TOOK SOMETHING EVERYBODY ALREADY HAD FOR FREE, gave it neat-looking packaging, bought celebrity endorsements for it, and sold it for a premium. What they sold, of course, was air. Nike's Air cushioning system was a triumph of technology and marketing, and, assisted by a basketball player named Michael Jordan, Nike grew from car-boot sales to the largest seller of sports shoes in the world—by quite a margin.

In 1962, Phil Knight, an accounting major and middle-distance runner from the University of Oregon, took a trip to Japan. There, inspired by a term paper he had written about importing sneakers, he struck a deal with a sneaker manufacturer called Onitsuka Tiger (later known as Asics) to become the brand's distributor in thirteen western states, later expanding to national distribution rights.

Under the company name Blue Ribbon Sports, Knight originally ordered 200 pairs, paying $3.33 a pair. On his return to the U.S. he teamed up with his running coach, Bill Bowerman, each contributing $500 to the enterprise. They sold the Tiger sneakers for $6.95 a pair from the trunk of Knight's green Plymouth Valiant at athletics meets and from a tiny shop next to the Pink Bucket Tavern in Portland; in 1964, they made $8,000. Knight, who was working part-time as an accountant, then hired a full-time salesman named Jeff Johnson, another runner, who would later come up with the name Nike after it came to him in a dream. Nike is the Greek goddess for victory.

Meanwhile Bowerman spent his spare time experimenting with homemade shoe designs, obsessing with shaving fractions of seconds off his runners' track times. In 1970, he mythically poured rubber onto his wife's waffle iron and created a new lightweight sole that offered athletes unprecedented cushioning and traction.

In 1971, Knight and Bowerman took Johnson's idea for the name and called the business Nike. The go-faster stripe that looked like a tick on the side—the "Swoosh"—came from a local design student who they paid just $35 (though she was later rewarded with Nike stock). In 1974, they launched the Waffle Trainer, which went on to become the best-selling training shoe in the United States.

Bowerman and Knight had a natural flair for marketing. After the 1972 Olympic marathon trials, they announced that four of the top seven finishers had worn Nike shoes (ignoring the fact that the top three places were filled by runners wearing Adidas, then the world number one). In 1973, Nike persuaded record-holding runner Steve Prefontaine to wear its shoes; then in 1974, with no paid endorsement, Jimmy Connors won Wimbledon and the U.S. Open wearing the Waffle Trainer. In 1978, John McEnroe signed up (paid at one time what was then regarded as a scandalous $100,000 a year) and Nike began its march to become a world-leading brand—in 1980 replacing Adidas as the country's top sneaker company. That was also the year Nike went public, turning several families who had invested $5,000 each in the early days into millionaires.

Nike's Air cushioning system first appeared in 1979 in a model called the Tailwind, after a former aerospace engineer called Frank Rudy had approached Blue Ribbon Sports with the idea of including a little air bladder in the heel of a shoe. After making around 1,000 prototypes to get the formula right, he licensed his patented idea to Nike. Marketed as "air travel" with images of the Wright Brothers' Kitty Hawk, the Tailwind was a success, but it missed a crucial marketing angle—you couldn't actually see the bubble of air inside the shoe. It was only when Nike eventually came up with a little plastic window in the side of the shoe—in 1987's Air Max—that Air became a phenomenon: you could now see that between your heel and the ground was a bubble of nothing. (The "air" was actually a gas called sulfur hexafluoride, made up of molecules that were too large to escape through the tiny holes in the polyurethane bubble. Instead of deflating over time, the bubble actually increased in pressure as other gases seeped in from outside.)

Nike hit a speed bump in 1986, when a sales slump forced it to lay off staff for the first time. Rival Reebok had hit upon soft shoes for the women's aerobics boom, which Nike misjudged, and Reebok moved briefly to the number one spot. Nike's marketing whiz Rob Strasser (who later helped to revitalize Adidas) had publicly remarked that Nike would never "make shoes for those [expletive] who like aerobics." Nike—and Strasser—did, however, predict another trend that would prove far longer-lasting: the kind of shoes worn by a little-known basketball rookie, fresh from the University of North Carolina, by the name of Michael Jordan. According to a *New York Times* report, "The Selling of Michael Jordan," a few weeks before Jordan started with the Chicago Bulls in 1984, Rob Strasser met with Jordan's agent to discuss how they might best expand Nike's range of basketball shoes. After mentioning Nike's new line of air-cushioned soles, they came up with a concept: "Air Jordan." As Jordan's career blossomed, the shoes Nike created specially for him—Air Jordans—became highly sought-after by young urban males as a fashion item, especially after the controversy that surrounded the first model, a black and red pair that were banned because they did not match the rest of the Bulls uniform. Nike ran an ad: "On October 15, Nike created a revolutionary new basketball shoe. On October 18, the NBA threw them out of the game. Fortunately, the NBA can't keep you from wearing them. Air Jordans. From Nike." The $65 pairs of shoes were soon changing hands on the street for $100, and one basketball executive told a newspaper he was afraid to wear his in case somebody mugged him for them. (The shoe was updated every year, and a recent model, the $200 Air Jordan XVII, came in its own metal briefcase.)

By the end of the 1980s, Nike had an unbeatable recipe: alluringly high-tech products, endorsements from athletes across a range of disciplines, an instantly recognizable brand, and a memorable slogan: Just Do It.

In 1996, Nike presciently signed Tiger Woods, then age twenty and largely unproven, to a reported $40 million five-year contract. The following year, Tiger won the U.S. Masters by a record twelve strokes and Nike's share of the U.S. sneaker market reached an all-time high. As a brand, though, Nike was no longer as young and fresh as its marketing might have you believe, despite the best efforts of the marketing geniuses at Nike's World Campus, a college-style cluster of buildings in Beaverton, outside Portland, Oregon, which featured jogging tracks, gyms, and child care. Perhaps life at Nike headquarters was too cushioned from the edgy, real world outside— what employees called "the biosphere." For all its counter-culture pretensions, Nike was now firmly mainstream—which began to turn off younger buyers. In 1998, Nike had its midlife crisis. The sneaker market was fragmenting. Soft, bulbous shoes designed for skateboarding and "classics," such as Puma's and Adidas's revamped 1970s styles, were now fashionable alternatives to Nike's high-tech athletic look. New Balance, with a wider range of sizes and fittings, was stealing hardcore runners who didn't care what shoes looked like as long as they were comfortable.

Nike's widespread use of labor in developing countries made it a target for anti-globalization campaigners, who revealed the company's contractors had employed children as young as eight, paying them just a few dollars a day to make sneakers that retailed for over $100. Nike may have been paying a premium over the usual local wages and provided much-needed employment, but it still jarred when customers learned Phil Knight alone was worth an estimated $5 billion.

Then the Asian economy tanked and Nike suffered a surprise bloody nose on the sporting field, when it sponsored Brazil for a reported $200 million at the 1998 soccer World Cup, only to have them lose to Adidas-sponsored France in the final. Profits slumped 50 percent from the previous year's all-time high. "So, what knocked us down?" Knight asked rhetorically, in his letter in the 1998 annual report. "Asia . . . brown shoes . . . labor practices . . . resignations . . . layoffs . . . boring ads." A little shaken, Nike responded by reevaluating its brand, so well recognized but now attracting negative associations. In 1998 it downsized its use of the ubiquitous Swoosh (dubbed the "Swooshtika" by Nike's opponents) and replaced the commanding "Just do it!" with the wimpier: "I can."

In 1999, the year Bill Bowerman died in his sleep at age eighty-eight, Phil Knight apologized to his staff at Nike's Portland, Oregon, headquarters for the loss of direction, and even admitted to the company's failings in the third world, conceding: "the Nike product has become synonymous with slave wages, forced overtime, and arbitrary abuse." With commitments to improving conditions for its factory workers and a new, humbler public demeanor, Nike refocused on the elements of its initial success—technology and endorsement.

To increase its appeal "Just Do It" returned as the main slogan, but otherwise Nike looked for ways to diversify the brand, rather than pitching the single, authoritarian message that had come to seem arrogant. In 2005, Nike announced it would post information on its website about the 700-plus factories it uses to make its products.

To increase its appeal to women, Nike launched a yoga shoe and the Nike Goddess brand (later renamed Nikewomen), and a chain of stores designed more like upscale fashion outlets than sports shoe shops (prompting worldwide clothing sales to increase 30 percent by 2004). For teenagers turned off by Nike's ubiquity, it launched a range of skateboarding shoes that were available only in limited numbers from specialist skateboarding shops (supported, naturally, by endorsements from Nike-sponsored skate pros). In 2003, it bought competitor Converse, but kept it operating under its own brand name.

Phil Knight also has a strong belief that Nike's future lies in soccer, both in the U.S. and worldwide. He first signed the U.S. women's star Mia Hamm, followed by an unknown fourteen-year-old soccer player named Freddy Adu (who became the youngest player ever signed to a U.S. professional team), then he paid English champion soccer team Manchester United a record $450 million to wear Nike shirts and shorts for fourteen years. But the athlete that best typifies today's Nike is the cyclist Lance Armstrong, who beat cancer, then broke into the insular world of European cycling to win the Tour de France in 1998. As he continued to dominate the sport, he attracted critics who claimed he had used drugs (even though he has never tested positive). But Armstrong toughed it out, remained focused on the basics, training hard in the mountains, and in 2005 came back to win the Tour for a record-breaking seventh time. Courageous. Unstoppable. And wearing Nike.

NOTES

"Make shoes . . ." Katz, Donald. "Triumph of swoosh," *Sports Illustrated*, 8.93, p. 54.

"On October 15, Nike created . . ." Patton, Phil. "The Selling of Michael Jordan," section 6, *New York Times*, 11.9.86, p. 48.

"The Nike product . . ." Gumbel, Andrew. "Can the Olympics Put the Spring Back into Nike's Step," Business section, *The Independent*, 9.13.00, p. 1.

REFERENCES

CIO Magazine, Fast Company, Financial Times, Footwear News, Forbes, The Guardian, The Independent, Los Angeles Times, Mail on Sunday, Mirror, New York Post, New York Times, Observer, Sports Illustrated, The Times, USA Today

Tiffany & Co.

How a cardboard box became an icon

WOULD IT HAVE BEEN THE SAME HAD THE BOX BEEN BLACK or white, instead of the trademarked duck-egg blue? All we know is that the color chosen by the jeweler Tiffany & Co. for its boxes not long after it opened for business in 1837 is today as recognizable as the name of the company itself. At least half the point of buying somebody a gift at Tiffany's is watching their face when they see the color of the box.

Charles Lewis Tiffany first opened for business on Broadway in New York selling stationery, Chinese goods, Japanese paper-mâché, walking sticks, and terracotta, but within a decade had repositioned himself as a purveyor of silver and as a jeweler. Tiffany made quite a name selling the valuables of French aristocrats fleeing the revolution; in 1887 Tiffany's bought a substantial number of the French crown jewels. The company also acquired the Tiffany Diamond in 1878, at 128.5 carats one of the largest. By the time Audrey Hepburn paid homage to the flagship Fifth Avenue store in 1961's *Breakfast at Tiffany's*, the company was still a New York-only destination; it opened its first out-of-state store in San Francisco in 1963. Tiffany's opened in Japan in 1972. There were still only eight stores in 1987. Ever since it has pursued a policy of expansion to become the leading—and perhaps the only—mass-market premium jewelry brand. By 2005, it had ninety-six stores worldwide on top of its fifty-five U.S. outlets.

Though it always prided itself on selling affordable items alongside heart-stopping diamonds, it has in recent years expanded its cheaper lines of jewelry, particularly silver, and trinkets such as mugs—all of which come in the distinctive packaging. As a result sales increased greatly between 1996 and 2005, from $174 million to $2.2 billion. The company's challenge now is to maintain its air of exclusivity while also making the most of its brand. And to avoid disappointing women the world over who open that elegant little package expecting a $500,000 diamond engagement ring and instead finding a $20 packet of playing cards.

REFERENCES
Atlanta Journal-Constitution, Australian Financial Review, Chicago Sun-Times, Contra Costa Times, National Post (Canada), *New York Post*

Levi's

A business cannot rely on its legend

LEVI'S JEANS WERE ONCE SO HIGHLY PRIZED AS A SYMBOL OF rebelliousness and freedom that during the Cold War western tourists could smuggle them into Moscow and sell them for the price of an air ticket back out again. In fact, Levi's reports its jeans are still used as currency in parts of Russia.

Levi's, particularly the 501 style, are still the jeans of choice for the Baby Boomers who grew up with images of Levi's-clad James Dean and Marlon Brando. But the market for denim has fragmented since 501s ruled supreme, with dozens of lesser-known labels offering an extraordinary range of styles. Levi's has struggled to reinvent itself for a new generation of customers who associate the brand with their parents' generation.

Levi's is still the market leader in volume, but it faces the predicament of many super-brands, such as Nike and Gap, which suddenly find their label is no longer fashionable. How does it regain marketshare without compromising its heritage and losing its traditional customers?

How much simpler it was for Levi Strauss back in the late nineteenth century, when his customers—miners, farmers, and laborers—were more concerned about pockets ripping off their jeans rather than whether their bums looked big in their new jeans.

Levi Strauss, who changed his first name from Loeb when he migrated to the United States from Bavaria, ran a wholesale dry goods store in San Francisco during the gold rush, selling handkerchiefs, blankets, and clothing to general stores throughout the American West. One of his customers was Jacob Davis, a Latvian-born tailor who had an idea to rivet the pockets onto pants to give them extra strength. He suggested to Strauss they go into business together, and in 1873 they successfully patented their design, which they called "waist overalls."

The riveted pants had buttons for suspenders and a single back pocket onto which was stitched a curved "V," a design now known as the Arcuate. In 1886, they introduced a leather patch on the rear waistline depicting two horses unsuccessfully attempting to tear apart a pair of pants, an enduring Levi's symbol. Around 1890, Levi Strauss numbered the waist overalls "501;" then in 1936 the company added the signature red tag to the rear pocket with the word *Levi's* stitched in white capitals. The stitching, the patch, the tag, and the number 501 were to become cornerstones of the brand.

Vogue magazine first decided working-class denim could be fashionable in the 1930s, but it was the youth of the 1950s who adopted blue jeans, particularly Levi's, as a symbol of rebellion. Levi's became the uniform of New York's art scene, while on the west coast the hippies decorated theirs with flowers. In Britain, denim became the uniform of the Mods.

In 1966, advertising agency Foote Cone & Belding produced Levi's first television advertisement. In the early 1970s, a copywriter named Mike Koelker started on the Levi's account. By 1984, when Bob Hass, Levi Strauss's great-grandnephew, was named Levi's chief executive, Koelker was on the account as executive creative director. He and Hass struck up a friendship that was to smooth over the usual quibbles between agency and client, often catching up after business hours to hammer out marketing problems. The 1980s was a fruitful period, with Koelker masterminding a series of campaigns that employed nostalgia and patriotism to brand Levi's, and particularly the 501 jeans, as quintessentially American. Between 1986 and 1996, Levi's enjoyed uninterrupted growth.

Meanwhile in Britain, Levi's advertising agency Bartle Bogle Hegarty had a hit with an advertisement that showed male super-model Nick Kamen stripping down to his boxer shorts in a laun-dromat to wash his 501s, to the strains of Marvin Gaye's "I Heard it Through the Grapevine." Levi's sold a reported 800,000 pairs of the jeans on the strength of the campaign, inadvertently sparking a rush on boxer shorts and sending Marvin Gaye to the top of the charts for the first time in decades.

Things began to go wrong for Levi's in 1994 when, back in the United States, Mike Koelker was diagnosed with lung cancer and left Foote Cone & Belding on medical leave. Levi's no longer received the same intimate attention it had enjoyed with Koelker. This was not a good time for a change in strategy: Levi's was facing increased competition from designer denim and was stuck with an aging product line.

In 1999, Hass brought in Philip Marineau to run the company. Marineau, formerly of PepsiCo, streamlined distribution and over-saw the closure of Levi's remaining American factories. He then focused on the product lines, replacing the old "one brand" approach with several splinter ranges sold from a diverse range of outlets: from the $300 "Red" and vintage labels available only at upscale boutiques, to the "Signature" line jeans, the first Levi jeans sold at mass discounter Wal-Mart, which offered them for as low as

$9. The new sub-brands still play on the old values of reliability and quality, but have largely dropped the "American legend" style of marketing. In its place is a Levi's that at least appears fresh and contemporary, with a manufacturing and distribution chain it hopes can respond effectively to changes in demand. Can it regain its dominance of old? That's what Marineau is hoping.

REFERENCES
Adweek, Chicago Tribune, Creative Review, Daily News Record, Financial Times, The Guardian, The Irish Times, LA Times, San Francisco Chronicle, Sunday Times, Time, WWD

THE BUSINESS DAREDEVILS

FedEx

"Being absolutely determined to accomplish something is a very, very important asset"

S OME PEOPLE ARE JUST DIFFERENT. MANY OF US, IF WE INHERITED $4 million, would retire to a tropical island or breed racehorses and swear never to do a day's work again. But Frederick Smith, age twenty-seven and recently returned from a tour of duty in Vietnam in 1970, took his inheritance and used it to fund a business so grand in its ambitions it was highly possible he would not only lose his own money but millions more besides.

His idea was Federal Express, a courier service that guaranteed overnight delivery of pretty much anything to pretty much anywhere in the United States, and, later on, express deliveries worldwide. He predicted that although no such service had ever existed, people would come to rely on it. Today, the business is so familiar and so widely used, people commonly say they "FedExed" something when they mean they sent it overnight.

Smith's father, who had founded a bus line, died when Smith was just four years old, an event that perhaps contributed to Smith's future drive. He first glimpsed his future while studying economics at Yale in 1965, when he wrote a paper about the growing number of uses for computers. He observed that as society became more reliant on them, it would be increasingly important for their computer manufacturers to repair them quickly should they fail. And to do that, they would need spare parts delivered quickly, preferably overnight. It was hardly a eureka moment; Smith can't recall the grade he received for the paper, but legend has it he received a C. Still, he filed the idea away.

Smith graduated in 1966, joined the Marines instead of attending Harvard Law School, and spent the next four years in Vietnam, serving first as a platoon leader on the ground, and later as a pilot. (He had learned to fly as a teenager and worked as a charter pilot while at Yale.)

When he returned to the United States, he took over his stepfather's airplane repair business in Little Rock, Arkansas. He discovered that getting spare parts for airplanes delivered to out-of-the-way Little Rock was a major problem and later he commissioned a study that found 80 percent of small, urgent shipments were to cities not currently serviced by airfreight companies.

He also recalled his Yale paper, observing that, as he had predicted, computers had become widespread, and that it was likely they required rapid delivery of parts, too. If you put the packages in jet planes, the former pilot figured, they could be anywhere in the United States within a few hours. But nobody was doing it.

So Smith took his inheritance, persuaded investors to come up with more funds in the order of another $90 million, and in 1971 at the age of just twenty-seven, launched Federal Express. He promised overnight delivery between any two points in the airline's initial network and went live on April 17, 1973, delivering—according to company history—183 packages to twenty-five cities. Why did he take the risk? In Vietnam, he said he had two hundred soldiers under his command, their lives in his hands. "Starting a business didn't intimidate me."

Smith concluded the most efficient way to service all points would be through a central hub where incoming packages would be unloaded, sorted, and sent out again. "My solution," he recalled, "was to create a delivery system that operates essentially the way a bank clearinghouse does: put all points on a network and connect them through a central hub. If you take any individual transaction, that kind of system seems absurd—it means making at least one extra stop. But if you look at the network as a whole, it's an efficient way to create an enormous number of connections." Smith chose Memphis, because the airport was seldom used between midnight and 6:00 a.m., and the weather was so predictable planes were grounded for only ten hours a year. FedEx, which shortened its name from Federal Express in 1994, is now the largest employer in the state, with one out of five of the Memphis workforce employed in airline-related industries. Memphis Airport is now the busiest cargo airport in the world.

The first years were particularly bumpy for Smith's investors: FedEx lost $29 million in its first twenty-six months and didn't return a profit until July 1975.

Initial plans to carry documents for bond houses fell through, as did plans to carry checks for Federal Reserve banks. According to the *Washington Post*, Smith was so hard up at one point that he traveled to Vegas with $200 in his pocket, won $26,000 playing blackjack, and used the cash to pay wages. In another episode, when a gunman held up the FedEx offices, Smith turned out his pockets to reveal a single dime. Other anecdotes recall employees leaving their watches with gas station attendants until they could return to pay for the gas.

FedEx went public in 1978 and by 1980 it was delivering 50,000 packages per night and expanding rapidly: just six years later it was delivering 1 million packages per night.

As Smith had predicted back in 1965, the world was becoming increasingly addicted to express deliveries, whether that meant vital medical equipment, monkey kidneys, or Maine lobsters. At the Manhattan headquarters of Merrill Lynch, it was revealed employees were sending internal memos via FedEx as it was often quicker than relying on their company's own mail service.

What FedEx had to do now was to keep up with demand. The potential for failure on a customer-to-customer basis is enormous. As one courier pointed out: "On Christmas Eve a lot of people call for the first and only time and they're desperate." Deliver on time and you're a hero, but delay a child's Christmas present for a single day and they'll never use you again.

One of FedEx's strengths has been an enthusiastic but realistic use of information technology. "Information about the package is as important as the package itself," Smith said as early as 1979. But its loyal workforce has been just as important. When its main rival, UPS, was crippled by a strike and FedEx received close to 1 million extra packages a day, thousands of workers showed up voluntarily at the hubs to sort the midnight rush. Smith saluted them in full-page newspaper ads with the military accolade "Bravo Zulu" and laid on extra bonuses. Executives report working 100-hour weeks, even 130-hour weeks, while implementing new systems.

FedEx experienced its own industrial relations hiccups in 1995, when the Airline Pilots Association banned overtime to disrupt the Christmas rush. Then, many of the remaining 110,000 employees rallied in the streets of Memphis in support of the company, half the pilots didn't take action, and some flew shifts on their days off. Smith said recently: "To me, the short definition of leadership is getting discretionary effort out of people."

Smith's other great skill appears to be persuading people who don't work for him to get the FedEx feeling, too. His close relationships with Washington lawmakers have seen FedEx invited to tag along on trade delegations to Latin America and China. President Bill Clinton's visit to the Philippines in 1994 smoothed the way for FedEx to build a cargo hub at the former U.S. Air force base at Subic Bay, a deal reported to be worth $300 million. Then in 1995 the company won authorization to act as sole U.S.-based air cargo carrier between the United States and China.

FedEx has sought to make customs clearances easier and it has won exemptions from certain trucking and noise abatement laws. In 2000, it struck a deal with the U.S. Postal service in which it gave the postal service access to FedEx planes in return for postal workers picking up and delivering FedEx packages, giving it access to an enormous network. In early 2004, FedEx also acquired the copy chain Kinko's, bringing it another 1,231 retail outlets across the country. Fred Smith has also maintained a relationship with a former fraternity brother from Yale, George W. Bush.

Smith, whose 7 percent of FedEx makes him worth some $1.1 billion (the company is valued at around $29 billion), has demonstrated repeatedly that his strategy is long-term. "Being absolutely determined to accomplish something is a very, very important asset," he says, adding: "Business is about money; it's not about life or death. When you have a lack of perspective you tend to get panicked or overly distraught about something that, in the scheme of things, is very small."

NOTES

"Being absolutely . . ."   Benjamin, Matthew. "Federal Express Fred Smith," *Investor's Business Daily*, 2.24.98, p. A1.

"My solution . . ."   Smith, Fred. "How I Delivered the Goods," Fortune.com.

"On Christmas . . ."   Moore, Martha T. "A Federal Express Night; Christmas Rush: How Firm Delivers," *Money, USA Today*, 12.14.89, p. 1B.

"Information . . ."   Gordon, Mark. "Next Day Change Guaranteed," *CIO Magazine*, 5.15.01.

"To me . . ."   Smith, Fred. "How I Delivered the Goods," Fortune.com.

REFERENCES

Air Transport World, AP, Arkansas Democrat-Gazette, BusinessWeek, CIO Magazine, CNN, Commercial Appeal, Computerworld, Edinburgh Evening News, E-Doc, Fast Company, Forbes, Fortune, Governing Magazine, Investor's Business Daily, Journal of Commerce, The National Journal, New York Times, The Record, South China Morning Post, Telegraph Herald, Time, The Times, USA Today, Washington Post

Esprit

Breaking up is hard to do

———

S USIE RUSSELL PICKED UP DOUG TOMPKINS HITCHHIKING NEAR Lake Tahoe, California, in 1963. She was a keen runner and he was a school drop-out who spent as much of his time as possible mountain climbing and skiing to Olympic standards. To pay the rent Doug painted houses, waited tables, and had been a mountain guide. They were both twenty-one and were married within six months. The Tompkins partnership would be the foundation for the Esprit brand, one of the most successful fashion labels of the 1980s with worldwide annual sales reaching more than $1 billion.

Esprit was not Doug's first business. He established outdoor clothing and mountain equipment brand The North Face in 1965 when he was just twenty-two. He sold the business in 1968 "because I had become bored with it and I hated being in the business of the sports I liked to do," says Doug, who never liked having to talk about equipment and gear rather than concentrating on the sport itself. He set off for a year in South America to make an adventure documentary doing high mountain skiing, climbing, and surfing.

When he returned to California, he worked with Susie and friend Jane Tise on a wholesale fashion business, a range of colorful, loose-fitting cotton clothes to suit the Californian lifestyle, working from an apartment in San Francisco. Doug put up the original capital. Initially, Doug worked part-time on the business while he finished his films. "This was an out-of-the-garage kind of business for the first few years," he says. Jane was more full-time and Susie was part-time. By 1970, two years after the company officially started, Doug took on a more active role with Jane.

Susie came on in a full-time capacity in 1971 when things started to take off.

For the next five years, the wholesale business steadily grew. Doug was soon bored with being another clothing maker. He wanted to turn these clothing ranges into a brand and try and make something of it. Susie and Jane supported the idea and he set about trying to create an image for these disparate brands. Doug hired a leading San Francisco graphic designer to work with the name Esprit de Corps, a company name from early on. Over the next few years, Doug assembled a groundbreaking team of designers and photographers and built a powerful brand of fresh-faced, beautiful people lying around in Esprit's unmistakably casual clothes.

Doug's strategy began to cause tension. Jane Tise and Allan Schwartz, the fourth partner in the business, were not happy with what Doug wanted to do. The business was turning over $8 million already, and Schwartz wanted to stay in a low-risk, profitable business model. They thought Doug's spending on advertising and image would sink the company. They sold out in 1975. The disgruntled former partners referred to the Tompkinses as a pair of "people shredders."

Today, Doug is adamant that Tise and Schwartz were wrong and that he was right. His strategy, he explains, was simply "the stock and trade of all the good brands in all markets from automobiles to perfumes, I just applied those principles to our business with good design, good discipline, and good professionals."

Without unhappy business partners, Susie and Doug got to work on their empire. As a team, Doug as chief executive and Susie as design director, they built Esprit into perhaps the most envied young fashion brand in the world during the 1980s. It was white hot in the twelve to twenty-five age demographic. Staff worked from a purpose-built office compound, enjoyed subsidized adventure travel, kayaking, language lessons, and time off for volunteer work. Doug built a reputation as a headstrong, intense, hyperactive visionary. He spent extravagantly on shop fitouts, photography, and the brand's image and was utterly focused on building the Esprit name. He left Susie to create the clothes and continued to spend up to six months each year on expeditions around the world.

Esprit wowed the junior sportswear fashion market for a decade with its fresh image of the California spirit, the Esprit logo and feel-good catalogs featuring staff and customers instead of models. Between 1979 and 1986, wholesale sales jumped from $75 million to $350 million. Up until the last quarter of 1986, the company enjoyed phenomenal growth, particularly in the U.S., with international Esprit sales reaching an estimated $1 billion.

Cracks in the business and the marriage began to appear in the early 1980s when Doug and Susie began to dispute the direction of the company. By 1985, Doug and Susie were living apart, and their growing rift began to seriously affect the business. Sales flattened, in line with the slump across the U.S. sportswear industry. Susie walked away from her Esprit role, and for two years the couple publicly fought for control of the business while Doug minded the shop. The fallout from investing too heavily in new retail stores in the U.S. blew out costs, and, for the first time, Esprit reported losses. Esprit began franchising stores to boost the company's fortunes, and 30 percent of staff were retrenched. In 1988, Doug said that the problems the company was facing were "textbook stuff" for a business. "We just wish we'd read the textbook." Says former Esprit sales director Lee Rosenberg: "Doug was a genius in forging our image and presenting our product. If our product had lived up to our image, we would be doing $2 billion. Our product never equaled our image." The problem, says Doug, was the designs weren't good enough. Even Esprit staff, who paid a fraction of retail for the clothes, were no longer wearing Esprit. "The products were not up to the image," he says. "It created very bad friction between Susie and myself."

Things became so bad between the Tompkinses that investment firm Goldman Sachs was appointed to find a buyer for the business.

In June 1990, at the eleventh hour, the Tompkinses agreed to keep the business in the family, and Doug sold his half share of the American business to Susie and a consortium for $125 million. This price was considered well below the company's total market value. "I took a $40 million bath to keep it with her," said Doug. He retained his stakes in the European and Asian Esprit operations, which were separate business entities. After the deal was done, Doug went rafting in the Soviet Union.

Over those last few years at Esprit, Doug had become heavily influenced by the radical ecological philosophers known as "deep ecologists," among them mountaineer philosopher Arne Naess. They believe that shallow ecology (e.g., pollution and resource depletion) is about protecting the health and affluence of the western world; deep ecology goes much further, encouraging the continuum of human and non-human life. The ethos also has a particular loathing for television.

In 1991, Doug began buying up parcels of pristine, virgin forest in southern Chile. His philanthropic gesture was greeted by Chileans with paranoia. (To deep ecologists he was Daddy Warbucks.) The Chileans wondered whether he was going to start a cult. He had to produce an advertisement to explain to the Chilean people what he wanted to do with the land.

The network of eleven parks over 738,000 acres of virgin forest, now known as Pumalin Park, only gained the status of nature reserve from the Chilean government in 2003 after more than a decade of fighting. Doug also set up the San Francisco-based Foundation for Deep Ecology, which supports biodiversity and sustainable agriculture. He lives part of the year in Pumalin with his new family, living on solar power and organic vegetables. The area is only accessible by boat or plane. He has also bought parcels of land in Argentina.

When Susie took total control of the American arm of Esprit in 1990, she took on a company that was up to its neck in debt, after paying Doug out. Sales were plummeting during a recession, but despite all these factors, Susie continued on with her breezy approach. Her reign was disastrous—characterized by resignations, firings, and rapid CEO turnover. U.S. sales fell from $360 million in 1990 to $200 million in 1995. She launched a Susie Tompkins signature line of clothing for older women, and an eco-range of clothing, collections that were so badly received that Susie was removed as design director. The following year, the U.S. operations (and debt) were bought out by former Tommy Hilfiger executive Jay Margolis and an investment consortium for $80 million. Margolis promptly banned Susie from Esprit headquarters. Susie remarried a hotel developer and has become a prominent San Francisco socialite and philanthropist since. Analysts have been scathing about her management of the Esprit brand that under her direction became allegedly insolvent.

The company would perhaps have perished if it were not for the solid performances of Esprit in Europe and Asia under the leadership of Michael Ying and Jurgen Friedrich. Ying, in particular has been a critical factor in the survival of Esprit. A former Hong Kong airport baggage handler, Michael is the brother of Mary Ying, one of the early employees in Esprit's first production facility in Hong Kong. Michael was Esprit's second employee in Hong Kong. He started working for the Tompkinses in 1971. He worked his way up to run the Hong Kong operations and became a partner in the Hong Kong arm of the business. He listed the Asian arm of Esprit, known as Esprit Holdings, on the Hong Kong stock exchange in 1993. He acquired the European arm of the company in 1996 and took control of the entire international Esprit operation in 2002.

The European and Asian arms of the company have enjoyed ten years of consecutive sales growth in both retail and wholesale operations. In 2002, the U.S. partners were bought out in a $150 million deal that will see the maestros of Esprit's success in Europe and Asia tackle the U.S. market under the Esprit Holdings banner. The group had revenues in 2004–05 of $2.6 billion, up 26 percent on the previous twelve months. Michael Ying, now a billionaire, remains the chairman and chief executive officer with a 16 percent stake in the company.

Esprit wholesales to 6,000 outlets in forty countries, and the company owns 2,500 retail stores. The plan now is to repeat the successful formula of European and Asian markets in the U.S. The financial headquarters is in Dusseldorf, with the creative headquarters in New York and finance operations based in Hong Kong. Under Michael Ying, Esprit is taking a bright and breezy brand, and continuing to make billions out of it.

Looking back, Doug finds it all "virtually meaningless. I luckily discovered the banality and senselessness of producing things that no one needs and just producing for the sake of it." On a recent trip to Paris, Doug visited an Esprit store in the Places des Victoires. "I was asking myself if I was in a time capsule. It all seems like an old dream."

NOTES

"Textbook stuff..." King Jr., Ralph. "How Esprit de Corp Lost Its Esprit," *Forbes*, 3.21.88, p. 91.

"Doug was a genius..." Ginsberg, Steve. "Esprit Saga," *WWD*, 2.12.90, p. 1.

"I took a..." Smith, Matt. "Esprit de Court," *San Francisco Weekly*, 10.8.97.

REFERENCES

Arena, BusinessWeek, Financial Times, Fortune, Fundacion Bosque Pumalin, *The Guardian, Harvard Business Review, Los Angeles Times, Miami Herald, New York Times, The Observer, San Francisco Business Times, San Francisco Chronicle, San Francisco Examiner, San Francisco Weekly, South China Morning Post, Time, Women's Wear Daily*

Playboy

Live and breathe the business

*P*LAYBOY WAS NOT SUCCESSFUL BECAUSE IT SHOWED MEN PICTURES of nude girls. It was successful because it managed to legitimize pornography by placing it in the context of an urbane bachelor lifestyle that included jazz, fine wine, literature, and elegant manners. What the early *Playboy* really offered its readers was schooling in a sophisticated way of life, spiced with the promise of freewheeling encounters with the opposite sex. The girlie pictures were just to get them in the door.

Its founder, Hugh Hefner, was very much a nonbachelor when he came up with the idea for his magazine in the early 1950s. His life had been pretty unremarkable until then: born in 1926 in Chicago, childhood in a Methodist Midwestern family, two years in the army at the end of World War II, and study at the University of Illinois under the GI Bill. He married his first real girlfriend, Mildred Williams, and they had two children, Christie and David. Hefner had had an interest in magazines from childhood (starting his own "newspaper" at age ten), and had edited a college magazine called *Shaft* that featured a "Coed of the Month." After working for the Chicago Carton Company and as an ad copywriter, he gravitated towards publishers for employment, landing a job as a promotions copywriter for *Esquire*, earning $60 a week, and then as the circulation director of a magazine called *Children's Activities*. But it was hardly glamorous, and neither was married life. Hefner later recalled: "A moment came when I thought, if I don't do something I'm going to turn into my parents."

He decided to start his own magazine. It would, Hefner decided, target the readers of his previous employer *Esquire*, but in a more contemporary fashion. At the time, all the other magazines for men were either aimed at the middle-aged or were obsessed with macho outdoor adventures. Hefner, who coveted life as an urban sophisticate, figured young men like himself might be more interested in such indoor pursuits as jazz, literature, and domestic competency— with an eye, of course, to using these skills as seduction techniques.

In 1952, Hefner scrounged up $8,000—$600 from a bank loan against his furniture and the rest from friends and relatives—and started putting together ideas, working at night at a card table in his apartment.

With virtually no money to spend on contributions, but some knowledge of copyright and syndication, he looked for material that was available as a cheap reprint or for free, in the public domain. He found a suitable extract from a Sir Arthur Conan Doyle story and bought it for just $25 from Doyle's estate. He reportedly convinced half of his contributors to accept payment in shares (which turned out to be the best decision they ever made). And then he heard about a nude picture of a young actress called Marilyn Monroe, which a nearby publisher had made into a calendar but had not been widely seen. Hefner drove out to the publisher on a cold call and somehow convinced him to sell the rights to the calendar for $500. That was the hook he needed to convince distributors to preorder a magazine they had never heard of.

That, and a terrific piece of salesmanship. "Dear Friend," Hefner wrote to the distributors, "I wanted you to be one of the first to hear the news. *Stag Party*—a brand-new magazine for men—will be out this fall and it will be one of the best-sellers you've ever handled." He signed it Nation-Wide News Company, Hugh M. Hefner, General Manager.

The Nation-Wide News Company was, of course, just Hefner and wife Millie, with Hefner variously describing himself as editor-publisher, publicity director, circulation director, and advertising director. Millie added a secretarial touch to letters by writing her initials in the lower left margin.

After he sent out the letter canvassing the distributors, Hefner received a not so pleasant letter from an outdoorsy magazine called *Stag Magazine*, which threatened legal action over the name *Stag Party*. Hefner gathered his friends around and after canvassing Pan and Satyr, came up with *Playboy*, the name of a recently failed car company. With orders for 70,000 copies on the strength of the Marilyn picture, Hefner was able to persuade two printers to publish the newly minted *Playboy* on credit.

Swigging Pepsi at his card table at 3:00 a.m., with a baby asleep down the hall, he knocked out an editorial that described life, *Playboy*-style. "We like our apartment. We enjoy mixing up cocktails, and an hors d'oeuvre or two, putting a little mood music on the phonograph, and inviting a female acquaintance for a quiet discussion on Picasso, Nietzsche, jazz, sex."

He figured he had to sell 35,000 to break even; with a retouched free picture of Marilyn Monroe on the cover to promote the centerfold, the first issue of *Playboy*, on the newsstands in December 1953, sold over 50,000 copies and introduced America to an irresistible world that was purely of Hefner's invention. Within a year circulation was up to 175,000; by 1960, it had hit one million and was overtaking *Esquire*. The first issue may have been an odd blend of material, but evidently it was working. Men may have joked, "I only read *Playboy* for the articles," but back in the 1960s there actually were far more articles than girlie pictures. Buyers of the December 1962 issue had to wade through 159 pages of advertisements and stories, such as an eleven-page feature on "The fine art of acquiring fine art" to reach the nudes, just ten pages of them in all. And *Playboy*'s pictures back then were tame, often showing nothing more than a single buttock or a hint of cleavage. What made them work was the attitude; it was Hefner's idea that the models be approachable, everyday women photographed in an unguarded moment, often with the suggestion of a man's presence—a pipe on a chair, a shadow in the background. The message: the girl next door likes sex as much as you do.

For the first years of *Playboy*'s life, Hefner worked non-stop, putting real strain on his marriage. He wrote in his journal, "*Playboy* consumes seven days of every week, more than a dozen hours a day and when I knock off at 1:30 or 2:00 in the morning I often stay right there."

By the end of the 1950s, Hefner decided he had been successful enough to start living the *Playboy* life himself, sponsoring a jazz festival and buying the first Playboy mansion. "It was something I thought would be fun that would also work as a marketing ploy," he said. "I started smoking a pipe and driving a 300SL Mercedes-Benz. Before long, I'd become world-famous." The first Playboy club opened in Chicago in 1960.

Hefner had made no secret of the fact he had enjoyed several affairs at the *Playboy* offices, which eventually contributed to the end of his marriage. *Playboy* was not just about good times, though. Hefner believed—or did a great impersonation of believing—that he was a liberal crusader, and to that end he spent the early years of the 1960s writing a series of editorials that came to be known as the *Playboy* manifesto, now available in their entirety on the *Playboy* website. A typical fragment: "If the human body—far and away the most remarkable, the most complicated, the most perfect, and the most beautiful creation on this earth—can become objectionable, obscene, or abhorrent when purposely posed and photographed to capture that remarkable perfection and beauty, then the world is a far more cockeyed place than we are willing to admit."

He took amphetamines and worked around the clock, producing 200,000 words to justify free sex and nude pictures.

"He did consider himself to be this deep thinker, this intellectual, this leader of the sexual revolution," said his biographer Russell Miller, author of the highly critical *Bunny: the Real Story of Playboy*.

Playboy's relationship with porn was, however, always touchy. Hefner may have philosophized at great length about the beauty of the naked female form, but he was still wary of crossing the line with advertisers, who accepted risqué but were turned off by sleaze. In the early 1970s, Hefner made two decisions that were to change *Playboy*'s course. He took the company public in 1971, which exposed it to nervous shareholders; and he declared the magazine "pubic"—showing full-frontal nudity for the first time—in what would become a circulation war with racier titles such as *Penthouse* and *Hustler*.

Playboy had by now grown into an empire that included the chain of twenty-three Playboy clubs populated by fluffy-tailed "bunnies," resort hotels, casinos, a modeling agency, a record label, and a limousine service. The magazine's circulation hit an all-time high of 7,161,561 copies in November 1972. But the company's profits were vulnerable, and Hefner's lifestyle, particularly the mansion, was an increasingly large overhead.

Hefner has admitted he was never really interested in running a vast conglomerate, and it showed as numerous ancillaries foundered. By 1975, despite huge income from the London casinos, the company was barely turning a profit. Scandals such as the conviction of Hefner's private secretary on drugs charges—and his subsequent suicide—and the murder of the 1980 Playmate of the Year, Dorothy Stratten, added to the impression that *Playboy* was no longer risqué and glamorous, but had slipped into sleaze. The darkest hour, though, was late in 1981, when police raided the London casinos following a tip-off from a rival firm. They found enough evidence of illegal behavior for a judge to revoke *Playboy*'s gambling licenses. In 1985, Hefner suffered a stroke. The era of the Playboy was apparently over.

Fast forward to 2003, though, and there's Hugh Hefner, age seventy-seven, partying at the Playboy mansion with his seven blonde girlfriends to celebrate the magazine's fiftieth anniversary. Hefner is still the editor-in-chief, but since 1982 the company has been run by his daughter, Christie, who brought much-needed business nous and an ability to negotiate with the boss unlike anybody before her.

"Hugh Hefner is still very involved in the company," says Christie Hefner today. "Moreover, Hef's lifestyle, legendary parties at the mansion, and public persona continue to interest the media and intrigue the public." She persuaded Hefner to close down the loss-making clubs, the last of which closed in 1986, and to expand into adult cable television, and, subsequently, online products. "*Playboy* was the first national magazine to go online (in 1994) and one of the first to carry advertising and launch a subscription service," Christie Hefner says. The brand's enormous recognition factor was an advantage in the transition to online, she says, but admits, "we learned to have patience"—it took five years before it started returning a profit. She believes the *Playboy* brand still "represents sophisticated, sexy fun" and it is leveraged into numerous licensed products worldwide such as sunglasses, jeans, and even shower curtains. "Two newer initiatives are creating physical expressions of the brand," she says. "In the first, we are planning to open three Playboy Concept Stores each year in major markets, via a licensing model. In the second, we are creating large-scale location based entertainment centers in major markets also via licensing."

Despite a new editorial approach designed to bring it into line with the new breed of men's magazines such as *Maxim*, *Playboy* remains highly anachronistic, yet is still the best-selling men's magazine in the United States. "Some might say we're antiquated," says Hefner. "But that's the price you pay for being around for a long time."

NOTES

"A moment came . . ." Atherton, Tony. "The Original Playboy," *Ottawa Citizen*, 12.6.03, p. A1.

"It was something . . ." Hefner, Hugh. "How We Got Started," *FSB Online*.

"He did consider himself . . ." Atherton, Tony. "The Original Playboy," *Ottawa Citizen*, 12.6.03, p. A1.

"Some might say . . ." Hefner, Hugh. "How We Got Started," *FSB Online*.

REFERENCES

ABC, *BusinessWeek*, CBS *Marketwatch*, *Chicago Sun-Times*, *Chicago Tribune*, CNN *Money*, *Daily Press*, *Fair Disclosure Wire*, *Forbes*, *Fortune*, *The Guardian*, *Hamilton Spectator*, *The Independent*, *Inside Media*, *International Herald Tribune*, *Los Angeles Times*, *Mediaweek*, NBC, *New York Times*, *Newsday*, *Orlando Sentinel*, *Ottawa Citizen*, *Playboy*, *Slate*, *Time*, *The Times*, *Vancouver Sun*, *Variety*, *Washington Post*, WWD

Section 17

THE LENNON AND McCARTNEY DUOS

Tupperware

Great ideas don't necessarily sell themselves

TUPPERWARE'S CREATOR, EARL SILAS TUPPER, MAY HAVE invented groundbreaking plastic food-storage containers but this demanding perfectionist from New England had no idea how to sell them. Tupper was said to feel physically ill if he found himself at a large gathering of women, so how on earth was he going to make money out of these milky-white airtight plastic bowls for housewives?

The early days of Tupperware were a long way from today's annual sales of $1.2 billion. The first Tupperware became available in 1946, and in the early years, the product was marketed in traditional retail stores. It did not sell well. Enter Brownie Wise, a single mother from rural Georgia, a dynamic babe with a beaming smile, and the antidote to the reclusive Tupper. She was excited about Tupper's bowls, and she had found a way to sell them, the Tupperware home party. (She needed the money to pay her son's medical bills.)

Wise argued that the brilliance of Tupperware needed to be explained to women, to be demonstrated to them, how it seals in freshness and how it "burps" (the characteristic sound when the lid is sealed properly); after all, the bowls themselves couldn't talk. Wise had been doing great business directly selling Tupperware for Stanley Home Products, and she convinced Tupper to switch to selling Tupperware at patio parties.

Despite their differences, Wise became the vice president in charge of sales in 1951 and began to build her army of Tupperware women.

Direct selling was the answer. By 1954, Tupperware sales had hit $25 million and there were 9,000 Tupperware salespeople in the United States, only 1,000 of whom were men. Wise was a celebrity and made the cover of *BusinessWeek*, the first woman ever to do so. She drove a pink Cadillac given to her by Tupper and had a Florida mansion complete with flamingos.

Wise cultivated the Tupperware lady persona, perfect for postwar American women embracing a new era of consumerism and affluence. The Tupperware lady always wore panty hose and heels, was immaculately groomed, intensely house-proud and charming—she became a role model for many women of the time as she was earning her own money while maintaining her role as homemaker. Said Anna Tate, a Tupperware recruiter, the man made the bread, the women "a little cake." Tupperware was able to ride the post-war boom, with housewives hell-bent on modern comforts and the latest consumer products.

Wise was almost religious in her zeal for Tupperware. She worked her sales troops up into a frenzy at her sales conferences, referred to by Tupperware as "Jubilees." There, Wise offered extravagant gifts, for star sellers (fur coats, jewelry, cars), "wish fairies" would present gifts and Wise even instigated a walk of fame to pay tribute to top sellers. There were fancy dress parties and trips to Europe. Wise offered thousands of women a source of income regardless of education or previous job skills.

Wise's success irked Tupper. "He didn't want the limelight for himself. He hated the limelight," says *Tupperware!* documentary maker Laurie Kahn-Leavitt. "He wanted the limelight for his product and it irked him when Brownie got all the credit for the success of his company." After all, he was the one who had invented the storage containers.

Tupperware was not Tupper's first invention. Tupper had devised a bizarre collection of inventions, from an entire theme park to a surgical procedure for removing the appendix through the anus. After his tree-surgery business failed, Tupper took a job with Viscaloid Co., a plastics company owned by DuPont. He worked there for just a year before starting his own plastics company, the Earl S. Tupper Company, in 1938. During World War II his company made such items as gas masks. His breakthrough came after the war when he began working with pure polyethylene pellets that would become the material for Tupperware products. For the first time, a plastic was made that was not smelly and brittle (it had been developed for weapons during the war). He then spent ten years improving the product and devising his patented tight-seal lid. After the war, Tupper could concentrate on making household items and the first Wonderlier bowl appeared in 1946.

Despite her influence, or because of it, Wise was fired in 1958 after continuing disagreements with Tupper. Despite Tupperware's sales tipping $100 million, she left with just $35,000 severance pay. With no stock options in the company, Wise lost her pink house and pink car. The company was so keen to disassociate itself from Wise that they buried all remaining copies of her book of motivational talks, *Best Wishes, Brownie Wise*, a drama reported in Laurie Kahn-Leavitt's documentary *Tupperware!* Tupper subsequently sold the company for $16 million to Rexall. (The company now has a market capitalization of $936 million.) Tupper moved to Florida, then Bermuda, then Panama, and finally to Costa Rica where he died in 1983. Wise died in 1992.

Today there are more than 800,000 Tupperware sales representatives in one hundred countries. A Tupperware party begins somewhere in the world every 2.5 seconds. There is a line of Tupperware cosmetics and, in an effort to reach more markets, Tupperware has set up kiosks in shopping centers to introduce new customers to the products. There are even online Tupperware parties. But the essence of the company remains the same. Wise's direct sales theory still stands today. Those bowls still don't know how to talk.

NOTES
"A little cake . . ." *Tupperware!*, a film by Laurie Kahn-Leavitt, 2004.

REFERENCES
Clarke, Alison . *Tupperware: The Promise of Plastic in 1950s America*, Smithsonian Institution Press, 1999.

The Age, Australian Financial Review, Bloomberg.com, *Boston Globe, BusinessWeek,* Canadian Review of Sociology and Anthropology, *Cincinatti Enquirer,* CNN, *Daily Objectivist, Evening Standard,* Everything2.com, *Financial Times, Fortune, The Guardian, Harvard University Gazette,* Hoover's Company Reports, *The Independent, International Herald Tribune,* Inventors.About.com, *Journal of Women's History, LA Weekly, Marketing Week,* Massachusetts Institute of Technology Engineering Department, *Metro Times* (Detroit), *Newsweek, New York Times, New Yorker, The Observer, Plastics News, Salon* magazine, *San Francisco Chronicle, Slate Magazine, The Sunday Age, Sydney Morning Herald, The Times,* Tupperware.com, *Washington Post, Washington Times*

Apple

A great idea is not always enough

DEPENDING ON YOUR AGE, YOU MAY OR MAY NOT KNOW THAT long, long before Apple started selling iPod Shuffles, it was poised to become the most powerful computer manufacturer in the world. If history had been slightly different, that computer on your desk today would be an Apple rather than an anonymous box running Windows.

The Apple Macintosh computer changed the world. Before the Macintosh, computers were mathematical, complicated, and arcane. You had to learn lines of complicated commands just to make them work. The first Macintosh, launched in 1984, was intuitive and friendly. You turned it on and a little smiling face appeared. If you typed words in Times New Roman font, then that was how they appeared on the screen, in black text on a white background—like paper. For the first time, a computer worked in a way that made sense.

Its advance over the competition, the IBM PC, was generational. Even Bill Gates recognized that as soon as he set eyes on the machine. The Macintosh soon commanded 20 percent of worldwide personal computer sales, and looked certain to set the new standard.

Except that Apple blew it.

Apple was founded in 1976 in California's Santa Clara Valley by Steve Wozniak and Steve Jobs, who met in 1973 in a mutual friend's garage. Wozniak, four years older than Jobs, had already graduated high school, but the pair seemed to click instantly.

Wozniak had been a technical whiz from childhood, when, unable to afford the parts, he designed computers in his head, drawing up plans for more than fifty variations by the time he graduated high school. Jobs, who made up for what he lacked in technical knowledge with an ability to hustle anything (secondhand computer chips, contraband, even, once he graduated, jobs at Hewlett-Packard and Atari). Wozniak attended Berkley; Jobs attended Reed College in Portland, Oregon. The college had a counter-culture focus where he became a "fruitarian," studied eastern philosophy, and refused to bathe.

Wozniak got a good job with Hewlett-Packard; Jobs eventually finagled his way into a position at nearby Atari, the video game maker, which was where the pair made a game in their spare time called Breakout. They were also members of a computer club called Homebrew, which met in (where else?) a friend's garage. Homebrew had been formed after the invention of the first personal computer, the Altair, which was featured on the cover of *Popular Electronics* magazine in January 1975—the same magazine cover that prompted Bill Gates and Paul Allen to start Microsoft, creating software for the Altair.

Wozniak built his own computer, which he offered first to Hewlett-Packard. When they declined, he showed it instead to the Homebrew Club—and Jobs, who immediately saw enormous potential in a business partnership with Wozniak. They founded a little company in 1976 and called it Apple; Jobs was just twenty-one. Wozniak was twenty-six.

Jobs sold his VW van and Wozniak his treasured Hewlett-Packard programmable calculator to fund their first design, the Apple I. They launched it at the Homebrew computer club and sold them for $666.66 per unit over ten months. Marketing manager Mike Markkula then invested $250,000 to become an equal partner and chairman of Apple, which was incorporated in January 1977. Wozniak next built the Apple II, which had a revolutionary color screen and could play games. Launched in April 1977, it was enormously successful, selling 50,000 in twelve months (and in its ever-evolving forms would prove a cash cow for Apple until its demise in 1993, making it probably the longest-lived model of computer in history).

In December 1980, Apple went public, selling 4.6 million shares at $22 each and creating enormous wealth for its founders: Jobs was worth $100 million at age twenty-five; Wozniak bought a Porsche and a movie theater. Wozniak also developed a passion for flying, which led, in February 1981, to a crash in a light plane that left him with head injuries. It took him five years to recover.

Exactly how Jobs and Wozniak got the idea for the Macintosh has become shrouded in myth. The generally accepted version is that in December 1979 Jobs and a group of Apple engineers managed to barter their way into Xerox's Palo Alto Research Center in exchange for discounted Apple stocks. On their brief tour, they saw an experimental computer that used a mouse to negotiate a desktop composed of overlapping windows, with realistic black text. Xerox did not seem to recognize the potential of its own invention, but Jobs certainly did—and went on to build the Macintosh.

The reality of the Mac's birth was probably a little more complicated. Jobs did get a look at the Xerox machine, but it had not exactly been a secret up till then, with Xerox publicizing its use of display graphics and a mouse for several years. According to Michael S. Malone, who wrote the enormously detailed account of Apple's growth, *Infinite Loop: How the World's Most Insanely Great Computer Company Went Insane* (Aurum Press, 1999), it was a programmer named Jef Raskin who had first visited Xerox in the summer of 1973. He joined Apple in 1977 and, inspired by what he had seen at Xerox, lay the foundation for the Macintosh. (Raskin, according to Malone's account, also tried out an embryonic version of the Internet at Xerox.)

After a false start with a machine called the Lisa (a good product that was far too expensive, at $12,000, for the small-business and home market Apple was aiming at), Apple launched the Macintosh in 1984 with an advertisement screened during the Superbowl football game. The ad, directed by *Blade Runner's* Ridley Scott and costing $500,000, portrayed a woman running through an oppressive future world where a Big Brother figure controls a mindless crowd from a giant screen. She throws a hammer at the screen, white light blinds the crowd, and the new Macintosh is introduced—easily understood symbolism that suggested freedom from the oppressive institution of the IBM PC.

As a brand and as a philosophy, Apple had arrived. Its product was indeed, in the words of Steve Jobs, "insanely great." And Jobs himself, always a charismatic entrepreneur, now assumed God-like status in the computer industry.

But some of his decisions were questionable. He specified that the Macintosh should launch with far less memory than it actually needed to work well, and it had no hard disk, which meant users were forever swapping floppy discs in and out. Under-powered and not as cheap as many had hoped ($2,495 at launch, $4,000 for a beefed-up version released later), it was seen by some as a novelty compared to the dull but ever-evolving IBM-family competitors and did not catch on with businesses.

As a company, Apple was in transition. Apple workers (literally) planted a pirate flag atop the headquarters to signify their rebellion from the corporate hegemony—a spirit of revolt that was to undermine the company's strategy for growth. Steve Wozniak lost interest in the ever-growing Apple and, while maintaining links with Jobs, left to become a computer teacher in February 1985.

Jobs then left Apple in September 1985 after repeated clashes with Mike Markkula and CEO John Sculley (who had come in from Pepsi-Cola), showing a mercurial side to his personality that created dissent and bitterness, in contrast to his usual winning charm. He went on to start another computer company called NeXT Software.

Without Jobs, his idealism, perfectionism, and charisma so strong it was described as a "reality distortion field," Apple foundered, torn between the commercial demands of growth and the idealism that still endured among the engineers. And IBM did not just disappear. Quite the contrary: because IBM's machines were made from readily available parts, there were suddenly numerous copycat versions— "clones"—on the market. Most used Microsoft's MS-DOS operating system, licensed to them by Bill Gates' fledgling company. Apple, conversely, chose to jealously guard its secrets, sealing cases of new Macintoshes closed with screws that required a special Apple tool to open them. Apple wanted to make everything in-house—hardware, operating system, even software.

In 1985, Bill Gates had offered to help Apple license its technology, sending the company a memo; Gates was interested in forming an alliance that would benefit both companies. Time and again the board met to consider licensing their technology, only to drown in internal politics. So the deal with Microsoft did not go ahead.

Apple's market share dropped from 20 percent in 1987 to less than 4 percent in 1997. Along the way, there had been opportunities to sell the business to Sun Microsystems, or to partner up with new-comers such as Sony. But the Apple board could not bring itself to relinquish its independence.

Microsoft launched Windows, its clunky but increasingly refined version of the point-and-click user interface. Apple attempted a legal challenge that eventually failed. Meanwhile, Apple suffered numerous production glitches, including a particular Powerbook laptop that had a tendency to catch fire. The Apple Newton personal digital assistant, chairman Sculley's big hope in 1993, flopped. True believers kept the faith, but converts were few and far between. In 1997, Apple made a loss of $1 billion.

After a succession of CEOs, Apple called once more on Steve Jobs, who had been engaged with making the animation studio Pixar a huge success (eventually bringing Jobs some $1 billion in share holdings) and trying to make a new company called NeXT Software fly (not so successful). In 1996, Apple bought NeXT for $400 million, which got them a new operating system that Jobs's team had designed, and the services of Jobs as an advisor, working half a day a week. The industry was abuzz with rumors Jobs wanted his old job back—which he denied. "People keep trying to suck me in," Jobs told *BusinessWeek* in March, 1997. "They want me to be some kind of Superman. But I have no desire to run Apple Computer. I deny it at every turn, but nobody believes me." Funny, then, that in September 1997 Jobs took the helm at Apple as "interim CEO" (on the now-legendary salary of $1) and set about redefining the company. At NeXT Software he had brought together a team of visionaries, five of whom came across to Apple with him, including Jonathan Ive (industrial design), Avie Tevanian (software), and Jon Rubenstein (hardware).

His first major public appearance as Apple's returning founder was at the Boston MacWorld Expo in August 1997. It was quite an occasion: in his keynote speech, Jobs brought up none other that Bill Gates on the big screen. While some in the crowd gasped and booed, Jobs told the gathering: "We have to let go of the notion that for Apple to win, Microsoft needs to lose. The era of competition between Microsoft and Apple is over, as far as I'm concerned."

Jobs whittled the existing product line down to just three computers, turning around 1996's first-quarter loss of $740 million to a profit of $30 million in the third quarter. Jobs made an alliance with Microsoft which included Microsoft making Mac versions of its software and with his new team he set to work on a new range. Jobs's first product was the iMac, a contemporary version of the original Macintosh. It may not have been technologically advanced, but it looked like no other computer, a one-piece design that combined screen and processor inside a candy-colored, translucent, organic-shaped shell. It was pitched as an Internet connection and entertainment device. Once again, Jobs had managed to turn a commodity into a must-have object and sales surged, bringing Apple into a profit of $601 million in 1999, though profits ebbed back to $65 million in 2002 as buyer enthusiasm for the new-look Apple once again gave way to the realities of the PC-dominated market.

Jobs pursued the entertainment-portal vision with the flat-panel version of the iMac (which offered buyers a then-revolutionary DVD burner), widescreen laptops, and—the biggest hit of all—the iPod personal music player.

Jobs had initially developed the music software iTunes, which made managing a database of tracks easier, then realized what it needed was a portable player to go with it. Nine months later, in a crash program reminiscent to the development of Sony's first Walkman, they unveiled the iPod in November 2001. Some criticized the price—$399 for the entry-level model—but its good looks and user-friendly design gave it "must-have" appeal. A hit with early adopters, it went mass market in 2003 when it was the essential Christmas gift, creating a world of "poddies" who downloaded their entire record collections onto the MP3 player's hard drive. By 2005 the iPod had some 33 percent of the total world market for MP3 digital music players by units sold and 51 percent by dollar value. In the first quarter of 2004, sales of iPods were up 900 percent on the same period a year earlier; Apple has now sold an estimated thirty-seven million iPods.

The entertainment crossover, particularly with Apple's iTunes Internet music service—the first music downloading service acceptable to both fans and artists alike—has proved so successful some analysts believe Apple will eventually redefine itself as a consumer electronics firm.

In June 2003, Apple finally appeared to have closed the price-technology gap in personal computers when Jobs launched the G5 range, stunningly fast machines that came in beautiful aluminum cases created by Jonathan Ive. But hardware is no longer the main game: what Jobs calls "digital lifestyle" is now Apple's modus operandi, covering music, digital pictures, and home video, integrated into a suite of complementary "i" programs including iMovie, iTunes, iPhoto, iDVD, and GarageBand, a digital music synthesizer; all of them easy to use. Significantly, Jobs offered versions of iPod and iTunes for Windows.

Apple is unlikely to ever have another shot at world domination but at least now it is again the best in the world at what it does: innovation.

NOTES

"People keep trying to suck me in . . ." Burrows, Peter. "Apple: What Is Steve Jobs Up To," *BusinessWeek*, 3.17.97.

REFERENCES

ABC News, *Apple: The Inside Story of Intrigue, Egomania, and Business Blunders,* by Jim Carlton, Crown Business, 1997.

Amelio, Gil, *On the Firing Line: My 500 Days at Apple,* HarperBusiness 1998.

Deutschman, Alan, *The Second Coming of Steve Jobs,* Broadway, 2001.

BBC, *Business 2.0, BusinessWeek, Cnet, Forbes, Freerepublic.com, The Guardian, Inventors.com, The Los Angeles Times, New Statesman, Salon.com, Stanford Library Interviews, Time, Wired*

id Software

Great companies don't necessarily need "adult supervision"

———

JOHN CARMACK IS AN INTROSPECTIVE MAN WHO SHUNS PUBLICITY. His name is unknown outside the world of hardcore computer gaming; yet when he decides to speak up on an issue, which he usually does in a low-key message on an Internet chat site, people like Microsoft's Bill Gates and Apple's Steve Jobs pay close attention.

The games created by Carmack and his partners—including the ultra-violent *Doom* and *Quake*—have sold millions of units, shaping an entire industry with their technical innovations, and helped countless teenagers to spend whole weekends at a stretch blasting aliens when they should have been studying.

Carmack's company, id Software, is based a long way from Silicon Valley, in Mesquite, Texas, and has just twenty-one employees. It makes, at most, one or two new products a year, and its business practices have often been quite counter-intuitive, such as when it gives away its products for free. Its management structure is occasionally anarchic—it's an industry joke that id "lacks adult supervision." So why does Carmack have so much influence?

Few people take computer games seriously, either as an art form or an industry. In terms of revenue, though, the games industry is fast approaching the movie and music industries and has an increasing influence over the rest of the technology sector—in a stagnating PC industry, the only people constantly upgrading their machines these days are gamers.

In 2005, the game spurring gamers on to upgrade was *Quake 4*, the latest in a series created by id Software, the company John

Carmack started with another twenty-something gamer, John Romero, and fellow enthusiasts. Carmack and Romero have been called the Lennon and McCartney of gaming, a reasonable analogy, describing their level of creativity and impact on the gaming industry.

Carmack grew up, in his own words, as a "stereotypical geek," with interests in computer hacking, science fiction, rockets, and bombs. "I was arrogant about being smarter than other people, but unhappy that I wasn't able to spend all my time doing what I wanted," he wrote in a posting on the industry news site Slashdot.org, explaining why he spent a year in a juvenile home (at fourteen he and some friends "borrowed" a computer from a wealthier school). Eventually, he wound up at a tiny software company called Softdisk, where he met John Romero. "I was happy," he said, "I was programming, or reading about programming, or talking about programming almost every waking hour."

Carmack, the technical genius, and Romero, designer extraordinaire, built their first game in their spare time, generating enough enthusiasm to quit their day jobs and start id Software with some other hard-core programmers, making their home in Mesquite, Texas in 1991. After a series of entertaining, arcade-like games, they created the game that was to redefine id—and the entire world of computer gaming. Called *Wolfenstein 3D*, it gave gamers their first view of a virtual world from the protagonist's perspective.

id was also one of the first companies to give away samples of its product. Instead of signing with distributors and spending money on advertising, id simply gave away part of *Wolfenstein* to gamers for free on floppy discs, called shareware. If consumers liked it enough, they could send a check for the rest. These days, demos and downloadable samples of software are commonplace, but in 1991 it was radical. And it worked.

When id launched *Doom* in 1993, it gave away roughly 100 million demo copies for free, but one in ten gamers bought the full

The Lennon and McCartney Duos | 321

version and id has since generated more than $100 million from the franchise, according to estimates.

Carmack and Romero also gave away what many would consider trade secrets, allowing other developers and hobbyists access to their code "engines," the building blocks of their games. That eventually translated into licensing fees (many commercial games use a licensed id engine at their core) and as gamers were able to modify and improve the original games, id was able to maintain a high profile in the marketplace, despite its own low product output. id helped to create communities that maintained interest in upcoming products. *Doom III*, for instance, was the most talked-about game for three years before it appeared on shelves: in 2002 it won the equivalent of an Oscar at the Electronic Entertainment Expo, voted Best of Show—and that was for a mere demo version.

Romero left id in 1996 to start a company called Ion Storm, which eventually became another leading developer, but only after its first, grandiose game proved a disaster, running years behind deadline.

Carmack stayed behind at id, which he now co-owns with Adrian Carmack (no relation), Kevin Cloud, Tim Willits, and Todd Hollenshead. He stuck to his original, teen-friendly formula, even when the media discovered that Columbine High School killers Eric Harris and Dylan Klebold, who shot twelve classmates in 1999, were obsessive players of *Doom* and another id title, *Quake*. Even President Bill Clinton expressed dismay at the violence of the shooter genre. Not that the controversy appeared to unduly bother John Carmack: his company's big release for 2004, *Doom III*, was, once again, an evolution of the horror-movie-themed first-person-shooter—and it has since sold over a million copies. Technically and graphically it is another example of an id product setting the agenda for the rest of the gaming industry.

John Carmack bought his first Ferrari at age twenty-two. He now owns several, but also funnels his need for speed into a band of volunteers called Armadillo Aerospace that is attempting to build a working space vehicle. Carmack has studied 1960s NASA manuals and makes rocket parts in his garage; he has spent some $1.5 million of his own cash, some of which went on a 1960s Russian Cosmonaut space suit he found on eBay, only to discover it had a broken zipper.

Apart from his hobbies, his wife Katherine Anna Kang (whom he met at id) and his little boy, Christopher Ryan, Carmack is still strictly a geek who lives to write computer code. "I get to drive a Ferrari to work but my day-to-day life is almost exactly the same as it was eight years ago," he once said. "I get up, go in to work, hopefully do some good stuff, then go home."

NOTES
"I was arrogant . . ." Slashdot.org, "Chat with John Carmack," 10.15.99.
"I get to . . ." Slashdot.org, "Chat with John Carmack," 10.15.99.

REFERENCES
Kushner, David, *Masters of Doom*, Random House, 2003.

Austin American-Statesman, The Australian, CNN.com, *Computer Gaming World, Dallas Morning News, Economist,* ExtremeTech.com, *Fort Worth Star-Telegram,* Gamespy.com, *Red Herring,* Salon.com, *Slashdot, Slate Magazine, Time, Wired*

Google

A dorm room is as good a place as any to start a multibillion dollar business

GOOGLE CAME RELATIVELY LATE TO THE INTERNET PARTY. IN the mid-1990s, search engines such as Yahoo!, AltaVista, and Lycos were generally regarded as equally useful and there didn't seem a particular need for a new one. Nobody was making much money out of search engines anyway.

In 1995, two twenty-something PhD candidates in computer science at Stanford University, Sergey Brin and Larry Page, the sons of a computer professor and a math professor, began exploring the relationships between pages on the Internet for a research project.

Looking at the hyperlinks that led from one page to another, they realized these formed a huge informal ratings system that funneled users towards useful pages. Using a computer-powered tool to crawl through the Web and evaluate the importance of these links, they built a search engine, initially called BackRub, which provided uncannily good results for users. With nobody interested in buying their idea, they decided to go into business for themselves.

Page found ways to build computer servers using cheap, easily available parts, rather than custom machines specialist companies charged hundreds of thousands of dollars for. Brin recalled in 2003: "We'd go down to the loading dock in the computer science buildings, sort of borrow the ones that were sitting there before, you know, the people who had really got them on their grants, like, got around to it. But eventually, that became kind of unscalable, and we decided we could get better resources if we started a company."

Page and Brin constructed their first data center in Page's dorm room from cheap PC parts and $15,000 borrowed on credit cards. They then moved to a Menlo Park, California, garage in September 1998 with four employees and $1 million in capital from friends, family, and investors who included Andy Bechtolsheim, one of the founders of Sun Microsystems. As Brin recalls on Google's website, "We met him very early one morning on the porch of a Stanford faculty member's home in Palo Alto. We gave him a quick demo. He had to run off somewhere, so he said, 'Instead of us discussing all the details, why don't I just write you a check?' It was made out to Google Inc. and was for $100,000."

In June 1999, Google announced it had secured seed capital including $25 million from venture capitalists Sequoia Capital and Kleiner Perkins Caufield & Byers, a stake that is now worth some $4 billion.

They rented the smallest space available, and ripped apart cheap computers to make their own space-efficient servers.

They were soon answering 10,000 search inquiries a day. By the end of 2000, that had increased to 60 million a day. By 2005, Google—the name comes from the number googol, a 1 followed by one hundred zeroes—was fielding over 200 million requests a day. For an Internet company, Google became profitable relatively quickly: after losing a reported $6 million in 1999, it turned a net profit of $6 million in 2001, up to $399 million in 2004, on revenues of $3.2 billion. Unlike the majority of Silicon Valley start-ups, Google resisted the temptation to go public early. Following a blaze of publicity, Google had its IPO in 2004 and was valued at $23.1 billion. In November 2005, the company was valued at $111 billion, making Google the world's largest media company by stock market value. Page and Brin, at least on paper, are multibillionaires.

So how did an Internet start-up with no obvious revenue stream succeed? From the outset, Page and Brin focused on a single goal: efficient search results. That meant accuracy and speed. Like a

Formula One racecar, where a few grams of unnecessary weight can mean the difference between pole position and also-ran, Google's home page is fanatically spartan: no images, no flashy graphics, and just thirty-seven words. Compared to the opposition, such as Yahoo!, who filled their home pages with graphics, newsflashes, and directories, Google was refreshingly simple.

Not to say it is perfect: Google indexes some four billion web pages, but that's a fraction of the total out there, which are constantly multiplying. And its machine-driven page ranking system is vulnerable to distortions such as "Google bombing," in which canny users link sites together for fun, political ends, or malice: in 2003 Google users who typed in the words "miserable failure" were directed to George W. Bush's biography on the White House website; and, prior to the Iraq war, entering the words "weapons of mass destruction" brought up a "computer error"-style page that read "These Weapons of Mass Destruction cannot be displayed." Still, most of the time it works pretty well: type in "Google critics," for example, and it will immediately find you the virulently anti-Google site googlewatch.com.

In the early days, Google spent virtually no money on marketing, relying initially on word of mouth among early adopters who loved its quirky, non-commercial look. Yet Google was anything but. Instead of amassing a paper fortune through a premature IPO, Google found a viable revenue stream from selling its search results to other search engines, including market leader Yahoo!, and from advertising, which it developed in its typically counterintuitive style. Ads are unobtrusive text-only affairs linked to search terms (type in "holiday," for instance, and travel company promotions will appear alongside your search results). Ads are limited to a handful down the right-hand side of the page; advertisers bid for the best positions. Pop-ups, graphics, streaming video, even logos are banned: too time-consuming, too irritating. Yet advertising doesn't have to occupy acres of real estate to succeed and Google claims a click-through rate five to ten times that of typical banner ads. They're neatly targeted and in style and content they appear more useful than annoying (to the extent some critics complain some users may confuse them with regular search results). Moreover, even in this typographical straitjacket there is room for ongoing improvement. Two Google employees constantly experiment to see which combinations of words work best: a Valentine's Day ad for flowers that read: "Fast. Fresh. Guaranteed" was changed to "Fast. Safe. Guaranteed" and sales doubled.

As a workplace, Google is obsessively focused on the core product, yet flexible enough to encourage a constant stream of new ideas. Engineers work in small, autonomous units, rotating the leadership and doing pretty much whatever they think needs to be done. Reportedly, nobody is allowed to talk in meetings for longer than ten minutes.

Google's headquarters in Mountain View, California, called the Googleplex, is a one thousand-employee paradise with free food, unlimited ice cream, pool and ping-pong tables, and complimentary massages, plus the options to spend 20 percent of work time on any outside activity and bring their dogs to the office. Before they moved in there was talk of doing without conventional telephones altogether, since everybody would be using their cell phones. Page and Brin completed the image of a "workplace of the future" by riding around on matching Segways.

Though it's not all frat-room stuff: Page and Brin hired former Novell CEO Eric Schmidt to run the operation as the "designated adult" (CEO and chairman). Page, who was Google's first CEO, became president of products in April 2001.

Google's approach to new technologies is freewheeling yet conservative. New ideas appear all the time on a part of the site called Google Labs, yet just a handful are allowed to pollute the purity of the home page.

Similarly, Google guards its core—the basics of the business—like virtual crown jewels, but it allows any developer out there to download the search engine for use in their own applications. Some might view giving the product away as insane but Google's hope is that its technology will wind up integrated in something interesting.

Going public has opened Google to criticism: some investors are nervous about the dot-com-boom-style workplace and the unorthodox management style. Others question whether the extraordinary growth can continue with one major product. But Google's dot-com-style work habits also mean exacting standards and an environment that attracts the best employees, in an industry that relies entirely on sharp minds. And while Google still sits behind its Spartan home page, in the background it is constantly launching new applications, such as desktop search, maps, free webmail, Blogger weblog software, and Picasa photo software—all of which move Google beyond search and into broader, perhaps even Microsoft, territory. In 2005, it announced an ambitious project to scan millions of library books around the world and make them available online, including titles from the New York Public Library, Harvard University, and Oxford University's Bodleian Library, causing a stink about potential copyright infringements and vague unrest about Google's growing scope.

Critics have also raised concerns about Google's email service, which offers users a large amount of free storage space, in return for which it attaches ads to emails that reflect the content of the message. Google claims its privacy policy is watertight, and that it would never release your personal details to anybody, but there is something slightly spooky about an organization keeping tabs on your Internet search habits and your emails—information that could both identify you and prove embarrassing if it fell into the wrong hands.

Still, if you don't like Google, there's a simple solution to the problem. "Some say Google is God," Brin once said. "Others say Google is Satan. But if they think Google is too powerful, remember that all it takes is a single click to go to another search engine."

NOTES

"We'd go down . . ." *Fresh Air* (TV), 10.14.03.

"Some say . . ." Ayers, Chris. "Google: Could This Be the New God in the Machine," Weekend Review, *The Times*, 11.1.03, p. 4.

REFERENCES

BusinessWeek, EContent, Fast Company, Financial Times, Fortune, The Independent on Sunday, Info world, New Yorker, Red Herring, Time, Vanity Fair, Wired

Seinfeld

"Originality is more valuable than plutonium"

NEVER THINK ABOUT THE MONEY. THAT'S THE RATHER IRONIC piece of advice Jerry Seinfeld gave when asked by a reporter in 1998 how he made his hundreds of millions. "I have never considered money," he said. "That's the most financially sound approach you can take in my business. When you don't consider money, then you make the right choice. And that always leads to money."

Was Seinfeld, then worth some $500 million and fast on his way to a billion, being facetious? Probably: this is not a man who likes to give a straight answer to anything. But it is true that in the early days, being on TV probably cost him money—it took him away from his day job.

In 1988, when he was first approached for a TV role, Seinfeld was already making a reported $2.5 million a year as a successful stand-up comedian, working as many as three hundred dates a year around the country. He had made some thirty appearances on the Carson and Letterman shows, doing his stand-up routines, and had appeared in his own television special.

The production company Castle Rock Entertainment first had Seinfeld in mind for a part on an ABC pilot called *Past Imperfect*. When that didn't work out, NBC, perhaps concerned somebody else would snap up Seinfeld if they didn't, set up a meeting in early 1989 where they loosely said, why don't you come up with a script for a new show, your own show, and we'll take a look? NBC executive Warren Littlefield, who was soon to become president of NBC Entertainment, later recalled that Seinfeld's response to NBC's offer was similarly vague, proposing a series about "just me and my friends hanging out and doing stuff."

Seinfeld, born in April 1954, grew up in Massapequa, Long Island, and attended Queens College in New York, majoring in communication and theatre arts. His first performance as a stand-up was ruined by terrible nerves—he famously remembered just four words: "the beach," "driving," and "shopping." Unlike comedians such as Robin Williams and the Scot Billy Connolly, both of whom can perform brilliantly with a stream of consciousness that changes from night to night, Seinfeld relied absolutely on his material, which he worked obsessively to perfect; the slightest tweak in his timing could make the difference between his gags—working, or falling flat. He took odd jobs to pay the bills, including selling jewelry on the street, waiting tables, and selling lightbulbs over the phone with his friend Mike Costanza (whose name he later borrowed for the *Seinfeld* character George Costanza). He made time to write an hour a day, come what may, and a strong advocate of self-improvement, he dabbled for a time with yoga, meditation, and even Scientology.

In 1976, Seinfeld met fellow stand-up Larry David, who also used observational material but could be far more acerbic than Seinfeld, with David walking off stage if an audience didn't like his act.

Larry David had been less successful than Seinfeld, at least financially, growing up in Brooklyn then living in subsidized housing on Manhattan's west side. He had nibbled at the big time, working stand-up for a decade, briefly landing a writing job on *Saturday Night Live,* and writing a screenplay that he had yet to see made into a movie. His material was like Seinfeld gone bad—he too put the magnifying glass onto everyday trivia, but while Seinfeld gently poked fun, David launched into angry raves. He also held down a series of odd jobs, working as a bra salesman for two months, and as a chauffeur.

One night, he and Seinfeld dropped into a Korean deli on the way to a comedy club and were riffing off each other about the bizarre impulse-buy products at the register. David turned to Seinfeld: this, he said, is the sort of stuff the TV show should be about.

Together, they sat down and wrote an episode for a pilot called *The Seinfeld Chronicles.* Their basic idea, thrashed out in a meeting in a coffee shop, was about a comedian who got his material from observing the absurdities of everyday life. There would be no main "story"; rather, the show would revolve around conversations. It would feature Seinfeld, playing himself; a character called George, who was played by Jason Alexander; and a character called Kessler (later renamed Kramer), who was played by Michael Richards.

NBC agreed to develop the show even before there was a proper format worked out, breaking all the rules. Why? "The more I learn, the more I realize success is extremely difficult to predict in television," Warren Littlefield wrote in 2001. "Originality is more valuable than plutonium, and we thought these guys deserved a shot at a pilot based on originality alone. So we rolled the dice on Jerry."

In May, 1989, NBC showed the pilot to a test audience who declared it "weak," with unlikable characters, according to the research document. "As one viewer put it, 'you can't get too excited about going to the laundromat.'"

Seinfeld was apparently unfussed about the show's chances, telling *USA Today* that if it flopped he'd give up on television for good. "If they want to do it my way—the right way—we can do a show together. I'm not interested in being a big star and that's working out real good."

NBC did in fact leave the show off the line-up for fall, 1989. But Castle Rock and several executives within NBC still thought it had potential, and later in the year Littlefield siphoned some cash away to make some more episodes of *Seinfeld*. Four more episodes—possibly the smallest number ever commissioned for a series. NBC requested that the show add a girl, the character Elaine, who was eventually played by Julia Louis-Dreyfus, and screened the first of the new episodes on May 31, 1990.

The four episodes—"The Stakeout," "The Robbery," "Male Unbonding," and "The Stock Tip"—performed tolerably, particularly with young men, a coveted audience for advertisers. Apparently NBC was still reluctant to persist: in 1997, Seinfeld told Larry King they had considered selling the show to another network, Fox. Only then, at the last minute, NBC ordered another thirteen episodes.

Seinfeld was not—as was commonly thought—about "nothing"; nor was it in any way typical of sitcoms in general. While a traditional sitcom had likeable characters performing two or three storylines and twelve scenes in half an hour, wrapped up in a happy ending, *Seinfeld* might have thirty scenes and five or six unconnected plots that would come together in a bizarre twist. Their motto (sewn onto jackets at one point) was "No hugging, no learning."

Seinfeld turned out to be about everything David or Seinfeld had ever found funny, weird, or odd, including David's careers as a bra salesman and a chauffeur, and even their experiences while making a pilot for NBC. David carried a notebook for recording everyday thoughts with comic potential, flipping through it when it came time to write a new episode (he wrote sixty episodes himself and oversaw many others).

Seinfeld gradually improved its audience share, and by 1991 was judged a success. By 1996, NBC was charging advertisers $400,000 for a thirty-second spot, and by 1997 it was making more than $200 million in revenue for NBC, attracting more than 30 million viewers a week. Castle Rock Entertainment, which owned the show (NBC only received advertising fees), made some $1 billion by 1998.

The performers were all on big salaries, but Jerry Seinfeld and Larry David also received part of the syndication rights, which were in another league entirely. David, who made a reported $200 million from syndication rights alone, left Seinfeld after the seventh season (though he came back to write the finale) and went on to star in HBO's *Curb Your Enthusiasm,* in which David plays himself, the successful writer of *Seinfeld,* as a well-meaning but cantankerous character who creates a daily pile-up of misunderstandings and social gaffes that inevitably leave him looking totally ridiculous. He has reportedly struggled with his wealth, selling a Porsche two weeks after buying it because he was embarrassed.

Seinfeld, who quit the show at the end of its ninth season in 1998 (despite an offer of $5 million an episode to continue), was less self-conscious about the financial rewards, amassing a collection of vintage Porsches and swank apartments, once reportedly paying $8 million in cash for a property. "Oh yes, I am overpaid," he told Larry King in 1987. "You know, I'd do this for nothing for many years. But as long as they're paying for it, you know, I should get a cut."

NOTES

"I have never considered money . . ." Taylor, Sam. "Jerry Seinfeld, Standing Up for Himself," Review *The Observer,* 7.12.98, p. 20.

"If they want to do it my . . ." Green, Tom. "Comic Seinfeld Stands Up for His Personal 'Chronicles,'" Life, *USA Today,* 7.3.89. p. 3D.

REFERENCES

Openheimer, Jerry. *Seinfeld, the Making of an American Icon,* Harper Collins, 2002.

Edmonton Journal, Electronic Media, The Guardian, Herald Sun, The Independent, Larry King Live, New York Daily News, New York Times, New Yorker, Newsweek, Observer, Record, Scotsman, Seattle Times, USA Today, Variety, Washington Post

FUNKY, INC.

Juicy Couture

"No amount of Madonnas can sell a product if it isn't good"

<hr>

THE "JUICY GIRLS" GELA NASH-TAYLOR AND PAM SKAIST-LEVY singlehandedly turned the humble, uncool tracksuit into a fashion phenomenon with their brand Juicy Couture. Just short of a decade after starting with an initial investment of $100 each, Nash-Taylor and Skaist-Levy sold their business to the Liz Claiborne group in a deal that includes a $53 million payment and ongoing profits that could tip $92 million. That is a lot of tracksuits.

The Juicy girls' business fairy tale has even made it onto a Juicy Couture T-shirt (where they live happily ever after of course), but Nash-Taylor admits that it has taken an "insane" amount of work for their "overnight" success. It was perhaps even more challenging for this start-up because of the pair's aversion to debt. Says Nash-Taylor: "We had very little investment because Pam and I couldn't have slept at night if we knew we owed anyone $10, let alone $60,000."

The "Juicys," as Nash-Taylor, a former actress and mother of three, and Skaist-Levy, a trained milliner and mother of one, like to call themselves (when they are not calling each other "Fluffy"), started their first venture in 1994 after meeting through a mutual friend. Their initial business, Travis Jeans, was built around a gap they saw in the market for stylish maternity jeans and other casual basics. For Nash-Taylor, the business was also driven by being a single mom and the need to earn a decent living. (She has since married John Taylor of 80s supergroup Duran Duran.)

Their Travis maternity jeans were basically old Levis with some extra elastic for the pregnant belly. The product sold well, and they built a strong network of retailers in California including upscale boutiques. They were advised to draw up a business plan and borrow $80,000, but Nash-Taylor and Skaist-Levy did not want to take on any debt. "We never want to owe anybody anything," says Skaist-Levy. "Instead we took our profits and put them back in. We didn't make a salary for probably the first two years." More than a decade on, and the pair still share an office in an unglamorous industrial estate in Pacoima, California.

"We're like sisters," says Nash-Taylor, still calling each other every morning at 6:30 a.m. Observers describe the success of their partnership as very much about their ability to focus on the task at hand. "When both of us focus on something, we have more energy than anyone on the planet," says Nash-Taylor.

The girls refuse to reveal where the idea for the Juicy brand came from. It debuted on a series of T-shirts in 1996, with a royal terrier logo. The tees sold out within weeks. The Juicy range was extended in 1999 to sweaters and scarves, each new range a huge publicity event with as many celebrities as possible roped in for the launches. While sales steadily increased, the business was not reaping the rewards, everyone was just working harder. "We had these huge orders and we still weren't making any money," says Nash-Taylor. The pair called their accountants. Despite having a healthy million dollars in orders, the costs structures meant that the business was only just breaking even. The accountants, who had worked with Juicy for twelve months, were fired on the spot for not explaining this fundamental error in the business strategy. To rectify the situation, Nash-Taylor and Skaist-Levy took a big risk, calling up all the clients who had ordered stock and said that they could not fulfill the orders. They changed their label from Juicy to Juicy Couture, hiked up their prices and went out into the market again, ready to make some money rather than just tread water. These days, a Juicy Couture cashmere tracksuit sells for around $500, and a basic sweat suit costs more than $150. "We learned how to make a profit and run a business," says Nash-Taylor. "We learned the hard way. My first piece of advice, before you invest a dime or borrow a penny from a bank, is to find out if anyone is interested in your product and find out how to price it so you can make money."

The company-making product, their range of velour, low-cut, comfy tracksuits was launched in 2001. They were a fashion phenomenon with Madonna, Oprah, and many other celebrities wearing custom Juicy Couture tracksuits. Paparazzi shots of Juicy-clad off-duty celebrities appeared in glossy magazines around the world, and a new, velour star was born. What made girls love these tracksuits even more was that they were not really made for going to the gym, they were made for slouching around watching DVDs, for low-key shopping, coffee, and other very girly pursuits.

Without big cash flows, Skaist-Levy and Nash-Taylor's marketing strategy had to be low cost. (Juicy Couture did not advertise until 2004.) The pair has always brilliantly used the cult of celebrity to sell their brand, sending out free customized Juicy Couture to people they knew could further their cause, particularly targeting movie stars and fashion editors. This approach, known as swag marketing, is not a new approach by any means, but the Juicys took this to another level. "They really know how to work it in terms of getting free product into the hands of people," says Rose Apodaca, West Coast bureau Chief of *WWD*. The Juicy approach was more than sending out a parcel of goodies; they would take a suite at a five-star Los Angeles hotel such as stylish Hollywood hotel Chateau Marmont and have people come through all day—celebrities, editors, assistants, and other key clients, handing out freebies that they would go away and wear, inadvertently promoting Juicy to a wide audience. The exclusivity of the events also added to the buzz about the brand. These events typically cost $20,000–$100,000 to stage but the return on investment was considerable with reams and reams of editorial coverage. Nash-Taylor says that while their address books are rather impressive, with the likes of Valentino and

Oprah Winfrey—both Juicy wearers—she says that they like the Juicy product for the same reason that their non-famous clients do. Nash-Taylor points out: "No amount of Madonnas can sell a product that isn't good."

Any positive editorial coverage would inspire Nash-Taylor to send the reporter even more free Juicy gear. "You better believe it," she says. Nowadays, this approach involves chartering private jets to fly in preferred clients to a new store opening in Las Vegas: same principle, just not exactly low-budget marketing.

What Nash-Taylor and Skaist-Levy did right from the start was to design girly, comfy fashion ranges that weren't meant to be reinvented every season. Juicy Couture pieces have a long shelf life and are not designed to be sensitive to seasonal trends. "Designers have to come up with entirely new looks each season," says Nash-Taylor. "We don't have to do that. If it works, we don't fix it."

By the end of 2002, Juicy Couture had racked up sales of $47 million and had 200 staff. It wasn't long before the company became a highly desirable acquisition for big fashion houses. Skaist-Levy and Nash-Taylor also knew that they would need a "sugar daddy" to continue to fund the rapid growth of the Juicy Couture brand. Their sugar daddy took the form of Liz Claiborne chairman and chief executive officer Paul Charrone, who paid an estimated $53 million in March 2003 for the company, plus offered the girls future earnings that could make the deal worth more than $92 million. The sale coincided with *Vogue* magazine describing Juicy Couture as the "future of fashion." The Juicys remain copresidents and retain creative control of Juicy Couture.

In the Juicy journey, the most stressful time for its founders was deciding when to let go. When it came to signing the contracts, Nash-Taylor remembers asking to be excused from the room. "I went into my bathroom and collapsed in tears and Pam came in and we collapsed hysterically. It was a horrible moment, it was like cutting off your arm and I wanted to take the business back instantly," says Nash-Taylor, who, of the two, was more inclined to hang on to the business a little longer. "Pam didn't want the stress of it on our shoulders anymore. There comes a point where your business outgrows you and you can't run it anymore."

Since Liz Claiborne took over the business, sales have skyrocketed. In 2004, sales moved past a reported $200 million and keep rising. Liz Claiborne does not reveal its division's sales but Nash-Taylor will say that the business has "way more than tripled its sales." When Juicy's first showroom opened in London in 2005, Nash-Taylor warned the Claiborne staff that they should brace themselves for the onslaught of buyers. "They were barely able to hold their heads above water," she says.

One of the major benefits of the sale is that Liz Claiborne has been able to help Juicy Couture cope with phenomenal growth, updating Juicy couture's "antiquated" systems, particularly in IT and distribution. "Now it is all very high tech rather than people running around helter skelter throwing things into boxes," says Nash-Taylor. Around 70 percent of the product is still made in the U.S. A new Juicy Couture flagship store in Las Vegas store has been so successful the company has had to double their forecast stock for the store.

While the company remains based in an unmarked building in Pacoima, California, Nash-Taylor and Skaist-Levy are living their dream. Designers John Galliano and Karl Lagerfeld wear their tracksuits, there are Juicy Couture Barbie dolls, and Nash-Taylor has another business idea bubbling away. "It is going to be huge," she says.

NOTES

"They really know . . ." Weddle, David. "Swagland," *Los Angeles Times*, 1.16.05, part 1, p. 14.

"You better believe . . ." Weddle, David. "Swagland," *Los Angeles Times*, 1.16.05, part 1, p. 14.

"Designers have to . . ." *The Record*, Kitchener-Waterloo, Ontario, Canada "Juicy Capitalizes on Desire for 'Sexy Basics,'" AAP, 8.21.03.

"No amount of Madonnas . . ." Bradberry, Grace. "The Women Who Made Velour Cool," *The Times*, London, 4.11.04, Times 2, p. 6.

REFERENCES

BusinessWeek, Financial Times, Los Angeles Business Journal, Los Angeles Times, New York Times, The Oprah Winfrey Show 4.12.03, Sunday Times, Vogue, Women's Wear Daily

Jamie Oliver

The world always wants to get naked

O NLY JUST REACHING HIS THIRTIES, THE SCRUFFY-HAIRED, rough-around-the-edges, frantically busy, cursing British chef Jamie Oliver has crammed a lot more than *Oprah* appearances into his lifetime. In 1966 Oliver was discovered by a television documentary crew while they were filming at the swank London restaurant The River Café where Jamie was working (and wise cracking) as a sous-chef. Immediately after Jamie's cheeky kitchen antics were screened on British television, he fielded offers from five different television companies. The concept of "The Naked Chef" was born—a down-to-earth lad with a mock Cockney accent in the kitchen, creating simple, tasty food, playing drums, and whizzing around on his Vespa with groovy inner-city Londoners. When Oliver signed up for his own television series, he says he was "shit scared and I thought I'd bitten off more than I could chew." But he did chew, and the program became a sensation in 1998. Audiences loved his turns of phrase, his jerky, pacy technique, and his simple recipes. He was everywhere, with several programs airing at once, writing cookbook after cookbook. All of a sudden Jamie Oliver was hot property.

The phenomenal demand for his pared-down recipes has him selling more books in some years than anyone else in Britain except Harry Potter creator J. K. Rowling.

Oliver became a celebrity, picking up lucrative sponsorship deals with all manner of companies, from saucepans to supermarkets. He had the stylish girlfriend (now wife, Jools), the wedding, and the cute offspring. All the while Jamie has stuck close by his family, even using his father's accountant to oversee his business dealings.

Early on, the hyperactive boy from Essex was cooking at The Cricketers, his parents' pub. "As soon as I could carry plates I was working," he says. At twelve he was training the catering school graduates coming to work at the hotel and at sixteen he dropped out of school and went to catering college.

More than 2,000 requests are made daily for bookings for his non-profit London restaurant, Fifteen. His books are available in twenty-one languages in fifty countries and his television programs are broadcast in fifty countries. He promotes Tefal saucepans, Royal Worcester tableware, Sainsbury supermarkets, and has an online daily diary. Vodafone offers cell phone recipes and there is a charity called "Cheeky Chops." It is very much Jamie Inc.

When Jamie told his family and his accountant that he was going to train a group of long-term unemployed youngsters how to cook in a restaurant he would create especially for them, they told him he was mad. But the resulting series *Jamie's Kitchen* was a ratings smash and saved Jamie's credibility. The workaholic, swearing, passionate, stressed-out, compassionate, communicative Oliver that shone through during the series added a whole new dimension to his image and has been well worth Jamie remortgaging his house to do it. Jamie has established other Fifteen-style restaurants in the Netherlands and there are plans for a restaurant in Australia. The lesson of the Oliver phenomenon seems to be that it is okay to be "shit scared" when offered a big opportunity, and that taking risks can be a beautiful thing.

NOTES

"Shit scared . . ." East, Louise. "Naked Ambition," *The Irish Times*, 11.21.02, p. 73.
"As I could . . ." Gerard, Jasper. "Now if Jamie Oliver ruled the country," *Sunday Times*, 1.26.03, p. 2.

REFERENCES

The Age, Australian Financial Review, Caterer and Hotelkeeper, Daily Telegraph, Delicious, The Economist, Evening Standard, FifteenRestaurant.com, *The Independent, International Herald Tribune, Irish Times, New York Times, Sunday Times, Sydney Morning Herald*

CollegeHumor.com

It's all about how you look at opportunities

———

EVER SINCE ITS INCEPTION, ONE OF THE INTERNET'S MOST commonly used features is the limitless pool of jokes and wacky pictures. Millions of people around the world devote large chunks of time to this phenomenon, particularly college students who can't get enough of dorm room gags, especially if they involve beer, bloopers, and topless girls. In the winter of 2000, connoisseurs of college humor and aspiring business students Josh Abramson and Ricky Van Veen created a website that would cater to this discerning demographic of eighteen to twenty-four-year-olds, giving students a forum for their often tasteless, crass comedy. The pair, friends since the sixth grade in Baltimore where they grew up, had the goal of finding enough online advertisers to pay for their beer (a considerable campus expense) and creating a website "fully dedicated to grinding your academic efforts to a halt." There was never a business plan. "The greatest thing about starting a business in college," says

Abramson, "is that there is very little risk." There was a $30 a month server fee and that's it.

CollegeHumor.com was launched with $200 of savings. Abramson and Van Veen spent their summer in a basement. They made flyers and let their campus know what they were up to. The workload was minimal until the pair started getting swamped with videos and photos of campus life from across the country. Only a month after it launched, CollegeHumor.com needed its own dedicated server to cope with traffic. Their hunch about the demand for the site was clearly spot-on. Van Veen says: "We just made it available to everyone. We just lifted up a rock and it was there." Their job is to filter the material—photos, movies, links, and columns—and serve it up on the basic website. Not that the filter is that rigorous. Expect to find plenty of photos of drunk students, animal bottoms, silly signs, and stories on such things as an outbreak of chlamydia at a San Francisco zoo. The CollegeHumor.com team has a list of things that aren't funny that includes midgets, Bill Gates, pimps, and Helen Keller jokes, but there is still a lot of room for bad taste.

Within three months it became clear that this business could pay for a lot more beer than Abramson and Van Veen could drink. The site gave advertisers direct access to the hard-to-please eighteen-to-twenty-four-year-old demographic of technology savvy, early adapters who were bombarding the site every day. The pair received several early offers to buy the business (one for $9 million), but Abramson and Van Veen were not interested. They were having too much fun. "We'd be doing this if we were making less money. The point is we are doing something we enjoy," says Van Veen. The buy-out offers inspired them to take the project more seriously. "We thought we could feed ourselves if we went full-time at it," says Van Veen. In 2003, revenue reached $250,000, and in 2004 it climbed to $2 million.

Early on, Abramson and Van Veen made an alliance with Zilo, a media company that specifically targets college and young adults through television, live events, and its online presence. "They never put us as a priority," says Abramson, who has constantly had to deal with not being taken seriously because of his age. "While young people don't necessarily have the experience to do certain things, this has no impact on their ability to be creative and have ideas." The Zilo alliance did not last.

Today, CollegeHumor.com is based in New York in a $10,000-a-month Tribeca loft, and the founders, now graduates, have been joined by Zach Klein and Jakob Lodwick. Advertisers on the site include DreamWorks, Toyota, Coca-Cola, and sports betting agencies that pay up to $60,000 a month. 2005 revenues are forecast to tip $5 million, a slice of that coming from the sales of irreverent T-shirts ("What would Ashton do?"). The site receives around six hundred pictures and one hundred movies every day. Staff numbers have deliberately remained low and margins, says Abramson, remain high. The partners apologize for some of the site's disorder. "This is how the Internet works when you have four people running a site that should have two dozen."

CollegeHumor.com now has a parent company, Connected Ventures, that collects the advertising revenue and product sales from the various websites it runs including Busted Tees (for all those crass T-shirts), Big Shocker (an in-joke hand signal that has been made into a range of Big Shocker products), a college dating site, and various other CollegeHumor spin-offs.

The boys are living the fantasy life of every college student—a New York loft, flatscreen TVs, positive cash flow, and meetings with high-level entertainment industry executives looking for ways to leverage the very marketable CollegeHumor.com brand. There are books, a possible Paramount movie in the pipeline, and 2005 has seen a surge in advertising revenue for the site.

Abramson, an accomplished jazz pianist who used to work in a piano bar, was always seen as an entrepreneur. He went to the Robins School of Business at the University of Richmond, but does not rate this academic experience as contributing anything significant to his business career. His former professor of economics Robert Dolan describes him as a "very laid back guy on the surface," but he was definitely someone with a plan. "You can tell the wheels are churning. He's an entrepreneur," he says. Abramson was selling string bracelets in high school, and later on he worked out that he could earn more in one night as a DJ with some sound equipment than his buddies were making in a fortnight as employees. "Ever since I was little kid it was my dream to run a company," he says.

Abramson is one of those who believes that the entrepreneurial spirit is something some people have while others don't. "Some people have the natural ability, some people don't. It is a way of looking at an opportunity. You could study business your whole life and still not get it."

NOTES

"We thought we could . . ." Mayhew, Melanie. "Laughing All the Way to the Bank," *Richmond Times Despatch*, Virginia, 4.4.05, p. D19.

"Very laid back guy . . ." Mayhew, Melanie. "Laughing All the Way to the Bank," *Richmond Times Despatch*, Virginia, 4.4.05, p. D19.

REFERENCES

Baltimore Sun, Broadband Week, BusinessWire, Multichannel News, *New Yorker, Richmond Times Despatch, University Wire, Wall Street Journal, Washington Post*

MAC Cosmetics
(Makeup Artist Cosmetics)

Two Franks are better than one

H OW A RANGE OF HOMEMADE MAKEUP BECAME A TRAILBLAZING global brand is the story of two Franks, partners in life and business: Frank Toskan, a fashion photographer/makeup artist and Frank Angelo, a successful hairdresser. Toskan was the makeup guru and Angelo the entrepreneur.

The flamboyant Angelo was running a successful chain of hairdressing salons in Toronto when he met Toskan. His first venture was a little movie business for neighborhood children that he ran when he was seven.

The Franks met in the early 1970s. Their quest for better quality makeup for their fashion shoots sent Toskan into their kitchen at the back of Angelo's hair salon in the Toronto suburb of Cabbage Town. "Commercial cosmetics weren't working for me, so I had to develop my own," he says. Toskan enlisted the help of future brother-in-law and nineteen-year-old chemist Vic Casale and they worked on a tiny range of lipsticks, eye pencils, bases, and powders.

Initially, the product was only distributed among friends in the fashion industry, but word soon got out about the dense pigment, the non-oily finish of the foundations, and the color range. The demand inspired Toskan and Angelo to liquidate their property assets and invest the proceeds in Makeup Artist Cosmetics. The business was formally established in 1984, with Toskan as creative director and Angelo as marketing director. MAC moved out of the kitchen into a 10,000-foot manufacturing plant that they grew out of within twelve months.

From the very beginning, MAC took a very clear position in the marketplace. The buzz about MAC was built at fashion shows, through Madonna video clips, on the cutting edge of the arts. Originally for makeup professionals, the brand became even more desirable because of its real links to the fashion frontline. The brand also stood for diversity, with its extensive color ranges to suit "all sexes, all races, all ages." Says Toskan: "I have always resented the image of the nineteen-year-old beautiful blonde, white model being shoved down people's throats." To prove the point, MAC's first spokesperson was 6'7" drag queen Ru Paul.

"MAC has broken the traditional industry way of selling product," says Toskan. MAC's radical approach also included going against the traditional cosmetic retailing strategy of high advertising spend and gift-with-purchase promotions. Toskan and Angelo's business model relied on a formula of low prices and word of mouth, no advertising, and no gift with purchase promotions. "I always believed in earning your customer, not buying her," says Toskan.

MAC's first big break was being offered space in a Toronto department store in 1984, albeit a very out-of-the-way counter. MAC continued to retail differently, with its black-clad trained makeup artists as sales assistants who were, for the most part, not working on commission. Without this sales pressure, the MAC people could concentrate on giving service that would keep the customers coming back.

Apart from maple syrup, MAC is one of the few Canadian exports that has had success out of its homeland. MAC's first U.S. sales were through the prestigious New York department store Henri Bendel, where women would wait in line for hours on weekends for the lip pencils. MAC opened its first store in New York's Greenwich Village in 1991.

Growth was exponential and caused serious problems for Toskan and Angelo. "We had created such a demand for the product that we were not able to respond," says Toskan. MAC was also dealing with product being sold in North America only to be taken offshore and sold in other countries, particularly in Asia, and sold on the black market for three times the price. There were also the challenges of expanding globally and negotiating to open new stores in retail environments the Franks knew nothing about. All these business distractions meant less time for product development and marketing and more time on company infrastructure.

Enter one of the world's biggest cosmetics companies, Estee Lauder, which had never distributed another company's products before. William Lauder, a senior executive at Lauder, recognized the potential for growth in this cult brand. "They started a category that no one saw coming," he says. In December 1994, Estee Lauder bought a 51 percent stake in MAC for $38 million with a view to outright acquisition. The deal was kept secret as Toskan and Angelo were terrified that an alliance with an industry giant might impact on the brand's street credibility, that MAC would be "Lauderized." The deal went ahead with MAC continuing to drive its image and Lauder focusing on the business side.

The marriage between David and Goliath was initially a happy one. The Franks worked on their ranges, promoted the brand, and kept up MAC's VIVA Glam AIDS campaign. Then came the shocking death of Angelo. In 1997, he died of a heart attack while having routine surgery in Florida. At the time, Toskan described Angelo as "the guy who pushed me out there. I was the more insecure one who wanted to stay in the background. He was my pedestal for many years."

By then the company was turning over $250 million annually. Toskan sold the whole company to Estee Lauder for an estimated $60 million in February 1998. In December 1998, Toskan resigned as creative director of MAC, no longer wanting to be a part of the company that he built.

Estee Lauder has continued to drive sales globally with MAC now sold in forty-six countries with sales of more than $500 million.

Viva Glam, the MAC range of lipsticks that donates all proceeds to AIDS research, has raised in excess of $32 million. Toskan still lives in the Toronto area.

NOTES

"Commercial cosmetics . . ." Krum, Sharon. "Shock Factor," *Courier Mail*, 5.10.97.

"I have always resented . . ." "This Is Not Your Mother's Maybelline," Manchester Guardian Service, *Albuquerque Tribune*, 6.6.96.

"MAC has broken . . ." *Managing with Lou Dobbs*, CNN, "Going Global in the Cosmetics Business," 7.9.95.

"I always believe in earning . . ." *Managing with Lou Dobbs*, CNN, "Going Global in the Cosmetics Business," 7.9.95.

"We had created . . ." McKay, Shona. "Marriages of Convenience," *The Financial Post*, 6.1.97.

"They started a category . . ." *Managing with Lou Dobbs*, CNN, "Going Global in the Cosmetics Business," 7.9.95.

"Lauderized . . ." Friede, Eva. "MAC Is Still the Insiders' Brand," *The Ottowa Citizen*, 6.1.01.

"The guy who . . ." Morra, Bernadette. "MAC Fashions Fine Funeral," *Toronto Star*, 1.23.97.

REFERENCES

The Financial Post (Toronto), *The Independent* (London), *London Free Press* (Ontario), *National Post* (Canada), *Scotland on Sunday*, *Toronto Star*, *Women's Wear Daily*

Section 19

FROM HIPPY TO HIP

Aveda

Bridging the gap between hippy and hip

I N THE 1970S, HORST RECHELBACHER STARTED MAKING SHAMPOOS in his kitchen because he couldn't find the all-natural products he wanted to work with in his hair salon in Minneapolis, Minnesota. This idea was the basis of a hair and beauty company that Horst would sell to the Estee Lauder cosmetics giant for $300 million in 1997. By filling this gap, the potential market for Aveda continues to be nothing short of huge.

Rechelbacher grew up in Austria with a mother who turned their kitchen into a place to make natural remedies from plants and herbs. "The kitchen was not just for making food. It was a little lab," he says. School life was hard for the dyslexic Rechelbacher, who dropped out at age fourteen to become an apprentice hairdresser. The handsome, competent Horst became a jetsetting, hardliving hairdresser, working in New York, Milan, and Paris in the 1960s, even tending to the tresses of Brigitte Bardot. In the bad old days, Horst fit the stereotype of the racy hairdresser—a long way from the meditating entrepreneur he would become.

Horst's life in Minneapolis began literally by accident. He was there for a hair show in 1965 when his car was hit by a drunk driver, leaving him so severely injured he was forced to stay to recuperate for six months. He set up a salon there called Horst of Austria. The salon was a hit, and he opened four more salons in the area.

In the late 1960s, Rechelbacher's life changed when he met a yogi who was passing through town. Rechelbacher began meditating and then spent time in India, where his whole outlook on life changed. Rechelbacher rediscovered his mother's natural remedies, inspiring in him enormous faith in the power of natural plant and herb remedies. He worked with an Indian herbalist to create a range of shampoos, conditioners, oils, a blood purifier, and a bowel cleanser. "Nobody was interested when we started," he says. His first product was a pungent, delicious clove shampoo.

Customers loved the Horst of Austria potions. Even snobby New York hairdressers were interested, as long as Horst changed the name of the products. (Why would they want to promote the name of another hairdresser?)

Rechelbacher rebranded the company in 1978 as Aveda, a word meaning "whole knowledge" in Sanskrit. Sales began climbing with products selling through a network of distributors to salons, retailers, and eventually, in Aveda's own stores. As the company grew, Horst was able to source plants and materials from Brazil, Nepal, India, Malaysia, Indonesia, and Africa.

In the 1980s, the growth of the company, while not the juggernaut of Anita Roddick's Body Shop, was steady. The products became more widely distributed to select salons throughout the United States, and by the mid-nineties, the privately-owned business had reported annual sales of $110 million (compared with The Body Shop's more than $700 million). Despite never liking the management side of running a business, Rechelbacher wanted his company to keep growing. "I was looking to get out. I had to sell to someone," he says.

In 1997, Rechelbacher received an offer he could not refuse. The cosmetics giant Estee Lauder bought his company for $300 million. Critics accused him of selling out his hippie-principled business to the enemy. But Horst argues, "If you want to change the cosmetic industry, you don't fight them. You join them and then work from the inside to change. We are doing more of what we have always done but now we can utilize Lauder's 300 scientists, use their infrastructure, and get the best retail locations globally. On my own it would have taken me twenty years to go global."

Today, Rechelbacher is setting up a string of health-related businesses through a company called Intelligent Nutrients that centers on organic food. He has an estimated fortune of $275 million and lives on an 800-acre estate in Wisconsin and has a New York City residence. He has eight dogs, takes lots of vitamins, meditates, does yoga, and has a beauty laboratory in his house. Meanwhile, the Aveda brand continues to appeal to both the fashion-conscious narcissus as well as the philanthropist, a bit like Rechelbacher himself. He appears to be a wonderful mix of principle and pleasure. He runs a charitable foundation and an education center, has an honorary doctorate in Ayurvedic medicine, and likes visiting far-flung places in search of herbs. On the other hand, he does not mind town cars and elegant clothing, and he has a taste for fine art. He is still a man who likes to bridge the gap between hippie and hip, and he showed the rest of the world how to do it.

NOTES

"The kitchen was not just..." Meehan, Thomas. "Horst of Fifth Avenue," *New York Observer*, 11.15.99.

"Nobody was interested . . ." Frankel, Susannah. "Horst sense," *The Independent*, 6.13.02, p. 12.

"I was looking to get out . . ." Frankel, Susannah. "Horst sense," *The Independent*, 6.13.02, p. 12.

"If you want to change the cosmetic industry . . ." Morra, Bernadette. "Aveda Founder Lauds Lauder Purchase," *The Toronto Star*, 6.4.98, p. E4.

REFERENCES

Adweek, The Age, Aveda.com, *Brandweek,* CNN, *Daily Mail, Dallas Morning News, The Guardian, Houston Chronicle, The Independent, Mail on Sunday, Minneapolis-St Paul CityBusiness, The Mirror, Newsweek, New York Times, The Observer, PR Newswire, Star Tribune, Sun Herald, Sunday Times, Toronto Star, USA Today, Women's Wear Daily*

Ben & Jerry's

Balding, nerdy hippies can build brilliant brands

L IKE MANY KIDS, BEN COHEN LIKED TO EXPERIMENT WITH HIS ICE cream by adding sweets, nuts, lollies, and even cake to it. Jerry Greenfield was not quite so experimental, but he was an expert scooper after manning the ice cream section of his school cafeteria. The boys, both from Merrick, New York, met in a seventh-grade gym class. They became lifelong friends, a pair of hippies who liked the Grateful Dead and making jewelry, pottery, and more unusually, ice cream.

Cohen and Greenfield are an unlikely entrepreneurial force, with their VW buses and left-of-center beliefs. Ironically, the super-premium ice cream brand they created juggernauted them out of their laid-back life into the burgeoning premium ice cream market that was taking off in the early 1980s. *The Guardian* newspaper describes their company as an "economic miracle." "In the annals of business history, they are recorded as the first company to turn a profit while behaving as a non-profit organization."

They both completed a $5 ice cream correspondence course from Pennsylvania State University before they opened the first Ben & Jerry's ice cream parlor (they like to call them scoop shops) in an old gas station in the university town of Burlington, Vermont. It was 1978.

Ben & Jerry's ice cream was made from locally supplied super-creamy, high-fat milk. Their ultra rich ice creams (some with twen-ty grams of fat per serving) had a similar sense of decadence as their ice cream nemesis Haagen-Daaz, but Ben & Jerry's cleverly pitched itself as the quirky, unpretentious brand run by the balding nerds. They marketed the ice creams not merely as flavors, more as personalities—think Cherry Garcia, Phish Food, and Chunky Monkey—and from its earliest days, Berry & Jerry's was preaching a brand of "caring capitalism."

The business was funded through a $4,000 loan, along with $8,000 in savings. Despite Cohen and Greenfield admitting that they had no idea what direction the business would take, they were optimistic about their scoop shop as there was no other ice cream parlor in the town of Burlington. In 1980, they took another step forward and began selling the ice cream in pint-sized containers. Ben distributed it in his VW bus.

The power of Ben & Jerry's brand may be in part to do with its record of social responsibility, but the quality of the product, and the company's ability to market it, is what set the company on a rapid ride to mainstream success. In the earliest days, Ben & Jerry's held summer movie festivals (gee, what goes well with movies on a hot summer's night?), and to celebrate each Ben & Jerry's anniversary, scoop shops served up free samples throughout the day.

When the brand launched outside the state in 1983, Cohen and Greenfield attempted to drive a purpose-built "Cowmobile," a modified mobile home, across the country to spread the word. The first Cowmobile was destroyed in a fire, but a second version was built.

In 1981, the first Ben & Jerry's franchise opened, and the ice cream was launched out of the state in Boston in 1983. In 1984, Cohen and Greenfield hired a former nightclub manager, Fred Lager, to help run the business, together raising $750,000 in a Vermont-only capital raising exercise, with money spent on building a much-needed new production facility. The factory immediately became the state's number-one tourist facility. Sales of the ice cream leapt 120 percent to $4 million and kept climbing from there as Ben & Jerry's distribution plans rolled out. The next year, 1985, sales were up 143 percent to $9 million, and just short of $20 million in 1986. A decade later, sales tipped $167 million with Ben & Jerry making the cover of *Time* magazine in 1991.

Part of the media's fascination with Ben & Jerry's was its continued commitment to corporate responsibility. As the company grew, it persisted in questioning the business world's single-minded obsession with the bottom line. While wanting to grow and turn a profit, Ben & Jerry's was always interested in the idea of being a good corporate citizen, both within and outside the company. To begin with, all staff earned at least 20 percent of the salary of the highest paid employee. The company backed local dairy farmers to supply the milk from cows not exposed to growth hormones and opened a series of PartnerShops owned by nonprofit organizations that offered job training and employment to disadvantaged people. It also offered staff three free pints of ice cream every day.

"Some of these people with strong social and humanitarian values—like Jerry and I—got into business by accident and were not sorted through that grid," said Cohen. "So through some quirk of fate, instead of ending up in a nonprofit social service agency, we happened to be trapped in a for-profit business."

Ben & Jerry's also committed 7.5 percent of pretax profits to philanthropic causes—a lot more than the 1 percent typically offered by big business. Ben & Jerry's set up all manner of revenue streams into nonprofit activities including an employee community fund and a foundation established with a parcel of company stock. The company also offered staff extended maternity and paternity leave and allowances for de facto and gay couples.

In 1988, they wrote a new company mission statement setting the expectation that the company should become a new role model of corporate responsibility, based on the ethos that business should improve the wider world's quality of life.

In April 2000, food giant Unilever bought the company for $326 million. The deal included a promise from Unilever not to tamper with the company philosophy, sack staff, or stop giving away a percentage of profits to charity (more than \$1.1 million per year). Ben & Jerry's has launched Climate Change College, a scheme offering scholarships to students to learn about climate change. There are still 450 U.S. scoop shops and stores in thirteen countries including France, Germany, Hong Kong, South Korea, and Malta. Cohen and Greenfield remain friends and, despite their fortunes, continue to live modestly, although Greenfield drives a Saab these days rather than a cowmobile. Cohen heads Business Leaders for Sensible Priorities (LSP), a coalition of business leaders, military experts, religious leaders, and entertainers including Ted Turner and Paul Newman. LSP lobbies for a shift in government spending towards education, job training, health, eradicating poverty, and other social advocacy issues.

NOTES

"In the annals of business history . . ." Elliott, Larry. "Greenbacks Love Green Business," *The Guardian*, 6.18.94, p. 27.

"Some of these people . . ." Rothman, Howard. *50 Companies That Changed the World*, Career Press, 2001.

REFERENCES

Cohen, Ben. *Ben & Jerry's Double Dip: How to Run a Values-Led Business and Make Money Too*, Simon & Schuster, 1998.

Lager, Fred. *Ben & Jerry's: the Inside Scoop: How Two Real Guys Built a Business with a Social Conscience and a Sense of Humor*, Three Rivers Press, 1995.

Older, Jules. *Ben & Jerry, The Real Scoop*, Chapters Pub Ltd, 1996.

Australian Financial Review, benjerry.com, *Burlington Free Press, BusinessWeek, Fast Company, Financial Times, Forbes, Fortune, The Guardian,* Hoover's Company Records, *The Independent, Los Angeles Times, New York Post, New York Times, The Observer, Time*

BEWARE OF
CHEAP IMITATIONS

Steinway

Go on, name another brand

ASK ANYBODY TO NAME A BRAND OF PIANO AND CHANCES ARE they will recall just one: Steinway. Why? Steinway & Sons does not make the most pianos—far from it. Its designs are not necessarily the most technologically advanced. Certainly it makes an excellent product; yet it has several competitors who make pianos to similar—some say higher—standards.

What the company has done so successfully has been to turn a nineteenth-century innovation into a twenty-first-century brand, using ingenious techniques of marketing and customer loyalty to ensure its name is widely recognized as number one.

Heinrich Engelhard Steinweg was born in Wolfshagen, Germany, in 1797, a harsh time: both his parents died young, along with several of his eleven siblings. After a stint in the army, he wanted to be a cabinetmaker but ended up making pianos, building his first grand piano in his kitchen in 1836. He migrated to New York in 1850 with four of his five sons, anglicized his name to Henry Steinway, and started his own piano company in 1853 in a Manhattan loft.

Thanks to a series of swift advances, by 1860 Steinway & Sons was the leading manufacturer of pianos in the United States, riding the middle-class home entertainment boom. Steinway studied the best techniques of his rivals and fine-tuned them, patenting numerous advances of his own. He built what was essentially a village in Astoria, Queens, to house his workshops. Then the family opened a branch factory in Hamburg, Germany, to produce pianos for the European market, as it does to this day. In its first fifty years,

Steinway made 100,000 pianos (number 100,000 was delivered to the White House in 1903).

During World War II, both plants were turned over to the war effort, with the New York factory churning out olive-green uprights for the armed forces and gliders that were employed in the Normandy landings. It was a tricky time, running an American business in Germany and a German-sounding business in the United States, but the firm survived and eventually benefited from post-war investment that put it ahead of its German competitors.

In the latter half of the century, the fiercest competition came from Japanese manufacturers such as Yamaha and Kawai, who were constantly developing new technologies that allowed them to build better, cheaper general-purpose pianos. Steinway cautiously incorporated some new techniques—such as computer-controlled saws to cut out components—but stubbornly stuck with tradition-al hand-assembling, a process that means it still takes a year to build a concert grand piano. It only produces around 5,000 pianos a year (in contrast, Yamaha makes around 100,000, most of them more affordable models).

In 1972, Henry Z. Steinway, the great-grandson of Steinway founder Heinrich Engelhard Steinweg, sold the business to CBS, and it passed through several hands before listing on the New York Stock Exchange in 1996. Today's prices start at $17,000 for the Professional Ebony upright, rise to $60,000 for a typical living-room grand, and continue onwards to $128,000 for a concert model. Custom and heirloom models from the "Crown Jewel" and "Legendary" ranges can cost up to $675,000, the price paid for a one-off special and, according to the company, a record for a new piano. An original 1880s Steinway sold at auction in 1997 for $1.2 million, even though, unlike violins, pianos do not improve with age, as their moving parts wear out.

The company's traditional ways of doing things have become increasingly prized by enthusiastic amateurs; then there are its longtime affiliations with top players. Even in the nineteenth century, Steinway courted artists' endorsements and managed its own roster of performers, much as brands Nike and Omega do with sports stars today. The company's Artist Roster now numbers some 1,300 world-class pianists and is a fearsome marketing tool.

Unlike most sponsorship deals, the Roster is not a contractual agreement; instead, in what the company calls a "gentleman's agreement," concert artists informally pledge to endorse and play Steinway pianos wherever they can (preferably with the maker's name plastered on the audience side of the case). In return, Steinway lends them pianos for performances, practice facilities, and perhaps more importantly, the services of its technicians, who perform vital tuning and customization. Many Steinway artists express their support—some slightly awkwardly—on the Steinway website, including Harry Connick Jr. who writes, "with a tone so rich, I would never be afraid of the dark. Steinway is the only and the best!"

The company claims 90 percent of the world's concert pianists bear the title "Steinway Artist" and play only Steinways (and before they enter an arrangement the company stipulates they must already privately own a Steinway). It also boasts its pianos are found in 95 percent of the world's concert halls. It has created a league of all-Steinway music colleges, such as the University of Maryland, which recently bought 103 Steinways. At store level, it encourages managers to promote high-profile sales, which often make the pages of local newspapers.

The Artist Roster and Steinway's presence in so many venues are major impediments to major rivals Yamaha and Kawai, which have both spent decades developing concert grands to compete with Steinway, and up-and-coming boutique makers such as the Italian firm Fazioli, which makes fewer than one hundred instruments a year, entirely by hand. Both Yamaha and Kawai have attempted to take on Steinway at its own game, donating pianos to music colleges and concert halls, and creating their own lists of artist endorsements (Yamaha signed Elton John). Their top-line products offer tantalizing technological advances, such as fourth pedals, extra keys, and high-tech materials. Kawai's Shigeru concert model even looks after the pianist's fingers with a soft-close lid that cannot be accidentally slammed down. To date, though, most of the big names have been prepared to risk their fingers with Steinway.

NOTES
"With a tone so rich . . ." Steinway.com

REFERENCES
Daily Telegraph, Financial Times, Forbes, Fortune, The Guardian, Los Angeles Times, Music Trades, New York Times, Plain Dealer, Sunday Telegraph

Lego

One brick at a time

LEGO IS SO COMMONPLACE TODAY (WITH FIFTY-TWO PIECES for every person on the planet) it is hard to imagine a time when these little plastic shapes were considered high-tech. But in 1947, when carpenter Ole Kirk Christiansen brought the first plastics injection-molding machine to Denmark, his fellow toymakers, who worked with wood, were horrified.

Yet Christiansen was on to something, and among his early experiments he produced what he called "automatic binding bricks." Thanks to the slightly flexible nature of the plastic, the bricks snapped together, and, more importantly, stayed together. Christiansen's company, Lego—derived from the Danish words for "play well"—refined the design, and patented its "stud and tube" locking system in 1958. The potential for play was enormous: just six eight-stud Lego bricks can be put together in 102,981,500 combinations. Take a few thousand and, thanks to what Lego calls "clutch factor" (the bricks' ability to stick together), you could make an airplane, a farm, a city—whatever you wanted. Ole Kirk believed passionately that the purpose of his bricks was to engage children in free-form play, to stimulate their imaginations.

After enormous initial success that took Lego from Scandinavia to Europe and then worldwide (in 1962 it bought its own plane) the company realized its business plan was flawed: the trouble was, a child who had a box of the stuff had absolutely no need for any more. Lego started cautiously expanding the core product, developing extra elements such as windows and wheels, which helped to make models more realistic. Then it moved into themed sets, including a farm, a medieval castle, and space models that came with genre-specific pieces. Philosophically, this was a great leap from Ole Kirk's original idea: instead of children dreaming up their own scenarios, Lego was now offering sets that came with step-by-step instructions.

While each new range usually generated an enormous sales boost, Lego remained cautious. No changes were considered lightly: it took, for instance, ten years for the company to consider giving its little human figures a range of expressions beyond the basic friendly smile.

For four decades, Lego built a brand that spoke of quality, reliability, and admirable principles (no Lego toy is allowed to represent a real, post-World War I weapon). For parents it was, and still is, a purchase they can feel good about.

In recent years, though, Lego began to look increasingly anachronistic. The company's only major attempt to diversify was through theme parks, the first of which opened in Billund, Denmark, in 1968, inspired by the stream of visitors who came to visit the Lego factory. Early ventures into new technology through the Mindstorms range of programmable robots foundered when the kits proved too expensive for children (though they were a hit in the adult geek community). This was, essentially, still a company reliant on little plastic bricks—a product easily imitated as the original patents expired.

American company Tyco advertised, "If you can't tell the difference, why pay the difference?" Moreover, these direct competitors, less concerned with quality and brand values, were able to turn over their ranges more quickly and certainly had no problems offering kits for warships and fighter planes—a niche Lego refused to enter.

In the 1990s, video games began to seriously compete for the toy dollar, along with characters linked to television shows. In 1998 and 2000, for the first time in its history, Lego lost money, despite turnover well in excess of $1 billion per annum. In 2000, a company spokesperson blamed some of Lego's fading fortunes on Pokémon, the trading card/video game hybrid that became a playground craze. Ironically, the same year, Lego was voted Toy of the Century by the British Association of Toy Retailers, *Fortune*, and *Forbes* magazines.

The profit slump proved a wake-up call for the family-run company, now run by Ole Kirk's grandson, Kjeld Kirk Kristiansen (who changed the spelling of the family name). Instead of relying on its own powers of innovation, which had been somewhat stifled by the cloistered atmosphere at Billund, Lego sought partnerships with those at the forefront of the digital revolution, offering suitors unimpeachable brand values and access to millions of children worldwide. First came George Lucas and a range of *Star Wars* kits in 1999. Then there was a partnership with Steven Spielberg (who had only once before allowed his name to be attached to an entertainment product) to produce a film-making kit for children. MovieMaker turned Lego characters—including a new range of *Jurassic Park* dinosaurs—into props for animated films, providing a bridge between the original product and the new world of multimedia. Lego then joined forces with Microsoft to develop games for the Xbox console, with plans to use Microsoft technology to power its movie-making products, now called Lego Studios.

In 2001, bolstered by the success of *Star Wars*, it launched a range of models based on the Harry Potter movie, which became the must-have toy of 2001. To prove it could still come up with its own ideas, it created its own Pokémon-style collectible called Bionicle, a range of robot-like creatures intelligently priced at pocket-money level that became the company's number one product in 2003, accounting for roughly 20 percent of turnover.

The company is still in transition to the digital era—despite some successes, it posted another loss in 2003 and announced job cuts. In 2004, Kjeld Kirk Kristiansen stepped down as CEO for thirty-five-year-old Jørgen Vig Knudstorp (Kristiansen, the company's majority shareholder, stayed on as vice chairman). Some question whether the company can survive while it still manufactures most of its bricks in Denmark, though it recently moved a factory from Switzerland to Prague. Others question the company's increasing reliance on fads and movie tie-ins, arguing that they lack replayability—once you have constructed the 3,104-piece *Star Wars* Imperial Star Destroyer you're unlikely to want to take it apart again. Meanwhile, the company admitted it had blundered by sidelining its Duplo line of larger bricks, a staple of preschools the world over, relaunching them in 2004 amid a renewed focus on the original bricks and playsets.

It's not all gloom—Lego recently set up the Lego Learning Institute, which funds research into play and learning, and Vision Lab, an internal thinktank, to plan the way forward and, in the words of one Lego executive, help the company loosen up a bit. The company has also sold off its theme parks to concentrate on the core business. But for Vig Knudstorp, a plain-speaking man who has promised to stabilize the decline and make the business profitable, rebuilding Lego's world will be a tough job, taken one brick at a time.

REFERENCES

Brand Strategy, Business2.0, BusinessWeek, Canberra Times, Cnet.com, Columbia Journalism Review, Fast Company, Financial Times, Forbes, The Guardian, Pause, Wired

Harley-Davidson

Be a Hells Angel for the weekend

M EMO: HARLEY-DAVIDSON TO HELLS ANGELS. SUBJECT: Thanks for all the bad publicity.

It hasn't quite happened yet, but Harley-Davidson certainly owes a debt of gratitude to the outlaw motorcycle club that adopted its products in the 1940s and gave them a bad name.

Harley-Davidson's checkered past holds tremendous appeal for Baby Boomers, who are attracted to the brand as a symbol of freedom and rebellion. The Hells Angels still ride Harleys, but the typical buyer is now a forty-something, well-heeled professional, looking to reclaim a little of his or her youth on the weekend. "Born to be Wild," proclaims a popular riders' T-shirt, adding in smaller letters underneath: "At least for a couple of days."

Nostalgia has offered the last remaining major American motorcycle manufacturer a second chance and its executives have made the most of it. As a maker of motorcycles, Harley-Davidson was long ago left behind by the competition, but as a luxury lifestyle brand, it has plenty of spark left.

For most of its one-hundred-year existence Harley-Davidson mirrored the fortunes of other great American industries. It was founded in a wooden shack in Milwaukee, Wisconsin, by twenty-one-year-old William S. Harley and twenty-year-old Arthur

Davidson, who in 1903 put the finishing touches on their proto-type for what was essentially a motorized bicycle. They were soon joined by two other partners, Arthur's brothers Walter and William. In 1909, the partners made an engineering breakthrough, designing a new engine called a V-twin that gave the bikes of the day a handy top speed of sixty mph. That basic configuration is still the heart of many Harley-Davidson motorcycles today, giving the machines their distinctive discordant rumble. (In 1994, Harley-Davidson even attempted to trademark the sound, described by the company's attorney as "potato, potato, potato.")

In World War I, the U.S. Armed Forces ordered 20,000 motorcycles from Harley-Davidson, and by 1920 the company was the largest manufacturer of motorcycles in the world. It sold another 90,000 to the army in World War II. The brand proved reliable and remained popular with servicemen on their return to the United States, some of whom banded together in motorcycle clubs.

On July 4, 1947, some 4,000 enthusiasts rode into a small town called Hollister, California, for a weekend of racing and drinking, events that were sensationalized by the press and later made into the Marlon Brando film *The Wild One* (though, for the record, Brando rode a British Triumph).

Another date not mentioned in Harley-Davidson's official company history is 1948, the year a group of enthusiasts in San Bernardino, California, formed a club called the Hells Angels. Several accounts claim they were former servicemen from a B-17 bomber known as Hells Angels; the club says that is untrue, though the name had been used by several bomber and fighter squadrons during World War II. Their ride of choice was the Harley-Davidson: big, loud, and most importantly, made in America.

The Angels and other clubs loved to customize, or "chop," their bikes, a look that was immortalized in the film *Easy Rider*. Not that Harley-Davidson wanted anything to do with it, according to former Hells Angels president and author Sonny Barger. "After we fixed our bikes the way we wanted them they didn't even want us inside their dealerships," he said. "Now they make them like we used to build them."

By the 1960s Harley-Davidson, since 1953 the sole American-based motorcycle manufacturer, was coming under increasing competition from Japanese brands such as Honda, which offered lighter, technically superior bikes at a lower price. In 1969 Harley-Davidson was bought by the American Machine and Foundry corporation (AMF), a move which at first seemed positive: AMF's capital would help Harley-Davidson see off its new challengers. But quality suffered, with as many as one in two bikes failing assembly line inspections, and Harley-Davidson lost its reputation for reliability. By 1981, Harley-Davidson's market share had dropped below 5 percent and it was even second to Honda in the super-heavyweight category that it had traditionally dominated. AMF wanted out, eventually handing the company back to thirteen Harley-Davidson executives in a highly leveraged management buyout.

The timing could not have been worse. A recession saw sales fall further and the company had to lay off half its workforce. In its first year and a half of independence, the company lost close to $30 million.

In a last-ditch move to save the business, Harley-Davidson successfully petitioned the government for tariff protection against Japanese imports in 1983, hoping to buy breathing space. President Reagan gave them five years, boosting the tariff on Japanese motorcycles over 700 cc from 4.4 percent to 49.4 percent.

The management team, including current chairman Jeffrey Bleustein and Willie G. Davidson, grandson of cofounder William Davidson, modernized the plant with Japanese-style just-in-time processes. Instead of spending millions on advertising (which they didn't have), they started a club called the Harley Owners' Group in 1983, to build on the fraternal feelings enjoyed by Harley riders. "We were doing 'close to the customer' marketing before it even had a name," Bleustein said in 2003. Today the club has over 900,000 members worldwide. The company also runs rider education courses and offers organized rides through its travel arm, including several U.S. French-language tours for fans from Europe.

Bleustein's team began to realize the potential of the brand when, from 1986, they began to encourage dealers to abandon the traditional layout of showrooms, where every inch of floor space was filled with bikes, in favor of airy spaces that showcased just four or five machines and used the rest of the space to promote Harley-Davidson merchandise. Today, the company makes around 15 percent of its sales from riding accessories, and up to another 10 percent in souvenirs such as bridal wear and—just in case you needed proof this had become a luxury brand—a $995 one-hundredth anniversary watch from Bulova.

Between 1995 and 2000, the company doubled capacity to meet demand, balancing its customers' nostalgic feelings for what a Harley-Davidson should be with technological improvements to meet expectations of reliability. In 1998, Harley-Davidson bought out the Buell sports bike company to expand its offerings to younger riders; to date, though, Buell is still a tiny part of the business.

Today, the company is America's second-largest motorcycle manufacturer, just behind Honda, with sales of over 350,000 bikes annually. More importantly, it once again owns the big bike market. So where to from here? When Harley-Davidson launched its first genuinely modern model in fifty years, 2001's futuristic V-Rod, it was derided by traditionalists as lacking the classic engine note. Meanwhile Harley-Davidson is stuck with a big-spending but aging core market of Baby Boomers. And even they are not entirely predictable. In 2003, a crowd of 100,000 riders—mostly mild-at-heart professionals—converged in Milwaukee for the company's one-hundredth anniversary concert. At the height of a successful evening, the company brought out its surprise special guest—not the Rolling Stones, as had been rumored, but Elton John. Thousands walked away early in disgust.

NOTES

"After we fixed . . ."   Zimmerman, Keith. "Hells Angels to Dad's Army: How Harleys Lost Their Street Cred," *The Times*, 8.28.03, Times 2, p. 4.

"We were doing . . ."   Barrett, Rick. "Harley-Davidson Aims to Keep the Wheels Turning," *Milwaukee Journal Sentinal*, 8.27.03.

REFERENCES

Associated Press, Brandweek, Canadian Press Newswire, CNBC/DOW JONES, CNN *Live, Colorado Springs Gazette, Fast Company, Fort Worth Star Telegram, Fortune, Hamilton Spectator, Houston Chronicle, The Independent on Sunday, Industry Week, Irish Times, Legal Times, Milwaukee Journal Sentinal, National Post* (Canada), *Newsweek, Salon, St. Petersburg Times* (Florida), *Sunday Times, Sunday Tribune, The Independent, The Times, Times Colonist* (Victoria Canada), *Toronto Star, USA Today, Washington Post*

Four Seasons Hotels

Never break the promise of your brand

I SADORE "ISSY" SHARP'S FIRST FOUR SEASONS HOTEL OPENED in a seedy district of downtown Toronto in 1961. In order to distract his patrons from the "nightlife" on the street, the former architect devised an inner landscaped courtyard with a pool, an outdoor café, and entertaining areas away from the fray. The hotel was buzzing from the start. Room rates were just $12.50 a night (around $75 in today's terms)—a far cry from the rates Four Seasons hotels charge today, typically the most expensive in their area. Over four decades, Four Seasons has become a $1.8 billion hotel group that manages more than sixty luxury hotels in twenty-nine countries.

Sharp is proud to report that his hotel chain has always been the first to break the $100, $200, $300, $400, etc. room rate barriers. "We can charge more," he says, not cockily. "It's about offering value."

Sharp opened his second hotel, Inn on the Park, in Toronto in 1963, but his real breakthrough came in 1970 when he opened a five-star hotel in London, also an Inn on the Park. By then, Sharp had crystallized the Four Seasons pitch—medium-sized hotels, with exceptional quality and service. The London hotel was filled with hand-picked antiques, wood paneling, and plush furnishings. The aesthetics were combined with the latest plumbing, technology, and climate control (a true novelty in London where spacious rooms and good plumbing were all too rare).

The Four Seasons brand has made its name not so much for the amenities and interiors, often designed by Isadore's wife Rosalie, but for the smallest details: the toiletries, overnight golf shoe repair, the high-thread-count sheets, roadside check-in, the health food, the comfort food, ultra soft toilet paper, someone to wash your motorcycle, to stock your favorite brand of toothpaste, the right kind of marshmallows. Sharp realized how valuable these small experiences were to a hotel stay. At the Four Seasons Sharm el Sheikh in Egypt, the hotel even has its own butcher for quality control. "Years back I said that in terms of guest satisfaction, 99 percent isn't good enough," says Sharp. "We determined that if you upset one percent of your customers throughout the system, each person would tell ten other people, and we could theoretically turn off over a million people a year. If we do that, how can we maintain a business?" Even the pool attendants at the Four Seasons Beverly Hills are interviewed four times for the job of handing out towels and Evian sprays. Why so picky? Because the Four Seasons brand needs to be protected: "Once you identify what it represents, you can never break the promise," Sharp says.

"There is something going wrong at this moment in a Four Seasons hotel somewhere," says Sharp from his head office in

Toronto. Having good staff is no guarantee against minor disasters, but switched-on employees know how to make things right. "It's not about smiling and 'have a nice day.' It is about dealing with things in a way that you would like to be treated," he says. Many senior managers left the company as Sharp tried to develop his ideal service culture. "These people couldn't walk the talk, they could not buy into the culture I was trying to create," he says. "This took a great deal of pain to accomplish."

Born in Toronto in 1931, Sharp spent his childhood playing sports—football, hockey, and track and field. Sharp says he played hard but was not overly competitive. He says he was into the "thrill of playing." As a young man, Sharp also helped his father out in his one-man construction business where he learned everything from digging ditches to plastering walls. Sharp's father would renovate houses, his mother would decorate them, and the property would be sold; then the process would start all over again.

To raise money while he was studying architecture, Sharp and a friend set up a vending machine business in bars around Toronto, selling green gum as a breath freshener rather than regular chewing gum (and charging three times as much for it). When he finished his studies, Sharp worked again in his father's construction business before launching his first hotel. Much of the initial capital came from friends and relatives who were constantly hearing Sharp's business pitch at Friday night dinners.

The Four Seasons business has changed dramatically over four decades. Sharp started out owning and operating hotels, and then dabbled in other, cheaper hotel markets and even aged care. The company first went public in 1969, but went private again in 1977 following share price volatility. Sharp decided to go public again in 1985. Today the business is primarily a management company, paid to manage hotels by their owners. Four Seasons also receives a percentage of each hotel's profits. Previously Four Seasons owned the properties as well, making the operation exposed to high levels of debt and risk due to the fluctuating fortunes of the hotel sector.

Post-9/11, the Iraq War, and the SARS outbreak have been diabolical for the travel industry. Even in the more risk-averse business model of the Four Seasons brand, surviving these periods has been "very tough," says Sharp. Despite two successive years of downturn in 2001 and 2002, Four Seasons refused to discount heavily, unlike its competitors. Rates were kept steady, and service levels were retained so that, as Sharp explains, when the climate improved rates wouldn't be 30 percent below what they should be. "Once you discount, it is very difficult to claw your way back," he says. Staff were retained by having them take annual leave, voluntary leave, or setting up job-share arrangements.

The slump has passed in the sector and Four Seasons has expanded. There are now expansion plans and a goal of one hundred Four Seasons properties under management within five years, targeting areas such as the Middle East, China, India, and Latin America. Sharp and his family retain 65 percent of voting rights (and 10 percent of stock) in Four Seasons, while Bill Gates has a 9 percent stake and billionaire Saudi Prince al-Waleed bin Talal owns 22 percent of the company.

Sharp, now in his seventies, is still very active in the business, traveling for 50 percent of his time to properties around the world on his private jet. He is known for being super-fit, an expert ballroom dancer, and competition bridge player. He is also known for constantly rearranging the furniture wherever he is. Succession plans for Four Seasons are unknown at this stage. Sharp's three surviving sons are not involved in the business, and Sharp argues that they should not have to be responsible for something he has created. He is also one of Canada's most prominent philanthropists, particularly in the area of cancer research, following the death of one of his sons from the disease in 1978. "It was never about the money," he says. "It still isn't."

NOTES

"Years back . . ." Kirkman, Alexandra. "Hotel for All Seasons," *Forbes*, 10.28.02.

REFERENCES

The Australian, BusinessWeek, Conrad N. Hilton College of Hotels & Resorts, *The Economist, Financial Post, Financial Times, Forbes, The Guardian, Hamilton Spectator,* Hoover's Company Capsules, *The Independent, Interior Design, Interiors, International Herald Tribune, National Post, New York Times, PR Newswire, Toronto Star*

Manolo Blahnik

Protect the brand, whatever the cost

IN THE 1990S, MARKETING GURUS BEGAN TALKING ABOUT "customer delight" as a benchmark for customer satisfaction and a successful service business. Manolo Blahnik has been concentrating on delighting his customers ever since his first shoe salon opened in Chelsea, London, in 1973.

This white-haired, debonair gentleman, known for his impatience, dogs, and love of Visconti films, has been able to pass on his own passion for shoes to his customers, who pay from $800 to an outrageous $24,000 for his shoe designs. Blahnik has initiated women into his ethos that celebrates the power of the stiletto and the seduction of the shoe in all its possible incarnations. Blahnik clients have an almost religious devotion to his work and to how his shoes make them feel: this is more than customer delight, it is customer ecstasy. Some women are even prepared to have toe surgery to ensure their feet fit into his pointy-toed styles.

Born in 1942, Blahnik's fascination (rather than fetish) with shoes began when he was a boy growing up in Spain's Canary Islands. He used to make strappy shoes for his dog and the local monkey and lizard population, sometimes out of foil, cotton ribbons, or muslin. His family were wealthy banana plantation owners (his mother is Spanish, his father Czech), and he grew up living a privileged existence, exposed to European culture, glamour, society, and lots of cinema. After briefly studying architecture and literature at the University of Geneva, he moved to Paris to study art before moving on to London in 1970, wanting to pursue his desire to become a set designer. He became involved with the elite fashion set including Paloma Picasso. His big break came in New York in 1971 when his path crossed American *Vogue* doyenne Diana Vreeland who suggested he design accessories and shoes. He designed his first shoe collection for hot London designer Ossie Clark in 1972. The following year Blahnik opened a store in London's Old Church Street and began his rise in the fashion world. As word of his salon spread, his social profile and fashion patronage increased and he carved alliances with important fashion designers.

Despite his success, he has no desire for Blahnik stores all over the world, or to sell Blahnik perfume, sunglasses, or jeans. He constantly knocks back offers from retailers wanting to stock his shoes, and politely declines invitations to buy out his brand, despite the wealth it would bring him. Blahnik wants to just keep doing what he loves: every part of the process of shoemaking from sketching to handcrafting the shoe. He has no interest in relinquishing control of the business to anyone except his sister, Evangelina, who is the business brains of the Blahnik empire.

The shoe business is no place for fashion flakes. "Fashion is a discipline," he says. Each shoe design must include sound engineering principles, particularly when it comes to constructing high heels. Blahnik's early shoes from his student days were known to be nigh impossible to walk in. He fixed that problem by taking further studies with master craftsmen in England. Blahnik estimates that it took him ten years of making his own mistakes before he had consolidated his craft. From then on his witty, whimsical sketches could become aerodynamic feats for feet. Today he still designs each of the styles he produces for each collection (picked from 250 prototype sketches). He spends four months each year crafting, to the very last stitch, the first of each shoe in the collection in his factory in Italy. Hence the price tags—these are among the most costly shoes in the world. But no one seems to be complaining.

Blahnik has continued to sell from an impeccable salon on London's Kings Road, and has added just three stores in New York, Beverly Hills, and Hong Kong to that list despite becoming the fashion world's shoe designer without peer, selling an estimated 100,000 pairs of his handmade shoes per year, and having free fashion and celebrity endorsements. Longtime client actor Sarah Jessica Parker and her television program *Sex and the City* at times appeared to be one long advertisement for all things Blahnik. He tends not advertise or hold fashion shows.

He remains inspired after more than thirty years, still working with young fashion design students that he believes in, calling them his "children." He lives, he says, a celibate life in a restored Georgian home in Bath that is reported to house 10,000 pairs of shoes, each pair its own fantasy for the feet.

NOTES

"Fashion is a . . ." Blanchard, Tamsin. "High on heels," *The Observer*, 1.12.03, p. H03.

REFERENCES

McDowell, Colin. *Manolo Blahnik*. Harper Collins, 2000.

The Age, British Vogue, Daily Mail, Daily Telegraph, Evening Standard, Financial Times, The Guardian, The Independent, Los Angeles Times, Mail on Sunday, New York Times, The Observer, Salon.com, *Sun Herald, Sunday Life, Sydney Morning Herald, The Times, Vanity Fair, Washington Post, Women's Wear Daily*

Porsche

"You sweep the steps from the top down"

————

IT SEEMS INCREDIBLE TODAY, BUT LITTLE OVER A DECADE AGO Porsche was in serious danger of collapse. In 1993, it sold just 14,000 cars, down from 53,000 in 1986, and in 1991 lost around $150 million.

Enter Wendelin Wiedeking. An engineer by trade, he came to Porsche in 1992 as head of its production and materials department. He had traveled to Japan and seen how car companies there ran their production lines; Porsche, in comparison, was back in the Middle Ages. Virtually everything was made by hand in-house, which brought the benefits of fine craftsmanship, but the downside of terrible inefficiency and occasional sloppy workmanship.

Brashly promising to deliver a 30 percent reduction in production costs, Wiedeking brought in a team of Japanese time and motion experts from Toyota to ruthlessly pull apart the existing system. He benchmarked the entire production process. Then, he cut the number of managers by 35 percent and fired 95 percent of the sales and marketing managers, in his version of an old German proverb, "You sweep the steps from the top down"—meaning effective change permeates the entire organization, starting with the bosses. Next, he went to the suppliers and pointed out their inefficiencies too, resulting in lower prices for Porsche. He may not have made many friends, but his methods were so effective and the results so obvious that the Porsche and Piech families, who still run the company, asked him to take over as CEO in 1993, at age thirty-nine. It was a job, as they say, for somebody looking for a challenge.

Wiedeking inherited a creaky, old-school factory and an ancient model range burdened with other people's mistakes. The company's heritage was closely tied to one model, the 911, a car thirty years old. Attempts to broaden the range in the hope of increased sales had failed—Porsche customers had refused to recognize any model but the 911 as a true Porsche. Wiedeking's genius was to recognize that the company did not have to abandon its heritage to move forward. Porsche had, after all, been in the sports car business for half a century, since Ferdinand Porsche built the first model, the 356, in 1948.

He cancelled plans to phase out the 911, instead dumping the models planned to succeed it, including a four-seater sedan. While hanging on to the 911's heritage, he also introduced a new entry-level model, the Boxster, a two-seater drop-top that was instantly recognizable as "Porsche." Lauded by the motoring press for its sharp handling, it was so popular with buyers that it still has a waiting list. If anything, there was a danger that the newer, cheaper Boxster would poach sales from the more expensive 911, but behind the scenes Wiedeking had it all worked out. The Boxster would, in fact, ensure the future success of its stablemate, while also paving the way for a new, more controversial model, the four-wheel-drive Cayenne.

It was all about efficiency. When he first planned the Boxster, Wiedeking knew Porsche could not afford to tool up a new factory of its own. So he took the previously unheard-of step of having the Boxster built by somebody else—in this case, a Finnish auto maker—leaving him more resources at the Porsche factory.

Then Wiedeking lent parts of the Boxster's design to the new 911, simplifying the production process. Again, Wiedeking read the market correctly: a handful of traditionalists complained that "their" 911 shared parts with its cheaper sibling, but to everybody else it looked like family resemblance. It now takes Porsche less than half the time it did in 1992 to assemble its flagship 911 Turbo, yet the car's build quality has improved.

When Porsche engineers are not working on their own product, they hire their skills to other companies including Harley-Davidson, Mercedes-Benz, Airbus, and even a forklift company—part of Wiedeking's philosophy to keep everyone busy. Today, around a third of Porsche's 2,300 staff are doing contract work at any one time, bringing in around $500 million extra revenue. On the factory floor, workers are paid above-union rates to work flexible hours: more when demand increases, less when it slackens off.

By the mid-1990s, Porsche was on the rebound, but as a niche provider of luxury goods it was still vulnerable to downturns in the economy—nobody "needs" a Porsche. Wiedeking decided to develop a third model as insurance. He plumped for the sports utility Cayenne to cash in on the enormous growth in sports utility vehicles and, on a more mundane level, to provide transportation for Porsche fans who also happened to have a child or two (advertisements were later to use the slogan: "cancel the vasectomy").

After his success outsourcing the Boxster, Wiedeking went one step further in 1997, entering a partnership with Volkswagen to develop the Cayenne simultaneously with the VW Touareg, with the two vehicles looking outwardly different but sharing much of the running gear underneath.

But would it be accepted as a true Porsche? Once again, the traditionalists railed against it. But Wiedeking was adamant that while it was no sports car, the Cayenne was "100 percent Porsche." It was, after all, powered by a Porsche V8 engine that made it the fastest SUV in the world. It now accounts for half of Porsche's sales.

Thanks to Wiedeking, Porsche is still the world's smallest mass manufacturer (every other mainstream sports-car maker including Ferrari and Aston Martin is now owned by a major group). It now sells around 70,000 vehicles a year, with customers queuing up for more. Demand is strongest with a one-year waiting list for the company's most expensive model, the 911 Turbo, which also happens to be its most profitable. Across the range, each car makes around ten times more profit than those made by General Motors—the highest of all manufacturers. Overall profits have increased for nine years in a row. And for the traditionalists still bristling at the Cayenne (one model of which now even comes with an engine sourced from VW), Wiedeking has a new model on the forecourt called the Carrera GT, a V10-powered, 600-horsepower monster capable of giving a taxiing jet fighter a run for its money. Porsche no longer a sports car company? Hardly.

REFERENCES

Automotive Intelligence News, Autoweek, BBC, BusinessWeek, Cigar Aficionado, Fortune, IndustryWeek, USA Today, Ward's Autoworld

Prada

Luxury with an edge

NOT EVERY SUCCESSFUL BUSINESSPERSON IS A NATURAL entrepreneur. Miuccia Prada, the quirky, beyond-cool fashion designer with the most futuristic store in the United States, isn't even sure she's in the right business. "I had many problems for many years doing this work," she said in 1998, "because I wanted to do something more serious."

Born into a well-to-do family in Milan, Italy, Prada studied political science, flirted with the Communist Party, and belonged to a theatrical troupe as a mime artist for six years before relatives encouraged her to direct her efforts into the family business, which her paternal grandfather, Mario, had founded in 1913, making such luxuries as walrus-skin bags with ivory fittings for the Italian royal family.

The leather goods business was still based around a single shop in Milan when Miuccia eventually took over in 1978. The same year, she met her future husband, Patrizio Bertelli, at a trade fair. Bertelli, the son of a lawyer and teacher, had studied engineering at Bologna University but dropped out to start his own business making leather goods. He first struck a deal with Miuccia to give him the exclusive license to make Prada products, then he wooed her, encouraging her to expand into shoes and fashion, giving the fashion house a new, inspiring edge.

The couple married in 1987 and today control the sprawling Prada group, a private company that owns the Prada and Miu Miu labels and has controlling interests in several other brands. Bertelli owns one-third of the business, Miuccia and the Prada family own the rest. Their relationship is famously stormy—"When they say we scream a lot, it's true," Prada said in 2004—but it has also been enormously productive, melding Prada's creativity with Bertelli's business sense.

One of Prada's breakthrough products was a bag that was determinedly utilitarian yet perfectly chic, a black nylon backpack that became the "must-have" accessory for fashionistas in the early 1990s. It was the ideal antidote to the excesses of the 1980s, yet its little triangular badge became as sought-after as any other luxury label—and was just as expensive.

The bag spawned enormous demand for the Prada range of nylon and leather accessories. Bertelli reportedly told boutiques that if they wanted Prada's accessories, they also had to carry Miuccia's minimalist line of womenswear, which he had encouraged her to design. Menswear, the Prada Sport range and the younger label Miu Miu (Miuccia's nickname), followed.

Prada expanded in the 1990s, buying up controlling interests in Jil Sander, Helmut Lang, and Church and Co. shoes. The Prada group now has over 250 retail outlets worldwide, including three flagship stores—called "epicenter concept stores"—that reflect its owners' growing interests in contemporary architecture, technology and the arts. The company's SoHo store in New York, designed by "difficult" Dutch architect Rem Koolhaas and built in 2001 at a cost of $40 million, came with glass changing room doors that turned opaque at the push of a button, a $1 million cylindrical elevator and clothes displayed in hanging cages—not a store in which to browse lightly. In 2003, Prada opened another "epicenter" in Tokyo, designed by Herzog and de Meuron, a six-story glass crystal, criss-crossed with lattice.

The Prada website, in contrast, is deliberately minimal, offering a home page with an image of current fashions and nothing else.

With annual revenue of some $1.6 billion, Miuccia and Bertelli are freer than most to explore their interests. Miuccia still lives in the same Milan apartment she was born in (admittedly it has been extended somewhat) and is an avid art collector. Bertelli, a competitive sailor in his youth, spent $50 million to get the Prada-sponsored yacht, *Luna Rosa*, to the finals of the America's Cup in 2000. The Prada-Bertelli partnership has been a formidable one.

NOTES

"I had many problems . . . "   Walker, Natasha. "The Bag Lady," *The Observer*, 7.26.98, p. 4.

"When they say . . ."   Frankel, Susannah. "The Feeling Is Miuccia," *The Independent*, 2.21.04, p. 20.

REFERENCES

Business, Evening Standard, Financial Times, The Guardian, International Herald Tribune, New York Times, New Yorker, Sunday Times, Vanity Fair

Alessi

Making the world a more beautiful place

I F EVER A COMPANY EXISTED ON FAITH, IT IS THE UPMARKET Italian homewares manufacturer Alessi. It freely admits there is no practical reason to buy its products, unless you really need the world's most beautiful flyswatter. Its designs are usually far more expensive than competitors that perform the same task. And sometimes they don't even do what they are supposed to, such as the kettle that burns your hand when you lift it off the stove. When that happens, Alessi does not cringe—instead, it celebrates. "I think it is essential for Alessi to have at least one fiasco every year," managing director Alberto Alessi often says. And the people who bought the failure are expected to understand.

If Alessi was a major car manufacturer, it would most likely have gone out of business a long time ago, chastised by consumer researcher JD Power along the way. But when somebody buys an Alessi lemon squeezer, they are not primarily interested in how well it extracts juice from a lemon. They are buying a little piece of what Alessi is about—and its contrary attitude to business is part of its appeal.

How did the company find itself in such a privileged position?

Alessi started life in 1921 as one of many metalwork businesses in the village of Omegna in the Italian Alps. Its founder, Giovanni Alessi, found a niche supplying high-quality equipment to commercial kitchens and hotels: salt-and-pepper stands, fruit bowls, bread baskets. During the second World War, Alessi produced insignia for uniforms and airplane parts, then, in the aftermath of hostilities, an enormous number of brass ladles for the U.S. Army. By the 1960s,

Alessi's stainless steel products were found in cafés throughout Italy, but nobody would think to remark on them.

In 1970, Giovanni's grandson Alberto came to the factory. He had just finished a law degree, but that was only because his father had refused to let him study architecture—and he resolved to inject some of his passion for modern design into the staid family business. He writes on the company website of his desire to produce "multiplied art" for the masses.

From the outset, he felt he had to call on outside expertise, an idea that is at the heart of the company's success today. His first attempts at hiring designer flair, which included commissioning Salvador Dali for a series of pressed steel artworks, were commercial flops. So Alberto, who took over management of the company with his two brothers in 1979, toned down his vision slightly, seeking instead to revitalize everyday homewares. "There is no reason to design another tray or teapot, but the search for perfection is what spurs people on to keep trying," he says. In the early 1980s, Alessi commissioned eleven architects to sketch their own versions of a tea and coffee service, drawing on the principles of architecture. It was another expensive folly for Alberto but in 1983 Alessi had some success with its first designer kettle, Richard Sapper's Kettle with a Singing Whistle. Then Alessi commissioned architect Michael Graves, one of the tea-set designers, to try a kettle, too.

The result was a seminal piece for Alessi, a stainless-steel cone with rivet-shaped bumps around its base and a cute plastic bird at its spout that whistled when the water boiled. With the 1980s fascination with all things "designer" now spreading to the kitchen, too, the Kettle with a Bird-Shaped Whistle became an inspirational must-have, and Alessi went on to sell over a million such kettles. Alessi's expanding range of designer kettles, minimalist trays, clocks, and ashtrays were now on every young professional's wedding list—and in serious danger of becoming a one-hit wonder.

Alessi's response was to reestablish the brand as a risk-taking leader in design, not just as a manufacturer of luxury goods. It continued to experiment through premier designers such as Philippe Starck, whose lemon squeezer, 1990's Juicy Salif, looked like a stainless-steel spider from outer space. It sold millions.

Starck's attempt at a kettle, the Hot Bertaa, was just as sensational, but for the wrong reasons: to look as amazing as it did—basically a cone with a shaft that was both a handle and a spout—it had to have complicated innards to channel the steam properly. But in practice it sputtered out boiling water when you tried to pour yourself a cup. Alberto Alessi called it one of the most important flops of the decade. "The kettle was much criticized," Alessi said in 2001, "but it was never a stupid project. I like fiascos because they are the only moment when there is a flash of light that can help you see where the border between success and failure is. It is a precious experience in the development of new projects."

In the early 1990s, Alessi opened its doors to young designers, soliciting proposals (it receives several hundred a year) and tip-offs on new talent from established names. It also diversified into plastic products that emphasized quirkiness and fun, and were much cheaper than the stainless-steel lines, much to the chagrin of long-time Alessi fans. Nutcrackers shaped like squirrels, bottle-openers with grinning cat's teeth, and flyswatters: designer chic for the mainstream. "Even in the area of ordinary household products, people require some art and poetry to add to their lives," says Alessi.

Alessi now has revenues estimated at $100 million and a catalogue of two thousand-odd products, adding three hundred and dropping eighty each year. Flexibility on the production line means a design can be profitable in runs of two thousand. The plastic range has helped Alessi to double its turnover every five years since the 1980s; Alessandro Mendini's 1994 Anna G corkscrew—with womanly arms and a smiling face—sold close to a million units in eight years. Alessi has also collaborated with other companies to produce, among other things, a range of bathroom fittings, watches, and electrical appliances.

Thanks in part to Alessi's success, though, every other manufacturer of homewares has realized the importance of aesthetics. The discount retailer Target brought this home when it commissioned Michael Graves to design, as part of a range of homewares, a kettle that looked a lot like his Alessi model but retailed for $30. It was a cheeky move, but Target was forgetting something: who went to Target to buy a kettle they didn't really need?

NOTES
"I think it is essential . . ." Paul, Donna. "Avanti," *Interior Design*, 11.1.02.
"There is no reason . . ." Alessi, Alberto. "Alberto Alessi's Perfect Design," Observer Life, *The Observer*, 1.14.01, p. 6.
"The kettle . . ." Wylie, Ian. "Failure is Glorious," *Fast Company*, 10.01, p. 35.
"Even in the . . ." Marsh, Peter. "Designed to Beat the World," *Financial Times*, 11.22.02, p.15.

REFERENCES
Birmingham Post, Daily Telegraph, Design Week, Fast Company, Financial Times, Forbes, The Guardian, The Independent, Interior Design, International Herald Tribune, Nottingham Evening Post, The New Yorker, Orlando Sentinel, Scotland on Sunday, South China Morning Post, Sunday Times, The Observer, Washington Post

NO EXPERIENCE NECESSARY

Subway

You can never have too many stores

F RED DeLUCA HAD EARNED HIS FIRST MILLION DOLLARS BY the time he was twenty-five. Today the Florida-based billionaire earns an estimated $1 million a week courtesy of the Subway fast-food business he cofounded when he was just seventeen years old. DeLuca's current earnings are a far cry from the $1.25 an hour he used to earn in the local hardware store, a wage that inspired him to earn some real money to pay for his degree in medicine from the local university in Bridgeport, Connecticut.

A family friend, scientist Peter Buck, put up $1,000 seed capital to fund the sandwich shop. (Today Buck, who sits on the board of parent company Doctor's Associates, earns similar amounts to DeLuca.) The plan was hatched at a family get-together, and the pair spent time looking at the successful delis in the area, deciding on a limited range of sandwiches served in foot-long or six-inch rolls. Family and friends helped set up the first store, calling it Pete's Super Submarines. The doors opened in Bridgeport in 1965, with the first day's trading excellent despite the fact that DeLuca only had one knife in the store.

The Subway business is now the second biggest fast-food chain in the world behind McDonald's, with a new store opening somewhere in the world every four hours. There are more Subway stores in the U.S. than McDonald's, but the chain is a long way behind the golden arches internationally. There are now more than 24,000 Subway stores in eighty-two countries around the world as opposed to McDonald's 30,000 outlets in one-hundred countries. Subway had annual sales in 2003 of $5.7 billion, McDonald's had sales in 2003 on $17.1 billion.

After the initial rush at the first Pete's Super Submarines, the weather turned wintry, and subsequent advertising and promotional campaigns failed to boost sales. "Nobody came into the first store," says DeLuca. DeLuca's instinct was to open more stores, working on the theory that more stores would increase recognition and help build the brand. Buck agreed to the plan. Subway's close-knit group of suppliers extended their credit to the business and DeLuca used the cash to open further stores. The second store opened in 1966. By 1968 there were five sandwich stores, now called Subway, and the business was looking healthier. DeLuca and Buck then set a goal of thirty stores.

In 1972, DeLuca was knocked-back from a bank for a loan and given the advice that he would never find any institutional support until he had a proper business plan and financial statements prepared by an accountant. The business was still not making any real money (although DeLuca had made his first million). DeLuca discovered that by being savvier about controlling costs, there could be bigger profits. He became a self-confessed penny-pincher, obsessively controlling costs, monitoring stock, supplies, and every facet of the business to minimize waste.

Franchising did not start until 1974 when DeLuca persuaded a friend to become a franchisee. DeLuca even paid the $14,000 fee as a sweetener. If he didn't like the sandwich business he could walk away and not owe a thing. DeLuca devised a franchise model that did not need much retail space, equipment, or elaborate fit-outs. Subway would receive a franchise fee and a royalty fee. (The royalty fee is currently 8 percent. In the early days the amount was much smaller.)

The business took off. In 1984, the first store opened offshore in Bahrain. By 1990, there were 5,000 Subways around the world. Subway's plans for growth were succeeding beyond DeLuca's and Buck's expectations. Every time they set a goal, they reached it way ahead of schedule.

The franchise model was far from perfect. For starters, there is always the risk that a franchised store will not work. An average of

1 percent of new Subway stores fail to thrive. Then, because of opening franchised stores in Japan, the business had an initial burst of sales but then failed to prosper. (The theory in Japan is that Subway rolls are too big for Japanese women to eat in public, it being considered gross to eat a giant mouthful of tuna sub.) Disgruntled franchisees sued Subway after pumping their life savings into the failed stores.

DeLuca also complicated the lives of franchisees by letting new Subway franchisees open stores wherever they liked, even if it was in the next block from an existing Subway store. DeLuca stuck with his belief that the more stores there are, regardless of whether some stores cannibalize another's sales, overall sales will be up. And the more stores, the more royalties for DeLuca. DeLuca now has a committee to handle problems, although franchisees must pay a fee to have their case heard.

DeLuca is the first to admit his company has made some mistakes with franchisee relationships, particularly over the territorial rules. Despite the controversy, and lawsuits in Japan, Canada, and the U.S. against Subway. There are still franchisees lining up to own a Subway store and 70 percent of new openings are by existing franchisees—just as DeLuca thought he needed several Subway stores to make a decent living, his recruits are thinking along the same lines.

DeLuca talks to his franchisees every month through "Fred's Home Video," the company has regular email updates, and new franchisees can attend Subway's sandwich school.

Subway has a very decentralized business model. DeLuca is chairman of Subway's parent company, Doctor's Associates. Then there is a separate company to handle Subway's administration, another to handle property leases, and another layer of independent agents acting as consultants to Subway's existing and potential franchises. These agents receive half of the initial franchise fee, one-third of royalties paid by franchises, and a transfer fee if stores are sold. They screen for new franchisees, scout for retail locations, and also manage teams of inspectors who anonymously visit Subway stores to ensure owners are sticking to Subway's guidelines.

Subway franchisees also pay 3.5 percent of their turnover to fund Subway's advertising budget. The company's advertising agency has a board made up of people elected by Subway franchisees to represent their interests. DeLuca himself cannot overrule the direction of this board. "At least half the time I would have done things differently," he says. "But this does not mean that I would have been doing things any better."

DeLuca has a secret weapon against other fast food rivals—a Houston, Texas, college student named Jared Fogle who used to weigh 425 pounds. Fogle noticed a local 1998 Subway advertising campaign promoting its sandwiches with less than six grams of fat. He started eating a low-fat Subway sandwich for lunch and dinner. A year later, he had lost 245 pounds. Fogle's mother wrote to Subway to thank them for his transformation. Subway did not respond to the letter. But the company did call after they noticed sales jumping in areas where newspapers had run stories on Fogle.

A campaign was launched around Jared Fogle that is arguably the most successful fast-food campaign ever. Fogle became a household name. Subway's pitch as the healthy alternative boosted sales by 33 percent, perfectly timed to cash in on a growing anti-fast food sentiment and the fears surrounding Mad Cow Disease. By 2001, Subway was selling close to 1 billion sandwiches annually. Fogle quit his day job with an airline and became a full-time Subway spokesperson. "And yes Fogle has been compensated very, very well," says DeLuca.

Despite his wealth, DeLuca has no plans to leave Subway. In the 1990s, he tried to launch other franchise ideas: budget hairdressers, spicy fried chicken, and a hamburger chain called Q burgers. They all flopped. He insists that Subway will not go public either. Since the late 1990s, DeLuca has been linked to the consortium Schaghticoke Tribal Nation, which planned to operate a casino in Kent, West Connecticut. The $12 million speculative investment has not paid off and has descended into a complicated, expensive legal battle. DeLuca lives in Orlando, Florida, with his wife and family. In 1996, he set up the Micro Investment Lending Enterprise (MILE), a non-profit seed funding organization to help entrepreneurs who do not have access to traditional loans. "We were never very sophisticated as business people," says DeLuca. And look where $1,000 took him.

NOTES

"Nobody came . . ." Davis, Stephania H. "Subway Owner Offers Business Advice at Westport Connecticut," *Connecticut Post*, 5.15.02.

"At least half . . ." Swann, Christopher. "Sandwich Chain Crams A Lot in 35 Years," *Financial Times*, 6.26.01, p. 4.

"And yes Fogle . . ." Francis, Bruce and Kathleen Hays. "Subway Passes McDonald's in Restaurants," *CNN Financial News*, 2.5.02.

"We were never sophisticated . . ." Brady, Diane. "Why Subway Is on a Roll," *BusinessWeek Online*, 8.19.02.

REFERENCES

DeLuca, Fred. *Start Small, Finish Big*. Warner Books, 2000.

BusinessWeek, CNN, *Fast Company*, *Financial Times*, *Forbes*, *Fortune*, *New York Times*, *Washington Post*

Mrs. Fields Cookies

"It's the lack of perfection that drives me crazy"

DEBBI FIELDS WAS JUST TWENTY WHEN SHE HAD HER BIG idea. Recently married and living in Palo Alto, California, she decided she was not cut out to be a housewife for the rest of her life. She had no business qualifications, but she had baked cookies at home since her early teens and figured it was her only marketable skill. So she decided to open a cookie shop. Success led to global expansion. And the rest is history.

Well, not quite.

Fields, the youngest of five girls born to a welder and a housewife in Oakland, California, grew up with a strong work ethic, working as a foul-ball girl for a baseball team at thirteen, in a department store, and, at seventeen, in a water ski show with the title Miss Marine World. At eighteen, she was at Denver airport on her way home from a ski trip when she met twenty-eight-year-old economist Randy Fields; they married a year later, reportedly after Debbi proposed. Married domesticity was not the be-all and end-all for Debbi, though. She later told a reporter she thought their circle of friends considered her "just a housewife."

"I knew my disadvantages," she told *Memphis Magazine* in 1999. "I was young, had no college credentials, came from little means. I was blonde and people figured I had no brains."

But she was persistent. In 1977, she managed to borrow enough money to start her business. She recalled: "The one thing I had to my name was a Volkswagen Bug, my collateral, and, basically, a dream. But I didn't care. I knew I would pay back my loan, even if I had to take three jobs."

At times she has recalled her husband saying her idea was stupid, though she has also claimed it was his support that got her the loan in the first place. "I thought she was loony," Randy said later. "She'd only been making cookies for my clients in the investment business. Her background was in English and History. She knew nothing about business." Later Debbi was to say, "The thing that really got me going was when my mom said I would fail."

Either way, on the day she opened the Mrs. Fields Chocolate Chippery, August 16, 1977, business was so slow that by 3:00 p.m., according to oft-repeated legend, she had not sold a single cookie. So Fields loaded up a tray with cookies and set off down the street, giving them away. It proved a successful strategy—by the end of the day she had lured customers back to the shop with her freebies and she had made $75.

Debbi Fields's homestyle, chewy, warm cookie, baked in-store, and her old-fashioned selling technique appealed to customers' nostalgia. Soft cookies were a new market, and the company expanded dramatically. By 1980, there were fifteen stores and headquarters had moved to Park City, Utah. By 1983, she had sixty-three stores. By 1986, husband Randy had quit being a consultant economist to work for her business, which now had 350 stores, bought 10 percent of the world supply of macadamia nuts, and even ran a "cookie college" to train managers (where eating a cookie was referred to as "having a Mrs. Fields experience"). Incredibly, Debbi, now pregnant with her fourth child, still found time to publish her autobiography, *One Smart Cookie*. (She and Randy eventually had five children, all daughters.)

Fields grasped early on that customer service was as important as the product itself. She learned her customers' preferences, remembered their birthdays, and hired staff who could do the same. She later refined her instincts into a three-step hiring process. First, she brought out a plate of cookies and asked the candidate to taste them, so she could judge their enthusiasm for the product. Next, she asked them to take a tray of cookies out onto the street and give them away, which gauged how outgoing they were. Lastly, she asked them to sing "Happy Birthday" in the store: something they would be required to do for customers. She called the process the three S's: sampling, selling, and singing.

Employees were also introduced to the mysterious "Mr. Thumb." Before selling each cookie, they had to squeeze it with their thumb to make sure it was still soft and chewy. Cookies more than two hours old were supposed to be given to charity.

"It's lack of perfection that drives me crazy," Fields once admitted. "The disappointment and frustration are indescribable when I find my cookie standards aren't being met. Perfection in a cookie is definable." She was known to drop into stores, throw out whole batches of cookies because they were too crunchy, then demonstrate to the staff how to make them properly.

They floated the company on the UK stock exchange in 1986 but the share price proved volatile, slumping in 1988 after it became apparent the company had expanded too quickly, leading to store closures. In 1993, the company, now with 780 stores, was restructured with four lenders effectively buying 79 percent of the business. Debbi Fields lost control, though agreed to stay on as its public face, finally retiring in 2000.

"That meant basically the bankers took over my business," she said later. "It was the worst, most devastating experience of my life, because it was like putting my child up for adoption."

In 1997, she divorced Randy and remarried, to retired company chairman Michael Rose, who also had five children from a previous marriage. No longer involved in the business that bears her name, today she is a keen horse rider and has reinvented herself as a popular speaker on the business seminar circuit, charging $15,000 an appearance.

NOTES

"I knew my disadvantages . . ." Sadler, Marilyn. "Baking a Name for Herself," *Memphis Magazine*, 6.99.

"The thing that really got me . . ." Bauer, Amy. "Fields Stresses Quality," *Capital Journal*, 10.5.03.

"I thought . . ." McKee, Victoria. "Is the Cookie Crumbling?" *The Times*, 4.14.89.

"The one thing . . ." *Indianapolis Star*, 10.2.03.

"It's lack of perfection . . ." staff writers, "Nibbles," Food, *St. Louis Post-Dispatch*, 5.17.93, p. 1.

"That meant . . ." *Managing with Lou Dobbs*, CNN, 11.23.96.

REFERENCES

Adweek, Brandweek, BusinessWeek, Chattanooga Free Press, Chicago Tribune, Christian Science Monitor, CNN, Commercial Appeal, Daily Oklahoman, Financial Times, Forbes, Fortune, Indianapolis Star, Kansas City Star, Knoxville News-Sentinel, Los Angeles Times, Ottawa Citizen, Pensacola News Journal, Portland Press Herald, Star Tribune, Times, Toronto Star

Diners Club

Credit where credit is due

THE FIRST DINERS CLUB CARD WAS DEVISED BY NEW YORK businessman Frank McNamara in 1950. It was made of cardboard, had the cardholder's signature on it, and was attached to a little booklet with a list of the fourteen New York restaurants that were part of the Diners Club scheme. Restaurants would pay a small service charge and offer customers a cash-free night out. At its inception, there were two hundred card members; by the end of the year there were 20,500 members; today there are more than eight million Diners Club cardholders in two hundred countries.

McNamara reportedly came up with the idea for the card after being caught short at a dinner at Major's Cabin Grill in Manhattan. He had left his wallet in another jacket. Acutely embarrassed, McNamara had to phone his wife in the suburbs and get her to drive in with the cash that he had left in his wallet at home.

Like many "legends" this story was actually a fairy tale, inspired by a savvy twenty-three-year-old spin-doctor, Matty Simmons, who would go on to write and produce the classic American comedy movie *Animal House*. McNamara knew he had a good idea, he just did not know how to sell it. So he and his lawyer Ralph Schneider cajoled Simmons into copywriting and media strategy for the fledgling charge card business.

"In 1950, press agents had very colorful imaginations," says Simmons. "We absolutely ad-libbed everything. None of us had ever done any of these things before, so we made things up as we went along." Simmons went on to become Diners Club's executive vice president, leaving the company in 1967 to start up the successful

Weight Watchers magazine before heading for Hollywood and the creation of *National Lampoon*.

While at Diners Club, Simmons's ads were so effective that each time they appeared thousands would apply for membership. By 1952, there were 42,000 Diners Club members. McNamara sold out his share of the business to Schneider and department store heir Alfred Bloomingdale for $200,000. Bloomingdale was already selling a charge card on the west coast in California. McNamara became a sales representative for a lumber company. Today Diners Club generates $30 billion in sales, though is way short of credit giants Visa and MasterCard. Frank McNamara died in 1957, seven years after the launch of Diners Club. He was just forty.

NOTES
"In 1950, press agents . . ." *Adweek*, 4.16.90.

REFERENCES
Simmons, Matty. *The Credit Card Catastrophe: The 20th Century Phenomenon That Changes the World*, Barricade Books, 1995.

Adweek, Australian Financial Review, Boston Globe, Chattanooga Times Free Press, CNN, *Daily Mail*, Hoover's Company Records, *New York Times, Ottawa Citizen, San Francisco Chronicle, Sunday Mail, The Times, Toronto Sun, United Press International, Weekend Australian*

Jani-King

The cleaning business is never going to disappear

B Y THE TIME JIM CAVANAUGH STARTED BUSINESS SCHOOL AT the University of Oklahoma in 1968, he was already a seasoned entrepreneur. As a kid he had run one of the largest paper rounds in his hometown of Norman, Oklahoma, where he employed his friends to help him do the jobs he didn't like, such as collecting fees. Cavanaugh preferred to go out and find new business, mow a few extra lawns, deliver more newspapers, or sell tickets to football games, than actually gather the money.

His $2-an-hour college job, working as a night auditor at the Holiday Inn in Norman, was a cinch for Cavanaugh. He would have all the accounts organized by 2 a.m., leaving him several hours to study, snooze, and contemplate his future. Twenty-year-old Cavanaugh used these midnight hours to think about the sort of business he wanted to create for himself and to hunt for the right opportunity. He read business books and financial magazines and devised plans for a childcare center and a hydroponic tomato business, but no one was going to lend a twenty-year-old money for such capital intensive ventures. He would have to find another way to get rich.

On the night shift, Cavanaugh got to know Don McGuffin, the man who came in each night to clean public areas of the hotel. They got talking about the cleaning business and Cavanaugh found out that this janitor was being paid $400 a month for his cleaning work (a lot more than Cavanaugh's $2 an hour). Commercial cleaning started to look very interesting to Cavanaugh. McGuffin told him that he hated the business side of his job, finding new clients, dealing with staff and administration. Cavanaugh thought he could help out and offered to make a brochure for McGuffin in return for a commission if Cavanaugh found him more work. It was a win/win deal. Cavanaugh's flair for sales quickly created more work than McGuffin could handle. Cavanaugh smelled opportunity and set to learning about the cleaning business, from how to polish a lobby floor to where to look for new cleaning contracts.

He set up Jani-King in 1969, drumming up business by day and cleaning by night. College would have to wait. While Cavanaugh was successful at bringing in new business he says in hindsight that he charged too little in fees to make the business one that he could live on. He also did not charge a finder's fee for new cleaning contracts. In the first five years of Jani-King, he was evicted from his apartment, had his car repossessed, and ended up living out of a station wagon borrowed from his father.

Cavanaugh always wanted a nationwide business but knew it would be next to impossible for him to raise the funds for a major expansion. He decided that franchising was his only option. He knew this would be a hard sell because so many franchise operations had been disreputable. To help potential Jani-King franchisees feel more confident that Cavanaugh was serious about making the business work (as opposed to just taking their savings), he devised a set-up proposition that was extremely low-risk for new Jani-King associates. The set-up fee of around $2,500 included cleaning equipment and products and could be paid off in installments so upfront fees were marginal. He pitched to the market that his national cleaning franchise would make cleaners "appear more professional," he said. "All they had to do was show up and clean." The suits went off to get the business and the cleaners just concentrated on cleaning.

Cavanaugh started selling Jani-King franchises in Oklahoma City in 1974. Within three months he had sold five franchises. He then moved on to Tulsa and began a cycle of moving to a new city, establishing a Jani-King presence and then moving on to the next city. It was a slow process putting Jani-King in cities such as Dallas, Fort Worth, Houston, Atlanta, St. Louis, and New Orleans. Jani-King moved into Canada in the 1980s and offshore in the 1990s.

There are now more than 10,500 Jani-King franchise owners in twenty countries including growth markets such as the United Arab Emirates and Turkey. Turnover in 2004 was an estimated $50 million. Franchisees must now pay a fee of $8,600–16,300 to join Jani-King and an ongoing royalty fee of 10 percent.

For Cavanaugh, it was a long, hard slog before his business was anywhere near stable. His reward for surviving those tough early years—he could afford to stop living out of his car and cut back on the cleaning.

NOTES

"More professional . . ." DeLuca, Fred with John P Hayes. *Start Small, Finish Big.* Warner Books, 2000. p.112.

REFERENCES

DeLuca, Fred with John P Hayes. *Start Small, Finish Big.* Warner Books, 2000.

Associated Press, Entrepreneur, Hoover's Company Records, janiking.com, *New York Times*

AND NOW
FOR SOMETHING
COMPLETELY DIFFERENT

Play-Doh

One person's trash can make a business treasure

―――――

P LAY-DOH STARTED LIFE AS A PRE-MIXED FLOURY PASTE CALLED Magic Wallpaper Cleaner, used from the beginning of the 1900s to remove sooty coal dust off wallpaper. As home heating evolved, demand for the cleaner lagged, and by the 1950s, the U.S.'s biggest maker of the cleaner, Kutol, was in real trouble. Kutol was run by a Cincinatti family, the McVickers, and, needless to say, a lot of talk around their dinner table centered on what to do with all this obsolete wallpaper cleaner. In 1955, the founder's son, Joe McVicker, listened to his sister-in-law, a teacher, complaining how hard it was for her younger students to use modeling clay. He sent her some of his doughy, nontoxic wallpaper cleaner to try out with the students. It was a hit. McVicker called his enterprise Rainbow Crafts and took his product, sold in a can and only available in off-white, to trade shows. The Play-Doh recipe was patented in 1956, and it was first sold in the Woodward & Lothrop Department Store in Washington, DC. Yellow, red, and blue Play-Doh were introduced the following year. Play-Doh made Joe McVicker a millionaire by the time he was twenty-seven.

First exported in 1964, Play-Doh is now available in seventy-five countries and sales have remained consistent. The total amount of Play-Doh sold is the equivalent weight of 159 fully loaded space shuttles and 95 million cans are sold each year. Play-Doh's parent company, Hasbro, which acquired the product in 1991, continues to use armies of lawyers to protect the precious, patented Play-Doh name from being accepted as the generic name for all modeling dough. More than two billion cans of Play-Doh later, Hasbro still wants to protect its turf. The formula for this soft, squishy play stuff remains top secret.

REFERENCES

AAO, Atlanta Journal and Constitution, Chicago Sun-Times, Courier Mail, FiftiesWeb.com, *Financial Times,* Inventors.About.com, *New York Times, Sarasota Herald-Tribune, Sunday Mail,* TVAcres.com, United States Patent and Trademark Office, *Washington Post*

Dippin' Dots

The ice cream from outer space

THE KEY TO MAKING THE BEST ICE CREAM IS EXTREME COLD— if you freeze the mix quickly enough, ice crystals don't have time to form and the end result is wonderfully smooth and creamy. Extreme cold, though, doesn't mean Siberian, or even Arctic: we're talking way down below -250 degrees fahrenheit—temperatures even a commercial ice cream machine can only dream of reaching.

One day in 1987, Curt Jones was making homemade ice cream with a neighbor at his home in Lexington, Kentucky. As he cranked the handle, he tried to explain to his friend what he did at work. Jones, a microbiologist, worked at an agricultural feed plant, where he experimented with ways of freezing enzymes and "good" bacteria to put into animal feed.

At the plant, he said, they were using liquid nitrogen to freeze the feed into pellets at -340 degrees fahrenheit. You could do the same thing with ice cream, he explained by way of example. Three weeks later Jones, intrigued by thought of making ice cream at temperatures colder than a chilly day on Pluto, took his friend and some ice cream mix to the lab. They mixed it up with liquid nitrogen and tasted the result. His findings were ambiguous—"It was really cold, about -200, and we burned our tongues," he recalls. But after it warmed up a little (to a relatively civilized -20) it was deliciously smooth.

Making nitrogen ice cream is a fairly well-known party trick among scientists: you just make up ice cream mix in a bowl, then pour in liquid nitrogen and stir with a spoon, preferably wearing gloves and goggles, and it freezes solid in moments. But Jones then put his ice cream mix through the nitrogen-freezing pellet machine, producing ice cream that was not only cryogenically frozen but formed into tiny beads—a unique, potentially captivating product. "I kinda put two and two together," he says. "I really felt from the very beginning that it might have a chance because it was so different."

Jones was by profession a scientist (he studied microbiology at Southern Illinois University), but he had grown up on a farm near Grand Chain, Illinois, where he had shown natural entrepreneurial flair as a youth running numerous enterprises including repairing radios, making brooms, raising livestock, and hauling hay and straw. "Growing up on a farm you do everything yourself," he says. "You are also exposed to risk—planting a crop is a risky venture every time you do it."

Jones was excited enough about his ice cream pellets that he sold his car and used some $12,000 in savings to have equipment built that would allow him to make ice cream pellets in his garage, including special freezers shipped from Europe that would keep the ice cream below -40.

The ice cream machine he designed—and later patented—was essentially a tank with a pool of liquid nitrogen in the bottom. Ice cream mix dripped through holes in the top of the tank, fell through super-cold evaporated nitrogen, formed into tiny beads like hailstones, then froze rock solid when they hit the liquid nitrogen at the bottom—a process Jones was later to describe the process on the *Oprah Winfrey Show* as "freezing raindrops."

Inventing the product was the easy part. Jones now had to convince people to buy it. And because Dippin' Dots—as he called it—was unique, it took a bit of explaining.

Jones, now twenty-eight, quit his day job and with wife Kay and daughter Tracey, opened his first store in Lexington, Kentucky, immediately making several potentially fatal mistakes. The builder they hired to fit out the store took them for a ride, leaving them with zero start-up capital for advertising and marketing when they eventually opened. And while they were in a busy location, with 20,000 cars driving past each day, what they needed was foot traffic—in particular, people who were in the mood to try a new, unusual product. "We lived on credit cards that first year," Jones says.

Jones figured the perfect place for the product was theme parks, where visitors would have time to try a sample cup and were in the mood for a treat. In 1989, he persuaded Opryland, in Nashville, to sell Dippin' Dots to their visitors, but, after two years, Opryland was considering dropping it. The problem, Jones discovered, was that the teenagers manning the booths weren't doing much to promote the Dots, basically expecting them to sell themselves. But most people don't just walk up and buy strange-looking food, especially ice cream that looks nothing like ice cream. They need a little persuading, and a free sample, first.

So Jones negotiated with Opryland to let him staff a booth with his own people. He and twelve others—some local, some from home—slept in sleeping bags in a nearby apartment in Nashville, spending their waking hours promoting Dippin' Dots at the park, with Jones riding around on his bicycle persuading visitors to check out his stand. It worked, though the night before they opened it snowed. "Then the next day we were trying to sell ice cream," says Jones.

As demand grew—albeit slowly—Jones needed money to expand his production facilities beyond his garage, opening a small factory in a former liquor store in Paducah, Kentucky, in 1990. Jones was always extremely reluctant to borrow money or bring in outside investors, raising cash instead from his father, who mortgaged the family farm, his sister, and a $40,000 credit card debt (before he quit his job at the feed plant, he had taken out six credit cards). The company is still owned privately, by Jones and his family. His wife, he admits, "was a little nervous at first."

The breakthrough came in 1992 when the Kennedy Space Center agreed to sell the product as "Space Dots," and they proved so popular visitors didn't bother with the free sample cups—they just wanted to buy some.

As the line-up of flavors grew—it now includes such variations as tropical tie-dye, watermelon, and chocolate chip cookie dough—so did the business. In 2003, the company made some $36 million, and by 2004 there were some six hundred Dippin' Dots franchises in the United States, with Dots now sold in amusement parks, movie theaters, fairs, malls, and even through specially designed robotic vending machines. Start-up costs in the United States for franchises are between $50,000 and $100,000 depending on location.

Jones has fought several legal battles to protect his patent and his brand. Instead of selling the Dots to retailers, Jones initially set up a network of independent dealers who would work hard to explain the product, and hunted down special trucking containers that required dry ice to keep the Dots in good condition.

In 2000, Jones decided to launch Dippin' Dots as a franchise, grandfathering over his existing dealers. Eight were apparently unhappy with the arrangement: according to court documents, on March 16, 2000, they simultaneously cancelled their contracts with Dippin' Dots and reopened under the name Frosty Bites, a competitor. Jones took them to court but suffered a setback when the court found that, while the dealers may have acted unethically, they had not technically broken the law. Jones estimates the patent battle, which is ongoing, has cost him some $5 million. Still, he's philosophical about it: "At the end of the day, the person who buys it is not going to worry whether you had a patent or not."

There are also licenses around the world: Jones first went global in 1995 with Japan, where a distributor had shown interest very early on, but nobody was sure how the Dots would fare on the voyage. So in 1994, Jones brought a shipping container into the parking lot, filled it with dry ice and Dippin' Dots and waited to see how long it took to melt. It lasted 15 days—just long enough to make the ocean crossing.

In 2004, Dippin' Dots had revenue of $40 million. It has a sister factory in South Korea, and sends its Dots worldwide in refrigerated containers, approximately 50,000 dots to the gallon. Jones, who likes golf and ballroom dancing and has five pets, hopes to grow the business to $100 million, and then see how he feels about it. "I'm still having fun with it," he says.

REFERENCES

BusinessWeek, Capital Times, Ice Cream Reporter, Kansas City Star, The Oprah Winfrey Show, Paducah Sun, Prep Magazine, The Tennessean, United States Court of Appeals, United States Patent Office, *Washington Post*

Build-A-Bear Workshop

It's never too late to rethink a timeless product

B Y THE END OF THE TWENTIETH CENTURY, THE COMMERCIAL potential of the humble teddy bear had been pretty well exhausted. Available everywhere from your local service station to FAO Schwartz, in any color, price, size, and even species you could think of, it seemed there was little room for a new "concept" in bears.

So when Maxine Clark, a recently retired retail executive from St. Louis, Missouri, started pitching her idea for a teddy bear shop to venture capitalists, it's not surprising she received a polite "thanks, but no thanks." So Clark invested $750,000 of her own cash, went ahead anyway and now, eight years later, is a majority shareholder in a public company with annual sales (in fiscal 2004) of some $302 million.

Clark's idea was Build-A-Bear Workshop, a chain of stores where instead of choosing and paying for a teddy bear, you build your own. Her stores are set up like mini versions of Santa's workshop. Assisted by staff, customers choose an unstuffed animal skin (anything from a teddy bear to a frog), then make a wish on a little satin heart, which goes inside, then they stuff the creature with as much filling as they want—loose and baggy or tight and plump. For an extra fee they can then dress their bear in a range of cute outfits. Build-A-Bear capitalized on two trends: customization and "retail-tainment," where you go to the mall to do something fun.

Clark opened her first store in October 1997. Meanwhile a local angel investor had read about her idea in a local paper and called up to offer her $4.3 million in growth capital. By Christmas so many investors were calling up, Clark didn't have time to return all their calls. "The day it opened we knew right away we had a winner," she says.

Build-A-Bear Workshop expanded rapidly to some two hundred company-owned stores across the country by the end of 2005, with franchises taking the concept overseas. Clark took the company public in October 2004, but remained the majority shareholder with some 18 percent of the stock. Why go public and endure the scrutiny and whims of shareholders?

"I had always eventually planned to be a public company as I had it in my original business plan," Clark says, adding, "I did have investors who would eventually need to exit. Buying out my partners to stay private would have been very costly and probably due to the debt involved, would have slowed our growth potential."

Clark says she had the idea when a ten-year-old friend was having trouble finding a particular Beanie Baby during the height of that craze and came up with a solution. "She said, 'I think we can make these,'" Clark recalls.

Clark was then age forty-seven and had recently retired from her position as head of Payless ShoeSource, the country's largest shoe retailer. She had grown tired of commuting from her home and husband in St. Louis to Payless's head office in Kansas—"That was no great way to live"—and was, she says, looking for a more creative outlet for her experience.

Born the daughter of a Coral Gables lighting store owner father and a social worker mother, Clark briefly flirted with becoming a journalist while studying at the University of Georgia, but majored in advertising and marketing and discovered she loved it. She spent the next twenty-five years of her career learning the ins and outs of retail, from marketing to manufacturing in factories in China, holding down executive roles at Venture Stores in St. Louis, Famous-Barr, and then Payless.

Clark had no children, and she and her husband had paid off their mortgage when she resigned from Payless, so she was under less financial pressure than many start-up entrepreneurs; nevertheless, she approached her germ of an idea cautiously. She checked out stuffed-animal factories, and, using the Internet, she first investigated whether there were any do-it-yourself bear businesses already in operation; there turned out to be several, all small. She says she approached a few to see if one might be worth buying; one, San Francisco's Basic Brown Bear Factory later filed suit against her, claiming in part her company had breached the terms of a nondisclosure agreement. It was later settled out of court with a confidentiality clause.

Wherever the idea really came from, it was Clark's execution that was the key, particularly little touches such as a barcode that allowed your lost bear to find its way home, via a scanner at the store—just like a real missing pet. She also built a database that sent out greetings on both the customer's and the stuffed animal's birthday, along with suggestions they might like to pop into the store for a celebra-tory new outfit, which helps to generate year-round business. Oprah Winfrey, for one, was taken with the feelgood factor idea, inviting Clark onto the show in February 2004 to build a bear for her. Sales exploded.

Clark drew heavily on her experience and contacts, using suppli-ers she knew already in China for the raw materials and, most importantly, she says, she had a detailed 10-year business plan that allowed for reinvesting profits in store improvements and new con-cepts. Build-A-Bear has also fiercely defended its brand against copycats, threatening legal action through cease-and-desist letters, though Clark herself doesn't seem too troubled by imitators. "People can only copy what they see in the stores now and in six months time we'll be way ahead," she says, adding, she says, "in addition, Build-A-Bear Workshop is as much about the experience as the product." And there's the bottom line, too: "You need a lot of capital to start a retail business."

Build-A-Bear is already expanding cautiously into another line called Friends2Bmade, in which girls can construct their own dolls. Dolls were at first part of a freestanding display in about sixty Build-A-Bear Workshop stores and based on the success, Build-A-Bear Workshop opened five Friends2Bmade stores in 2005.

REFERENCES

The Australian, BusinessWeek, Display and Design Ideas, Mail on Sunday, Messenger-Inquirer, New York Daily News, New York Post, The Oprah Winfrey Show, Retail Week

Disposable Diapers

Necessity is the mother of invention

WITH DISPOSABLE DIAPERS HAVING A 95 PERCENT MARKET penetration in the United States, where 18 billion are sold each year, diapers have come a long way from the animal skins, leaves, and weeds used as makeshift diapers throughout the ages.

A former assistant beauty editor of American *Vogue*, Marion Donovan found that there was nothing beautiful about cloth diapers when she had her first child. From a family of inventors, Donovan set about trying to avoid leaking diapers being a part of her life. She began creating plastic coverings for the cloth diapers to stop the leakage, using shower curtain material. In 1946, she patented the "boater": made from parachute cloth, it covered the cloth diaper. It was successfully marketed from 1949. Donovan also invented plastic snaps as an alternative to safety pins.

When she then began using absorbent paper inside the boater instead of cloth, manufacturers were not interested in her idea, saying that the product would be too expensive to manufacture. So Donovan went into business herself. She sold her invention for $1 million a year later. This is not to say Donovan was the only inventor of the disposable diaper; she was more an important part in the evolution of the product. Procter & Gamble was the first company to make serious money out of the diaper when it launched Pampers in 1961, a product so successful that the company could not meet demand for years.

REFERENCES

Associated Press, Australian Magazine, Carlos Richer, *Chicago Sun-Times, Columbus Dispatch, Fort-Worth Star, The Guardian, The Independent, Milwaukee Journal Sentinel, National Public Radio, Newsweek, New York Times,* PR Newswire, *Radio Times, Seattle Times, Sunday Telegraph, USA Today*

Neopets

How to make money in a virtual world

B ORED ONE AFTERNOON IN 1997, A TWENTY-YEAR-OLD BRITISH college student came up with an idea for a new website that he thought might entertain his fellow students. Adam Powell, a student at Britain's Nottingham University, dreamed up an imaginary universe called Neopia, which visitors could explore with their own online pet. These creatures, best described as a cross between a Pokémon and a Tamagotchi, were cute and needed looking after—to feed them, you had to play games and solve puzzles on the site to win money you could exchange for food and medicine in the shops in the town square. Forget to feed them, and they got sick—to keep your Neopet in good health, you had to visit the site constantly.

It was a fun idea, but one that lay dormant while Powell started some other, less fanciful, Internet businesses, mainly focused on online advertising. In November 1999, though, he and his girlfriend, Donna Williams, finally launched what they named "Neopets" as a live website, with the vague aim, they told Britain's *Guardian* newspaper, to "keep university students entertained, and possibly make some cash from banner advertising." It was cute, it was mildly addictive, and friends of Powell and Williams loved it. As did thousands of others who created a pet in the first few weeks it went online.

Word spread as far as southern California, the home of Douglas Dohring, who had for fourteen years run a market research company that produced surveys for automakers. Dohring didn't see the site as an infantile diversion for college students. He saw it as a fledgling children's brand that offered numerous opportunities for making money, including market research, advertising, and product spin-offs. "I saw it like Disney in the early days," he recalled in 2003. "You introduce characters in an entertainment medium, create a world-wide following, then create products to generate a business model."

Dohring made Powell and Williams an offer for the operation—reported as $1.1 million—and shifted Neopets and its founders to Glendale, Los Angeles. "Andrew and Donna were doing Neopets for their own enjoyment," Dohring said. "They didn't want to make a business out of it, but I talked them into it."

In early 2000, Dohring made an announcement to his staff: instead of car surveys, he said, they were now in charge of imaginary creatures with weird names. Executive vice president Rik Kenney, who had started the research company with Dohring, later said he had been stunned by the announcement. Dohring played down the shift, saying it fitted in with his general move to conduct more market research online, where it was far cheaper than over the phone.

The privately held Dohring Company said Neopets was profitable within three months and grossed $6 million by the end of 2000; by 2005, the company claimed more than 75 million people (most of them children, but not all) had created their own pet.

How does it make money? It is free to users—at least, free in the sense they don't have to pay anything to create a pet and enjoy the site. They pay by unwittingly volunteering to take part in interactive advertisements, an innovation Dohring even trademarked as "immersive advertising," described on the Neopets site thus: "Neopets' Immersive Advertising programs are successful because members interact directly with the advertiser's product, which is embedded within the customized site content."

Most of the content on the site, which resembles a cartoony map of a world, surrounded by moons and space stations, is plain good fun, if a rather sobering indictment of what passes for fun for a child in 2005. Users can play simple puzzle and shooting games to win Neopoints, buy food for their pet at imaginary stores, play at share trading on the NeoDaq stock market, search for rare items to sell in eBay-style auctions, and chat with other users though the chat room guilds. Virtually everything has a silly name: the hospital sells sporkle syrup to cure ugga-ugga disease.

Amid the folksy shops of the main village, there's a McDonald's outlet that sells regular Happy Meals (linking users to a slick animated advertisement) and a Disney theatre where users can preview real-world movie releases. Some of the games have been branded, too—rolling a Reece's peanut butter ball into a hole, or racing a Mattel Hot Wheels car. To demonstrate the effectiveness of Immersive Advertising, Dohring surveyed Neopet users and found that 35.8 percent had sampled Kraft's Capri Sun drink. They introduced it to the site, then resurveyed users, finding that 43 percent had now tried the drink. (Neopets users who take part in surveys are rewarded with Neopoints for answering such questions as, have you been to a Wal-Mart store in the past two months?)

More recently, Neopets introduced good, old-fashioned banner ads, including the "powered by Google" mini ads that are rapidly taking over the Internet, which caused some complaints from users.

Neopets has also successfully propagated its own brand, signing deals with Warner Bros for movies, Sony for PlayStation games, and a Japanese phone company for a hand-held version of the site, based on the synchronicity between Neopets, kids, and mobile phones. In 2004, McDonald's gave away millions of Neopet plush toys in its Happy Meals in a triumph of cross-promotion.

There was a blip in 2002, when it was revealed in an English court that former U.S. Marine Toby Studebaker, who was charged with abducting and having sex with a twelve-year-old English schoolgirl, had met the girl in a Neopets chat room at Neopets in July 2002. While that had nothing to do with Neopets per se, stories abound of how children using the site can fall prey to scammers and hackers who gain access to their accounts and steal their Neopoints or attempt to extort their virtual valuables—an important early lesson, perhaps, on the dangers of e-commerce, but not exactly what a nine-year-old is expecting from her Neopets experience. In Australia, in 2004, after a cross-promotion with McDonald's Happy Meals exposed thousands of children to Neopets for the first time, some parents complained that the games of chance on the Neopets website were exposing their children to gambling; in response, Neopets removed some games from the Australian version of its site.

There have also been concerns raised by users about the site's restriction of discussion of religious and political issues. "We don't want to allow things that could be controversial among the community," Doug Dohring told the *Wall Street Journal* in February 2005, which also reported Dohring's long-time membership of the Church of Scientology. According to the *Wall Street Journal*, Dohring said his religion did not influence the site, but he did use some of the principles of Scientology in his business dealings.

And not everybody is comfortable with the site's unashamed commercialism in the guise of children's entertainment. The Ralph Nader group Commercial Alert, for one, has encouraged parents to keep their children away from Neopets; numerous psychologists have warned, albeit weakly, about the dangers of Neopet addiction and insidious advertising. The company's standard response is that commercial children's television exposes children to a far greater number of advertisements, in proportion to the content. Yet Neopets, as Dohring points out, has pioneered a new form of advertising that children don't just watch, but participate in, and he has the results to back up its success. In June 2005, obviously inspired by this unusual form of access to a youth market, MTV Networks bought Neopets for $160 million, in a deal that kept Dohring on as CEO.

Parents, don't, of course, have to buy things just because their children ask for them. And if their children nag too much there is an easy solution—turn off the computer.

NOTES
"Keep university students entertained . . ." Headon, Martin. "Pet Hates," *Guardian Online,* 10.21.02, p. 7.

"I saw it like Disney . . ." Hopkins, Brent. "Pet Project: Virtual Land of Animal Fantasy Turns Real Profits for Next-Generation Internet Hit," *The Daily News of Los Angeles,* 12.16.03, Business B1.

"Andrew and Donna were doing . . ." Weingarten, Marc. "As Children Adopt Pets, a Game Adopts Them," Circuits, *New York Times,* 2.21.02, p. 7.

"We don't want to allow things . . ." Wingfield, Nick. "Web's Addictive Neopets Are Ready for Big Career Leap," *Wall Street Journal,* 2.22.05.

REFERENCES
Advertising Age, BusinessWeek, CNN.com, *Daily News of Los Angeles,, Daily Telegraph, Hamilton Spectator, Hollywood Reporter, The Independent, International Herald Tribune, Kansas City Star, New York Times, Philadelphia Inquirer, The Times*

Super Soaker

NASA research finally pays off

Y OU DON'T HAVE TO BE A ROCKET SCIENTIST TO BUILD A BETTER toy . . . but didn't hurt Lonnie Johnston, inventor of the Super Soaker water pistol—one of the biggest-selling toys of all time. Johnston came up with the idea while he was working at NASA's Jet Propulsion Laboratory in Pasadena, California, where he helped design three space probes including the Galileo and Mars Observer spacecraft.

Johnson grew up in Marietta, Georgia but attended high school in Mobile, Alabama. His father was a driver for the Air Force and his mother was a nurse's aide. He was a natural experimenter: at thirteen he built a missile from a television antenna (it blew up on the launch pad); at fourteen, police interviewed him about a rocket-fuel fire in his high school hallway (he made it from potassium nitrate and sugar, but insists it was his brother who took it to school); and at eighteen he won a national science competition with a robot called "Linex" that he built from scraps. "I was always tinkering, building, and making things," he recalls. "They nicknamed me 'professor' by the time I left school." He trained as a mechanical engineer at Tuskegee University, then completed a Master of Science degree in Nuclear Engineering, before joining the Air Force.

In inventor folklore, however, Johnson's training and career achievements were just preparation for the day in 1982 when he was home from work and experimenting with a side project he had for an environmentally friendly heat pump that ran on water. He went into the bathroom, attached a homemade high-pressure nozzle to the sink and was startled when it fired a blast of water across the room. His first thought was: gee, that would make a great water pistol.

Johnson built his first prototype from a soda bottle, plexiglass, lengths of PVC tubing, and a bicycle-style pump, to create pressure inside the water reservoir, machining the parts himself.

The key to the design was a built-in pump that a child could use easily, yet still create enough pressure for a strong jet of water. Johnson's six-year-old daughter Aneka proved he had got it right by soaking her neighbors.

From the beginning, Johnson believed his idea had commercial value, and in 1983 he filed for a patent for what he called the "Pneumatic Water Gun." But it took another eight years before what eventually became known as the Super Soaker went into production.

In 1987, he quit the Air Force with an understanding that an investment capital firm would help him start his inventing business.

They backed out at the last minute, leaving Johnson unemployed. He was forced to ask the Jet Propulsion Laboratory if they would have him back; they did so, immediately.

Meanwhile, Johnson had discounted producing the gun himself after a factory quoted him $200,000 to build the first 1,000 units. "I knew I couldn't afford that, so I looked for someone to license it to," he says. He wrote to some two dozen companies; two showed interest, but the first went through several restructures and never quite signed the licensing agreement. The second went bust before they could put it into production. In 1989, Johnson, now back to square one, took his idea to the American International Toy Fair in New York, where he met one of the owners of Larami, Al Davis.

He was wary of giving away too much on the spot. "I didn't have a non-disclosure agreement with me," he told *Black Enterprise* magazine in 1993, "So I talked very superficially. I just said I had an idea for a new type of water gun and asked if they would be interested."

Davis loosely invited him to demonstrate his invention to Larami's president, Myung Song, in the boardroom at their headquarters in Philadelphia. Johnson remembers the invitation as something like this: "Don't make a special trip, if you're in the area, drop by." Johnson did drop by (at the first opportunity), pumped up his prototype, and squirted a blast of water across the room. Song's reaction was one word: "Wow!"

Larami agreed to license the squirter, and brought in another engineer, Bruce D'Andrade, to refine the design for manufacture, and the Power Drencher (later renamed Super Soaker) went on sale in late 1989 for $10. (The new design, rendered in bright orange and lime green plastic, was patented under the names of D'Andrade and Johnson in 1991.)

Larami sent a Super Soaker to Johnny Carson on the *Tonight Show*, who had an annual segment where he demonstrated—and occasionally ridiculed—unusual new products. He picked up the Soaker, sprayed sidekick Ed McMahon and several girls in the audience and made a joke about using one to hold up a retirement home. Viewers reacted much as the executives at Larami had—wow! —and sales exploded. Larami asked Johnson to suggest improvements to the original, so he came up with a new way of pumping that produced a more powerful squirt and an even more successful water gun. One chain reported selling 225,000 Soakers in a single week.

There was more publicity in May 1992 when a fifteen-year-old in Boston was shot dead after Super Soaker horseplay. The Mayor pleaded with stores to pull them from the shelves, and two local chains complied. Two youths in Harlem, New York, were similarly wounded after soaking a man carrying a real gun; and there were reports of teen gangs filling up their Soakers with bleach, in one case squirting a mother and her four-year-old child. In a follow-up article titled "The Soaking of America," *Newsweek* quoted a Harvard psychiatrist who earnestly claimed the popularity of Super Soakers mirrored the escalation of violence in society: "It's kind of like drug dealers moving up from handguns to Uzis."

Even talk show host David Letterman paid homage in June 1992, in his satirical "Top 10 Items on the Bush/Yeltsin Summit Agenda"—number ten was "Sign arms pact limiting number of Super Soaker squirt guns."

The controversy may have dented sales—or the extra publicity may have simply added to the Super Soaker snowball. Johnson remembers his first royalty check: "It was huge—I had to stop and sit down." He was able to quit his day job to concentrate on his company Johnson Research and Development and has since developed several more toys, as well as numerous "serious" technologies such as rechargeable batteries. Johnson says today retail sales of the Super Soaker have totaled close to $1 billion. Does he think he will ever have another success on that scale? "It's difficult to predict," he says, "because I'm an engineer and what appeals to people is very subjective."

NOTES

"I didn't have a non-disclosure . . ." "Making Money Making Toys," *Black Enterprise*, p.68, November 1993.

"It's kind of like drug . . ." Mathews, Jay, Debra Rosenberg, Nichole Christian, "The Soaking of America," *Newsweek*, 6.22.92, p. 58.

REFERENCES

Black Enterprise, Charlotte Observer, Ebony, Financial Post, iSoaker.com, Legal Intelligencer, MIT Inventor of the Week, New Jersey Law Journal, New York Times, Newsweek, NPR Weekend, Philadelphia Inquirer, Science World, Washington Post

INDEX

ABOUT THE AUTHORS

Emily Ross and Angus Holland's *100 Great Businesses and the Minds Behind Them* was devised in Melbourne, Australia, where they both live and work.

Emily Ross is a senior writer with the country's leading national business magazine *BRW*. She specializes in leadership, innovation, and entrepreneurship. Angus Holland is a senior editor with *The Age* newspaper.

Between them they have lived in Abu Dhabi, Hong Kong, Kuwait, London, Lantau Island, Milan, Paris, Mauritius, Qatar, Singapore, and Tokyo. They live in Melbourne with their two children.